HOLDING
SCHOOLS
ACCOUNTABLE

HOLDING SCHOOLS ACCOUNTABLE

Performance-Based Reform
in Education

Helen F. Ladd
Editor

THE BROOKINGS INSTITUTION
Washington, D.C.

Copyright © 1996 by
THE BROOKINGS INSTITUTION
1775 Massachusetts Avenue, N.W., Washington, D.C. 20036

Library of Congress Cataloging-in-Publication data:

Holding schools accountable : performance-based reform in education / Helen F. Ladd,
    editor.
        p.   cm.
    Includes bibliographical references and index.
    ISBN 0-8157-5104-4 (cloth : alk. paper). — ISBN 0-8157-5103-6 (pbk. : alk. paper)
    1. Competency based education—United States.   2. School management and
organization—United States.   3. Education change—United States.   I. Ladd, Helen F.
LC1032.H65   1996
371.2'00973—dc20   95-46845
                                                                                          CIP

9 8 7 6 5 4 3 2 1

The paper used in this publication meets the minimum
requirements of the American National Standard for
Information Sciences—Permanence of Paper for Printed
Library Materials, ANSI Z39.48-1984

Typeset in Sabon

Composition by Automated Graphic Systems
White Plains, Maryland

Printed by R. R. Donnelley and Sons, Co.
Harrisonburg, Virginia

Ꞵ THE BROOKINGS INSTITUTION

The Brookings Institution is an independent organization devoted to nonpartisan research, education, and publication in economics, government, foreign policy, and the social sciences generally. Its principal purposes are to aid in the development of sound public policies and to promote public understanding of issues of national importance.

The Institution was founded on December 8, 1927, to merge the activities of the Institute for Government Research, founded in 1916, the Institute of Economics, founded in 1922, and the Robert Brookings Graduate School of Economics and Government, founded in 1924.

The Board of Trustees is responsible for the general administration of the Institution, while the immediate direction of the policies, program, and staff is vested in the President, assisted by an advisory committee of the officers and staff. The by-laws of the Institution state: "It is the function of the Trustees to make possible the conduct of scientific research, and publication, under the most favorable conditions, and to safeguard the independence of the research staff in the pursuit of their studies and in the publication of the results of such studies. It is not a part of their function to determine, control, or influence the conduct of particular investigations or the conclusions reached."

The President bears final responsibility for the decision to publish a manuscript as a Brookings book. In reaching his judgment on the competence, accuracy, and objectivity of each study, the President is advised by the director of the appropriate research program and weighs the views of a panel of expert outside readers who report to him in confidence on the quality of the work. Publication of a work signifies that it is deemed a competent treatment worthy of public consideration but does not imply endorsement of conclusions or recommendations.

The Institution maintains its position of neutrality on issues of public policy in order to safeguard the intellectual freedom of the staff. Hence interpretations or conclusions in Brookings publications should be understood to be solely those of the authors and should not be attributed to the Institution, to its trustees, officers, or other staff members, or to the organizations that support its research.

Foreword

Despite more than a decade of piecemeal reform in response to harsh criticism of American schools in the early 1980s, many people believe that our system of elementary and secondary education is still not preparing students at reasonable cost for the challenges of a global economy. Students are graduating from high school without the cognitive skills increasingly valued by employers or the background required for success in college. Test scores of U.S. students have remained relatively constant at the same time that real per pupil spending has been rising rapidly.

Given the projected upturn in enrollments and the outlook for intensified competition for funds at the state and local level, per pupil spending on elementary and secondary education cannot continue to grow at the rapid rates of the past. At the same time, educational outcomes need to be improved to ensure that all children leave school with the skills and flexibility required to compete in the modern labor market. Therefore the U.S. education system must become more productive: resources must be used more effectively to achieve greater academic learning.

To reach this end, many people believe that schools should be held more accountable for the academic performance of their students. This results-oriented reform effort seeks to encourage schools to use their limited resources more effectively in the pursuit of the common goal, high levels of learning for all students. One approach is to introduce into the existing school system accountability and incentive programs that reward the most effective schools and generate increased scrutiny of the least effective ones. An alternative approach is to empower parents to hold schools accountable through the introduction of more choice, perhaps in the form of school voucher programs.

In this book, the authors examine what can be learned from recent experience with both approaches to accountability. Their analyses of administered accountability systems in South Carolina, Mississippi, Kentucky, and the city of Dallas highlight a variety of thorny design and implementation issues such as whether and how to adjust for the socioeconomic backgrounds of students and how to minimize incentives for teachers to teach narrowly to the test or otherwise manipulate the accountability program. The authors conclude that although such programs have potential for improving student outcomes, they should not be viewed as a substitute for additional resources or increased capacity to deliver educational services, especially in schools serving disadvantaged students. The analyses of parental choice programs imply that if vouchers are desirable, they should be distributed to families based on economic need. In addition, the book provides new evidence that educational inputs such as class size and teacher quality—both of which cost money—do affect learning, especially of students who are performing poorly.

This book is the outgrowth of a two-day conference at the Brookings Institution in April 1995, organized by Helen F. Ladd. The conference brought together researchers from various disciplines—most notably economics, educational policy and management, and political science—to present new empirical evidence on performance-based strategies for reforming education.

Helen F. Ladd undertook this project while she was a visiting fellow at the Brookings Institution during a sabbatical leave from Duke University. She thanks Brookings and Duke University for financial support. Anita Whitlock served as the administrative assistant for the conference. Nancy Davidson shepherded the manuscript through the editorial process. Timothy Taylor provided additional editorial assistance to ensure that the book would be broadly accessible. Gerard Trimarco verified the manuscript's factual content; Lisa Guillory and Gemma Park prepared the manuscript for publication; and Max Franke prepared the index.

The conference was an activity of the Brown Center for Education Research at the Brookings Institution. Brookings gratefully acknowledges financial support from the Brown Center, the Spencer Foundation, and an anonymous donor.

The views expressed in this book are those of the authors and should not be ascribed to the funding sources or the trustees, officers, or staff members of the Brookings Institution.

MICHAEL H. ARMACOST
President

March 1996
Washington, D.C.

Contents

Figures

HOLDING
SCHOOLS
ACCOUNTABLE

CHAPTER ONE

Introduction

Helen F. Ladd

Past efforts to reform elementary and secondary education in the United States have often focused on changes in educational governance, process, and inputs. Thus the suggestions for reform included ideas like introducing site-based management of schools, promoting the development of professional standards for teachers, or hiring more teachers. In contrast, present efforts to reform elementary and secondary education in the United States are focusing heavily on the outcomes of the educational system. This interest in performance-based reform reflects in part a general preoccupation with managerial efficiency. Citizens and taxpayers seem to be increasingly concerned with how to use resources more efficiently to get more output for fewer inputs in large corporations, hospitals, the military, and elsewhere. But interest in performance-based reform for education also reflects patterns and trends specific to elementary and secondary education in the United States.

First, many people believe that the K–12 system of education is not adequately preparing students, at reasonable cost, for the challenges of a global economy. One concern is that the skills of high school graduates do not match the needs of employers. In a previous era, low-skilled workers could find well-paid jobs in manufacturing and hope to stay there throughout their working lives. Today, global competition increases the demand for workers who are sufficiently well educated to have the flexibility to move from one job to another as opportunities change job demands. The value of an education is rising; recent work shows that basic cognitive skills were more important predictors of wages six years after high school in the mid-1980s than in the late 1970s.[1] Yet U.S. students are lagging behind students in many other countries in their performance on international

1. See Murnane, Willett, and Levy (1995).

tests of science and math.[2] These problems are especially serious in many large inner cities. But any student who receives a poor education today runs a high risk of being unable to compete for well-paid jobs.

Second, outcomes-oriented proposals are drawing attention because resources to increase K–12 education are expected to be tight in the next decade. During the 1970s and early 1980s, declining enrollments allowed the country to increase per pupil spending without much increase in total spending. The enrollment picture has now changed. By 2004, enrollments are projected to rise by 13 percent at the K–8 level and by 24 percent at the high school level.[3] Moreover, cutbacks in federal aid to state and local governments will put increasing pressure on taxpayers at the state and local level. These trends will exert increasing pressure to limit the growth of per pupil spending on education.

Third, outcomes-based research has gained impetus from a feeling that the U.S. educational system has not been especially efficient in turning resources into educated students. Test scores of U.S. students have remained relatively constant at the same time that spending per pupil has risen quite dramatically. Test scores published by the National Assessment of Educational Progress (NAEP) provide a more accurate picture of national trends than SAT scores, which are contaminated by a varying mix of students who take the exam, because the NAEP scores are based on nationally representative samples of students aged 9, 13, and 17. During the twenty-two-year period from 1971 to 1992, NAEP scores improved only slightly in math and remained essentially constant in other subject areas.[4] In contrast, education spending per pupil (adjusted for inflation) rose significantly—50 percent in the period from 1974 to 1992.

However, these trends provide an oversimplified picture of the productivity trends of the education system. Actually, real resources devoted to the average pupil have increased by significantly less than 50 percent. One reason is that the costs of inputs used in the education system have gone up faster than general price deflators, a phenomenon that is common throughout the labor-intensive service sector of the economy. The costs of educational inputs increased by over 310 percent between 1974 and 1991, while general price indicators increased by only 260 percent. Conse-

---

2. For example, on the second International Assessment of Educational Progress (IAEP), conducted in 1990–91, thirteen-year-old U.S. students were outscored in math by students in all of the other countries except Spain and in science by students from Korea, Taiwan, and the former Soviet Union. Congressional Budget Office (1993, p. 17).

3. U.S. Department of Education (1994b, table 3).

4. U.S. Department of Education (1994a, pp. 50–56).

quently, if per pupil spending were deflated by a price index for elementary and secondary education rather than a general deflator, real per pupil spending would have increased not by 50 percent (or at an annual rate of 2.3 percent), but rather by 29 percent (or an annual rate of 1.5 percent).[5]

But even this 29 percent growth in real per pupil spending overstates the growth in resources available for the average student, because some of the increase in spending reflects the growth in funding for special education students. Reasonable people can disagree how much money should be spent on students with special needs. Nonetheless, the Americans with Disabilities Act provides such children with a legal entitlement to appropriate education services,[6] and on average, it costs about twice as much to educate a student in a special education program as a student in a regular program. Special education students now account for about 11.8 percent of total pupils, up from about 8.7 percent in the late 1970s.[7]

Finally, educating children has become more challenging over time because of the increasing proportions of children who are raised in poverty or in single-parent households, or both. Hence, some of the increase in resources simply reflects the fact that schools are being asked to do more today than in the past.

In sum, the past productivity picture in K–12 education may not be as bleak as some people claim. Student performance has not increased much, but neither have the resources aimed at the average student. But given that resources are not likely to increase much in the future, and there is a need for a better-educated work force, most people agree that schools need to become more productive in the future.

Focusing on Outcomes as a Way to Improve the System

How can schools do a better job of educating American children? The answer of many school reformers is to clarify the mission of elementary and

5. Calculations by the author based on data from the U.S. Department of Education (1994b, tables 38, 165). A recent study by the Economic Policy Institute supports this analysis. Looking at the period from 1967 to 1991, that study concludes that real per pupil spending, appropriately adjusted for inflation, grew by 40 percent less than conventionally reported. See Rothstein and Miles (1995, p. 7).

6. In 1975 Congress passed the Education for All Handicapped Children Act (currently the Individuals with Disabilities Education Act) through which the federal government became involved in the regulation of and partial financing of education programs for children with disabilities.

7. U.S. Department of Education (1994b, table 52).

secondary schools. Although the K–12 education system clearly has multiple missions—including, for example, the training of students to be good citizens—a consensus is emerging that more attention needs to be focused on the cognitive learning of students. Moreover, many reformers would redefine the nature of that learning to make it more consistent with the needs of an information-based and globally competitive economy. Much of the current reform effort is driven by the call for high academic expectations for all children and ambitious learning standards that emphasize problem solving and thinking rather than basic skills. For example, the Goals 2000: Educate America Act—initially proposed by a bipartisan group of governors, supported by President Bush, and passed in 1994 during President Clinton's administration—sets eight goals, including two core goals related to student performance. One calls for all students to achieve high levels of competency in various subjects by the year 2000, and the other calls for the United States to be number one in math and science by the year 2000.

A reform agenda along these lines begins with ambitious academic goals or standards for all children and curriculum frameworks that describe what all children should know and be able to do—that is, with a definition of the desired outcomes. Such standards come from many sources. For example, the National Council of Teachers of Mathematics (NCTM), a private organization of teachers and scholars, developed voluntary standards designed to transform the teaching of math. Using the NCTM standards and process as a model, the U.S. Department of Education has made grants to groups of teachers and scholars to create voluntary national standards in a variety of fields including history, science, English, and civics.[8] The Goals 2000 legislation also sets up funding and procedures to develop voluntary national standards, to monitor progress toward the goals, and to encourage states to develop their own standards.

Systemic reform then requires that schools and school systems be held accountable for the progress of students toward the goals. Thus, states would shift the focus of their school accreditation efforts away from attention to inputs, such as the number of books in the library and the qualifications of teachers, and toward student outcomes. At the local level, the role of the school board at the district level would shift away from monitoring educational inputs to setting outcome goals and providing financial, technical, and professional support to achieve those goals. These outcomes

8. For a full discussion of standards, see Ravitch (1995).

might be measured on an absolute standard (certain scores on certain tests) or on a standard relative to certain other schools or districts.

Clarifying the mission of an organization is only a first step toward reform. The challenge within the educational system is to find the specific strategies and policy levers that will change enough parts of the complex educational system to increase student learning. This book brings together researchers from various disciplines—most notably economics, educational policy and management, and political science—to present new empirically based research on these issues.

Overview of Book

The many performance-based strategies for reforming schools can be broadly divided into two groups. One type of reform involves the introduction of accountability and systemic reform programs designed to work within the existing administrative structure of the schools. A second major type of performance-based reform strategy is choice or voucher systems that operate by holding the schools accountable to parents who have choice in the selection of schools for their children. Included here are programs that provide choice within the public school system, those that offer vouchers to small numbers of disadvantaged students, or those that open up the system more generally to market pressures. These proposals involve some change, and perhaps a substantial overhaul, of the existing administrative structure of schools.

With either strategy, one can take the perspective of managerial efficiency, which starts with the existing level and distribution of school resources and asks how accountability, incentive, or voucher programs can be designed to maximize student learning. Alternatively, one can start with some specific educational outcome goals and ask how many more resources would be needed in some districts or schools relative to others to achieve those goals. The costs of achieving a specific educational outcome are likely to vary across schools because when students have parents with little income or education, the schools face a more formidable educational task than when students come from more advantaged backgrounds. This perspective highlights the issue of costs and resources, which, along with student achievement, occupies a central place in this book.

Strategies That Work within the Existing Structure

Part I of the book focuses on strategies that work within the existing administrative structure of the schools. These strategies come by various names, like "the new educational accountability" and systemic change. In general, these approaches emphasize measures of student performance as the basis for school accountability; the creation of technically complex approaches for evaluating schools; the creation of systems of rewards, penalties, and intervention strategies to introduce incentives for improvement; and a stress on high academic expectations and challenging curriculum frameworks for all children.

Chapter 2, by Charles T. Clotfelter and Helen F. Ladd, uses as examples the state of South Carolina and the Dallas Independent School District, both of which reward schools for their contribution to the year-to-year gains in student performance. They point out several challenges for such accountability programs. One is to develop ranking systems that make fair adjustments for the socioeconomic backgrounds of the students, but to have those ranking systems be understandable and justifiable to parents and educational staff. A second design challenge is to develop clear measures of outcomes to maximize the incentive for schools to increase student learning, yet minimize the incentives for the system to be corrupted through narrow teaching to the test, the failure to test some students, and outright cheating. Clotfelter and Ladd discuss how South Carolina and Dallas have dealt with these issues. Also, they provide evidence that the Dallas program appears to have increased the performance of students on the state test relative to that of students in other large Texas cities.

Chapter 3, by Richard F. Elmore, Charles H. Abelmann, and Susan H. Fuhrman, highlights a broader set of design, implementation, and political issues involved in the new educational accountability by comparing and contrasting Kentucky's ambitious reform effort with the less ambitious accountability efforts of Mississippi. The authors focus first on the design issues that would confront any state in shifting from input and process to performance as the basis of accountability; for example, should a state choose a relative measure of student performance, as did Mississippi, or an absolute measure of proficiency, as did Kentucky? They also emphasize many of the same issues addressed by Clotfelter and Ladd, such as perceptions of fairness and the nature of the incentives. In addition, they raise a question of whether states are truly willing to intervene in or perhaps to take over schools or districts with low performance. For educational reforms to survive, the authors argue, states are faced with the formidable challenge of creating a stable and long-term political environment for reform.

Chapter 4, by David Cohen, sheds additional light on outcome-oriented reforms. Based largely on his observations in three states—South Carolina, Michigan, and California—Cohen examines what happens to systemic reform, with its attempt to focus on educational outcomes and policy coherence, when it is implemented within the fragmented, decentralized, and incoherent educational system. He finds that although systemic reform does affect education, the reforms themselves are affected in turn by the system they seek to reform. Moreover, Cohen points out that when many levels of the educational system are attempting their own reforms, the result is that guidance grows more ambitious, but instruction becomes more variable. Given the recent shift in political orientation toward the right, Cohen predicts that the whole systemic reform movement could be swept away by a movement that stresses parental choice and local control rather than administered forms of accountability.

Strategies That Work by Changing the System

An alternative to administrative procedures as an accountability mechanism is to give parents some freedom to select the schools their children attend. Under such a system of parental choice, schools presumably would have strong incentives to be accountable to parents and students. Part II of the book addresses the extent to which this form of accountability is likely to lead to higher academic achievement for students and how it compares with administrative procedures as an accountability mechanism.

In chapter 5, John Witte summarizes what is now known about the links between choice and academic achievement based on existing public school choice programs, comparisons between student performance in public and private schools, and various experiments with voucher programs, including the Milwaukee parental choice program for which he has been serving as the chief external evaluator. His first question is the extent to which parents seek academic quality in making their choices, as opposed to a good fit in some other way. Witte then looks at whether students in schools of choice do better than students in other schools. After controlling for the various factors affecting school selection, Witte finds little or no difference on test scores for students in Catholic schools relative to students in public schools. On the other hand, Witte cites some new and convincing evidence from other studies that conclude that two alternative outcome measures, graduation rates and subsequent enrollment in four-year colleges, are significantly higher for students in Catholic schools than in public schools and that these improved outcomes emerge primarily for students at the lower end of the achievement distribution. Witte discusses possible reasons for these effects. He also emphasizes that none of the research he reviews can measure the potential dynamic effects of a full-scale, widespread choice program.

In chapter 6, Caroline Minter Hoxby attempts to measure the medium- and long-run general equilibrium effects that might be generated by a voucher program. Her ambitious and innovative strategy involves interpreting the variation across metropolitan areas in subsidies for Catholic school tuitions as a proxy for variations in voucher payments. In particular, she estimates the relationship between tuition subsidies and each of the following policy-relevant variables: the percentage of students who attend private schools, the characteristics of students who attend private schools, total and per pupil spending on public schools, and the performance of students as measured by test scores, educational attainment, and hourly wage rates. She then uses these estimated relationships to simulate the effects of a school voucher program.

Her results imply that a $1,000 voucher would increase the percentage of students in private schools from about 10 percent to 14 percent and that the increase would be distributed among both well-educated and more poorly educated families. Her most striking conclusion is that the voucher would improve student performance across the board: both public and private school students would stay in school on average two years longer, average test scores would rise by about 10 percent, and hourly wages would rise by 14 percent. Thus, Hoxby's results imply that the voucher program would serve as a powerful accountability device.

Resources and Costs

Parts III and IV address resource and cost issues as they relate to attempts to achieve high levels of outcomes for all students. In chapter 7, Hamilton Lankford and James H. Wyckoff use a rich fourteen-year panel data set for New York State to look closely at the use of resources, with special attention to the growth of special education spending. They confirm the view that the growth in overall spending per pupil greatly overstates the growth in classroom spending for regular pupils, which is the more relevant measure for statements about productivity. In New York

City, for example, while overall spending per pupil increased by about 24 percent, spending on regular students increased by only 7 percent. A large increase in spending on special education accounts for much of the differential. The authors explore in some detail the explanations for this rise in special education spending, whether it appears to crowd out spending on behalf of regular students, whether school officials are gaining some advantage by categorizing students as in need of special education, and what it implies for future budget pressures.

The Lankford-Wyckoff chapter provides a useful transition to the final three chapters, which examine the linkages between inputs or spending and educational outcomes. Whether higher student achievement is sought through centralized accountability systems or decentralized choice programs, policymakers will need more information than they currently have about how specific inputs such as class size or teacher quality affect educational outcomes, how much it costs to implement various existing models for educating disadvantaged youth in urban areas, and how state policymakers could measure differences in the costs of educating different types of students so as to provide appropriate amounts of compensatory aid to districts serving high-cost students.

In chapter 8, Ronald F. Ferguson and Helen F. Ladd provide new evidence that schooling inputs, such as class size or teacher quality, affect educational outcomes as measured by student test scores and that the effects are large enough to be relevant for deliberations about the adequacy and equity of educational spending. Their major contribution is to estimate a true value-added model, with a number of methodological improvements over earlier studies, based on student-level data from Alabama. They conclude that higher-quality teachers and smaller class sizes lead to greater learning, especially for math. Their results for the student-level analysis are reinforced by a district-level analysis of Alabama data.

Given that the relevant school inputs cost money, these findings imply that "money matters" for student achievement. In a more direct test, Ferguson and Ladd reinforce this conclusion by showing that, after appropriate statistical adjustments, per pupil instructional spending is positively associated with student test scores, especially in low-spending districts. These findings indicate that the provision of additional resources in resource-deficient districts can lead to increased student learning, even without major restructuring of the education system.

Of course, even the alternative of restructuring education programs is not without cost. In chapter 9, W. Steven Barnett assesses three well-known models designed to improve educational practice for disadvantaged students in urban school districts: Henry Levin's Accelerated Schools program, which attempts to narrow the initial educational deficit of at-risk children by moving them faster than traditional remedial programs; Robert Slavin's Success for All program, which assigns a high priority to reading skills and emphasizes prevention and early intervention; and James Comer's School Development program, which strengthens the links between schools and the children, families, and communities they serve. All three programs attempt to reallocate existing resources to accomplish their ends. Barnett examines the evidence on how effective these models have been in increasing student achievement, and the extent to which these programs may be generalizable to all elementary schools serving disadvantaged children.

Chapter 10, by William D. Duncombe, John Ruggiero, and John M. Yinger, takes a different and innovative approach to the problem of estimating the differential costs of educating various types of students or students in different types of districts to achieve a given level of outcomes. Building on and advancing the existing literature, they focus on seven sources of cost differentials: differences in teacher salaries that do not reflect local decisions, the size of the district as measured by enrollment, and the percentages of children in poverty, households with a female single parent, children with limited English proficiency, students with disabilities or severe disabilities, and students in high school. Using data for New York state, they estimate that costs in the 10 percent of the districts with the highest costs exceed average state per pupil costs by almost 53 percent. They also compare their preferred index with other approaches, and find that while simpler indexes can produce similar results, the ad hoc cost indexes of the type currently used in New York and elsewhere are seriously flawed.

Issues and Lessons about Performance-Based Reform

What lessons emerge from this new research on performance-based reform of schools? The following discussion addresses seven questions, reflecting the material in the chapters, comments by formal and informal discussants, and my own perspectives.

Who Should Be Held Accountable?

The "new state accountability" generally starts from the view that the school is the most appropriate unit of accountability. For example, the school is the centerpiece of the accountability systems in South Carolina, Dallas, and Kentucky. Clotfelter and Ladd make the case that accountability at the school level has greater potential for success than programs such as merit pay for individual teachers, because merit pay creates morale problems and provides inappropriate incentives for teachers to compete against each other, rather than to cooperate in the joint endeavor of educating students. In contrast, programs that focus accountability and incentives on the school as a collective body are potentially more productive because they encourage teachers, principals, and staff to work together toward a common mission; they could conceivably change the school culture and norms in a desirable direction; and, to the extent that school officials have power over key decisions, such as budgetary and curriculum issues, schools can be more responsive to incentives than can individual teachers.

However, Eric Hanushek argued that merit pay programs for teachers might be more beneficial than other participants believed. He pointed out that 80 percent of the U.S. work force receives some form of merit pay, and merit pay programs are playing an increasing role in some educational institutions such as business schools. More generally, he suggested a closer inquiry into who merit pay incentive policies are designed to influence and over what time frame one should evaluate results. For example, if merit pay is intended to change the characteristics of future teachers by making the profession more attractive, evaluations of effects would require a relatively long time frame.

More generally, why does it make sense to try to hold either teachers or schools accountable for the performance of students? Would it not make more sense to try to make the students themselves more accountable for their own performance? After all, students are not inanimate objects like blocks of wood that can be acted on by a carpenter, but instead are people with their own motivations and will.[9] If the goal is to raise the academic performance of students, why not increase the incentives for students to work harder? As John Bishop has documented, the United States is unusual in its failure to hold students accountable. Except for students applying to elite colleges, performance in high school has little effect on students'

9. This image comes from Cohen (1995, p. 30).

opportunities after high school. Many colleges attach little or no weight to high school grades, and employers essentially never look at high school transcripts. Moreover, because no state except New York has externally graded and demanding tests for graduating students, employers and colleges have no good signals of student effort and accomplishment. Recent research by Bishop on Canadian provinces appears to document the potential role of such tests in stimulating student achievement.[10] Emerging from the conference discussion was the conclusion that an effective incentive strategy should be directed at all three groups: students, teachers, and schools.

Are Administrative Accountability Systems Desirable and Sustainable?

Tremendous emotion surrounds attempts to make school systems more accountable for educational outcomes. Although economists typically endorse greater use of incentive programs, a well-known theorem in organizational economics demonstrates that when only one of the multiple goals of an organization can be measured, and hence rewarded, incentive programs are undesirable because they will encourage people to focus all their attention on the measurable and rewarded goal to the exclusion of other goals.[11] Many educators are implicitly evoking this theorem when they express fear that the concept of outcome-based accountability threatens the complex fabric of education.

The fact that such administered accountability and incentive programs are currently in vogue directly reflects the general consensus that the major mission of elementary and secondary education should be academic learning. Such programs will remain viable only to the extent that this consensus is maintained.

To the extent that a major focus on academic achievement conflicts with other educational goals valued by various subsets of the population, an alternative strategy might be to follow the Dutch model. In that model, all schools are held accountable by the state for educational outcomes, but they are also free to pursue other goals. In the U.S. context, this model might be implemented by an expansion of the quasi-public charter schools, which would be free to pursue whatever goals they wished—provided their students met certain state-determined academic achievement goals.

10. These results are reported in Bishop (1994, p. 24).
11. See, for example, Milgrom and Roberts (1992, pp. 228–31).

What Are the Crucial Components of a Well-Designed Accountability System?

A number of thorny issues arise in the design of performance-based accountability systems. The first is whether in constructing measures of school effectiveness, average student test scores should be adjusted to take account of variation in the students' prior knowledge or socioeconomic background. Clotfelter and Ladd pose the issue in terms of perceptions of fairness: an accountability system would be deemed unfair if it typically favored schools serving one type of student rather than another. As they illustrate with data for South Carolina fifth graders, the use of average unadjusted test scores as the ranking measure would disproportionately favor schools with above-average proportions of whites and below-average proportions of poor students.

The discussant for their chapter, Robert Meyer, posed the question somewhat differently. In general, the key is to separate the goals for students from measuring the performance of the school system. Thus, if the purpose of an accountability system is to induce school officials to change their behavior, the accountability measure should reflect primarily the factors under their control and not factors that are outside their control, such as the socioeconomic backgrounds of students.

Nonetheless, many policymakers believe that any adjustment for socioeconomic differences could be misinterpreted to suggest that some children are more able to learn than others or that some schools are being let off the hook for the poor academic performance of their students. For example, the Black Caucus in Mississippi opposed any adjustments to the district-level outcome measures for that state and supported instead a uniform student outcome measure as the performance measure for all schools in the state. Kentucky tried to address the problem by setting the same high absolute outcome standard for students in all schools. However, because the state wants all schools to achieve the standards within twenty years and schools with lower-performing students have further to go, this strategy requires schools serving low-performing districts to show greater gains in improvement than other schools to be deemed effective.

A second issue is whether performance-based accountability systems are compatible with the more ambitious and experimental forms of "authentic" assessment that reformers advocate as essential for encouraging higher-order thinking and problem solving. Experience in Kentucky illustrates the problems. Assessment of a portfolio of student writing work, for example, puts a heavy burden on teachers, can typically be implemented in only a few key grades because of the expense, and generates scores that may be unreliable and inappropriate for comparisons across schools. In addition, ambitious systems typically lead to very high failure rates that are politically difficult to accept. Authentic assessment was designed to improve teachers' ability to diagnose what they need to do in the classroom. As noted by Richard Elmore, it may well not be compatible with accountability systems.

A third issue relates to whether the undesirable side effects of accountability and incentive system can be kept to a tolerable level. Research on Dallas indicates that the design of the program matters a lot. To avoid providing an incentive for narrow teaching to a specific test, accountability should be based on a range of test and other outcome measures. Programs should rank schools on their value-added rather than absolute test scores, to reduce the incentives for schools to exclude low-scoring students from the school or the testing program. Programs should focus on all grades rather than just a selected few, to reduce incentives for school administrators to focus resources on selected grades to the detriment of others. Finally, a balance must be found so financial awards are large enough to change behavior, but not so large that they induce outright cheating.

A fourth issue is the extent to which the technical complexity of a well-designed accountability system is compatible with political and implementation demands. As illustrated by the experiences of both Dallas and Kentucky, many educators within the system do not understand how their accountability system works. This lack of comprehensibility can be a problem. It makes educators suspicious of the system, and makes it difficult for them to make the link between what they are doing in the classroom and what is being rewarded. It also means that technocrats who control the system effectively end up making policy decisions. Dallas addressed the last problem by setting up an Accountability Task Force composed of principals, teachers, and representatives of the business community to serve as the link between the technical experts and the school board, to hear appeals, and to make policy decisions such as how to weight the different outcome measures. In this way, Dallas appears to have achieved a healthy balance between overly politicizing decisions or insufficiently accounting for different values.

Finally, it is clear that administrative accountability systems and incentive systems are not a panacea for the challenge of school reform. The success of such programs in generating change is dependent on the capacity of the state to follow through in providing the necessary assistance and support to individual schools and teachers. Moreover, since most of the experience with such systems comes from states with weak or nonexistent teacher unions, almost nothing is known about implementation issues or effectiveness in a situation with strong unions.

Discussant Jane Hannaway neatly summarized the conclusion. Performance-based reform of education makes sense because so little is known about the specific relationships between educational inputs and outputs. If those relationships were better understood, outcome goals could be achieved by focusing attention on the inputs to the educational process. Without such knowledge, a preferred strategy is for policymakers to focus on outcome goals and to let schools experiment with ways to become more effective. At the same time, the challenge of developing acceptable measures of student and school performance, combined with other design and implementation challenges, makes it advisable for states to move with caution as they implement performance-based strategies.

Which Is a Better Way to Hold Schools Accountable: Parental Choice or an Administered System?

Achieving accountability through parental choice rather than through an administrative system has considerable intuitive appeal. Although Witte points out that the test scores of private school students may not greatly exceed those of public school students, private school students have higher graduation rates and are more likely to go to college. Moreover, according to Hoxby's analysis of subsidies for Catholic schools as a proxy for vouchers, competition from private schools may make the public schools more efficient. While these results are certainly suggestive, it is still too soon to reach the conclusion that parental choice should be the preferred mechanism for educational reform.

Many of the key issues are raised in the comments by Thomas Kane, who has a number of methodological concerns about Hoxby's analysis. He argues that a wide variety of voucher schemes is possible and that the existing evidence offers little guidance in choosing among them. In addition, Kane points out a well-functioning parental choice system requires that parents have good information about the quality of schools. Producing such information may thus lead back to the problems of constructing and publicizing measures of school performance that would be analogous, although not identical, to the ones required in a centralized accountability system. In the absence of a value-added measure, parents may simply choose schools with the highest test scores and thereby in effect base their choices on the socioeconomic background of the students rather than on where their children will learn the most.

The main difference between parental choice and an administered system is that under a choice program, accountability would be achieved by the mechanism of student exit. Advantaged and academically motivated students are more likely than other students to leave. Thus, to the extent that a child's learning is enhanced by the presence of advantaged and motivated students in the classroom, the departure of such students would generate a negative externality by reducing the learning of other students.

Kane argues that if the effect on student learning of attending a particular school is fairly uniform across students, then centralized performance systems are likely to be superior since they avoid the costs inherent in a choice program borne by the students who remain behind when other students leave. In contrast, the more the contribution of a school varies among students, the more effective a choice program will be in promoting student performance.

Should Voucher Programs Be Based on Need?

The research reported here supports the view that if we are to have voucher programs, the distribution of the vouchers should be based on need. Hoxby's simulation analysis shows that even with a universal voucher program, the share of children attending private school would rise only from 10 percent to 14 percent. Hence, a large share of the voucher funds would go to families who would have sent their children to private schools without the program. Second, Witte's survey shows that, in general, the students selecting private schools are disproportionately from advantaged families. Third, Kane's observation that students from high-income families may generate positive externalities while students from low-income families may generate negative externalities suggests that some form of public intervention into the private school market may be appropriate. Hence, to minimize wasteful use of resources, to provide equal opportunity to disadvantaged students, and to compensate schools for any negative externalities, children from economically disadvantaged families should be provided much larger vouchers than those from families with higher income.

How Can Policymakers Ensure Schools in High-Poverty Areas Adequate Resources to Achieve High Standards?

William Clune's commentary on the last three chapters of this book focuses on what they imply about state strategies to ensure that students in high-poverty schools have an opportunity to meet minimum state standards of student achievement. In particular, these chapters suggest that spending more on smaller class size or higher-quality teachers can generate returns in the form of greater learning and that investing in new forms of teaching and organizing schools that focus on academic performance seems to be worthwhile in some situations. In addition, these chapters provide additional evidence that, even after controlling for variation in efficiency, districts with higher poverty rates must spend more than others to generate a given level of student achievement.

However, many questions remain unanswered. There is much to learn about the interactions between basic inputs, like teachers, and changes in process or management. Moreover, while the three models of educational restructuring evaluated by Barnett may well be effective in some situations, it is not clear how generalizable they are to other schools serving poor students. None of the chapters directly addresses two key cost issues in typical high-poverty areas: the disastrous physical condition of many of the older schools, which require substantial amounts of new capital investment and maintenance spending, and the costs involved in maintaining a stable set of high-quality teachers in schools where working conditions are often far from ideal.

How should policymakers ensure that schools serving disadvantaged children have adequate resources to meet minimum outcome standards? One response, discussed further below, is for more experimental research on how to achieve adequate outcomes for these children in the most cost-effective manner. In the meantime, quantitative research of the type undertaken by Ferguson and Ladd and by Duncombe, Ruggiero, and Yinger could be used to determine an average additional amount of spending required in these schools to achieve minimum outcomes without special management reforms—that is, in ordinary schools—so that states and districts could allocate this additional amount to schools serving disadvantaged students.

Can More Experimentation and Evaluation Provide Some Answers?

A frequently recurring theme is the need for more experimentation and evaluation to find out what works and under what conditions. Education reform is plagued by the problem that policymakers introduce full-blown systems without thinking about how to evaluate them and what needs to be known about their effectiveness. As a result, lots of half-baked schemes to reform education get introduced before it is clear if they are likely to be effective. Educators can easily (and with some justification) become cynical about new innovations and view them as fads that soon will pass. As a consequence, they are less likely to respond to such reforms.

In some areas, experimentation will be easier than in others. For example, while more direct experimentation with large-scale voucher programs might be desirable, it may be hard to design an experiment to illuminate the feedback or dynamic effects that are of such interest. Experiments may work better for more narrowly defined questions such as the effects of class size. Both Steven Barnett and William Clune strongly advocated more experimental or quasi-experimental research on programs to deal with schools in high-poverty areas. Charles Abelmann noted that while such research could provide useful evidence of how various approaches work in specific schools, even more challenging for the researcher is to determine how to design and evaluate programs so that the results can be broadly applied.

Some conference participants emphasized the challenge of persuading policymakers to understand the value of experimental research. Most policymakers do not want to hear that their pet program is ineffective. Many want to retain the flexibility of modifying a program as they implement it and hence may be unwilling to support formal experimental designs. Given this challenge of convincing policymakers, one approach is to seize the opportunities provided naturally whenever there are queues of students who want to attend particular schools or programs. Provided that there is no systematic pattern to the queue or that children are taken off it randomly, the children in the program can be compared with those who were excluded.

Given the decentralization of the U.S. system of education, a strong argument can be made that the federal government should provide the push for and funding for a wave of such experiments. However, in the current political environment in which the federal government is turning more and more responsibilities back to the states, states will probably need to take on some of the responsibility for experimentation and evaluation.

Devoting more resources to research and evaluation is particularly important in the light of the shift in policy focus to educational results. In a system in which schools are held accountable for results—either through an administered system or by parental choice—school officials need reliable information on the contributions of various strategies to student learning. In addition, within a results-driven system, policymakers need information so that they can assure that adequate resources are available for children to learn in all schools. The success of performance-based reform of education is certainly not guaranteed. However, its chances of improving academic outcomes will be enhanced with knowledge from carefully controlled studies of the effects of specific educational strategies on student performance.

References

Bishop, John H. 1994. "The Impact of Curriculum-Based Examinations on Learning in Canadian Secondary Schools." Working Paper 94. Cornell University, Department of Economics.

Cohen, David. 1995. "Rewarding Teachers for Students' Performance." Paper prepared for a forum on incentives and systemic reform, sponsored by the Consortium for Policy Research in Education (CPRE) and the Pew Forum on Education Reform.

Congressional Budget Office. 1993. *The Federal Role in Improving Elementary and Secondary Education.*

Milgrom, Paul, and John Roberts. 1992. *Economics, Organization and Management.* Prentice-Hall.

Murnane, Richard J., John Willett, and Frank Levy. 1995. "The Growing Importance of Cognitive Skills in Wage Determination." *Review of Economics and Statistics* 77 (May): 251–66.

Ravitch, Diane. 1995. *National Standards in American Education: A Citizen's Guide.* Brookings.

Rothstein, Richard, and Karen Hawley Miles. 1995. *Where's the Money Gone? Changes in the Level and Composition of Education Spending.* Washington: Economic Policy Institute.

U.S. Department of Education, National Center for Education Statistics. 1994a. *The Condition of Education, 1994.*

U.S. Department of Education, National Center for Education Statistics. 1994b. *Digest of Education Statistics, 1994.*

PART ONE

Performance-Based Incentive Programs

CHAPTER TWO

Recognizing and Rewarding Success in Public Schools

Charles T. Clotfelter and Helen F. Ladd

FEW AREAS of public policy in the last decade have witnessed the flurry of reforms and innovations that have characterized K–12 education. Spurred by national concern about the quality of American public education, states and local school districts have undertaken hundreds of reforms, touching not only traditional topics such as curricular content, instructional methods, and teacher training but also fundamental issues of organizational structure and finance. Some of these reforms, such as merit pay for teachers, have sought to change the structure of financial incentives. Other reforms, like mandated standards and state "report cards," have sought to engender accountability by shifting the focus away from inputs to measured student outcomes.

In this chapter, we examine programs that combine the focus on outcomes with the use of financial incentives to recognize and reward the most effective schools. We examine such recognition and reward programs by focusing on the experience of two jurisdictions, the state of South Carolina and the Dallas Independent School District. By looking closely at two particularly sophisticated school-based programs, we are able to shed light on a variety of issues that apply more broadly to recognition and reward programs in education, such as how to pick winners, whether and how one should adjust for socioeconomic differences among schools, what sorts of

The authors would like to thank seminar participants at Brookings and Duke for their helpful comments and suggestions. In addition, they are extremely grateful to Adrian Austin and Rebecca Rund of Duke University and Anthony Shen of Brookings for superb research assistance. They also are grateful to John Suber, Garrett Mandeville, and John May of South Carolina and Robert Mendro and William Webster of Dallas for their assistance in obtaining and interpreting the data for South Carolina and Dallas. In addition, they thank Sandy Kress and a long list of teachers, principals, and other school officials who shared their time and insights about both programs.

incentives are generated, and whether the programs are in fact likely to increase student learning. The fundamental questions we address are whether such programs offer the potential for improving the performance of public schools and, if so, how they are best designed to fulfill that potential.

Issues Related to the Design of Recognition and Reward Programs

Among proposals for school reform, perhaps the most prominent are those calling for competition where parents and students would choose among public and (sometimes) private schools. In contrast to this approach, recognition and reward programs work within the existing administrative structure of the public school system. Their goal is to provide signals and incentives similar to those that might emerge from a market system with the purpose of holding various actors accountable and improving all schools in the system. Although often introduced as part of a larger comprehensive reform package, as in South Carolina and Kentucky, they sometimes are the centerpiece of the reform effort, as in Dallas. For example, one kind of recognition and reward program would focus on school "report cards," which publicize measured outcomes of student performance. In some states, such measures are tied to financial payoffs for schools or school officials.

Any recognition and reward program must answer several basic questions. What will be measured? Will adjustments be made for socioeconomic factors? How will the measures be linked to the rewards for educators? Before examining the particulars of the South Carolina and Dallas programs, it is useful to say a few words about these general questions.

What Will Be Measured?

The education literature offers a wide array of theories, measures, and studies about measurement and testing. Conventional practice, however, is solidly on the side of standardized tests as a measure of achievement. Not surprisingly, such tests constitute the basis for most programs for recognition and reward. Clearly, the use of such tests reflects the widespread belief that they can provide data that are useful in measuring the extent and success of any organizational change. This new focus on data-centered standards is epitomized in the Goals 2000: Educate America Act passed in the spring of 1994 with its emphasis on the establishment of goals and the measurement of progress toward those goals.

Such tests can vary in a number of dimensions. They may be "norm-based" or criterion-based. They may cover different subject matter. Some states have experimented with tests that are not machine-readable, such as North Carolina's writing test, but the difficulty of calibrating, let alone grading, tests of this sort precludes their widespread use. More generally, the call for more "authentic" assessment in the form of student portfolios exacerbates the problem of making fair comparisons across schools or districts.[1]

Some recognition and reward programs have used other measures in addition to standardized test scores. As we discuss below, South Carolina uses attendance rates, for both students and teachers, in its reward program. A predecessor of that state's program also included measures of student and parent attitudes.

In deciding what should be measured, two important considerations are how closely the measure corresponds to the actual or desired outcome and whether the targets of the program (such as the schools or the parents) can affect the outcome measures. One potential pitfall of any such measurement program is the "narrowing" of the curriculum or "teaching to the test," if in the process of preparing their students teachers devote their attention excessively toward the subjects to be covered by tests. One may also worry about the integrity of the test administration itself, if those subject to the rewards are administering the test instrument.

Despite these genuine concerns, the greatest advantage of using measured results and standardized tests may be that teachers, other school officials, and the public can understand the measure and comprehend at some level how the evaluations are made.

Will Adjustments Be Made for Socioeconomic Factors?

The 1966 Coleman report showed that the socioeconomic characteristics of students explained far and away the largest share of measured differences in educational achievement.[2] While most scholars continued to be-

---

1. For an evaluation of Vermont's experience with authentic assessment, see Koretz and others (1994). Also see the chapter by Elmore, Abelmann, and Fuhrman in this volume on Kentucky's attempt to incorporate an ambitious assessment mechanism into its accountability system.

2. Coleman and others (1966).

lieve that teachers and schools exert an influence on students' measured achievement, the large estimated effect of socioeconomic factors had a chastening influence on the optimism of educational reformers.[3] It also implies that it would be unfair to compare schools or school systems simply on the basis of their students' test scores. Thus, most recognition and reward programs perform some kind of adjustment of the absolute scores in an effort to give all participants a reasonable chance to be a winner.

Various approaches to adjustment can be distinguished. One approach is to focus on improvement—changes in scores over time—thereby letting each student, school, or district define its own benchmark. One serious criticism of this approach as a measure of the contributions of schooling to learning is the observation that any change in a student's test scores from year to year is attributable not only to what goes on in the school but also to what goes on at home, which reflects the student's economic and social background.[4]

An alternative approach is to compare actual scores with a predicted score. This prediction might be arrived at by regression analysis. Essentially, this means comparing schools with others that are similar as measured by factors like social and economic background or educational achievement in a prior year. For this approach, one must decide what constitutes legitimate predictors. If one uses socioeconomic status as a predictor, the effect is to set a lower threshold for success for poor students than for rich ones. Does that imply that poor students do not have the capacity to achieve at the levels observed among the affluent? Or that society does not expect as much from them? For a variable like race, these issues may be even more pointed.

Another issue in how to adjust is the appropriate level of observation. Because of the normal movement of students into or out of schools, using data aggregated by school or district (the most common approach) may lead to comparisons of different groups of students over time. Thus schools with more migration might face special problems or have to take responsibility for the performance of more students who were not under their influence for much of the year. The trade-off is that any approach that starts with data on individual students, who can then be assigned to the right schools for the purpose of the ranking, will be more difficult and expensive to carry out.

3. See, for example, Firestone (1991, p. 22).
4. For further discussion of this point, see Meyer (1994).

These questions are real and difficult, but not making some adjustment for socioeconomic differences among students will surely result in rankings that have identifiable socioeconomic bias. However, there is inevitably a trade-off with simplicity: as absolute scores are adjusted for a variety of reasons, the measures of achievement become less straightforward and comprehensible, which makes it harder for both parents and educators to evaluate the results.

How Will the Measures Be Linked to the Rewards for Educators?

Various measures, and the way they are used, can create different kinds of incentives. Some of these issues have already been mentioned; for example, if poorly conceived measures encourage narrow "teaching to the test," then the overall process of education can suffer.

One issue is whether the purpose of this measurement is recognition or reward. If the purpose of the information is simply to highlight which schools and districts are doing well, then one needs to decide if schools or districts should be explicitly compared with one another or instead with some absolute level of performance. Should results be shown in ways that allow rankings of schools, districts, or groups of students? If rewards are to be given, then the schools must be explicitly ranked either overall or by type of school, such as elementary, middle, or high school. When categories of schools are used, the categorization of magnet schools or special academies must be addressed.

If rewards or incentives are a part of the program, what should they be and to whom should they be given? It may be that symbolic forms of recognition—say, flags in the front hall of a school—can provide a powerful incentive. Experience shows that financial incentive programs directed toward individual teachers—like merit pay—have not worked well, and teachers have disliked them. The limitations of such programs are well known: the lack of consensus about what makes for effective teaching; the fact that gains in student achievement often reflect not just the actions of an individual teacher but also the more general environment for learning in the school; and the growing recognition that rewarding individual teachers encourages them to compete with one another rather than to work cooperatively. For these reasons, many believe that schools would be a more appropriate target for incentive programs than individual teachers.[5]

5. See Johnson (1984); Garms (1986); Murnane and Cohen (1986); and Cohen and Murnane (1985).

The past decade has also seen a growing belief among those who studied corporations and other large organizations in the importance of decentralized management and its corollary concept, accountability. Under such names as "continuous improvement" and "total quality management," the idea took hold that improvements in the efficiency of production and the quality of outputs could best be achieved by pushing decisionmaking down in the hierarchy. This urge to decentralize within public education found substance in "site-based management" and handing over to teams of teachers more discretion in deciding what and how to teach.[6] The bureaucracies of public school systems, like the hierarchies of giant corporations, were increasingly seen as impediments to improvement.[7]

As a result, there has been a change in the way public schools are managed. Increasingly, structures are being established to give principals and other local school officials more authority to make changes. The flip side of this increased authority is that they need to be rewarded for their successes and held accountable for their failures.

School Incentive Programs in South Carolina and Dallas

Recognition and reward programs in South Carolina and Dallas illustrate how such school-based programs might work in practice. Both programs are based on sophisticated approaches to ranking schools, and both have been in place long enough for strengths and weaknesses to emerge.

South Carolina's incentive award program began with the South Carolina Educational Improvement Act of 1984. This sweeping piece of legislation contained dozens of initiatives, including increased pay for teachers, beefed-up course requirements for high school graduation, universal kindergarten, a new basic skills exit exam for high school seniors, a performance incentive program for principals, school improvement councils with elected representatives, new tests and remedial help for low-scoring students, and increased support for capital expenditures. Taken together,

6. For a discussion of site-based management and other innovations in public schools, see, for example, Elmore (1991).

7. For example, Theodore R. Sizer states (1984, p. 209): "Bureaucracies lumber. Once regulations, collective bargaining agreements, and licensure get installed, change comes hard. Every regulation, agreement, and license spawns a lobby dedicated to keeping it in place. The larger and more complex the hierarchy, the more powerful the lobby becomes, ever more remote from frustrated classroom teachers, poorly served students, and angry parents."

the initiatives in the act represented more than a 20 percent increase in state spending on education, financed by a percentage-point increase in the state sales and use tax.[8] Although South Carolina was the first state to introduce a school performance incentive program, other states that have adopted such programs include Georgia, Indiana, Kentucky, Tennessee, and Texas.[9]

As far as we know, Dallas has one of the most complete and sophisticated accountability and incentive program of any big-city district in the country.[10] The Dallas program emerged from the work of a special commission appointed by the Dallas School Board in 1990. The commission, which had strong involvement and support from the local business community, set as a goal "to hold all levels of the district accountable for results and thus to simulate continuous quality improvement over time."[11] As part of this accountability system, financial awards were to be given to the personnel in the most effective schools, with half of the $2.5 million cost of the awards initially to be funded by the local business community. Dallas officials hope that their focus on accountability will generate a variety of other changes throughout the system.

Dallas's introduction of a sophisticated accountability and incentive system for the 1991–92 school year was facilitated by the statewide orientation toward testing and accountability, the absence of strong teacher unions that might have opposed it, the presence of competent statisticians and evaluators within the Dallas Independent School District (William Webster and Robert Mendro), and the fact that the chairman of the commission (Sandy Kress) successfully ran for chairman of the school board and thereby was in a position to implement the program. An Accountability Task Force made up of teachers, principals, parents, and members of the community and appointed by the school board has played a central role in legitimizing and implementing the program.

8. Kirk (1985).
9. Cornett and Ganes (1994).
10. Dallas schools are also subject to the state of Texas's recognition and reward program. Because criteria of the two programs differ significantly, Dallas schools are significantly underrepresented among the high-ranking schools in the state. Compared with Dallas, the state of Texas places much more emphasis on the absolute performance of the students and on the state's criterion-referenced test, the Texas Assessment of Academic Skills (TAAS). As a result, of the nine Dallas elementary schools that were winners of state monetary awards in the 1994 school year, only four were winners of Dallas awards. Among the other five schools that won state awards, three placed in the lowest 30 percent of the Dallas rankings.
11. Commission for Educational Excellence (1991, p. 3).

Ranking Schools and Picking Winners

Recognizing the strong effects of family and community background on the academic performance of students, neither South Carolina nor Dallas bases the school rankings on the absolute test performance of students. Instead, both places begin by measuring the difference between each student's absolute performance and his or her predicted performance on a particular test. In both places, a "gain" signifies a change from a benchmark or predicted score rather than from an actual score in the previous year.[12] However, Dallas and South Carolina differ significantly in how they predict student test scores and, consequently, in how they incorporate family background information into the overall school ranking and determination of winning schools. These student "gains" are then aggregated into school "gains" for all students who were enrolled in a school for the whole year. In both states, students who changed schools during the year or for whom prior-year test results are not available are excluded from the analysis and the ranking calculation.

SOUTH CAROLINA'S APPROACH. To include students in all grades, South Carolina relies on two main tests, typically given in different grades: the Basic Skills Assessment Program (BSAP), which is a state criterion-referenced test, and the Comprehensive Test of Basic Skills (CTBS), which is a nationally normed standardized test. South Carolina uses student-specific "gains" in test scores as the basis for the school ranking but also incorporates student and teacher attendance and, in the higher grades, dropout rates in determining the size of the award.

As we noted earlier, South Carolina and Dallas differ in how they calculate a student's predicted score, which in turn is the point of comparison for calculating student "gains." In South Carolina, the predicted score is based exclusively on a student's performance in the previous year as measured by test scores. The equation includes a constant and both squared and product terms. For example, the calculation for student i's predicted reading score R in year t uses that student's reading and math scores in the previous year $t-1$, in the following equation, where R indicates a reading test and M a math test:[13]

---

12. In the special case in which test scores are measured in commensurable units and T_i^* is set equal to the student's test score in the previous year, the difference would represent a true gain.

13. Even had South Carolina wanted to define the student "gain" as the difference between scores in year t and scores in year $t-1$, it would not have been able to do so because of the noncomparability of the tests given from year to year. The BSAP is given in grades 1, 2, 3, 6, 8, and 10 (exit exam), and the CTBS is given in grades 4, 5, 7, 9, and

$$R_{it} = a + bR_{i,t-1} + cM_{i,t-1} + c(R_{i,t-1}M_{i,t-1}) + dR_{i,t-1}^2 + eM_{i,t-1}^2 + u_{it}.$$

The parameters *a, b, c, d,* and *e* are estimated by regression analysis on the basis of all students for whom both current and prior-year test data are available. Clearly, a predicted score in South Carolina is not simply a linear function of scores in previous years.

To compute a "school gain index," South Carolina aggregates by using the median of the student "gains." The use of the median keeps teachers from focusing attention on students they perceive as fast learners who could make the school look good. However, it also gives them little incentive to give attention to students they perceive as slower learners whose small "gains" would not affect the calculation of the median.

No socioeconomic variables are included in the South Carolina approach to projecting scores. However, it is not immediately obvious what effect this omission would have on disadvantaged students. One possibility is that test scores of students living in economically disadvantaged family situations might increase at a slower rate than those of other students. In this situation, the predicted scores for such students would be systematically too high, which would result in small or negative "gains" for such students and a corresponding low estimate of the effectiveness of the schools they attend. Working in the other direction is the possibility that a ten-point "gain" in test scores might be easier to attain in the middle or the bottom of the test score range than at the very top of the range. If this is true, the average "gain" in schools serving students from advantaged households, who are likely to be high scorers, might be smaller than those serving disadvantaged students. In short, the direction of any bias arising from the lack of socioeconomic variables in the South Carolina approach is an empirical question.

In fact, experience with the program in South Carolina shows that when schools are ranked using this approach, the schools serving pupils with low socioeconomic status (SES) are much more likely to be near the bottom than are the schools serving more advantaged students. Hence South Carolina officials found that if they did not introduce SES information into the process for measuring the effectiveness of schools, the low-SES schools would seldom win incentive awards.[14]

---

11. In addition, the state gives a school readiness test in grade 1. Richards and Sheu (1992, p. 75).

14. See Richards and Sheu (1992). The positive correlation between the school gain index (SGI) and SES might possibly be explained as follows. Because achievement scores are measured with error, the regression explaining fifth grade scores as a function of fourth grade scores is subject to errors-in-variables bias, which tends to bias the coefficients toward zero. The greater the error, and thus the greater the downward bias, the more the SGI

To deal with this situation, South Carolina chose to classify the schools into five groups based on four variables that are intended to reflect the socioeconomic characteristics of the students: the percentage of students approved for free lunches, the percentage approved for reduced-price lunch, median years of education for teachers, and (for schools with a first grade) the percentage of students judged during pre–first grade screening not to be ready for school. Relying heavily on the extent of free or subsidized school lunches as a measure of student SES is appealing because it is available in administrative records, but it is obviously a less than full or complete measure of socioeconomic status. South Carolina chose not to use race of the student or the school as a proxy for socioeconomic status, presumably out of concern about the adverse signals it might send. Within each group, the top 25 percent of the schools with the greatest gains were eligible for incentive awards.[15]

Because of the positive correlation between the gain score and socioeconomic status, the score a school needs to win differs across the groups, with the cutoff set higher for the schools serving high-SES students than in those serving low-SES students. Principals soon realized that the group into which their schools fell could be of considerable significance. Schools that ended up near the bottom of a higher group rather than at the top of a lower group naturally felt that they were being treated unfairly. In response to such criticisms, the state introduced in 1992 an alternative method of adjustment, referred to as "exceeding expectations," which compared the size of a school's actual gain with the gain that was predicted based on the absolute level of scores in that school. A school could win an award either by being in the top quartile of the socioeconomic group into which it was placed or by being in the top 25 percent of the distribution of schools in the degree to which it "exceeded expectations."[16]

---

variable will resemble the absolute fifth grade score. The result would be a positive correlation between the calculated measure and the absolute level of the fifth grade scores and hence SES. We are grateful to Christopher Jencks for pointing out this possibility.

15. The variables are weighted by the results of a school-level regression equation of test scores on the grouping variables. In effect, the schools are grouped by the expected performance of their students on the various tests, aggregated across grades. Initially, a funding variable, namely local funding over the state required amount, was included in the ranking equation (Richards and Sheu [1992, p. 73]), but it was later dropped from the equation. In addition, winners have to exhibit a positive school gain index, which has the effect of excluding some schools in the top 25 percent of the lower groups from winning.

16. The SGI for each school was regressed against average absolute test scores in the school. The greater the positive residual, the more the school "exceeded expectations."

THE DALLAS APPROACH. Dallas also relies on two main tests: the Texas Assessment of Academic Skills (TAAS) and the Iowa Test of Basic Skills (ITBS). Both are typically administered in all grades (except the TAAS is not given in the lower elementary grades). To determine gains for individual students, Dallas uses a methodology somewhat similar to the South Carolina metholodology. Dallas also supplements the test score gains with a variety of schoolwide measures such as student attendance and promotion rates in elementary schools; those variables plus dropout rates and enrollment in accelerated courses in middle schools; and those plus average SAT and PSAT scores and the percentage taking the tests in the high schools. For each of these school-level variables, Dallas calculates the difference between the school's value and a predicted value, where the predicted value is based on a school-level regression equation. The Accountability Task Force determines which outcome measures are used each year and how they are to be weighted.

The Dallas district's methodology for looking at the gains in student scores is a two-stage procedure.[17] In the first stage, all test scores are purged of the effects of socioeconomic characteristics, including the race of the student. The second stage replicates the South Carolina approach of regressing test scores on prior-year test scores, except that adjusted test scores, based on the residuals from the first-stage regressions, are substituted for the actual test scores.

The first stage regressions to adjust for socioeconomic factors include characteristics both of the student and of the school. Individual factors include whether the student is black, Hispanic, limited-English proficient, male, and approved for free or reduced-price lunch, and also various interactions among these variables. The school-level variables include the mobility rate (the number of students entering or leaving the school per 100 students) and the degree of overcrowding. As is the case in South Carolina, the equations are based only on those students who are enrolled for the full year and for whom prior-year test data are available.[18] The mobility

17. The following discussion is based on Webster, Mendro, and Almaguer (1993); Webster and others (1994); Webster and Mendro (1995); and personal discussions with Robert Mendro and William Webster of the Division of Research, Planning and Evaluation of the Dallas Independent School District.

18. Dallas counts students as enrolled if they are enrolled in the school from October to June. Provided test score data are available for that student for the prior year, the student is included in the analysis, even if he or she attended a different school the previous year. Because Texas exempts from testing all students with limited English proficiency until the third grade, none of those students can be included until the fourth grade. The district is currently developing a strategy for testing those children at an earlier age so that they can be included in a school's effectiveness ranking.

rate is in the equation to control for the adverse effect that the movement of children into and out of the class has on the other students.

The first-stage regressions are run not only for test scores in the current year but also for test scores in the previous year. The residuals from these regressions are treated as adjusted test scores. By construction, variation in these residuals reflects something other than variation in the socioeconomic characteristics of the students.

At the second stage, students' adjusted test scores for the current year are regressed on students' adjusted test scores for the previous year, with no squared or interaction terms. The difference between each student's actual (adjusted) test score for the present year and the predicted (adjusted) test score represents the student's "gain." To develop its "school improvement indices," Dallas aggregates to the school level by using the mean of the student "gains," appropriately standardized across all tests and grades for all students enrolled in the school during the year. Dallas's use of the mean of the student "gains" is designed to indicate to teachers and the public that the performance of all students counts and to avoid providing an incentive for teachers to teach to a subset of the students.

Thus the main difference between the South Carolina "gain" approach and the Dallas approach is that the latter explicitly adjusts for the characteristics of individual students, including the race of the student. Moreover, South Carolina's adjustment for socioeconomic status is based exclusively on school-level aggregates, not individual characteristics.[19] But although the Dallas methodology ensures that student "gain" scores are uncorrelated with the measured socioeconomic characteristics of the students, an evaluation of the approach by the school district's research and evaluation department suggests that some small school-level effects remain. For example, the ranking of reading scores for, say fifth graders, is slightly correlated with the percentage of the students in the school who are minorities. In an attempt to reduce this correlation, the district has since replaced the second stage of the current analysis with the technique of "hierarchical linear modeling," which permits the introduction of more school-level variables as conditioning variables.[20]

19. In practice the Dallas approach is much more complicated than described here. In its attempt to be responsive to a variety of statistical concerns that could undermine the perceived fairness of the program, Dallas has introduced a number of refinements that increase the complexity of the approach. For example, at two points during the calculations, a structure is mechanically imposed on the errors in the regressions to eliminate any problems of heteroskasticity. In addition, the method involves multiple standardizations and various weightings. See Webster, Mendro, and Almaguer (1993).

20. See Webster and others (1994, p. 17).

Two aspects of the Dallas methodology are worth highlighting. First, in its attempt to be scrupulously fair to schools, Dallas has developed an approach that is incomprehensible to most participants in the process and to most outside observers. Even the straightforward form of the two-stage approach as described above is difficult to explain and discuss. The addition of a variety of sophisticated adjustments and refinements may serve to counter various concerns, but in the process it makes the approach even more opaque. Outcome measures that school officials see and understand—such as test scores—go into a black box, and there they are adjusted in various complex ways, standardized, and then restandardized. The indicators that emerge bear little resemblance to the data that originally went into the black box. School officials neither understand the process nor have any idea what sorts of gains would have been required for them to achieve a high ranking.

The second aspect worth highlighting is the role of race. By including the race of the student in the prediction equations, Dallas is explicitly accounting for the possibility that minority students may learn less in any given year than their white counterparts, even after other indicators are taken into consideration. With this procedure, the district avoids the criticism that its accountability system is biased against schools with high proportions of minority students. However, the danger arises that the approach may reinforce the notion that some students are less able to learn than others.

The Awards

Both South Carolina and Dallas provide financial and other rewards to the winning schools, determined primarily by the schools' ranking. In both areas, schools must also show positive growth in test scores to be eligible for an award.

The centerpiece of the Dallas program is bonuses to the staff of the winning schools. In each winning school, the principals and teachers each receive a bonus of $1,000, and the nonprofessional staff, such as secretaries and janitors, each receive $500. In addition, $2,000 is given to the school activity fund. Winning schools are also recognized at an elaborate luncheon in downtown Dallas. Each year about 20 percent of school personnel receive awards. Given the fixed pot of money, the proportion of the schools that win each year depends on the number of teachers and other staff members in the winning schools.

For 1994–95, a two-tier system of awards was established. The top tier received the current level of awards, and personnel in a second tier of schools, made up of all the nonwinning schools whose performance exceeded predicted performance, won smaller awards: $450 for professionals and $225 for others. This change was designed to create more winners and to give more hope of winning to those schools far down in the ranking.

In South Carolina, the winning schools essentially share a given pot of money in proportion to their enrollments. Winning schools that fail to reach state goals for attendance (for both students and teachers) receive somewhat smaller awards. In addition, schools falling just short of the threshold for winning are given "honorable mention" citations and a token $1,000 award. All winning schools are also awarded colorful flags suitable to be displayed.[21]

In contrast to the awards in Dallas, the awards in South Carolina are given explicitly to the schools, with the use of the funds determined by schools in consultation with local school committees, and they cannot be used for direct payments to teachers. Typical awards are in the range of $15,000 to $20,000 per school. In addition to the monetary awards, winning schools in South Carolina receive an extra payoff. After a school wins, and for as long as it continues to achieve positive gain scores, it is excused from the requirement of petitioning the state for exceptions to the labyrinth of rules covering its operation. For example, if a school wants to use some of its budget for a part-time language teacher, use some mandated physical education time for unstructured recess, or combine science and math classes, it can do so without submitting a formal request for a waiver.

In addition to recognizing and rewarding the schools that are performing well, school ranking programs of this type also provide information on the schools that are performing poorly. In Dallas, a low-performing school receives additional scrutiny from the superintendent. Such attention focuses on the school's improvement plan and progress toward achieving school goals. In addition, the central office closely monitors the school's leadership and, in some cases, provides additional resources to the school.

---

21. Because winning is based on a school's ranking relative to other schools and awards come out of a fixed pot, schools can never be sure before the fact whether they will be winners or, if they are, how much money they will win. Awards for winning schools not reaching either 96 percent attendance for teachers or students are reduced by 10 percent and awards for those failing on both counts are reduced by 20 percent. The per student prize amount cannot be calculated until after the prizes are allocated to honorable mentions and attendance results are tabulated.

Significantly, low performance does not trigger automatic sanctions, as it is designed to do in some other states, such as Kentucky.[22]

Adjusting: A Closer Look

As this discussion has doubtless suggested to the reader, many possible measures of school performance exist. Some of these measures may be closely related; others will give quite different results. In this section, we explore these issues by examining nine different measures of school performance. For the purpose of illustration, we use actual data from South Carolina's recognition and reward program to understand how these different measures would have functioned, and then look briefly at the patterns in Dallas.

Alternative Measures of Student Achievement

We wish to consider alternative measures of school performance, all based on the standardized test scores of students, and apply these measures to the scores of fifth graders in South Carolina schools. The first measure is the average absolute score of fifth graders in the school. The other eight measures represent various attempts to correct for differences among schools that may lead to perceptions that comparisons of average scores are unfair. Measure number 2, the average change in test scores from one year to the next, uses only the students for whom data were available in both years. Measure 3 uses the difference between the average fifth grade score and the average fourth grade score for all students in each school in those grades, thereby ignoring the in- and outmigration of students. Measure 4 calculates the change in the logarithm of the score, which approximates the percentage change in scores, rather than the absolute change.

Measure 5—the school gain index, or SGI—comes directly out of the South Carolina program itself. As described above, this measure is calculated for each test taken by each student as the difference between the student's fifth grade score minus the predicted score for that student, where the predicted score is a function of the student's reading and math scores from the previous year. Here, we calculate the arithmetic mean SGI for fifth graders in each school, separating the reading and math averages.

22. For a criticism of the Kentucky proposal, see Darling-Hammond (1992, p. 255).

Although our measure differs somewhat from the actual measure calculated in South Carolina (which the reader will recall uses the median score), the basic idea is the same.

Measure 6 is based on one of the forms of adjustment built into South Carolina's approach, referred to above as "exceeding expectations." This measure uses the residual from a regression of each school's SGI on the school's average test scores. It adjusts measure 5 for any tendency of the school gain index to correlate systematically with average scores.

The seventh and eighth measures are based on the adjustment method used by North Carolina between 1991 and 1993 for its report card on the performance of school districts.[23] In North Carolina's approach, a district's effectiveness is measured by the difference between its actual test scores and predictions of the district's scores, given the socioeconomic characteristics of the students. The predicted scores are referred to as the par scores. We apply this approach here at the school level. In the case of measure 7, the regression includes the percentage of students receiving free lunch and the percentage receiving reduced-price lunch. For measure 8, the racial composition of the school is added as an additional regressor.

Measure 9 approximates the method used by the Dallas Independent School District. As explained above, it is calculated from the residuals of a regression of adjusted test scores on adjusted prior-year test scores, where the adjustment involves purging all test scores of their correlation with the socioeconomic characteristics of the students.[24] The measure of the school's performance is the mean of the residuals, which represent the portions of each student's performance not explained by socioeconomic characteristics, across all students in the school.

Adjustment Calculations

Through the South Carolina recognition and reward program, we found that matching data were available for 41,650 fifth-grade students

23. For a description and analysis of this methodology, see Clotfelter and Ladd (1994).
24. The variables in the first-stage regressions include 0–1 variables for race, gender, free lunch, and reduced-price lunch, interactions between free lunch and race and between reduced-price lunch and race, and a proxy for the mobility rate for the entire grade within the school. The mobility rate was calculated as the number of nonmatched students (those who took the test in the fifth grade but who were not in the school in the fourth grade) divided by the total number of fifth grade students taking the test in the school.

in 571 schools.[25] To see how the various measures correlate with each other, we report the correlation matrix for the nine measures in table 2-1.

Among the alternative adjusted measures, the measures that are variants of each other—those based on changes (2, 3, and 4) and those based on residuals from a cross-section regression (7 and 8)—are highly correlated with each other, and thus will tend to produce similar rankings. But otherwise the patterns are not uniform. Column 1 of the table shows that the absolute average score is much less correlated with the other measures than they are correlated among themselves. Its correlation with the others ranges from 0 for the adjusted South Carolina measure (by construction) to 0.58 for measures 7 and 8.

Apparent Bias in the Measures

Whether any of these measures are judged as fair will likely depend on several criteria, including how closely the outcomes correspond to the judgments of close observers. But any measure of school effectiveness that is highly correlated with the racial or economic composition of the student body will be difficult to defend.

To give a sense of the association of the various measures with race and economic status, we report in table 2-2 the correlation coefficients of each of the nine measures with two demographic variables, the percentage of students receiving free lunch and the percentage of students who are black within each school. As shown in the first row of the table, these two demographic measures are highly correlated with the average absolute scores. By contrast, the correlations with all of the adjusted measures are much smaller. Among the remaining measures, the one most subject to a bias in favor of more affluent and whiter schools is the South Carolina school gain index. In fact, most of the adjusted measures show some bias in the direction of more affluent and whiter schools, though the correlation coefficients are generally low. Measure 8 is essentially uncorrelated with the

25. The data set itself includes 47,000 students—all of the state's fifth graders in 1994. Choosing the fifth grade had the advantage that, in contrast to every other pair of grades, the state used the same kind of achievement test in both fourth and fifth grades. After dropping from the sample students for whom test data were missing or incomplete, information on 45,872 students remained. Of these, 41,650 had matching test results for fourth as well as fifth grade. (The remaining 4,252 fifth graders changed schools between fourth and fifth grades.) In 1994 these students attended a total of 595 elementary schools, of which 571 had students the previous year as well. The average school had 77 fifth grade students.

Table 2-1. *Correlations among Alternative Measures of School Performance*[a]

Measure[b]	1	2	3	4	5	6	7	8	9
(1) Average score	1.00	...	...	...	...	...	...	...	...
(2) Change (matched)	0.42	1.00	...	...	...	...	...	...	...
(3) Change (unmatched)	0.36	0.94	1.00	...	...	...	...	...	...
(4) Log change	0.31	0.99	0.94	1.00	...	...	...	...	...
(5) SGI	0.51	0.97	0.90	0.95	1.00	...	...	...	...
(6) Adjusted SGI	0.00	0.89	0.86	0.93	0.86	1.00	...	...	...
(7) Relative to par, without race	0.58	0.46	0.43	0.40	0.47	0.20	1.00	...	...
(8) Relative to par, with race	0.58	0.47	0.44	0.42	0.48	0.22	0.99	1.00	...
(9) Student residual	0.17	0.90	0.86	0.92	0.85	0.89	0.40	0.39	1.00

Source: Authors' calculations based on unpublished data from South Carolina Department of Education.

a. Using reading scores.

b. Measures are as follows: (1) mean fifth grade score; (2) change in mean score, matched students only; (3) mean score based on all fifth grade students minus previous year's mean for matched students; (4) log change in mean score, matched students only; (5) mean student gain index using South Carolina methodology; (6) residual from "exceeding expectations" equation using South Carolina methodology (SGI for the school regressed on average test scores in the school); (7) difference from "par": residual from cross-section equation using North Carolina methodology; (8) same as 7, with race added as explanatory variable; (9) mean of student test score residuals using Dallas methodology.

Table 2-2. *Correlations of School Performance Measures with Demographic Characteristics of Students*

	Percentage receiving free lunch		Percentage black	
Measure[a]	Reading	Math	Reading	Math
(1) Average score	−0.81	−0.61	−0.71	−0.55
(2) Change (matched)	−0.18	−0.07	−0.10	−0.11
(3) Change (unmatched)	−0.13	−0.05	−0.06	−0.09
(4) Log change	−0.08	−0.04	−0.02	−0.09
(5) SGI	−0.29	−0.10	−0.21	−0.13
(6) Adjusted SGI	0.14	0.27	0.17	0.20
(7) Relative to par, without race	0.00	0.00	−0.09	0.07
(8) Relative to par, with race	0.00	0.00	0.00	0.00
(9) Student residual	0.08	0.01	0.03	−0.04

Source: See table 2-1.
a. See table 2-1 for definitions of measures.

Table 2-3. *Characteristics of Winners and Nonwinners Resulting from Alternative Measures of School Performance*[a]

	Percentage receiving free lunch		Percentage black	
Measure[b]	Top 25 percent	Remainder	Top 25 percent	Remainder
(1) Average score	23	51	22	51
(2) Change (matched)	40	44	42	44
(3) Change (unmatched)	41	44	43	43
(4) Log change	43	44	44	43
(5) SGI	38	45	39	45
(6) Adjusted SGI	48	41	51	40
(7) Relative to par, without race	44	43	43	44
(8) Relative to par, with race	44	43	46	42
(9) Student residual	46	42	46	42

Source: See table 2-1.
a. Using reading scores.
b. See table 2-1 for definitions of measures.

demographic variables because these school-level variables were accounted for explicitly in the measure's construction. As we have implemented it, the Dallas approach (measure 9) shows no bias toward white or affluent schools and in fact may slightly overcompensate for these factors. The anomaly among these measures is the corrected SGI (measure 6), which appears to overcompensate significantly for race and affluence.

We next carried out simulations to find out which of our districts would end up in the top quartile given different measurements (see table 2-3). We then compared the top quartile with the rest of the schools to determine if the two sets of schools differ systematically. The first row of the table shows that if absolute reading scores were used, winning schools would have 23 percent of their students on free lunch, whereas the nonwinners would have over 50 percent. In addition, the winning schools would have a markedly smaller proportion of black students. Under this ranking scheme, winning schools would differ systematically from nonwinners.

In contrast, the remaining rows show that once the adjustments are made, these readily measured differences between winning and nonwinning schools almost disappear in most cases. Of the remaining measures, the ones that produce the biggest differences between winners and losers are the South Carolina measures (5 and 6), with the school gain index leaning in the direction of whiter and more affluent schools and the adjusted version going the other way.

In carrying out this analysis, we also found a difference between larger and smaller schools. When ranked according to absolute test scores (measure 1), schools in the top quarter tended to have fifth-grade classes about 14 percent larger than those in the nonwinning schools. But according to many of the other measures, smaller schools appear to have an advantage. We have no ready explanation for this curious result.

Actual Patterns in Dallas

In Dallas, winning schools accounted for about 20 percent of the schools at the top of the rankings for each category, such as elementary, middle, and high school. During the first three years of the Dallas program, 57 percent of the schools were not in the top 20 percent of their categories in any of the three years, 28 percent won once, 11 percent won twice, and only 4 percent won three times. The relatively low rate of repeat winners is not surprising, given that if a school makes large gains one year, it is harder to maintain that high level of gains the next year.[26]

We looked for bias in the pattern of winning from two directions: whether demographic characteristics could explain the results, and whether schools with a higher level of scores consistently ended up as winners. No clear patterns or differences emerge. Hence, the actual results

26. We hypothesized that we would find more repeat winners at the middle school level than at the other levels because middle schools have fewer grades and take a big chunk of their students from feeder schools. If those feeder schools are doing a poor job, the middle school can look good year after year. In fact, we found a slightly higher percentage of repeat winners in middle schools, 19 percent, versus 15 percent in elementary and high schools, but the difference was not statistically significant.

for Dallas confirm the simulated results reported above, that the Dallas methodology appears to generate no clear bias among schools with different average test scores or demographic characteristics.

Incentives and Unintended Effects

To be effective, recognition and reward systems must change behavior in ways that encourage student learning. For several reasons, school-based incentive programs could conceivably generate more favorable behavioral responses than more narrowly based programs of incentives for individual teachers. For example, in contrast to a teacher-based program, a school-based incentive program could encourage teachers to support and learn from each other. A schoolwide program might also have a better chance of changing the school culture and norms, helping teachers to demand more from students.[27] To the extent that school officials have actual power over key decisions, schools can be more responsive to incentives than can individual teachers. For example, school officials can move around existing resources, hire and fire teachers, encourage professional development, commandeer additional resources, and force changes throughout the system. Finally, given the observation that teachers often know better what they need than do central administrators, school-based incentive programs could lead to more teacher involvement in decisions about the form of teacher training and thereby to better programs.

Despite the potential of school-based incentive programs—especially in the context of a school system where significant power has been decentralized to the school level—a number of concerns remain. These include "teaching to the test," program manipulation and outright cheating, and effects of the program on teacher morale.

Teaching to the Test

Of the possible undesirable side effects of recognition and reward programs, perhaps the most serious is the possibility that teachers will focus too narrowly on the measures that are used in the ranking system, to the detriment of a broader goal of student learning. At an extreme, this would

---

27. As elaborated by Bishop (1994), in many schools the amount of work done in any classroom may be viewed as the outcome of a negotiation between the students and the teacher.

involve teaching actual questions that will appear on the test, which is clearly undesirable. On the other hand, if the test reflects a well-designed curriculum, then teaching to the test may be exactly what the state or district intends.

Both Dallas and South Carolina use in their ranking system a test that is related to the state curriculum. For example, the Texas Assessment of Academic Skills (TAAS) is explicitly linked to the state's essential elements curriculum. School officials in Dallas believe that the essential elements curriculum represents a reasonable baseline, so that, at least at the elementary and middle school levels, teaching to the objectives of the TAAS requires teaching the basic curriculum.[28] Even at the elementary school level, however, Dallas bases its rankings on performance on a nationally normed test as well so that it can signal the schools and teachers that good performance on a single test is not sufficient.

At the high school level, Dallas officials were less willing to defend the TAAS as being closely linked to the curriculum. Although the district includes student performance on the TAAS exit exam as one element of a school's ranking, it tries to minimize the incentive for teachers to focus narrowly on the basic skills on the TAAS by including a range of other outcome measures, including scores on end-of-course exams, in the ranking procedure. There is clearly concern that standardized tests are more oriented toward basic skills than higher-order thinking skills, and thus that rewarding progress toward one learning objective and not the other could lead teachers to focus their attention on the rewarded activity, perhaps to the exclusion of the other.[29] Thus recognition and reward programs may be limited by the quality of the available assessment methods.

Many of the problems related to teaching to the test can be solved by using more than one test, by paying attention to the link between the tests and the teaching goals for the schools, and by developing better assessment systems. However, the concern about teaching to the test may also reflect a more fundamental unease among some educators with the fact that recognition and reward programs focus on academic achievement. To the extent that schools have other goals, such as training students to be good citizens, rewarding academic performance alone could be viewed as undesirable.

28. However, Dallas officials are concerned that the TAAS has not been subject to a formal validation. See Anderson and others (1994).
29. Milgrom and Roberts (1992, pp. 228–31) discuss this topic under the rubric of the equal compensation principle. Also see Hannaway (1992) for a proposal to resolve the problem by separating the tasks and providing financial incentives only for the teachers of basic skills.

Program Manipulation and Outright Cheating

One can imagine a variety of ways that school officials might manipulate school-based incentive programs of the type used in South Carolina and Dallas. Extreme examples might include altering answers after tests have been turned in, having teachers assist students during the test, or discouraging certain students from taking the test at all.

Anecdotes from South Carolina illustrate some other possibilities. One former high school principal pointed out that the system could be gamed by emphasizing the tests in alternating years, so that gains would be exceptional every second year. To increase the chances of big gains, tests in "off" years would be administered in poor environments such as the gym or cafeteria. In years when gains were anticipated, the tests would be talked up and administered in more comfortable surroundings such as the students' own math and English classrooms. In addition, school officials can try to affect into which of the five groups their school is classified (remember, awards in South Carolina are given within five different groups). One official pointed out that teachers giving screening tests to entering first graders can try to increase the proportion of students evaluated as unready for first grade. Similarly, principals have strong objectives to enroll as many students as possible in the free and reduced-price lunch program. Both steps would increase the likelihood that the school will be placed in a low group, and thus affect its likelihood of winning an award.

Dallas's concerns about the manipulation of student numbers are clear from its requirement that a winning school test at least 95 percent of its eligible students and its inclusion of the following warning: "Schools that, in the opinion of the Accountability Task Force, attempt to manipulate their continuously enrolled student population will be disqualified from the Awards Program."[30] Dallas officials, however, downplay the potential problem by pointing out that schools have to be pretty clever to figure out who to try to exclude from the testing or from the school count. For example, a student who scored low in the previous year could easily have a larger "gain" than a high-scoring student. A sophisticated method of adjusting for student background that counts gains rather than average scores is not as easy to manipulate.

Given the relatively high stakes for teachers and principals in the Dallas incentive program, it is not surprising to find evidence of outright cheating in that city. In at least two situations, the district found evidence that school

30. Dallas Independent School District (1993, p. 3).

personnel had tampered with the tests in an attempt to raise the performance of the school's students. However, as district officials examine test scores by school and teacher each year, they can readily flag exceptionally large gains in a particular classroom or school. Further investigation of the original test papers is then usually sufficient to determine whether the school was phenomenally successful or whether fraud was involved. The district has publicized cases of cheating discovered in this manner and has punished the guilty parties, in some cases by firing them, in the hope of deterring similar cheating in the future.

Effects on Teacher Morale

The morale problems in programs of merit pay for individual teachers are well known: teachers who win bonuses may be happy, but those who do not may resent the others or believe they were more deserving.[31] A school-based incentive program of the type used in Dallas avoids some of these problems by giving bonuses to all teachers in a winning school. However, other potential morale problems remain. One is the free rider problem that occurs because all teachers win an award regardless of their contribution to the overall effort. However, since it is easier to fire teachers in Dallas than elsewhere because of the absence of unions, a nonperforming teacher may benefit from a bonus in one year but find his or her job in jeopardy in a subsequent year.

A second morale problem arises in part because the school rankings are based on performance relative to that of all the other schools. As a result, teachers in a school can work extremely hard to win an award and in fact increase student performance more than in the previous year, only to find that other schools did even better. In some cases the result is extreme frustration, anger, and disappointment.[32] The small number of winners each year also contributes to this problem. Only about 20 percent of the schools in Dallas win awards each year, and over the three years of the award program, more than half the schools have never won an award. This large proportion of nonwinners means that many teachers may come to believe that they can never win. Dallas's recent introduction of a two-tier system of winners, which increases the proportion of winners to about 50 percent each year, responds to this concern.

31. See, for example, Cohen and Murnane (1985).
32. Based largely on interviews in one Dallas school.

Effects of the Dallas Program on Student Outcomes

The ultimate test of recognition and reward programs is their effects on student outcomes. Because the school incentive program in South Carolina was introduced as part of a comprehensive package of school reform, isolating the effects of the incentive program on student outcomes in that state would be impossible. However, the accountability and school incentive system is the centerpiece of the school reform effort in Dallas. Hence, to measure the effects of recognition and reward programs, we focus attention on Dallas.

However, even in limiting our attention to Dallas, there are difficulties in measuring how the accountability program affects student outcomes. For example, while student test scores may increase in the short run as teachers focus more attention on academic achievement and test-taking skills, the three years since the beginning of the program is probably too short a time for the program to induce the types of changes in culture, personnel and teacher training necessary to promote and sustain long-term gains in test scores. Dallas's testing arrangements are dictated largely by state decisions, and the state has altered its testing program, especially its use of nationally normed tests, in significant ways during the past five years.[33] Consequently, results on nationally normed tests in Dallas for each year since the introduction of the Dallas reform are not directly comparable to test results for any year before its introduction.[34] Finally, there is always the possibility that any results are affected by other changes occurring in Dallas, some of which may not be related to the accountability program.

These concerns cannot be avoided. But to minimize them, we decided to focus on a single test, the Texas Assessment of Academic Skills, which

33. Through 1990–91 Texas used the full Iowa Test of Basic Skills and the Tests of Academic Proficiency (ITBS/TAP). For 1991–93 it used the Norm-Referenced Assessment Program for Texas (NAPT), which by 1993 was a bit of a hybrid between a nationally normed test and a test referenced to the state curriculum. Distressed by the inappropriate norming of the NAPT, the Dallas district requested a waiver from the NAPT in 1993–94 and replaced it with a short form of the ITBS/TAP. Although the short form was normed to the full ITBS, it includes a higher proportion of more challenging questions. See Anderson and others (1994).

34. In a recent internal study comparing Dallas test scores on the Iowa Test of Basic Skills in 1994 with scores in 1991, the authors had to make some rather arbitrary adjustments to account for the fact that Dallas used the long form of the test in 1991 and the short form in 1994. The results were at best mixed. See Anderson and others (1994, p. 5) for the adjustment and throughout for the results.

is linked to the state's curriculum. Then, we used panel data techniques to comparate the performance of Dallas students in specific grades with that of students in the other five large Texas cities.

Comparisons with Other Cities

Specifically, we compared the performance of Dallas students in specific grades on various components of the state-administered TAAS with student performance in the other five large Texas cities—Austin, El Paso, Fort Worth, San Antonio, and Houston—for the school years 1990–91 to 1993–94. The 1990–91 school year represents the year before the Dallas program was introduced, and 1993–94 is the third year of the program.[35] The six Texas cities vary in size and racial makeup. But they are all urban areas, and all Texas schools are subject to the same statewide curriculum, the same statewide testing requirements, and the same statewide reform and accountability efforts. Remaining city and school-specific differences can be controlled for statistically.[36]

Our basic outcome measure is the pass rate on various parts of the TAAS, such as reading and math. While we would prefer to use data on raw test scores, which would reflect gains by all students, we view the pass rate as an acceptable alternative outcome measure, especially given that average pass rates are relatively low.

35. We would prefer to focus on changes in performance for specific cohorts of students. Unfortunately, the data for that type of study design are not available. Although we have information on gains by cohorts after the introduction of the program, we do not have comparable information on gains by similar cohorts before the program. Hence no direct inferences about program effects can be made from the postprogram changes in test scores by cohort in Dallas.

36. Although the Dallas Independent School District (ISD) is virtually coterminous with the city of Dallas, cities and school districts are typically not coterminous in the other big Texas cities. To cover as much of each city as possible, we have combined the major school districts in those cities that are served by more than one district. The cities' ISDs were used for Austin, Dallas, and Forth Worth, respectively. For Houston, we combined the ISDs of Houston, Alief, and Spring Branch; for El Paso, the ISDs of El Paso, Canutillo, and Ysleta; and for San Antonio, the ISDs of San Antonio, Edgewood, Harlandale, South San Antonio, and Alamo Heights. The 1992 population of the six cities ranged from 1.7 million in Houston to 454,000 in Forth Worth. Dallas is the second largest city with 1 million people. Dallas has the highest proportion of black students (44.4 percent), followed by Forth Worth (34.0 percent) and Houston (31.7 percent). San Antonio has 83.8 percent Hispanic students, El Paso 78.6 percent, Houston 45.0 percent, and Dallas 39.7 percent. With respect to economically disadvantaged students, Dallas ranks second with 71.2 percent to San Antonio's 82.8 percent. Population figures are from U.S. Bureau of the Census (1994). All other figures are from 1993–94 and originate from the MicroAEIS (Academic Excellence Indicator System) computer data base and the AEIS.

We focus here on reading and math results for seventh graders.[37] For the years 1990–91, 1991–92, and 1992–93, collecting the data is straightforward. However, starting in the spring of 1993, the TAAS was administered in the spring rather than in the fall. Thus, for the 1993–94 school year, we adjust for the timing change by using spring 1994 sixth grade scores. The adjustment is imperfect in at least two ways. A test taken in the spring of the sixth grade is not exactly equivalent to a test taken in the fall of the seventh grade, given that students tend to forget material during the summer vacation. However, we can correct for the discrepancy statistically. A second difficulty with the sixth grade substitution is that our panel of schools is not identical over time, because sixth grades are typically not in the same school as seventh grades.

Model of Seventh Grade Pass Rates

Our panel analysis focuses on pass rates at the school level for seventh (and sixth in 1993–94) grade scores in reading and math. For each subject, we look at pass rates for the following groups of students: all students, children from economically disadvantaged households, blacks, Hispanics, and whites. To simplify the presentation of the basic model, we use the subscript i to denote the school and exclude subscripts for the subject or subgroup. The basic model takes the following form:

$$PASS_{it} = \alpha + \beta_1(YR92_t \times Dallas) + \beta_2(YR93_t \times Dallas) + \beta_3(YR94_t \times Dallas)$$
$$+ \Sigma_k X_{kit}(\gamma_k + \delta_k YR94) + \Sigma_m \theta_m + \Sigma_r \eta_r + \mu_{it}.$$

The variables are defined as follows. The dependent variable $PASS_{it}$ is the seventh grade pass rate (sixth in 1993–94) in school i in year t (for a specific subject and subgroup), expressed relative to the statewide average pass rate for that subject in that year. At the beginning of the independent variables, α is a constant, and at the end, μ_{it} is a random error term that varies by school and by year.

The crucial variables for this analysis are the three terms that interact the Dallas indicator variable with the year, that is, the first three variables

37. We report the full analysis in Ladd (1995). Based on a model similar to that reported below for seventh graders, for third graders we find significant gains in Dallas relative to other districts during the first year of the program. An alternative analysis based on specific cohorts of students moving from third to fourth grade, however, suggests that any positive effects the Dallas program may have had have been insufficient to offset what otherwise would have been a decline in the success rate of Dallas students relative to those in other Texas cities.

in the equation. *YR92$_t$* is an indicator variable that takes on the value 1 if it is the 1991–92 school year, and 0 otherwise. Similarly, *YR93$_t$* is an indicator variable that takes on the value 1 for the 1992–93 school year, and *YR94$_t$* is an indicator variable that takes on the value 1 for the 1993–94 school year. *Dallas* is an indicator variable that takes on the value 1 if the school is in Dallas and 0 otherwise. Given that the Dallas program was initiated during the 1991–92 school year, and the TAAS was given during the fall of that year, we take the coefficient, β_1, of the 1992 interaction term to measure effects before the introduction of the Dallas program. A positive coefficient on the 1993 or the 1994 interaction term, β_2 or β_3, would indicate that pass rates went up more in Dallas than in the other five cities in that year relative to the base year, 1991.

The other variables serve as control variables. X_{kit} represents the *k*th characteristic of school *i* in year *t*, which includes the percentage of the students in the school who are black, the percentage who are Hispanic, the percentage with limited English proficiency, the percentage who are economically disadvantaged, and the mobility rate of students. The school characteristic variables control for differences among schools and over time in the characteristics of the student body. These variables are interacted with the 1994 school year to allow for the effects of the spring test to vary by subgroup of the student population and by the amount of movement into and out of the school. City effects control for any differences in the average performance on the TAAS across cities. As a result, the observation that Dallas schools typically may have either lower or higher pass rates than schools in the other cities does not affect the measure of program effects. Here, γ_k (for $k = 1 \ldots 5$) and δ_m (for $m = 1992, 1993, 1994$) are parameters to be estimated.

θ_m represents year effects for 1992, 1993, 1994, where 1991 is treated as the base year. Year effects control for all the factors that affect average pass rates from year to year—for example, a change in the passing standard. Since the dependent variable is expressed relative to the state average, the year effects are expected to be small.

η_r represents city effects for Dallas, Austin, El Paso, Fort Worth, and San Antonio (Houston is left out). Given the inclusion of the city and year indicator variables, it is reasonable to assume that the error term is uncorrelated with the explanatory variables and that it has a mean of zero.[38]

38. The variation in school sizes across the sample makes it unreasonable to assume that the error terms are drawn from distributions with the same variance across schools. Consequently, all equations reported below were weighted either by the number of students in the school or by the number of students in the school in the particular subgroup. Ideally, the weights should reflect the number of students tested in each grade rather than the

Estimated Program Effects

Before turning to the coefficients of primary interest, we briefly summarize the other coefficients. For the reader who wants all the details, two tables in the appendix present the full set of estimates for reading and math. In almost all cases, the school characteristic variables enter with negative and statistically significant coefficients. In other words, the relative pass rate for all students in a grade falls as the concentrations of black, Hispanic, limited–English proficiency, and disadvantaged students rise. Furthermore, mobility always enters negatively and highly significantly; this finding suggests that schools with more students moving in and out during the year have lower pass rates than schools with more stable student populations.[39] The signs on the 1994 school interaction terms are typically positive, indicating that the test scores for various groups are higher in 1994 than they would have been had the 1994 test been more similar to the other tests.

The key results, as mentioned earlier, are the coefficients of the three major interaction variables. However, the results here are complicated to interpret. For the category of all students, the reading coefficients (that is, β_2 and β_3) are in the range of 10 to 12 percent of the state average for all three years. In other words, compared with pass rates in the 1991 base year, pass rates in the next three years rose by about 11 percent more relative to the state average in Dallas than they did in the other big Texas cities. This outcome at first appears consistent with the existence of a large program effect in all three years. However, this interpretation is complicated by the unexpected finding that the 1992 coefficient β_1 is the same order of magnitude as the 1993 and 1994 coefficients. Because the 1991–92 TAAS

---

number of students in each school. However, we do not have data on the number of students in each grade. In general, school size would be correlated with grade size except for those elementary schools that have fewer grades than the average elementary school. A case can also be made that weighting is undesirable on the ground that within-school correlation offsets the effect of schoolsize on the variance of the error term. In any case, unweighted equations yield results that are similar to the weighted results reported here. See Dickens (1990).

39. In contrast to the other school characteristics, data for the mobility rate are available for only one year, 1992–93. Hence the coefficient reflects only the effects of variation among schools and not the effects of changes over time. Note that in contrast to the methodology used in the Dallas program, the test results used in these regressions include all children tested, not just those enrolled in the school throughout the year. This observation implies that the negative coefficient measures both the adverse effects of mobility on the children who are not continuously enrolled in the school and also the effects on the other students.

was given in the fall of 1991, the pass rates for 1992 represent gains that occurred before the Dallas accountability program was officially under way.

The explanation for the positive 1992 coefficient is unclear. One possibility is that Dallas schools would have improved their scores in 1992 whether or not the accountability program was enacted. An alternate possibility is that the higher scores resulted from the considerable publicity as the commission's reform proposals were debated during the spring and summer of 1991, and it became clear that the reforms would emphasize test scores. On this explanation, the 1992 estimate would represent a program effect, but one that would not represent new learning. Therefore, the fact that the 1993 and 1994 estimates are similar to the 1992 estimate could be consistent with little or no effect of the accountability program on the average learning of students in Dallas.

This overall pattern hides some significant variation across subgroups. As of 1994, the largest effects emerge for Hispanics and whites. For both those subgroups, the 1994 effects relative to the 1991 base year are large— 0.18 for Hispanics and 0.22 for whites—and remain large (but less significant) when compared with 1992—a difference of 0.08 for Hispanics and 0.09 for whites.[40] Thus, to the extent that the 1992 coefficients indicate what would have happened in the absence of the program, we conclude that the program may have increased pass rates in Dallas 8 percent relative to the state average for Hispanics and 9 percent for whites. For blacks and economically disadvantaged students, the results are far less encouraging: there may have been some positive effects in 1993, the first year of the program, but those effects disappear by the spring of 1994.

The math results generally parallel those for reading. Positive coefficients emerge for the category of all students in 1993 and 1994, but once again the large 1992 coefficient argues against interpreting them as measures of program effects. The 1993 coefficients are positive and larger than the 1992 coefficients for economically disadvantaged students and Hispanics, which provides weak support for the view that the program improved test results for those two groups during its first year. As of the spring of 1994, pass rates had increased more in Dallas than in the other cities compared with 1991 and for all the subgroups other than blacks. How-

---

40. Based on an *F* test to determine whether the 1992 and 1994 coefficients are similar, we can reject the null hypothesis of similarity only at the 15 percent level for Hispanics and at the 33 percent level for whites.

ever, only for Hispanics and whites were the 1994 coefficients larger than those for 1992. Again, to the extent that the 1992 coefficient measures what would have happened without the accountability program, program effects emerge only for Hispanics and whites.

Other Modifications

In working with this basic model, a variety of modifications were suggested by theory, evidence, and curiosity. Details of these regressions and calculations are available on request from the authors. Here, we seek to give the reader a sense of which modifications made some difference and which did not.

One possible criticism of our research methodology is that other large Texas cities may also have been engaged in significant local school reform initiatives during the relevant period; in fact, both telephone inquiries and perusal of follow-up information suggest significant reform efforts in Fort Worth, Houston, and in one school district in El Paso called Ysleta.[41] In the analysis just presented, the Dallas program was evaluated relative to the typical reform effort in other large Texas cities. To the extent that the other reform efforts generate gains in student performance, students in Dallas would have had to do even better for the Dallas program to generate statistically significant positive effects.

By modifying the basic model, we can determine the magnitude of the Dallas reform effects relative both to the average change in districts not engaged in local reform efforts (the base case) and to those in other districts with local reform initiatives. In general, we found that the measured program effects for Dallas typically exceed those for the other reforming cities, and exceed the cities without reforms by even more. In addition, the changes in Dallas for subgroups of students also typically exceed those for the other districts. The main exceptions are blacks in Houston and

---

41. Fort Worth started a significant reform initiative in 1989 that engaged the local corporations and the community in a program to ensure that students are prepared for the workplace. In 1992–93 Houston introduced a multiyear school improvement plan under which schools submit goals and implementation plans and receive school report cards from the district based on their performance relative to their goals. Finally, while El Paso ISD has no special reform initiative, Ysleta ISD, which serves 50,000 students in El Paso, has a school incentive program that provides awards to high-performing schools.

economically disadvantaged students in Ysleta, both of whom apparently gained more than comparable students in Dallas in 1994.[42]

To check the sensitivity of our results, we experimented with other modifications to the basic model. We added information on two teacher variables: pupils per teacher and the percentage of teachers with more than five years of experience. We initially excluded these two resource variables from the basic model because the city indicator variables pick up systematic differences in resources available per student across cities, and the year variables capture systematic differences over time. In addition, changes in the amount of resources available to schools in Dallas are endogenous to the extent that Dallas's accountability system generated pressure for a different set of resource decisions. When we reran the equations with the two teacher variables, their inclusion had little effect on the results for the key variables.

Another possible complication arises from the fact that during the study period, the state of Texas became more aggressive in identifying low-performing schools and trying to remedy their problems. To the extent that the state's program was successful, it would be difficult for schools in this low-performing category in Dallas to outperform comparable schools in other Texas cities. To account for this possibility, we eliminated the 25 percent of the schools with the highest proportion of disadvantaged students, on the grounds that high disadvantage is likely to be associated with low pass rates on the TAAS, and recalculated our regressions. The results are that the coefficients on the 1994 interaction terms fall slightly from the levels in the basic model, but the patterns across years and across subgroups are similar to those for the full sample. Thus it seems that the existence of the state program does not account for the observed results.

A final extension of our basic analysis was to bring in dropout rates and attendance. Since the relatively high dropout rates among high school students will contaminate the concept of a pass rate, we cannot report a similar analysis of pass rates on the high school TAAS exit exam. Instead, we used a panel data analysis similar to the pass rate analysis to look at changes in high school dropout rates in Dallas relative to the other cities

---

42. For reading scores in the category of all students, Dallas exhibits a 1994 coefficient of 0.143; Houston, 0.061; Fort Worth, 0.051 (not statistically significant); and Ysleta, 0.123. For the category of all students in math, the 1994 interaction terms are 0.164 for Dallas, 0.020 for Houston (not significant), 0.007 for Forth Worth (not significant), and 0.089 for Ysleta. The one possible exception to the generalization of greater gains in Dallas is for black students in Ysleta, who, according to the regression results, experienced extremely large gains in 1994. However, this result should be discounted because of the erratic behavior of the coefficient on blacks in that district over the three years.

from the 1990–91 school year to 1992–93. Starting from an overall drop-out rate of 11 percent in Dallas in 1990–91, which was substantially higher than that in the other five cities during that year, dropout rates declined more in Dallas than in other cities in both 1992 and 1993. The extent to which these reductions should be attributed to the accountability program is unclear. Nonetheless, the decline for each of the subgroups is quite clear.

We used a similar approach to examine attendance at both the elementary and middle schools. Because we do not have attendance broken down by student subgroup and because we have comparable data for only 1990–91 and 1992–93, our comparison is between those two years alone. For elementary schools, we find that the attendance rate increased by about one quarter of a percentage point more in Dallas than it did in the other Texas cities during the two-year period, an outcome that may well reflect a separate incentive program in Dallas to promote school attendance. For junior high schools we find no effect.

Summary

The results of comparing changes in student outcomes in Dallas with those in other big Texas cities is consistent with the view that the Dallas program has exerted some positive effects on student outcomes since 1991 and in some cases since 1992. What proportion of these gains should be attributed to the accountability program is hard to assess. In future work, we plan to extend this discussion of effects by looking at whether the program induced particular changes, such as principal turnover rates, that could ultimately affect student outcomes. Our preliminary analysis of principal turnover shows that the rate has increased significantly since the introduction of the program, but there is only limited evidence to support the conclusion that turnover rates have been significantly higher in the low-performing than in the high-performing schools.

Conclusion

Supporters view school-based recognition and reward programs as desirable because they provide recognition to deserving but sometimes under-appreciated school officials; they provide incentives for school officials to focus attention on student learning and to increase that learning; and, in some cases, they may facilitate or drive other changes, such as site-based management, that could lead to better schools. Their detractors in the education community view them as undesirable primarily because they focus so much attention on the outcomes that can be measured most easily. For example, Anthony Bryk and Kim Hermanson offer a memorable image of the schools as a rich and complex tapestry, with the danger that such programs will pull on only the most visible strands of the tapestry and in the process introduce undesirable "stress, strains, and distortion."[43] Our research uncovers several trade-offs inherent in the design of these programs.

The first trade-off is between treating schools fairly, by adjusting for all the factors outside their control that influence test scores, and possibly sending the undesirable message that the state or district has lower expectations for some groups of students than for others. Our analysis shows that even adjustments using students' previous performance generally will not meet the fairness test unless test scores are adjusted for the students' socioeconomic status. This conclusion emerges because socioeconomic status affects not only the level of achievement but also its rate of growth. Thus, South Carolina found that focusing on gain scores calculated solely from student test scores would result in concentrating the winners among the schools serving high-SES students. The state responded by grouping schools into categories defined by SES, but this adjustment then created an additional set of problems. Dallas's approach of fully incorporating SES (including the race of the student) into the gain scores treats the schools fairly, but may raise the broader concern about lower expectations for some groups of students.

A second trade-off is between the complexity of the adjustment methodology and its transparency. The attempt by Dallas to treat schools fairly has resulted in an incredibly complex methodology that participants view as a black box. This lack of transparency could lead to perceptions that the approach is unfair, but it need not do so in all situations. Dallas officials have effectively countered some of the concerns about the black box by documenting that all schools have virtually the same chance of winning and that the socioeconomic characteristics of the winning schools mirror those of all schools. The district's extensive use of the Accountability Task Force to legitimize the methodology and to keep decisions about the methodology from being made exclusively by the technocrats also mitigates concerns about unfairness. Nonetheless, to some the lack of transparency is a potential source of friction and perceived unfairness. In addition, and

43. Bryk and Hermanson (1992, p. 463); also see Darling-Hammond (1992), who uses the Bryk and Hermanson image to highlight the same point.

perhaps more important, opaqueness is a problem for incentive programs because it makes it difficult or impossible for school officials to make the link between behavior that they can directly observe or affect and the types of performance needed to win an award. Thus the lack of transparency could weaken the incentive effects of the program. Moreover, it undermines morale and confidence in the program because school officials do not understand why their schools jump around in the rankings from one year to the next.

A third trade-off relates to the magnitude of the awards. The larger the financial rewards attached to good performance or the severity of the sanctions associated with poor performance, the greater the incentives for people to change their behavior in response to the program. The challenge is to provide a large enough incentive to generate the desired effects without creating too large an incentive for outright cheating and manipulation. Our evidence suggests that the incentives in the Dallas program seem to be large enough to generate higher student performance, but they have also engendered some less desirable responses. Design features such as multiple outcome measures, linkage of tests to the curriculum, and the use of "gain" scores rather than absolute test scores can mitigate some of the undesirable responses. Nonetheless, the greater the incentives, the more likely is it that they will lead to "stress, strains, and distortions."

Finally, there are two benefits of reward and recognition programs that we have not emphasized in the text but that deserve mention. First, when they are well designed, reward and recognition programs force the state or district to compile information that can be used to improve local school management. For example, the process of compiling data for the school rankings in Dallas generates information by class, subject area, and even by teacher that principals can use to determine weaknesses within the school. Because this disaggregated information is based on small sample sizes, it must be used with care. Nonetheless, we believe that this disaggregated information can lead to better decisions at the school level.

Second, we believe that programs that appropriately adjust for the background of the students serve an important public relations role, especially for the schools serving disadvantaged students. The low average test scores of students in schools serving students of low socioeconomic status often make it easy for parents, citizens, and taxpayers to be highly critical of such schools. Such criticism can be unfair and detrimental to the morale in the school. However, a well-designed recognition and reward program can recognize those schools that are effective, independent of the absolute level of student test scores.

Table 2A-1. *Estimated Effects of Dallas Program on Pass Rates on the TAAS, Seventh Grade Reading*[a]

Variable	All students	Economically disadvantaged	Black	Hispanic	White
YR92 × Dallas	0.1020*	0.0330	0.1062*	0.0995	0.1314
	(1.91)	(0.54)	(1.75)	(1.52)	(1.25)
YR93 × Dallas	0.1227*	0.1188**	0.0777	0.1155*	0.1197
	(2.32)	(1.99)	(1.62)	(1.81)	(1.13)
YR94 × Dallas	0.0966**	0.0448	−0.0797	0.1800**	0.2236**
	(2.15)	(0.87)	(1.56)	(3.28)	(2.39)
Percent black	−0.0085**	−0.0033*	−0.0025**	−0.0001	0.0028**
	(15.24)	(4.52)	(3.15)	(0.09)	(2.46)
Percent Hispanic	−0.0091**	−0.0030**	0.0004	−0.0026**	−0.0048**
	(12.78)	(3.39)	(0.35)	(3.25)	(3.47)
Percent LEP	−0.0010	−0.0030**	−0.0031	−0.0037**	0.0116**
	(0.95)	(2.70)	(1.30)	(3.82)	(4.90)
Percent disadvantaged	−0.0029**	−0.0008	−0.0037**	−0.0021**	−0.0039**
	(3.82)	(0.85)	(3.57)	(2.62)	(2.35)
Mobility rate	−0.0144*	−0.0092**	−0.0151**	−0.0124**	−0.0204**
	(11.35)	(6.04)	(9.20)	(8.56)	(7.29)
YR92	0.0032	0.0361*	0.0465*	0.0228	−0.0449
	(0.17)	(1.63)	(1.66)	(1.16)	(1.42)
YR93	−0.0243	0.0008	0.0465*	−0.0184	−0.0684**
	(1.30)	(0.04)	(1.64)	(0.94)	(2.13)
YR94	−0.4981**	0.0307	0.0714	−0.0872	−0.6642**
	(9.19)	(0.40)	(0.73)	(1.19)	(7.36)
Dallas	−0.0775*	−0.0518	−0.2000	−0.0479	−0.1890**
	(2.03)	(1.13)	(0.47)	(1.00)	(2.47)

Table 2A-1 (continued)

Variable	All students	Economically disadvantaged	Black	Hispanic	White
Austin	-0.0133	-0.0897**	-0.1039	-0.0685**	0.1537**
	(0.55)	(3.09)	(2.70)	(2.34)	(4.26)
El Paso	0.0700**	0.0271	0.0468	0.1213**	0.1463**
	(3.23)	(1.13)	(0.72)	(5.94)	(3.25)
Fort Worth	-0.0191	-0.0460*	-0.0375	0.0130	0.0155
	(0.82)	(1.65)	(1.22)	(0.43)	(0.42)
San Antonio	0.0669**	-0.0035	0.0254	0.0700**	0.1657**
	(2.23)	(0.11)	(0.42)	(2.46)	(2.53)
YR94×percent black	0.0034**	-0.0002	-0.0022*	-0.0006	-0.0014
	(4.21)	(0.24)	(1.85)	(0.45)	(0.73)
YR94×percent Hispanic	0.0029**	-0.0012	-0.0079**	0.0	0.0015
	(2.83)	(0.90)	(4.03)	(0.02)	(0.69)
YR94×percent LEP	0.0017	0.0034**	0.0041	0.0030**	-0.0025
	(1.50)	(3.02)	(1.47)	(2.96)	(0.76)
YR94×percent disadvantaged	0.0029**	0.0019*	0.0063**	0.0015	-0.0006
	(3.03)	(1.64)	(5.00)	(1.43)	(0.26)
YR94×mobility rate	0.0068**	0.0036*	0.0046*	0.0066**	0.0182**
	(4.12)	(1.86)	(1.94)	(3.46)	(4.27)
Constant	1.95**	1.1113**	1.23**	1.2174**	1.9488**
	(50.84)	(19.99)	(20.80)	(23.58)	(30.93)
N	783	753	573	707	492
Adjusted R^2	0.72	0.42	0.45	0.55	0.46

*Significant at the .1 level.
**Significant at the .05 level.
a. Observations are weighted by pupils in the subgroup in the school. The dependent variable is fall seventh grade pass rates relative to the state average for the school years 1991, 1992, and 1993, and spring pass rates for 1994. Numbers in parentheses are absolute values of t-statistics.

Table 2A-2. *Estimated Effects of Dallas Program on Pass Rates on the TAAS, Seventh Grade Mathematics*[a]

Variable	All students	Economically disadvantaged	Black	Hispanic	White
YR92 × Dallas	0.1565** (2.39)	0.1192 (1.54)	0.2193** (2.94)	0.1444* (1.73)	0.1320 (1.29)
YR93 × Dallas	0.1711** (2.64)	0.1873** (2.45)	0.2111** (2.85)	0.1867** (2.28)	0.0648 (0.63)
YR94 × Dallas	0.1434** (2.60)	0.1101* (1.67)	0.0410 (0.65)	0.2074** (2.95)	0.2078** (2.29)
Percent black	−0.0092** (13.26)	−0.0039** (4.12)	−0.0011 (1.14)	0.0001 (0.07)	0.0013 (1.22)
Percent Hispanic	−0.0096** (10.89)	−0.0030** (2.57)	0.0015 (0.96)	−0.0032** (3.09)	−0.0073** (5.41)
Percent LEP	−0.0006 (0.43)	−0.0032** (2.21)	−0.0038 (1.27)	−0.0036** (2.82)	0.0106** (4.62)
Percent disadvantaged	−0.0020** (2.17)	0.0004 (0.31)	−0.0044** (3.39)	−0.0006 (0.63)	−0.0024 (1.50)
Mobility rate	−0.0125** (8.20)	−0.0084** (4.22)	−0.1509** (7.49)	−0.0093** (5.03)	−0.0183** (6.75)
YR92	−0.0322 (1.40)	−0.0223 (0.78)	−0.0059 (0.17)	−0.0330 (1.31)	−0.0693** (2.27)
YR93	−0.0370 (1.60)	0.0258 (0.91)	0.0047 (0.13)	−0.0349 (1.38)	−0.0933** (2.99)
YR94	−0.2699** (4.05)	0.0600 (0.61)	0.0528 (0.44)	0.0125 (0.13)	−0.3998** (4.57)
Dallas	−0.0247 (0.53)	−0.0077 (0.13)	0.2800 (0.54)	0.0078 (0.13)	−0.1382* (1.87)

Table 2A-2 (continued)

Variable	All students	Economically disadvantaged	Black	Hispanic	White
Austin	−0.0954**	−0.1377**	−0.1158**	−0.1386**	0.0037
	(3.20)	(3.71)	(2.45)	(3.68)	(0.11)
El Paso	0.0761**	0.0403	0.0062	0.1287**	0.1151**
	(2.84)	(1.31)	(0.08)	(4.90)	(2.63)
Fort Worth	−0.0716**	−0.0735**	−0.0435	−0.0153	0.1042**
	(2.49)	(2.07)	(1.15)	(0.40)	(2.95)
San Antonio	0.0205	−0.0641	−0.0795	0.0206	0.0712
	(0.55)	(1.56)	(1.07)	(0.56)	(1.12)
YR94×percent black	0.0020**	−0.0004	−0.0329**	−0.0004	−0.0014
	(2.01)	(0.31)	(1.93)	(0.25)	(0.77)
YR94×percent Hispanic	0.0020	−0.0011	−0.0377**	0.0001	0.0039*
	(1.55)	(0.68)	(3.21)	(0.07)	(1.90)
YR94×percent LEP	0.0018	0.0041**	0.0340	0.0043**	−0.0043
	(1.30)	(2.78)	(1.16)	(3.24)	(1.37)
YR94×percent disadvantaged	0.0010	0.0006	0.0071**	−0.0005	−0.0030
	(0.86)	(0.40)	(4.56)	(0.40)	(1.31)
YR94×mobility rate	0.0047**	0.0016	0.0009	0.0033	0.0137**
	(2.31)	(0.61)	(0.32)	(1.35)	(3.34)
Constant	1.9284**	1.1054**	1.2066**	1.1656**	2.0203**
	(41.26)	(15.40)	(15.91)	(17.62)	(33.09)
N	781	745	571	703	493
Adjusted R^2	0.63	0.30	0.35	0.41	0.42

*Significant at the .1 level.
**Significant at the .05 level.
a. Observations are weighted by pupils in the subgroup in the school. The dependent variable is fall seventh grade pass rates relative to the state average for the school years 1991, 1992, and 1993, and spring pass rates for 1994. Numbers in parentheses are absolute values of t-statistics.

References

Anderson, Mark and others. 1994. "Longitudinal Achievement Trends: 1989–94," Division of Research, Planning and Evaluation, Dallas Public Schools.

Bishop, John H. 1994. "The Impact of Curriculum-Based Examinations on Learning in Canadian Secondary Schools," Working Paper 94. Cornell University, Department of Economics.

Bryk, Anthony S., and Kim L. Hermanson. 1992. "Educational Indicator Systems: Observations on Their Structure, Interpretation, and Use." *Review of Research in Education* 19: 451–84.

Clotfelter, Charles, and Helen F. Ladd. 1994. "Information as a Policy Lever: The Case of North Carolina's School 'Report Card.'" Paper prepared for 1994 meeting of Association of Public Policy and Management.

Cohen, David K., and Richard J. Murnane. 1985. "The Merits of Merit Pay." *Public Interest* 80 (Summer): 3–30.

Coleman, James S., and others. 1966. *Equality of Educational Opportunity.* U.S. Department of Health, Education and Welfare, Office of Education.

Commission for Educational Excellence. 1991. *Final Report to the Board of Trustees, Dallas Independent School District.*

Cornett, Lynn M., and Gale F. Ganes. 1994. *Reflecting on 10 Years of Incentive Programs.* Southern Regional Educational Board.

Dallas Independent School District. 1993. "School Performance Improvement Awards, 1992–1993."

Darling-Hammond, Linda. 1992. "Educational Indicators and Enlightened Policy." *Educational Policy* 6 (September): 235–65.

Dickens, William T. 1990. "Error Components in Grouped Data: Is It Ever Worth Weighting?" *Review of Economics and Statistics* 72 (May): 328–33.

Elmore, Richard F. 1991. "Innovation in Education Policy." Paper prepared for Conference on Fundamental Questions of Innovation, Duke University.

Firestone, William A. 1991. "Educators, Researchers, and the Effective Schools Movement." In *Rethinking Effective Schools: Research and Practice,* edited by James R. Bliss and others, 12–27. Prentice Hall.

Garms, Walter I. 1986. "Merit Schools for Florida, A Concept Paper." *Education and Urban Society* 18 (May): 369–90.

Hannaway, Jane. 1992. "Higher Order Skills, Job Design, and Incentives: An Analysis and Proposal." *American Educational Research Journal* 29 (Spring): 3–21.

Johnson, Susan Moore. 1984. "Merit Pay for Teachers: A Poor Prescription for Reform." *Harvard Educational Review* 54 (May): 175–85.

Kirk, L. Roger. 1985. "The South Carolina Improvement Act of 1984." *Journal of Education Finance* 11 (Summer): 132–45.

Koretz, Daniel, and others. 1994. "Can Portfolios Assess Student Performance and Influence Instruction? The 1991–92 Vermont Experience," RAND/RP-259. Santa Monica, Calif.: RAND Corporation.

Ladd, Helen F. 1995. "The Dallas School Accountability and Incentive Program: An Evaluation of Its Impacts on Student Outcomes." Paper prepared for a workshop at the Harris School of the University of Chicago.

Meyer, Robert H. 1994. "Can Schools be Held Accountable for Good Performance? A Critique of Common Educational Performance Indicators." Minneapolis Public Schools, Workshop on Evaluation Methods.

Milgrom, Paul, and John Roberts. 1992. *Economics, Organization and Management*. Prentice-Hall.

Murnane, Richard J., and David K. Cohen. 1986. "Merit Pay and the Evaluation Problem: Why Most Merit Pay Plans Fail and a Few Survive." *Harvard Educational Review* 56 (February): 1–17.

Richards, Craig E., and Tian Ming Sheu. 1992. "The South Carolina School Incentive Reward Program: A Policy Analysis." *Economics of Education Review* 11 (March): 71–86.

Sizer, Theodore R. 1984. *Horace's Compromise: The Dilemma of the American High School*. Houghton Mifflin.

Webster, William J., Robert L. Mendro, and Ted O. Almaguer. 1993. "Effectiveness Indices: The Major Component of an Equitable Accountability System." Paper prepared for annual meeting of the American Educational Research Association.

Webster, William J., and others. 1994. "Alternative Methodologies for Identifying Effective Schools." Paper prepared for joint meeting of the Arizona Educational Research Organization and the Rocky Mountain Educational Research Association.

Webster, William J., and Robert L. Mendro. 1995. "Evaluation for Improved School-Level Decision Making and Productivity." Paper prepared for Hawaii Institute on Assessment and Accountability.

CHAPTER THREE

The New Accountability in State Education Reform: From Process to Performance

Richard F. Elmore, Charles H. Abelmann, and Susan H. Fuhrman

A NEW MODEL of state and local school governance is evolving that we call "the new educational accountability." The model has three major components: a primary emphasis on measured student performance as the basis for school accountability, sometimes accompanied by other indicators of success; the creation of relatively complex systems of standards by which data on student performance are compared by school and by locality; and the creation of systems of rewards and penalties and intervention strategies to introduce incentives for improvement.

What is new is an increasing emphasis on student performance as the touchstone for state governance. In principle, focusing on student performance should move states away from input regulations—judging schools based on the number of books in the library and the proportion of certified staff, for example—and toward a model of steering by results—using rewards, sanctions, and assistance to move schools toward higher levels of performance. In other words, the new educational accountability should focus schools' attention less on compliance with rules and more on increasing learning for students.

The work on this chapter was funded in part by the Consortium for Policy Research in Education (CPRE), under grant #R11G10007 from the Office of Educational Research and Improvement, U.S. Department of Education. The opinions expressed are those of the authors and are not necessarily shared by CPRE, its institutional partners or the funding agency. The three authors contributed equally to this chapter.

What States Are Doing

In 1993, the Consortium for Policy Research in Education (CPRE) conducted a survey of superintendents and commissioners in the fifty state agencies to inquire about regulation and methods of certifying or accrediting schools. Questions concerned changes in methods and criteria used for accrediting schools, the use of rewards and sanctions, the approach to low-achieving schools, and the role of regulations concerning inputs and process in accreditation. Respondents in at least forty-three states claimed that they were revising or expecting to change their accountability systems to focus more on performance. Most of these states were also undertaking standards-based reform by developing expectations for student learning and aligning other policies, such as assessment and accountability policies, to support the standards.

A number of design features distinguish new performance-based approaches from more traditional accountability systems.[1] For example, many states that accredit or certify schools or districts are trying to place more emphasis on student performance.[2] Traditionally, accreditation has been determined by compliance with input and process standards, monitored through district self-reports, periodic visits, and inspection of syllabuses and other paperwork, such as local board minutes indicating adoption of specific curricula. More recently, the focus on performance has led to using outcome data, such as test scores and dropout rates, as criteria for accreditation. The purpose is to provide schools flexibility so that they can maximize student performance on new standards.[3]

Most new accreditation approaches rest on state-determined performance standards or benchmarks of adequate progress. However, a related approach involves school-site determination of and planning toward specific performance targets, such as improved test scores in reading and math. In Kansas, for example, the state provides assistance to schools in developing the plan. A team then visits in the fourth year of the five-year improvement cycle to determine if accreditation will be granted.

More states publicly report district or school test scores along with other outcome measures such as attendance and dropout rates. According to the

---

1. See, for example, Hetrick (1993). The following discussion includes excerpts from Fuhrman (1994a, 1994b).

2. A few states have no formal approval process and leave accreditation up to private agencies.

3. For example, see the National Governors' Association (1986) concept of a "horse trade" swapping accountability for performance for regulation.

Council of Chief State School Officers (CCSSO), twenty-eight states have included school-level test scores in public performance reporting.[4] Public reporting energizes parents and other community members to pressure schools for higher performance, particularly when data show differences in performance among schools that are roughly comparable in the public's eye.

Increasingly, consequences are being attached to various accreditation and performance levels. In addition to public reporting, some states also provide tangible nonmonetary recognition, such as flags or pennants, for excellent performance. A 1993 survey revealed that six states—Georgia, Indiana, Kentucky, North Carolina, South Carolina, and Texas—provided monetary rewards for improved school performance.[5] The chapter by Charles Clotfelter and Helen Ladd in this volume discusses the use of fiscal incentives for achievement.

With respect to sanctions, the ultimate punishment for failure of accreditation in the past was loss of state aid, a step rarely taken. In the 1980s, six states developed programs for state intervention in severely troubled school districts, sometimes referred to as "academically bankrupt" districts.[6] Additional states adopted such approaches in the 1990s. Generally, a series of interventions such as visits by technical assistance teams and the appointment of on-site monitors or conservators precede the ultimate sanctions: state takeover or removal of local governance. For example, low performers in Illinois will be placed on an academic watch list and be required to develop a correction plan. Eventually the local board could be removed. In Maryland, sanctions include reconstituting schools, bringing in new staff, or privatization.

Even for acceptable performers, some states are trying to focus school and district visits on teaching and learning. Instead of paper reviews and central office visits, the new forms of inspection are to consist of lengthy peer visits that include classroom observation and involve feedback and extensive discussions about practice. Examples are the New York school quality review and the California program review.

Over 80 percent of the states claim they are engaged in developing, piloting, or implementing such new approaches to accountability, but few performance-based systems are actually up and running. In September 1994 we made follow-up inquiries in seven states that appeared to be far along

4. Council of Chief State School Officers (1994).
5. Southern Regional Education Board (1994).
6. U.S. Department of Education (1988).

based on the 1993 survey. In most cases, the plans that were being drawn in 1993 were still in a developmental or experimental phase. The delay in moving to new systems did not appear to be simply a matter of phase-in. In some states, fundamental aspects of the system, like definitions of adequate performance or progress, had not yet been established. In others, politics altered the plans being made in 1993. It appears that many states are encountering problems putting performance-based systems into effect.

To understand the issues surrounding the establishment of performance-based accountability, we decided to study emerging approaches in some depth by visiting two states, Kentucky and Mississippi.[7] We chose these states because they represent relatively advanced stages of development compared with other states, and they represent two very different policy environments.[8] Kentucky launched possibly the country's most ambitious educational reform in 1990 as the result of court action. The centerpiece of this reform is a new system of educational assessments, standards, incentives, and sanctions that together form an ambitious new accountability system. Mississippi, on the other hand, has evolved toward its present system by a series of incremental changes since the early 1980s. Although it has the major elements of a new accountability system in place, it has constructed its system in a way that requires lower expenditures on new assessments and less administrative overhead than Kentucky. These two states, in other words, represent relatively well developed accountability systems at very different levels of resources.

Our approach to understanding the new educational accountability takes its point of departure from the observation that all attempts to change relationships among actors in complex governance structures entail three distinct types of problems: the design of new systems, the implementation of new systems, and the politics of new systems. Thus, the next three major sections of this chapter will discuss issues of design, implementation, and politics in the Kentucky and Mississippi educational reforms.

---

7. Over a two-month period, we interviewed approximately twenty-five people from each state, including key legislators involved in education, legislative staff, state board members, members of the state departments of education, staff of educational organizations in the states, local school and district personnel, members of the academic community, and journalists who cover education. Interviews lasted approximately one and one-half hours each and were tape-recorded and transcribed.

8. We use the term "relatively" advisedly here. As the survey evidence shows, many states have pieces of the new accountability systems in place, but few have systems that are fully developed. Thus the fact that Kentucky and Mississippi have both fully developed systems, even though they are both in early stages of implementation, makes them relatively advanced systems.

Design Issues in New Accountability Systems

The design of new educational accountability systems brings a demanding set of technical and conceptual issues. Changes in state accountability systems are occurring at the same time as major changes in the understanding of how to measure educational performance. These changes signal a move away from traditional measures of student learning, with their emphasis on testing students' recall of discrete bits of information, toward less traditional measures that attempt to capture whether students understand and can apply knowledge to relatively complex problems. States must decide whom to hold accountable, for what levels of performance, on the basis of what types of performance indicators, with what consequences. Mississippi and Kentucky represent distinctly different solutions to these design issues, although they share a common focus on the central characteristic of the new educational accountability systems: an attempt to move away from input and process regulation to performance-based systems of accountability. In general, Mississippi can be viewed as the lower-cost, basic version of the new state accountability, while Kentucky can be viewed as the higher-cost, more complex version.

Essential Elements of Design

Mississippi's system focuses on state accreditation of districts as the main mechanism of accountability. Until recently, the state used the Stanford Achievement Test in grades 4, 6, and 8 and a combination of criterion-referenced tests to cover other grades. However, an alternate performance assessment system went into effect in the 1995–96 school year. It tests all children in grades 4 through 9. The new system adds additional criterion-referenced subject area tests for high school students. A functional literacy examination and an Algebra 1 test will continue to be part of the system for assigning accreditation levels, and additional subject area tests are in development. The state also continues to use a variety of process regulations.

Mississippi's accreditation system is designed to identify how well or how poorly a school district is performing.[9] Districts are ranked on five levels, based on a combination of performance and process variables. Districts at level 3 are considered to be successful. To reach accreditation levels

9. Letter from Judy Rhodes, director of Office of Educational Accountability, Mississippi Department of Education, June 2, 1995.

4 and 5, districts are held accountable for additional variables, including performance on a national test taken by college applicants, a graduation rate of at least 75 percent, and a college enrollment that includes 35 percent of the senior class. Levels 1 and 2 are considered less than adequate.

These accreditation levels are set in part by creating a distribution of the norm-referenced test scores in a given year and assigning level 3 to a point one-half of an individual standard deviation below the average of all Mississippi students taking the test. While the annual minimum values for the norm-referenced test are thus established in a relative fashion, absolute minimum and maximum values were established in 1987 and 1988 so that the annual minimum values must fall within a very narrow range. For a school district to be level 3, its students must have on average at least 70 percent of the answers correct on criterion-referenced measures and cannot fall below the thirty-second percentile for standardized, norm-referenced measures; the district must also pass 100 percent of the process regulations.[10] Other levels are then determined on the basis of whether they have met the required percentage of performance standards and process variables. The Mississippi system provides limited incentives for high-performing districts, at levels 4 and 5, in the form of deregulation. The State Department of Education provides intensive assistance for districts at level 1 in the form of outside technical assistance in analyzing deficiencies and proposing remedies.

The Kentucky system focuses on holding schools accountable for specified performance standards in eight domains, including reading, writing, mathematics, science, social studies, arts and humanities, practical living, and vocational studies, and in a noncognitive domain that includes attendance, retention at a grade level, dropping out, and transitions from secondary school to further education or work. Performance is measured at grades 4, 5, 8, 11, and 12. The difference between the school's actual average performance in each domain at a baseline period (academic year 1991–92) and a standard representing all students scoring at the "proficient" (as opposed to novice and apprentice) level was determined. This difference was then divided by ten, and each school is evaluated on whether it achieves one-tenth of the difference between its baseline performance and the standard every two years over a twenty-year period. In other words, the average performance of each school should improve until it reaches the proficiency level in no more than twenty years.

10. Letter from Judy Rhodes.

Each biennium, schools are judged by the amount of improvement expected during the two-year period. Schools scoring at least a one-point improvement over the threshold receive substantial financial rewards for exceeding their performance targets; these rewards were given out in spring of 1995 for the first time. Those scoring below the threshold but above the baseline are to develop improvement plans. Schools below their baseline (from zero to 5 percent) are required to develop improvement plans. They receive assistance from the state in the form of improvement funds and assistance from a state-selected "distinguished educator." Schools at the lowest level (more than 5 percent below the baseline) are classified as schools in crisis. They also receive assistance, but are subjected to the additional sanctions of staff being placed on probation and students being given transfer rights to other schools. The "school in crisis" provision was suspended by the legislature for the first biennium of the system's operation.

The design features of the two states' accreditation systems are outlined in table 3-1. The Mississippi system focuses on districts as the unit of accountability, while the Kentucky system focuses on schools and districts. The Mississippi system defines a "floating" index of performance as one that falls between a narrow range that has been secured by the absolute minimum and maximum values pegged to the yearly average performance of students in the state, while the Kentucky system defines an absolute index of performance by setting a fixed proficiency level in each performance domain. The Mississippi system classifies districts annually based on their performance on that year's test, while the Kentucky system sets up a baseline measure of performance and defines a twenty-year trajectory between the baseline and the proficiency standard, rendering an accountability judgment of schools every two years on the basis of their progress toward the proficiency standard. The Mississippi system used the Stanford Achievement Test from 1988 through 1994 and in 1995 began to use the Iowa Test of Basic Skills, the Tests of Achievement and Proficiency, and some other criterion-referenced tests, while the Kentucky system uses an advanced version of performance examinations and portfolio assessments that have been custom developed for that system. The Mississippi system provides limited incentives for high-performing districts and limited assistance and sanctions for low-performing districts, while the Kentucky system provides substantial financial incentives for high-performing schools and significant assistance and sanctions for low-performing schools. The Mississippi system does, however, have a takeover provision, which has not been exercised.

Table 3-1. *Design Features of Kentucky and Mississippi Accreditation Systems*

Design feature	Kentucky	Mississippi
Goal of system	Every student, school and district be at least proficient in twenty years (five student levels from novice to distinguished)	Every school district be at least at level 3 (successful)
Level of accountability	Schools and districts (each school has its own threshold it must meet every two years)	Every district is ranked each year (five possible levels)
Standard of accountability	Fixed standards	Floating standard for norm-referenced tests with absolute minimum and maximum values
Types of assessments	Criterion-referenced and portfolios	Criterion-referenced and norm-referenced
Subject areas	Reading, writing, mathematics, social studies, science, arts and humanities, practical living and vocational studies	Reading, language, mathematics, high school subject tests
Grades tested	4, 5, 8, 11, 12	4, 5, 6, 7, 8, 9
Graduation test	Not required	Required
Noncognitive index	Attendance, retention, dropouts, transition	School process standards (different percentages for different levels)
Rewards	Cash rewards for teachers in schools that meet or exceed set threshold	Process regulations lifted for level 4 and level 5 schools
Sanctions or assistance	Distinguished educators go to schools in crisis; parents have the right to transfer a child out of the school; certified staff are placed on probation	Office of Conservatorship, takeover provision

Sources: Alston and others (1994); Burnham (1995); Guskey (1994).

These two designs entail different levels of technical complexity. In Mississippi, the main technical problem was designing the indexing system that allows the state to classify districts. The state made a decision to use existing testing technology and to minimize the cost of incentives and sanctions by limiting them to deregulation for high-performing districts and assistance for the lowest-performing districts. However, Mississippi is in the process of upgrading the tests it uses, in part due to a realization that the curriculum had been narrowed by reliance on traditional multiple-choice tests.[11] In Mississippi, test data are meant to be used to inform individual instruction.

Kentucky, on the other hand, set out more or less intentionally to create one of the most advanced, and hence one of the most complicated, assessment and accountability systems in the country. It developed a new "authentic" assessment system in the form of performance exams requiring students to provide complex open-ended responses to questions and portfolio assessments requiring multisample collections of student work and teacher participation in assessing that work.[12] It developed a complex and expensive system of rewards and sanctions that imposed high demands on the technical capacity of the assessment system and the resources of the state to oversee school improvement. In Kentucky, these data are used to make school-level judgments and there is no attempt to use the tests to inform instructional needs of individual students. Focusing on schools and districts means that the state is potentially dealing with many more units of accountability.

Problems of Design

Embedded in both these designs is a series of problems that virtually any state would confront if it were to attempt to shift from input and process to performance as a basis for accountability. One central issue is the signals

11. Massell (1995) provides an extensive list of references for this topic. These references include Shepard (1990); Herman and Golan (1991); and Madaus and others (1992).

12. The terms "authentic assessment" and "performance examinations" refer to the forms of assessment in which students are asked to provide open-ended responses to relatively complex problems and in which responses are evaluated both for the depth of understanding demonstrated by the student and whether the student gets the correct answer. These assessments are said to be more "authentic" because they are thought to approximate more closely the kinds of problems students will be expected to solve outside of school, and they are said to focus on performance because they ask students to demonstrate their knowledge through application rather than through recall of facts. Because of their open-ended nature, performance assessments are more expensive to administer and score.

these performance accountability systems send to schools and districts about what constitutes acceptable performance. The Mississippi system sends the message that acceptable performance is a relative phenomenon. Districts are evaluated and assigned to levels on the basis of their position in a distribution of other districts in the state. In fact, the acceptable level of performance is significantly below the norm-referenced average for the state. The Kentucky system, on the other hand, sends the message that acceptable performance is an absolute phenomenon, defined in terms of proficiency levels on performance-based measures. In fact, these proficiency levels are set well above the average performance of schools, so that virtually all schools have a substantial majority of students scoring below proficiency levels in most domains.

Neither system provides a ready answer to the question of why students should be expected to achieve at the levels prescribed by the system and what value would follow from their achievement. The Mississippi system, in effect, uses the standard of average performance on a norm-referenced test, but knowing that does not answer the question of what a given level of performance means in terms of a student's actual ability to do something. The Kentucky system says, in effect, that acceptable performance is defined in terms of a level of proficiency determined by experts who construct the assessment. These experts use standards of performance like whether a student can construct an intelligible paragraph or devise and explain a solution to a problem of mathematics requiring long division. While these criteria have more meaning in terms of what students are actually able to do, no evidence yet exists to link proficient performance on the Kentucky assessment to students' performance in the world outside of school.[13]

Another question about what constitutes satisfactory progress relates to the rate at which student performance is expected to improve. The Mississippi system sends an ambiguous message on this score. Because districts are evaluated on the basis of their performance relative to a floating average of annual test results, they have no certain picture of what level of test performance is adequate in any given year until the distribution of scores is set for that year, nor do they have any sense of what rate of improvement

13. In fact, as is discussed later on, the Kentucky Instructional Results Information System (KIRIS) scores do not necessarily correlate highly with other measures, such as SAT scores, accepted by the public as predictive of future success.

is satisfactory.[14] To account for differences in performance among school districts assigned to the same level, the state has recently created an annual performance index to enable performance comparisons within accreditation levels.

In Kentucky, on the other hand, the assessments are designed to show how schools are approaching the proficiency standard. However, the performance target of moving schools to an average proficiency level over twenty years is politically determined, and no one knows whether it is educationally or technically feasible. As a staff member on the Kentucky assessment team said, "We'll have to see, after several rounds of this thing, if our expectations were too high. . . . The first thing we need to figure out is if it really is possible to close this gap by 10 percent a biennium. And the answer right now is that nobody knows whether it is possible."

There also seems to be some disagreement among Kentucky policymakers about whether the goal of the system is to achieve average proficiency in each school or to achieve average proficiency for each student, a considerably more difficult task. A journalist observed that the Kentucky education commissioner at the time was quoted as saying initially that all students would ultimately score at the proficiency level. "Now what he's saying is that the average will be proficient, which is very different." So even within a system in which performance targets are stable, there is considerable disagreement and ambiguity over what constitutes satisfactory progress.

Yet another important design issue has to do with the technical complexity of the accountability system, which affects public confidence in the system. Questions inevitably arise as to why various tests are weighted the way they are, what various assessments actually measure, to what extent indicators other than test scores should count, and how much year-to-year progress is sufficient. The answers to these questions should reflect learning and beliefs about schooling, such as how much growth in achievement can be expected of students at different levels and ages, what kinds of questions demonstrate learning, how many of those questions need to be asked, and which skills and understandings are important. If these issues are not well understood and accepted, the policymakers and educators who run the system cannot explain or defend judgments about school performance.

---

14. As we will note later, the Mississippi system also involves accountability measures designed to improve the performance of low-achieving students, so districts have incentives not only to improve average performance but also to do so without lowering the performance of students in the lowest-scoring part of the population.

In Mississippi, very few policymakers, educators or members of the general public understand the indexing system by which a school or district's performance is evaluated each year. The scheme for classifying schools into levels was designed by a professor from Alabama and could not be explained by most people we interviewed. So while there seems to be a relatively high level of confidence in the system among key actors, that confidence may be somewhat fragile, since it is based on a relatively low understanding.

In Kentucky, the problems are similar. Design issues are raised by the manner in which measures of performance are aggregated into an index of school performance, which is in turn used to mete out rewards and sanctions. Why should each component of the index be weighted as it is? Why should schools make equal increments of progress toward their targets every two years over a twenty-year period? What is the educational justification for these decisions? How do the formulas relate to commonsense understanding of educational improvement?

Many educators and members of the public do not understand the index. As a highly informed Kentucky state educator said, "It's too complicated. That's one of the most serious problems of it, and one of the reasons it's not trusted, other than some of the technical reasons, is that people do not understand it. The superintendents and assessment coordinators say they know how it operates, the teachers are not sure, the parents are not sure." When one superintendent was asked about the accountability formula, he responded, "If you ask me do I understand the formula, no. No I don't . . . for me to sit here and you ask me to explain it to you, I'd be in deep trouble."

Because Kentucky is using state-of-the-art assessment methods, those methods are subject to fairly continuous scrutiny and criticism by educational measurement experts from within and outside the state. Of course, this does not imply that the methods are always easy to understand or to explain. For example, Kentucky relies on a cohort approach, comparing each group of fourth or eighth graders with previous groups at those levels, instead of a longitudinal approach that would involve tracking the same group of students over the grades. Some experts prefer a longitudinal approach, although it is more complex and expensive.[15] Another concern is that Kentucky's only tool for evaluating student writing consists of a portfolio of between five and seven pieces of a student's best work, accompanied by a letter to the reviewer. No two student portfolios need be the same;

15. Western Michigan University (1995).

portfolios differ both by the type of writing and in the nature of what prompted the writing. Local teachers, in many cases the classroom teacher of the student, score the portfolios using a state-developed holistic rubric that is applied across all pieces, multiple genres, and grade levels. Are such scores a reliable way of comparing schools?

Overall, then, the Mississippi and Kentucky systems represent very different solutions to the basic design problems embedded in the new accountability. Mississippi has chosen to construct a relatively low-cost system that focuses on districts and existing testing technology, with relatively low incentives and sanctions. In doing so, it has opened up problems of how to use a combination of traditional norm-referenced tests, criterion-referenced tests, and process standards to stimulate cumulative performance over time. Kentucky has chosen an ambitious, some would say high-risk route, in which it is using performance assessments and portfolios, and a complex multiple index, to deliver significant rewards and sanctions for school districts. In both states, schools are sorted into groups or assigned index values by formulas and calculations that are not clearly understood, which makes it difficult for such measurements to motivate useful reform. Statisticians and psychometricians may be in the driver's seat with the policymakers and educators unable to understand or explain the rationale behind the formulas and assessment approaches.

Implementation Issues in New Accountability Systems

The implementation of new accountability systems imposes new demands on policymakers and practitioners. Educators in localities and schools are being asked not just to accommodate new types of student testing and assessment, but to use the results of those assessments to change what they teach and how they teach it. New governance arrangements are being put into place that focus accountability more explicitly on school-level performance. As policymakers and educators put new accountability systems into place, the match between the design on paper and the state's ability to implement it is tested, frequently leading to adjustments in the design.

Incentives for Student Performance

Kentucky focuses on both schools and districts, and Mississippi focuses only on districts, which means that their incentive systems also differ. In Kentucky, the school site acts as an autonomous unit. It is held accountable for the performance of students tested as part of the Kentucky Instructional Results Information System (KIRIS). The school can earn cash rewards if it can demonstrate its ability to move beyond its designated threshold, or can fall into receivership if it fails to meet its threshold. The first rewards were announced in February 1995 for the 35 percent of the state schools that improved by more than their threshold. In March 1995 the state distributed $25.5 million directly to 14,100 teachers and administrators across 480 schools and 42 districts that achieved reward status. The most money went proportionally to teachers in schools and districts that showed the most improvement. Assuming teachers decided to distribute the dollars to themselves, individual rewards would have varied in size from $1,301 to $2,602 per teacher.[16] There is an appeal procedure for schools who believe that they deserve rewards, and the state was holding some money in reserve in case any appeal succeeds.

In Mississippi, high-performing school districts are extempted from certain process regulations, such as days required for staff development; districts at the lower levels are subject to assistance and intervention. Unlike in Kentucky, a good Mississippi school in a bad district can go unnoticed, as can a poor school in a good district, because the incentives operate at the district level. Despite this difference, both states are betting to a considerable extent on similar motivational strategies to influence teachers and administrators: public reporting of test scores, rewards for top performers, and sanctions as deterrents for low performance.

Some evidence exists to test the power of these incentives, although Kentucky's system is quite new and Mississippi's has evolved over time. For example, the institution of deregulatory rewards for Mississippi schools in levels 4 and 5 is quite recent, and it is not yet possible to offer anything other than tentative estimates of the effects of these systems.

In Kentucky, our interviews and surveys conducted by others indicate that, as a result of the assessment's emphasis on writing, the number of students writing and the quality of their writing has improved.[17] Teachers at the tested grades are very aware of the performance standards and what threshold must be met. Similarly, in Mississippi, teachers know what level their school district is in and how their school performs in relationship to others.

What encourages this attention to performance? First, it appears that the reporting of data in both states has been very powerful in attracting public and press scrutiny. According to a Mississippi journalist, when the

16. Mark Scharer, "KERA Improvements Pay Off for More Than 14,100 Educators," *Louisville Courier-Journal,* April 5, 1995, pp. 1, 6.
17. See, for example, Western Michigan University (1995).

report card first came out everyone wanted a copy: "I mean nobody could keep them. It was probably the most read thing in the state." Although KIRIS was designed for judging a given school's progress toward a standard, not as a system for comparing schools, the press ranks the best and worst schools in the state.

The potential sanctions also appear to have heightened attention to performance issues. One district staff person in Kentucky commented, "I know we've got an attitude of we're not going to let any of our schools get into sanction. . . . If we have to send out central staff to sit in the school to do what we can do to help them do better, we're going to do that." One superintendent described a school that would have been sanctioned but realized the threat and made tremendous strides. According to the superintendent, "They got serious in terms of analyzing the way they were teaching, analyzing what questions are posed with the KIRIS assessment."

In Mississippi, level 1 districts have been forced to make certain changes. When Mississippi at one point considered taking over a number of poorly performing school districts, "the whole attitude and the whole atmosphere in these communities changed all at once," according to one respondent. A top official in the state department reported, "We witnessed communities beginning to come to unify and business and industry coming together and boards of supervisors coming together and just a host of people in these communities rallying together with the issue of saving the schools." A researcher in the state commented, "The threat of takeover is a powerful threat, especially in conjunction with the High School Activities Association's rule that, if you lose accreditation from the state, you lose the right to compete in athletics." As one level 1 superintendent commented: "They didn't give me a choice. . . . We got a letter demanding you come to Jackson and go through this training. . . . They suggested some workshops and that kind of thing that I should do to bring up my leadership ability. . . . You look at your curriculum and you center your staff development for teachers around things that you need to improve on."

Few teachers or administrators talked about the incentives created by the possibility of rewards, probably because the reward aspects of the system were relatively new and uncertain. In fact, teachers in Kentucky were skeptical that rewards would actually be doled out, as they were in the late spring of 1995. As one respondent explained the cynicism, "In 1986, the state promised $300 for all teachers that had a satisfactory evaluation. It never happened. Today teachers are still waiting for the $300." Additional research will be needed to examine reward systems as they come on line.

Problems with the Operation of Incentives

In both states, certain elements of the systems raise questions about the strength and effectiveness of the incentive structure. One important issue is the extent to which the systems focus only on the top and the bottom of the performance distribution, leaving out those schools and districts falling in between.

In Mississippi, for example, the vast majority of districts are at level 3 and very few are at levels 4 and 5. The state usually has around ten districts at level 1 and around thirty at level 2. Districts often flip-flop back and forth between level 1 and level 2, but when a district moves from level 1 to level 2, state assistance stops. A state board member commented, "So in effect we have a small cluster of carrots at the very top and a small cluster of extremely clumsy sticks at the very bottom and as a practical matter under the current regime not many carrots or sticks of real significance in the middle ground." One of the designers of the Mississippi system commented that Level 3 districts "are achieving a minimum and it is up to the local community to force them to go above the minimum. If the local community is satisfied with the minimum, the state is satisfied with it. The state has limited resources and limited staff, so they have to concentrate on those who are below 3."

In Kentucky, although the system is designed to encourage growth in schools at all performance levels, only exceptional growth is rewarded and only exceptional lack of progress is penalized. As in Mississippi, the money in the system is at the extremes. For those progressing at roughly the expected rate, the main lever appears to be public reporting.

A second issue is the degree to which these systems might provide perverse incentives for schools or school districts to respond to these policy changes by focusing on only the best or average students or schools, neglecting the weaker ones. A Kentucky high school—particularly a small one, where each individual's score counts—might do better if weak students drop out (or are pushed out), because dropout rates account for a much smaller part of the accountability index than cognitive measures. One assessment coordinator recognized this design problem: "I'm concerned because we have fewer students after grade 9 and it looks like it's to a school's advantage to get a kid to drop out rather than to keep him on the rolls and have poor test scores at grade 12." Similarly, a school district in Mississippi can reach level 3 by placing an emphasis on the best students. As a senior staff member commented, "You could be teaching to the upper 25, 30, 40 percent of your students, and pull your scores above the mean and show a pretty significant level of performance, and yet . . . a large percentage of your population would be in that bottom quartile." A large district might be able to reach level 3 while having one or two very low-performing schools.

To counter actions harmful to the original intent of these state reforms, both Kentucky and Mississippi have added a screen to encourage attention to the lowest-performing students. In Kentucky, schools might reach their thresholds without moving up any of the novice students, but unless they demonstrate moving all students forward, they do not qualify for an award. In Mississippi, a school district hoping to reach level 4 or level 5 must demonstrate that it does not have more than 25 percent of the students in the bottom quartile or, if that is not possible, at least a steady reduction of the number in the bottom quartile. Senior staff members of the State Department of Education in Mississippi hope to be able to include this same screen as part of the requirements for being a level 3 school. It is not clear whether these attempts to avert perverse consequences will be sufficient.

Perceptions of Fairness

Local educators often raise questions about the fairness of the accountability system. In Kentucky, teachers raise questions about students who are transient and might have just arrived in a school the year testing takes place. Others raise concerns about holding special education students accountable and the inequitable distribution of special education students within a district.

In Mississippi, some educators believe that poorer districts are at a disadvantage. One educator explained:

> Basically, when you look at about three factors, and that is the number of students on free lunch, the economic base of the district, and then the amount spent per child for instruction, it correlates just almost 100 percent with the districts who fall at level 1, 2, 3, 4 and 5. The ones that are level 4 and 5 have very few students on free lunch. . . . So, it's really not fair to compare these kids down here that are predominantly minority students, very low income. They get just the minimum that the state provides and very little else spent on them.

The relationship between school districts' accreditation levels and the percentage of their students eligible for free lunch is shown in table 3-2. Indeed, level 1 school districts on average do have the highest percentage

Table 3-2. *Mississippi Performance-Based Accreditation Levels, by District Spending and Percentage of Students Eligible for Free Lunch*

School level	Number of schools	Percent eligible for free lunch			Per pupil expenditure (dollars)[a]		
		Mean	Standard deviation	Median	Mean	Standard deviation	Median
1 (probation)	16	88.1	5.5	89.3	4,143	484	4,078
2 (warned)	33	76.1	12.4	77.0	3,833	382	3,796
3 (successful)	100	51.2	16.2	49.8	3,773	463	3,674
4 (advanced)	0	...	...	...	...	...	...
5 (excellent)	4	27.9	11.2	28.3	3,480	290	3,425

Sources: Data from Mississippi Department of Education, *Mississippi Report Card, 1994;* and October School Lunch Monthly Report.

a. An average per pupil expenditure calculated by using the total current expenditures from all sources of revenue divided by nine-month average daily attendance.

of students on free lunch, and level 5 school districts have the fewest. Unlike the jurisdictions treated in the Clotfelter and Ladd chapter in this volume, Mississippi currently does not control for any measure of socioeconomic status in calculating its accreditation levels. According to a member of the State Department of Education, "We pushed very hard to have an SES [socioeconomic status] factor, but the State Board cut it off at the gap . . . as some members said it would present a double standard."

In Kentucky, the State Department of Education explicitly searched for a relationship between rewards and the geographic location of the school, racial-ethnic composition of the students in the school, economic status of students in the school, original baseline score, or school size. The technical report (issued a few months after the rewards were announced) acknowledges that baseline scores for schools were highly correlated with socioeconomic status, as measured by the percentage of students receiving free lunch, but nonetheless found, "Schools with high proportions of low income students were as likely to achieve reward status as schools with low proportions of low income students."[18] The *Lexington Herald-Leader* did its own study of the percentage of the state goal each school achieved in relationship with each district's amount of assessed property value per student and also concluded that poor and rich schools were equally likely to do well.[19]

18. Kentucky Department of Education (1995, p. 266).
19. Lucy May, "Poor Schools as Likely as Rich to Hit KERA Goals, Earn Rewards," *Lexington Herald-Leader,* February 9, 1995, pp. A1, A10.

The State's Capacity to Deliver

Both states place great stress on state-level intervention in schools or districts on the low end of the performance scale. But actual assistance is falling short of what is envisioned in the accountability plans.

In Mississippi, districts that fall to level 1 must work with the state to develop an improvement plan. While the state has an extensive mandate to hire consultants, make field visits, interview everyone from community leaders to students, set up required training programs, and more, this type of intervention is typically short-lived. A senior official explained, "With limited resources, both human resources and financial, we have had to make some decisions. . . . Our inability to stay with those districts is a weakness of the system."

In Kentucky, the original Education Reform Act specified that each school in crisis would have a distinguished educator assigned to work with it. Currently, since sanctions have been delayed, poorly performing schools in Kentucky can voluntarily select whether they wish to have a distinguished educator. The State Department of Education went through an exhaustive and highly competitive search and selection process to identify fifty distinguished educators, and then to put them through a training program in leadership skills, methods of personnel evaluation, school budget and finance, and school curriculum and assessment. But when funds were requested to place all fifty distinguished educators, the General Assembly cut the request by 40 percent. Twenty-three distinguished educators were funded for the 1994–95 school year to work on a voluntary basis with approximately 150 schools, which implies that each distinguished educator has had to work with 8 or 9 schools. In addition, the department has been forced to reduce its staff. The state does seem to be trying to address this issue. In 1995–96, 46 distinguished educators were funded to work on a voluntary basis with 53 schools designated as in decline.

Quite aside from the resource issue, it is not clear that states have the technical capacity to improve low-performing schools and districts. In 1990, Mississippi came very close to taking over a number of school districts. But senior department staff were actually relieved when the state board backed down, recognizing the bleak prospect of the state department running school districts across the state. One senior official explained his response: "I continue to try and argue before you take over a district, you better be real sure that you can do a better job running it than the people who are there." One superintendent from a level 1 district commented, "You know what I'd like to see? I'd like to see them come in and take over. . . . I'd like to see how they could perform on the firing line here."

How Experience with Implementation Influences Design

In both Kentucky and Mississippi, the implementation of these new accountability systems has required continual tinkering with the design, including both the nature and timing of the tests.

Mississippi was the first state to have an accreditation system based primarily on student performance. Although legislation for the system was passed in 1982, it did not really take effect until the 1987 school year. It took time to develop the system and more time before the tests could be used for accountability purposes. Initially the state used the Basic Skills Assessment Program (BSAP) in grades 3, 5, and 8, but, according to a staff member, "It lived out its usefulness because it was strictly bottom-line, basic criterion reference and everybody was doing pretty well on it." As one staff member described it, "You had many school districts that obtained a minimum level in their basic skills and unfortunately when they got there they thought they had achieved nirvana."

The state pursued other tests. According to one member of a task force appointed to address issues of assessment, "The best way to raise the level of expectation was to bring in a new testing program that significantly increased the level of expectation." The state will continue with the norm-referenced test but will add a performance-based component to it and extend the testing to all students in grades 4 through 9.

Kentucky also has had to grapple with how to balance the different measures in its accountability system. Initially, multiple-choice tests were included as part of the Kentucky assessment design to ensure and protect a level of reliability that would be acceptable to educators. As the reliability of the performance-based parts of the assessment has risen, many participants have wanted to remove the multiple-choice testing, feeling that it contradicts the type of instructional change the state is seeking. The state board voted to keep the multiple-choice test in June 1994, but then reversed the decision in the fall of 1994. Others assert that it is still needed for technical reasons.

Kentucky has adjusted the grades tested, as well. The fourth grade teachers were overwhelmed by the implementation and grading of both writing and math portfolios. As a result, the math portfolio was moved to the fifth grade. The writing assessment, which involved a ninety-minute response to a question, or "prompt," although not part of the baseline, will now be incorporated into the writing component of the assessment. The state must decide how to value portfolio products compared with a ninety-minute writing prompt. The state is also in the process of shifting part of the twelfth grade assessment to the eleventh grade. This shift, predicated on a perceived need to improve student motivation, presents a technical challenge of equating scores from before and after the transition.

Even when such changes are fully defensible, they also present an opportunity for critics to question the staying power of the accountability reforms. According to one respondent, change is a chance for teachers to say, "See, they don't know what the hell they're doing. They're changing their mind all the time." One staff member in Kentucky commented,

> The problem is getting the system to work in a reliable and valid manner. . . . And so the question is, Are we going to throw this out and start something else, or are we going to be able to maintain this? And it's a real touch and go issue. We're at a very critical state right now. Because if we don't fix some of the things, we'll lose support of people who are supporting the change.

Political Issues in New Accountability Systems

Decisions about accountability are intensely political. They carry within them policymakers' understandings of what state responsibility for education means: what schools must deliver and what the state must guarantee they deliver. Decisions about those indicators, and the consequences related to their achievement, are profoundly important to local educators, to key stakeholders and their associations, and to policymakers. One would expect the existing array of political interests to have difficulty adjusting to a new distribution of expectations, power, and authority. The issues surrounding the design and implementation of performance-based systems recur often in state education politics: constituency pressures, resource constraints, an unstable policy environment, a lack of public understanding, even the possibility of turning away from performance standards and returning to input and process standards.

Constituency Pressures

Although legislators and governors frequently "talk tough," they are very susceptible to pressures by school people to back down and soften policies perceived to be restrictive or punitive. After all, schools are located in every legislative district. School and district leaders are often sophisticated political actors who are quite skilled at influencing policy development. All legislators, governors, and state board members hear frequently from these constituents, and very often the nature of the message is to "get the state off our back" (matched in frequency by "send more money").

In Kentucky, for example, the State Department of Education originally planned for outside audited scores on writing portfolios, which would prevail over teacher scoring. There were discrepancies between teacher-scored portfolios of work collected throughout the year and the independently scored writing exercise given during the statewide assessment. It is possible that teachers, knowing their students, were giving credit for effort and mentally comparing the pieces included in the portfolio with other work done during the year, while the contractor focused solely on the pieces submitted. When the new scores from the testing contractor were released, with some significant differences from school scores, educators protested vociferously. According to an evaluator of the Kentucky reforms, "All of a sudden their scores were lower, and [it seemed as if] they were cheating, and that was really tough on them. . . . So the department came up with options." For example, schools could accept the audited scores, adjust their own, or go through rescoring. But the legislature and the State Department of Education felt the educators' pressure and permitted districts an added option—keeping their original scores.

In another action during the 1994 session, the Kentucky legislature, at the department's suggestion, delayed the onset of the sanctions for "schools in crisis" for two years. Doubts about the reliability and validity of the assessment contributed to the decision. In an independent evaluation of KIRIS released in January 1995, the evaluators suggest that reliability and validity be demonstrated before the accountability index is used for high-stakes decisions related to rewards and sanctions.[20] But while these doubts led to suspending sanctions, rewards based on the same tests were scheduled for implementation in the spring of 1995 as originally planned. The state felt under intense pressure to get the rewards out, in part because of the skepticism referred to earlier about previously unfunded rewards.

In Mississippi, the legislature was reluctant to authorize the state to put failing districts into conservatorship. Once the authority was granted, the state was reluctant to use it. Between the time the Commission on School Accreditation recommended takeover in 1993 and the board's consider-

20. Western Michigan University (1995, p. 11).

ation of takeover, a flurry of activity took place in the local districts. Seeing this as evidence of "the deterrent effect" of conservatorship in action, the state did not take over any districts. As noted previously, many respondents thought that the department questioned its own capacity to make the necessary changes in failed districts and that the political flack was not worth the effort.

Resource Constraints

Hard-pressed state agencies do not have the human or fiscal resources to carry out the elements of the new accountability systems: assessment design and scoring; audits, visits, and reviews of local schools; explaining new systems to the public; and technical assistance to troubled schools or districts. Such constraints have always hampered accountability approaches, creating gaps between what states said they were holding districts accountable for, what they could actually observe, and what they could realistically enforce. Most reviews of districts have been on paper, and visits have been infrequent and superficial. Now the resource constraints are more apparent and troublesome, both because the systems are more complex and demand more capacity and because there are more meaningful rewards and sanctions attached to accountability processes.

In Kentucky, some initial features of the accountability system have been scaled back for lack of financial support from the legislature. For example, initially students were to be tested in off-years as part of a testing program to monitor continuous improvement, but the commissioner was unsuccessful in getting additional resources during the 1992 legislative session. As a result, some districts have gone ahead and purchased the off-year scrimmage tests directly from the testing company, while others use only the mandatory testing program.

Similar financial constraints affect Mississippi. In 1994–95 only about $100,000 was available for the twelve districts in level 1, which is not very much money for the task of turning around the lowest performers. Furthermore, some of the funds that the state uses come from a federal program that supports school improvement initiatives but could easily be reduced by federal budget cuts.

Districts and schools sometimes use resource deficiencies to explain low performance. For example, a principal in a Mississippi level 2 (formerly level 1) district said that school improvement was a difficult endeavor in a district like his, with insufficient resources to hire the specialists needed to make progress in curriculum and pedagogy:

> We don't have the human resources. I can have all kinds of good things going
> on in my head, and I can share with you, with my faculty . . . where I am.
> But if I do not have the time to sit with you, monitor with you, model for you,
> sometimes those things just end up in my head or on a piece of paper. . . . So
> there are systems that no doubt have reading supervisors, curriculum coordi-
> nators, . . . math supervisors. . . . I don't have that.

Mississippi is working on establishing a new funding formula directly
linked to the accreditation system. The state has determined what it costs
a district to achieve level 3 by examining twenty-five level 3 districts. The
state hopes to secure an additional $128 million to fund this formula. Ac-
cording to a member of the legislature, "Once that is in place, then a school
district cannot use the excuse, we do not have enough funds."

Political Stability

Accountability reforms, like education reforms in general, are vulnerable to political shifts, both because of a change of political leadership or a
change of public mood.

Initially, Kentucky's expectations for students were set forth in six
learning goals and further specified in seventy-five valued outcomes to be
assessed through KIRIS. The goals and outcomes were scrutinized by a
variety of critics, and those relating to character traits—such as self-suffi-
ciency and responsibility—drew the most fire. Ultimately the backlash led
to the removal of two goals along with the associated outcomes from the
assessment system, the renaming of "outcomes" as academic expectations,
and the rewording of some of the statements.

Many educators felt that changes altered the goals substantively. A
member of the Kentucky State Department of Education staff said, "There
is a lot of concern that by making them more in the common vernacular,
they've lost a lot of the technical meaning that teachers needed in order to
teach them. . . ." Without the technical language, some teachers believe
they cannot really understand what is being asked of them. One of the
originators of the standards complained:

> How can you cave in to these people when we had three and four years of
> work to develop these outcomes; we had representatives from all the stake-
> holders, teachers, administrators, etc., and this represented the best thinking
> of 150 Kentucky educators, and then you can give them away because you
> get political pressure from a very small group?

Mississippi has not yet faced the anti-outcome outcry, but policymakers worry about it. A senior legislator said:

> Now in my opinion, the term "outcome" engenders . . . such a connotation that in many parts of the country, and now in some parts of our state, is viewed somehow as a very liberal approach to doing certain things in the schools that are unacceptable to conservative society. We do not believe we're doing those things, and in fact, our direction from our committee . . . is that on all tests remove any portions of the test that would tend to inflame these issues. . . . We don't use the term "outcome" because (1) we don't understand it, and (2) we do not want opposition to programs that are legitimate, that are good, that anyone in any political spectrum would adopt and agree are valid objectives for a school to accomplish.

The political turmoil surrounding standards reform indicates that much of the public is ambivalent and confused about standards and related policies. The public appears to believe in high standards but may be thinking about basic skills rather than the more complex, ambitious visions of learning expressed in the Kentucky outcomes and assessed through KIRIS.[21] Furthermore, many parents appear to be worried that the intrusion of "values" into education will usurp family prerogatives, and they suspect all state-level standards of posing such a risk. Such suspicion means that accountability systems will receive continuing criticism.

Public and Educator Understanding

A segment of the public fears that standards represent a threat to family values. The technical nature of these systems poses further risks. Remember, the structure and workings of the accountability systems are not well understood by many key policymakers and educators in Kentucky and Mississippi. Consequently, they cannot explain them to the public in a way that inspires confidence.

Kentucky parents are confused about the difference between the new tests and the familiar norm-referenced standardized tests. They are accustomed to reports telling them the percentile in which their children and their school scores and how that compares with other students, schools, districts, and states, even if most parents do not understand the basis on which these scores are computed. In contrast, KIRIS scores indicate how children are doing in comparison with an absolute standard. Parents have

21. Johnson and Immerwahr (1994).

little basis on which to understand a rating of "proficient" or "novice." A researcher who works closely with KIRIS commented on the "need to let parents know where their children are in relation to some kind of national standard, or some standard they understand."

Furthermore, KIRIS is given in only a few grades, while the traditional tests were given yearly. Norm-referenced tests are much less expensive and time-consuming than tests composed of lengthy tasks and open-ended, difficult-to-score questions, so yearly administration was more feasible. The solution adopted by many schools is to continue with a more traditional norm-referenced test while also adopting the new KIRIS requirements. But multiple testing may fuel rather than alleviate parental confusion. For example, Kentucky parents complained when their college-bound youngsters' high scores on the SAT or the ACT were matched with less-than-proficient KIRIS scores. They did not know, or perhaps care, about differences between the tests. They also overlooked the fact that KIRIS tests were not taken until the end of senior year and deemed to have no consequence by many students who took them much less seriously than college entrance exams.

In Mississippi, too, people are used to comparison, not to a focus on one's own scores over time. As one state agency official said, "I think from a weakness standpoint, we still haven't gotten down to helping people focus on their own improvement as opposed to how they relate to the district next door or to the district across the field."

Without public backing, the new systems are even more vulnerable to political attack. States may have to amend their plans to meet parental expectations, such as the desire for regular information about individual students, if they wish to generate sustained support.

Persistence of Input and Process Standards

States that design performance-based systems intend to substitute performance criteria for process regulations. But removing existing regulations is difficult. Regulations protect constituencies and serve as important statements about minimal services to be provided to all children, especially children in poor or troubled districts where access to educational services is not assured. They also serve the state's desire to limit corruption, inefficiency, and waste.[22]

22. Fuhrman and Elmore (1995).

In both states, we saw evidence of ambivalence about regulation. Kentucky is trying to pare legislation by reviewing rules and trying to move more strongly to a focus on performance. But the Kentucky Education Reform Act includes many new requirements about practice along with its performance focus, such as the mandates for school-based management and for multiage primary classrooms. Each requirement and element of the act creates a need for a plan to be submitted to the state. All these plans are perceived as additional process burdens. As one policymaker predicted, "If you talk to superintendents and principals, and coordinators, they'll tell you one of the biggest problems that needs attention is the amount of paperwork. So they have to do a transformation plan, they have to do a professional plan, they have to do a technology plan, they have to do this and that."

Although administrators perceive a burden, they are not sure that these requirements and others should be dropped, especially not for the traditional "bad apples," the corrupt or troubled districts that are the focus of much current regulation throughout every state. A Kentucky superintendent said, "Kentucky is east, west and central. There's a whole different philosophy and culture. And the culture in eastern Kentucky and western Kentucky is, they need monitoring."

In the fall of 1994, as a part of Mississippi's effort to further reduce the process standards, the State Department of Education sent out a survey to school districts and state-level officials to see which process standards were viewed as absolutely necessary. As the results were described, "Consistently on every person that has completed one of the questionnaires, when you ask them if there should be a requirement, while they say in general that we ought to decrease these, when they go through and they look at them one on one . . . they come back to the bottom line, this is absolutely necessary."

Mississippi's policymakers do offer some deregulation as a reward for schools in levels 4 and 5. However, they continue to regulate nonetheless. In the 1994 session, the legislature mandated that in order for a school district to be accredited, all its classrooms had to be air-conditioned by July 1, 1995, and that a certain number of librarians had to be employed.

Prospects for the New Educational Accountability

The new educational accountability, or the movement of state accountability systems from emphasizing inputs and processes to emphasizing performance, is at a critical stage of development in the United States. Many states have introduced elements of accountability for performance, but few have yet introduced fully developed systems in which performance measures are linked explicitly to incentives and processes for improvements that cover all schools and districts. Since Kentucky and Mississippi have relatively well-developed systems, their experience can help to identify key issues that emerge in the design, implementation, and politics of accountability systems.

We perceive five main challenges for states as they move toward educational accountability: making accountability systems understandable and defensible to policymakers, educators, parents, and students; resolving issues of fairness in the design and implementation of accountability systems; focusing incentives for improvement; developing state capacity to implement and maintain accountability systems; and creating a stable political environment.

Making Systems Understandable and Defensible

Performance-based accountability systems are technically more demanding and complex than input- and process-based systems, because they require the construction of defensible measures of performance and the creation of systems for evaluating schools and districts. This technical complexity causes two major problems. First, the systems can be very difficult to understand, even for administrators and policymakers who are close to them and whose work brings them into regular contact with the systems, much less for parents and members of the public at large. Some of these technical issues, such as what the assessments actually measure and how composite indexes are used to classify schools and districts, have potentially large administrative and political consequences.

One might argue that people do not necessarily have to understand accountability systems, as long as they have confidence that they are well designed and fair. We think this argument is questionable.

First, performance-based accountability systems depend heavily for their success on whether school administrators, teachers, parents, and students know *what to do* to improve performance. To the extent that the systems themselves do not convey information about what to do to improve performance, they are not likely to be viewed as helpful by the people who are charged with that responsibility. In addition, poorly understood systems are politically vulnerable because they often produce surprises that only the experts can try to explain, and surprises undermine the credibility of the systems. When schools move down in performance levels while they are struggling to improve, school administrators, teachers, parents, and students justifiably want to know whether they are actually failing or whether the results are artifacts of a measurement system they do not understand.

Second, the technical complexity of performance-based accountability systems, coupled with the fact that they entail relatively new assessment and evaluation techniques, means that they require constant revision in their early stages. Mississippi is moving away from its use of norm-referenced tests toward standards-based assessment, which will entail major changes in how schools and districts collect and interpret performance data. Kentucky has changed the grade levels at which assessments occur, the mix of assessment techniques, and the way portfolio results are audited. Although these changes are an inevitable consequence of the development and fine-tuning of performance-based accountability systems, advocates often see them as evidence of a retreat on the strategic aims of the systems, while critics interpret them as evidence of fundamental flaws. Explaining and defending such changes is an important task for policymakers and high-level administrators.

Resolving Issues of Fairness

New educational accountability systems raise issues of fairness that are politically and technically complex. The central issue is the extent to which schools or districts should be rewarded or penalized for student performance, without regard for the prior knowledge or social background of their students. One side of this issue, represented in this volume by the Clotfelter and Ladd chapter, argues that schools can fairly be held accountable only for factors that they control, and therefore that performance accountability systems should control for or equalize student socioeconomic status before they dispense rewards and penalties. A related point of view is the "value-added" argument, which says that schools should be accountable only for the performance gains or losses they contribute to students; hence performance accountability systems should control for prior student achievement.

The other side of the issue argues that controlling for student background or prior achievement institutionalizes low expectations for poor, minority, low-achieving students. Controlling for social background or prior achievement, in effect, holds schools with large proportions of such students to a lower standard of performance. Instead, this view holds that policy and resources should be used to create incentives for schools with high proportions of poor, minority, low-achieving students to improve learning at a faster rate than other schools.

These points of view are fought out in the design of state accountability systems. Mississippi has clearly decided against controlling for social background. Since it is clear that student achievement in Mississippi is related to the socioeconomic status of students, the accountability system adversely affects school districts with high proportions of low-income, disadvantaged students. The Kentucky system is more complex on this issue. By holding schools accountable for closing the gap between a baseline measure of performance and a standard over a twenty-year period, Kentucky is, in a way, controlling for prior student achievement. On the other hand, schools with high proportions of low-performing students are implicitly held to a higher standard of performance than schools with lower proportions, since they must go further to meet the proficiency goal.

We are agnostic about this debate. If performance accountability systems are seen as ways of rewarding and penalizing schools for what they are able to do, then it is fair to control for student background and prior achievement. On the other hand, if the systems are supposed to be useful in driving resources toward schools that have the largest gap between performance standards and actual performance, then controlling for student background or prior performance is counterproductive, because it allows schools and school systems to, in effect, conceal the pockets of greatest need by adjusting standards. If this debate can be resolved, it will require either a clearer focus on what the performance goals of the educational system are to be, or the development of systems that reward both added value and attainment of an absolute standard.

Focusing Incentives for Improvement

Underlying the new educational accountability is a belief that states should reorient their relations with schools and districts away from passive, maintenance-oriented oversight to the active creation of incentives for improvements in student learning. However, the creation of such incentives is an extraordinarily complex task and even relatively well developed state systems are just beginning to grapple with it. The Mississippi system, for example, focuses most of its attention on the bottom level of districts and consequently offers weak to nonexistent direct incentives for districts at middle and higher levels to improve. Mississippi decisionmakers are frank in their admission that the system does not speak to districts in the middle where the community thinks average performance is good enough, even though "middle-level" districts in the Mississippi system are at only the thirty-second percentile of performance on nationally normed standardized achievement tests. In addition, the Mississippi system mediates all incentives through districts, rather than focusing directly on schools.

The Kentucky system provides relatively strong incentives for high-performing schools, in the form of recognition and monetary rewards, and relatively strong sanctions and support for low-performing schools. For schools in the middle range, the incentives are more ambiguous. If such schools are satisfied with their performance, there is little in the middle range to encourage them to improve. Recall that schools are evaluated in Kentucky based on their *progress* toward a standard of proficiency. One source of uncertainty in the incentive structure of the Kentucky system is whether schools will be able to move at a steady pace toward the standard, or whether, given such factors as student mobility and diversity in learning patterns among students, some schools will find it difficult to make steady progress.

Developing State Capacity

Performance-based systems of accountability are high-maintenance in another respect: they require technical expertise in assessment and evaluation issues, and special competence in assisting districts and schools in improving their performance. States can solve this capacity issue either by contracting with experts or by developing the expertise themselves. Both Mississippi and Kentucky have contracted heavily with outside firms for development of assessment technology. Kentucky has also decided to contract with distinguished educators for assistance to low-performing schools. While contracting allows states to run performance-based systems relatively efficiently, it also contributes to the problem (alluded to earlier) of a separation between technical expertise about assessment and evaluation and the policymakers and high-level administrators who are responsible for the systems.

A more serious problem is whether states are willing to invest in the capacity to meet the established goals of their systems. Kentucky set up a system to provide assistance to low-performing schools and then underfunded the distinguished educators program that was to provide that assistance. Mississippi has created an assistance requirement for low-performing districts, but it is far from clear that the State Department of Education has the resources to deliver the required assistance or to take over districts if necessary. There is a serious mismatch between goals and capacities in some parts of these states' accountability systems.

Creating a Stable Political Environment for Reform

Because performance-based accountability systems are technically complex and aimed at relatively long-term improvements in schooling, they require sustained development and support. Thus the political stability around these systems will be a key factor influencing their chances of success. This stability involves both rhetorical and financial support from elected officials and educators' and parents' acceptance of the results of assessments and evaluations of their schools as legitimate. This issue could be critical in Kentucky, where, because of the extraordinarily high performance standards embedded in the assessment system, schools that were previously considered to be excellent may be classified as in need of serious improvement.

The new emphasis on accountability in both Kentucky and Mississippi marks a significant departure from state systems that previously gave little attention to student, school, or district performance. In each state, one can find both critics and supporters of these new systems. In both states, the attention to accountability has resulted in desperately needed additional state support for education. The attention to accountability has resulted in a new public dialogue around schools and student performances, in part because of close scrutiny by the press in its new role of messenger of results. Public attention on high-performing and low-performing schools and districts is highlighting model practices and is ensuring that poor practices begin to change. Low-performing districts want to get out of the spotlight. Both states have provided significant funding for staff development to assist teachers and administrators. Both states have also shown a willingness to revisit and revise the accountability systems to improve their functioning.

As Mississippi, Kentucky, and other states continue with the development of performance-based accountability approaches, policymakers need to face both the technical demands of the system and the practical requirements of explaining and justify it to the public and to key constituencies. They need to adapt and improve the systems to provide solutions to emerging problems.

References

Alston, Ethel, and others. 1994. *The Kentucky Education Reform Act.* Frankfort, Ky.: Legislative Research Commission.

Burnham, Tom. 1995. *Mississippi Accreditation Requirements of the State Board of Education.* Bulletin 171, 12th ed. Jackson, Miss.

Council of Chief State School Officers. State Education Assessment Center. 1994. *State Education Accountability Reports: Results of CCSSO Survey.* Washington: CCSSO.

Fuhrman, Susan. 1994a. "Evaluation of Performance in the United States: Changes in Accountability." Prepared for Organization of Economic Cooperation and Development.

———. 1994b. "New Accountability Systems and Evaluating Systemic Reform." Prepared for U.S. Department of Education, Planning and Evaluation Service.

Fuhrman, Susan H., and Richard F. Elmore. 1995. "Ruling Out Rules: The Evolution of Deregulation in State Education Policy." New Brunswick, N.J.: Consortium for Policy Research in Education.

Guskey, Thomas R., ed. 1994. *High Stakes Performance Assessment. Perspectives on Kentucky's Reform.* Thousand Oaks, Calif.: Corwin Press.

Herman, J. L., and S. Golan. 1991. *Effects of Standardized Testing on Teachers and Learning: Another Look.* CSE Technical Report 348. Los Angeles: University of California at Los Angeles, National Center for Research on Evaluation, Standards, and Student Testing.

Hetrick, Beverly. 1993. "Fifty State Survey on Regulation and Accountability." New Brunswick, N.J.: Consortium on Policy Research in Education.

Johnson, Jean, and John Immerwahr. 1994. *First Things First: What Americans Expect from the Public Schools.* New York: Public Agenda.

Kentucky Department of Education. 1995. *KIRIS Accountability Cycle I: Technical Manual.* Frankfort, Ky.

Madaus, G. F., and others. 1992. *The Impact of Mandated Standardized Testing on Minority Students.* Boston: Boston College, Center for the Study of Testing, Evaluation, and Educational Policy.

Massell, Diane. 1995. "What We Know about Assessing What Students Know: A Literature Review on Assessment." Prepared for the Annie Casey Foundation. Cosponsored by Consortium for Policy Research in Education, Rutgers University.

National Governors' Association. 1986. *Time for Results.* Washington: Center for Policy Research and Analysis.

Shepard, Lorrie A. 1990. "Inflated Test Score Gains: Is the Problem Old Norms or Teaching the Test?" *Educational Measurement: Issues and Practice* 9 (Fall) 15–22.

Southern Regional Education Board. 1994. *Reflecting on Ten Years of Incentive Programs: The 1993 SREB Career Ladder Clearinghouse Survey.* Atlanta: Southern Regional Education Board Career Ladder Clearinghouse.

U.S. Department of Education. Office of Educational Research and Improvement. 1988. *Measuring Up: Questions and Answers about State Roles in Educational Accountability.* PIP 89-820.

Western Michigan University. The Evaluation Center. 1995. *An Independent Evaluation of the Kentucky Instructional Results Information System (KIRIS).* Report conducted for Kentucky Institute for Education Research. Kalamazoo.

CHAPTER FOUR

Standards-Based School Reform: Policy, Practice, and Performance

David K. Cohen

T HE YEARS between 1980 and 1994 saw a remarkable realignment in American education. During the 1980s, a conservative president vowed to abolish the federal Department of Education and turn schooling back to states and localities. But the Department of Education persisted, and Ronald Reagan's administration exerted an impressive nationalizing influence on public education. It helped to mobilize powerful national pressures for better academic performance, stiffer standards, and even national tests. In the 1980s conservatives began to push public education toward some sort of national and perhaps even federal system. Some even attacked local control of schools as a dangerously outmoded idea.

The same years also saw dramatic changes in ideas about the purposes and content of schooling. In the mid-1970s and early 1980s, school improvement had focused on the "basics."[1] By the end of Reagan's first term, however, researchers, school reformers, and advocates from business had begun to argue for more intellectually ambitious instruction. They contended that teaching and learning should be more deeply rooted in the disciplines and much more demanding. Teachers should help students to understand mathematical concepts, to interpret serious literature, to write creatively about their ideas and experiences, and to converse thoughtfully about history and social science. Reformers also began to argue that

This chapter has profited from the comments of several conference participants and from the persistent attention of Helen Ladd. I also owe James P. Spillane many thanks for his close reading of an earlier draft and many helpful suggestions.
1. In the 1970s and early 1980s, in response to worries about relaxed standards and weak performance by disadvantaged students, states and the federal government pressed basic skills instruction on schools, supporting the idea with technical assistance and enforcing it with standardized "minimum competency" tests. Those tests were America's first postwar brush with performance-oriented schooling.

schools and school systems should orient their work to the results that students achieve rather than to the resources that schools receive.

No less remarkable, reformers proposed fundamental changes in politics and policy to achieve these goals. Beginning with California, state education agencies began to exercise more central authority for instruction by devising and implementing intellectually ambitious curriculums and assessments. By Bill Clinton's inauguration, reform efforts that envisioned some version of coordinated change in instructional frameworks, curriculum, and assessment were under way in several dozen states. Reformers came to call this combination "systemic reform," and it entailed several key ideas: that instruction should be intellectually much more ambitious; that those ambitions should hold for all students; and that learning and teaching should be pressed in that direction by a coordinated set of instructional guidance mechanisms, including means to hold schools accountable for students' performance.[2] That vision of reform was given a central place in federal education policy in 1994 with the passage of Goals 2000 and the reauthorization of title 1.

Systemic reform rested on several key assumptions. First, reformers assumed or hoped that if state and federal education agencies set ambitious goals and created new instructional frameworks, curriculum, and assessments, then professionals would get the message and instruction would become more demanding and coherent. Reformers conceded that teachers would need help to learn, and most argued that schools should be made accountable for students' performance as measured in the new assessments.[3] But no state envisioned teacher education as the engine of reform. In most cases, the central focus was reserved for some combination of standards, curriculum, and assessments.

A second key assumption was that intellectually ambitious instruction was a reasonable enough goal for American public schools that reformers could propose attainment in a relatively short time—perhaps by the year 2000 or soon thereafter. That seemed quite astonishing, given the nation's long history of devotion to basic skills and relatively low-grade intellectual ambitions for most students. A third assumption was no less remarkable: that state and federal agencies could carry the burden of standards-based

2. O'Day and Smith (1993).
3. Most state and federal reformers seemed to accept some version of this idea. Various mechanisms to enhance accountability were included in the reforms, but they seem to play a central role only in Kentucky. The notion of accountability also is prominent in title 1 of the Elementary and Secondary Education Act and Goals 2000, though not tightly defined.

reform. This implied that they could quickly mobilize the capabilities to write and promulgate standards, devise instructional frameworks, compose assessments, and thus change teaching and learning. A fourth idea was that systemic reform would reduce inequality in educational achievement if disadvantaged students were held to the same high standards as everybody else and if schools could be made to improve education across the board.

Systemic reform, therefore, is broader than performance reward schemes, which focus on a single mechanism for change—incentives for improved student performance. Systemic reform embraces a linked set of mechanisms in instructional guidance that includes such incentives but reaches far beyond them. But both approaches involve a fundamental reorientation of public education toward results produced, rather than resources allocated, and toward somehow holding schools accountable for students' achievement.

Systemic reform is nothing if not ambitious. The present system of education is marked by weak and inconsistent standards, incoherent guidance for instruction, little consensus about goals, and great inequality in educational achievement. Systemic reformers envision the rapid creation of a system marked by strong and consistent standards, coherent guidance for instruction, strong consensus about goals, and much greater equality in educational achievement. That stark contrast frames the central issue in this chapter: will systemic reform succeed in fundamentally revising public schools, or will public education impose fundamental changes on systemic reform? My answers to this question are not conclusive, since the reform movement is young and much of the evidence is not yet in.[4] But a good deal

4. One main basis for my report is a continuing study of how intellectually ambitious state instructional policies develop and are enacted by state and local educators and teachers, a study conducted in more than a dozen districts in Michigan, California, and South Carolina. The districts range from large to small and from highly urban to semirural. They include several cities—one very large and several others of medium size—and two fairly conventional suburbs. All of the districts include schools in which there are an appreciable number of disadvantaged children, and more than half are heavily attended by such children. The research team of which I am a part has observed and interviewed in second and fifth grades, and in most cases we followed teachers' work for three to five years.

I am indebted to my colleagues in that study, including Deborah Lowenberg Ball, Carol Barnes, Jennifer Borman, James Bowker, Daniel Chazan, Pamela Geist, S. G. Grant, Ruth Heaton, Nancy Jennings, Nancy Knapp, Susan Luks, Steve Mattson, Penelope Peterson, Sue Poppink, Richard Prawat, Jeremy Price, Ralph Putnam, Janine Remillard, Peggy Rittenhouse, Angela Shojgreen-Downer, James Spillane, Sarah Theule-Lubienski, Karl Wheatley, and Suzanne Wilson. The study has been supported in part by Michigan State University, and by grants to Michigan State University and the University of Michigan from the Pew Charitable Trust (Grant No. 91-04343-000), the Carnegie Corporation of New York

of evidence has been collected, and I consider it in four areas: guidance for instruction, teaching practice, accountability and the political context, and conflicting goals.

Guidance for Instruction

Systemic reformers seek more coherent and powerful state guidance for instruction, but power and authority have been extraordinarily dispersed in the U.S. education system. The school "system" is in some critical respects a nonsystem, a congeries of more than 100,000 schools situated in 15,000 independent local governments, 50 state governments and hundreds of intermediate and special district governments in between, as well as several federal agencies and countless private organizations. It is reasonable to wonder if proposals for high standards and instructional guidance could have a coherent effect on practice in such an incoherent system.

Although systemic reform has had significant effects, it does not seem to have made guidance for instruction more coherent. At the federal level, certain reforms made impressive progress between the mid-1980s and 1994. Chapter 1 (now title 1) was reauthorized in 1988, and it encouraged state and local programs to adopt intellectually more ambitious instructional goals for disadvantaged children. The governors met with President Bush at Charlottesville at roughly the same time and agreed on national education goals—an unprecedented idea. But after several years of partisan scrapping, congressional Democrats rejected President Bush's proposal, titled America 2000. Only in 1994, after Bill Clinton was elected president, was the Democratic version passed into law as Goals 2000.

From one vantage point, Goals 2000 seemed a giant step. Title 2 of the bill created a federal certification agency, the National Education Standards and Improvement Council (NESIC), for national content and performance standards, and title 3 created a program of grants to state education agencies to support the development of state instructional goals, state content and performance standards, and state and local plans to meet those

(Grant No. B 5638), the National Science Foundation (Grant No. ESI-9153834), and the Consortium for Policy Research in Education (CPRE), which is funded by a grant from the U.S. Department of Education, Office of Educational Research and Improvement (Grant No. OERI-G-008690011). I am indebted to the granting agencies for their assistance, but the ideas expressed here are mine, and are not necessarily shared by the grantors or my colleagues in the research.

standards. These steps would have been politically unimaginable just a few years earlier. But politics had not changed much at all in other respects, for Goals 2000 deferred broadly to states: NESIC was voluntary, and states could get their title 3 grants without meeting many requirements related to Goals 2000.

Title 1 was reauthorized again shortly after Goals 2000 became law, and this time it pushed much further toward systemic reform. It required state title 1 programs to set high instructional goals for students, to devise or adopt intellectually ambitious content and performance standards, and to create local programs that would push all students to high standards and hold schools accountable for the results. Title 1 is a roughly $7 billion annual formula-grant program that operates in all states and more than 90 percent of all local districts, and it offers monies that states and localities want for the education of disadvantaged students. Reformers expected that state and local desire for title 1 funds would lead them in the direction of Goals 2000.[5]

Varied Reforms in the States

Title 1 and Goals 2000 may mark the beginning of a fundamental shift in the federal role in schooling. But that will depend partly on what happens in the states, which so far has been a very mixed story. The state versions of these reforms made progress between the mid-1980s and 1994, as guidance for instruction moved in the direction of reform. For instance, California produced a series of ambitious new instructional frameworks in the core academic subjects between 1985 and 1994 and made large changes in the content and format of the state assessment program. Vermont made similarly impressive changes in assessment and other guidance for instruction, though educators there have relied on much more extensive professional involvement than did those in California. Kentucky drastically overhauled its entire school system in response to a court order, installing new systems of assessment, accountability, and professional development. Many other states have moved in the same direction—South Carolina, Arizona, New York, Connecticut, and Delaware among them—though with varying strategies and speeds.

In fact, differences among these states are as noteworthy as the similarities. For instance, Michigan—which for most of its history had a very de-

---

5. See Education Funding Research Council (1995).

centralized school system—moved toward more central guidance, but it did so in a much more piecemeal fashion than California, Kentucky, or Vermont, with few signs of the guiding vision of reform that could be found in those three states. Michigan revised its guidance for reading quite dramatically in the mid-1980s and a few years later revised the state reading tests, almost as an afterthought. Revisions in mathematics and science guidance and assessments followed several years later, but at roughly the same time the legislature initiated a core curriculum measure (Public Act 25) that required local districts to devise their own approaches to core subjects. Shortly thereafter, and for different reasons, the governor and legislature overhauled the state school finance system, which reduced local property taxes and increased the state's role in school finance. Thus Michigan moved toward reform in a distinctly disjointed manner.[6]

South Carolina, by contrast, seemed to move quickly from a well-established and highly centralized 1980s state program that pressed schools to teach facts and skills and rewarded them for test score gains, to a program in the early 1990s that focused on intellectually much more ambitious instruction within a more decentralized state structure. But the new system of frameworks and assessments is still incomplete, and important elements of the previous system remain on the books. The state did not dismantle its previous system of rewards for performance on statewide standardized tests, and at the moment it is unclear what sorts of performance will be rewarded.[7]

California differed from both Michigan and South Carolina. The state took an aggressive approach to developing new state guidance, and it sustained the clearest vision of intellectually ambitious instruction for the longest time—between 1985 and 1994. But the state education agency also changed its strategy and tactics for implementing that guidance several times. In mathematics it initially published a brief new framework in 1985 that offered innovative but very broad guidance. In 1992 the state authorities published a new framework that offered much more detailed and somewhat different guidance. In the mid-1980s state education leaders seemed to place most of their bets on changing textbooks through the state adoption system, but when that produced only modest changes, they promoted the development of alternative curriculum materials, an approach that seems to have done more to make dramatically revised curriculum

6. Cohen and others (forthcoming, chap. 7).
7. This report is based on several papers by members of the study mentioned in note 4 above, including Jennings, Spillane, and Borman (1995); Jennings and Spillane (1995).

available. Next, state officials gave much more emphasis to revising the state testing program, partly with the aim of increasing accountability: officials argued that once the assessments were changed and the results published, the low scores on more ambitious tests would "drive" school professionals to improve instruction. But that sort of accountability could work only if teachers noticed the results and decided to change, or if parents noticed and encouraged teachers to change, and, in either case, if teachers had the wherewithal to learn how to change.[8]

State guidance for instruction in systemic reform thus varies considerably. States differ in the comprehensiveness, speed, approach and depth of their reforms, and they have rather different histories. Systemic reform has brought a broad drift toward intellectually more ambitious instruction at the state level, but thus far it has not brought more coherence to state guidance for instruction.

Local Responses to Reform

These points gain force from consideration of the local responses to systemic reform. The guidance for instruction that local central offices offer to schools has begun to shift in the direction of reform, but that shift has so far not been accompanied by greater local coherence in guidance for instruction, for districts' responses differ significantly within states, and schools' responses differ significantly within districts. Our research team observed these patterns in Michigan, California and South Carolina: a few districts aggressively tried to capitalize on the state reforms for their own reasons, a small fraction were indifferent, and most responded in piecemeal and modest fashion.

James Spillane has shown that change was fragmentary within districts.[9] Many local central offices sent mixed signals, since their offices included both reformers and traditionalists. Since many subunits in central offices have quite different missions, they tend to make use of higher-level policies in ways that fit with those missions. For instance, professional development administrators in one city school district saw the state reforms as just one of many possible sources of demand for their services and thus gave them a modest priority. But the district reading coordinator focused on the

---

8. Despite some ingenious efforts and a good deal of organizing, California education agencies had at best modest capacity to help teachers to change. This account is based on field notes from the study mentioned in note 4 above.

9. This account is drawn from Spillane (1993). See also Spillane (1996a).

extraordinary need for professional development if the reading reforms were to succeed. She tried to get local help with that task, but the central office curriculum leaders resisted the state reforms and refused fiscal support for her work because they believed that most students needed basic skills instruction. At the same time, administrators in the district's chapter 1 office took the state policy as an opportunity to change chapter 1 instruction significantly, including the initiation of a significant professional development effort for chapter 1 teachers and aides. Thus four subunits in the same central office—which incidentally had recently settled on a single mission statement—broadcast quite different messages about the new state policy to schools and teachers.[10]

That story was repeated with local variations in all three states. Scholars habitually write as though school districts are unitary and internally homogenous organizations, but they are not.[11] Administrators work in subunits that specialize in prior policies like title 1, bilingual education, or special education, or that reflect professional subspecialities like the reading curriculum, secondary education, or vocational education, or that reflect functional distinctions like budget, evaluation, or professional development. Organizational context does not determine everything, but it does shape perceptions and judgment. An internally fragmented local organization means that when state agencies send one message, the local office receives it in many different ways.[12]

Another final source of variation is differences among school principals within districts: some embrace reforms and use them as an opportunity to try to change instruction; others maintain their attachment to traditional classroom methods; and still others are neutral. Only one of the school systems that we studied made anything that might approach a serious and sustained effort to shape principals' decisions about instruction.

Reasons for Variability

The very reforms that seek more coherence in instructional policy thus have helped to create more variety and less coherence. While there has been a broad movement toward intellectually more ambitious instruction, there also has been great variability within that movement. Looking across

10. See Spillane (1993).
11. Spillane (1996b).
12. For a general account of these organizational patterns in American education, see Cohen (1982); Cohen and Spillane (1992); and Spillane (1993).

districts, one used to see a fairly homogenous embrace of basic skills. Now, some districts employ "literature-based" curriculums in reading and "hands-on" approaches to mathematics while others retain more conservative approaches. One also can see significant differences within districts. Some districts, central subunits, and schools are working in much more ambitious ways than they did five years ago, many more have changed somewhat, many have changed only a little, and some not at all. Quite a few are displaying all of these reactions at once.

So far, then, the growth of state instructional policy has not constrained local instructional policymaking.[13] The states have used a diverse array of policy instruments—new instructional standards or frameworks, new curriculum guidance, revised testing programs, and even revamped professional education—but local educational authorities have continued to act as though they had undiminished authority to make instructional policy. Some have rewritten local standards or frameworks, revised professional education, and changed testing programs; others have continued as before. Stronger state guidance for instruction has not reduced local instructional policymaking or weakened local school governance. Local school policymaking generally is more active and influential now than it was in the late 1960s and early 1970s, despite more active state guidance for instruction.

That pattern of growing activity everywhere owes a good deal to the fragmented organization of schooling, for it tends to amplify differences in what educators make of the messages that flow around them.[14] Although states have all the formal authority in schooling, they usually delegate most of it to localities, most of which delegate a great deal to individual schools, which until very recently left many decisions to teachers. Governments also are divided by the separation of powers: since legislative, executive, and judicial branches of state and federal governments respond to different incentives and operate in different ways, professionals working in them often see the same issues differently. Local schools embody elements of that division, with full-time professional executives struggling to work with the part-time legislatures known as school boards. Finally, chronic distrust of government and carefully designed weakness in it has opened a large role for private-sector organizations to do much of the work that state agencies do in Asia and Europe, including such central matters as student assessment, materials development, and text publishing.

13. See Cohen (1982); Fuhrman, Clune, and Elmore (1988); Fuhrman and Elmore (1990); Spillane (1996a).
14. Scott and Meyer (1983); see also Schwille and others (1983).

As reform ideas became popular and played through this fragmented structure, they were picked up by an astonishing variety of organizations—all concerned with schools, but each in its own way. Many organizations responded by offering their own programs for systemic reform, their own ideas about standards, goals, and curriculum, and their own views of how to achieve greater coherence. The result was a veritable deluge of critiques, reform ideas, proposals, and materials.[15] Although much of it tended in the same very broad direction of higher standards and greater coherence, the aggregate was a blizzard of different and often conflicting ideas. The result resembled the disease as much as the cure.[16]

A second explanation for more varied guidance for instruction is that state reform proposals often point in several different directions at once, because they embody divergent political tendencies. For example, South Carolina's recent systemic reforms prominently featured an effort by the state education agency to strengthen and streamline state guidance for instruction, yet at the same time the state legislature adopted a scheme to decentralize state government and increase individual schools' influence and involvement.[17] It also sought to bypass district central offices, channel some state funds directly to schools, and make the decisionmaking process at each unit of government more participatory by involving representatives of various interest groups in governing the schools. This reform package moved in several directions at once. If the decentralize-and-enhance-school-influence elements of the reforms were to succeed, they would run counter to the streamline-governance-and-enhance-state influence elements.

Systemic reform seems likely to carry these contending tendencies into practice. More school-level power and participation in hope of strengthening individual schools' capacity for improvement could be consistent with streamlining and simplifying governance, if it were balanced by large sub-

15. Although government is one source of the deluge, the private sector has been no less important. Ideas, materials, services, and proposals flood into local districts from nongovernmental sources—such as the education professions, university researchers, and text and test publishers—and the private sector in American education is no more coherent than government. Many private organizations create and merchandise tests, school texts, and supplementary materials, all of which typically are unrelated. Some private organizations try to reduce taxes while others organize to promote changes in the curriculum. All these and many other private organizations cluster around the fragmented formal governance structure of public education, performing a great variety of essential and peripheral functions while adding to the complexity of policy, politics, and administration.

16. For a fuller account of this phenomenon, see Cohen and Spillane (1992).

17. See O'Day and Smith (1993).

tractions from local, state and federal governance and policy.[18] But politicians find it much easier to add than to subtract. Agencies scheduled for reduction or elimination always have advocates and often do something useful. Addition without subtraction produces efforts to simplify that also complicate and efforts to decentralize that also centralize.[19]

A third source of incoherence in the response to reform has been the reform ideas themselves. While reformers agree that more demanding standards are desirable, they hold different views about what such standards are, how they might be developed and used, and how they might affect education. For instance, ideas about the way to realize new standards of performance vary wildly. Many reformers argue for the "alignment" of assessment, curriculum, and instruction, but some believe that alignment should be defined and enacted one school at a time, while others contend that it should be accomplished for all schools together statewide or district-wide, by integrating the content and methodology of tests, curriculum frameworks, and teacher education and texts and requiring professional compliance.[20] Still others try to blend the two visions. Such disagreement extends to nearly all elements of the reform agenda.

That sort of disagreement arises both from the different conceptions of educational change that are embraced by various advocates of reform and from the weakly specified reform agenda. Even in mathematics, where the National Council of Teachers of Mathematics (NCTM) standards are commonly believed to mark unprecedented agreement about the purposes and methods of better education, practitioners and policymakers hold many different ideas about what the standards mean and what they suggest for practice. One reason for such different ideas is that the NCTM standards are phrased in general terms. That is no oversight, for the ambitious and complex instruction that NCTM wants to encourage could not be closely specified without being transformed into something much less am-

18. O'Day and Smith (1993).

19. One can find parallel instances in almost all state reform efforts. Late in 1993 the Michigan legislature passed a large package of reform legislation. In certain respects it expanded state influence in curriculum and sought to clarify lines of responsibility over matters of curriculum and instruction. But Public Acts 335 and 339 also reflected a deep tension between efforts to simplify instructional governance by establishing stronger state-level leadership over curriculum and instructional matters and efforts to preserve local control on these matters. See Thompson, Spillane, and Cohen (1994).

20. The differences are quite sharp. Clune (1993) and Darling-Hammond (1996) both favor some sort of decentralized reform process. But O'Day and Smith (1993) advocate a much more structured and "systemic" process of change that would have significant uniformities, at least within states.

bitious and complex.[21] But general guidance necessarily encourages ambiguity and disagreement about what it entails for state and local implementation and classroom instruction.[22]

Systemic reform thus has begun to change guidance for instruction in American education, nudging it in the direction of more ambitious goals, higher standards, new assessments, and more substantial curriculums. But American education has also begun to change systemic reform, turning proposals for leaner, more focused, and more coherent guidance for instruction into a gathering babel of reform ideas and practices. That should be no surprise, for American government was designed to frustrate exactly the sort of coordinated action within and among governments that systemic reformers seek. But the consequences are troubling. The growth of new public and private organizations in education since the 1950s has been fragmented and diffuse, spawning more agencies and increasing political and administrative traffic without greatly increasing the capacity for instruction.[23]

One irony in this story is that carefully designed barriers within American government have kept public education agencies weak as they have grown in the wake of expanding policy.[24] Another is that while advocates of systemic reform speak of reducing and streamlining government, even the strongest state and local agencies have only modest capacity in such central areas as curriculum, assessment, and teacher development. The recent reforms could not succeed unless state and local governments and pri-

21. There are other consequences of weak specification. For example, the ambitious new NCTM standards assume that adopting teachers and students would need a good deal of room to devise academic tasks, revise lessons, and improvise responses to each others' work; but all that would be attended by much uncertainty. In order to make good use of the standards teachers also would need much deeper knowledge of mathematics, of mathematics teaching, and of students' mathematics learning than most American teachers now have. They would require rather different beliefs and professional values than most American teachers now hold with respect to these matters, and they would need ways to work together on mathematics instruction—that is, social and professional structures that could enable teachers to engage in continuing professional work concerning what the standards might mean and how they might be enacted. Lacking such knowledge, beliefs, and collective work, most teachers would be free to interpret the standards as they liked.

22. There is much more that reformers could do without great additional specification. They could, for example, offer many examples of key reform practices; these would further exemplify the reform in particular domains without offering recipes, rules, or requirements. Such examples could greatly increase the richness of advice about reform without restricting practitioners' work.

23. See Scott and Meyer (1983).

24. That result has been observed in past reforms. See Cohen (1982).

vate-sector agencies became vastly more knowledgeable and effective, which they hardly could do by becoming smaller.[25]

A final irony is that education governance has moved toward systemic reform while also moving away from it. Many observers expected that more pressure for coherence at the state level would diminish local action and bring localities into line with state guidance, for they think of power as a zero-sum game. But that view is more an expression of Americans' abiding skepticism about government than a result of careful observation. In this case, as in others before it, power, organization, and activity expanded at several levels of government at once, frustrating reformers' ambitions in some respects while beginning to realize them in others.

Teaching and Reform

Advocates of systemic reform propose radical change in the nature of instruction, but the agents of change on whom they must rely are the very teachers and administrators whose work reformers find so inadequate. Reformers want students to be active problem solvers rather than passive absorbers. They want teachers to coach and conduct rather than to pour knowledge into passive brains. In these ways and others the reforms envision an instructional revolution. But most classroom work was relatively didactic and routinized on the eve of reform, as it had been for generations before. Teachers are the problem that policy must solve, for their modest knowledge and skills are one important reason why most instruction has been relatively didactic and unambitious. But teachers also are the agents on whom policy must rely to solve that problem.

One plausible criterion for the success of systemic reform in changing practice is teachers' awareness of new policy directions, and by that measure the new state policies are doing well, for many teachers have heard about them. For example, in California in 1994, 44 percent of elementary teachers reported that they "had read much or all of the 1992 mathematics framework," which is remarkable after only two years.[26] Another criterion

---

25. Cohen (1982); Spillane (1996a).

26. These data arise from a survey of California elementary school teachers sponsored by NSF (Grant No. ESI-9153834) and jointly carried out by Joan Talbert at Stanford University, Deborah L. Ball, Penelope Peterson, and Suzanne Wilson at Michigan State University, and myself at the University of Michigan. The data analysis reported here has been done by Heather Hill at the University of Michigan. The percentages are based on an unweighted sample and may change slightly when sampling weights are applied.

for success is practitioners' attitudes toward the reforms, and here again there are strong signs of progress. In the same 1994 survey of California elementary school teachers, 51.6 percent reported that they were "positive" or "strongly positive" about the state's new standards and assessments for mathematics. Only 4 percent report a negative view of the state's new standards and assessments, and the remainder are neutral or have no opinion.

Still another criterion for success is practitioners' awareness and conversation, for if the new ideas seep into teachers' and administrators' knowledge and discussions, there may be some basis for understanding and thus further change. By that criterion as well, the reforms have made significant progress. Many teachers report that they have learned to think and talk about reading and mathematics differently as the reformers' vision has gained currency within education. For instance, 54 percent of California elementary school teachers were able to distinguish quite accurately between leading reform ideas and other conceptions of mathematics instruction.[27] Most of the teachers studied in Michigan also reported that they now use the new reading ideas and view reading in more complex terms. They also seem to have a better sense of how deeply children can think about what they read than teachers did fifteen years ago, and they seem to appreciate how readers' knowledge and experience can shape the sense they make of text.[28]

A more stringent criterion of success is incorporation into practice, but even there the reforms have made progress. Many teachers report that they are using the new ideas in instruction. In reading, for example, many no longer use basal reading texts, but instead use what they refer to as "real" books and stories. Some recent reading texts no longer entail ability grouping, and the once ubiquitous reading groups have disappeared from some classrooms. One also finds improved texts and other materials in mathematics. Many teachers report that they expect their students to make sense of their assignments, and many use the language of mathematical understanding to describe their purposes and methods. For example, in the survey of elementary school teachers in California, more than 90 percent report that they use at least one set of the new curriculum materials that are

27. The criterion here was that teachers had to get two or fewer incorrect answers on a thirteen-item list of quite diverse ideas about mathematics teaching.
28. These conclusions are based on studies of more than sixty teachers in a dozen districts in three states. For detailed studies of a few of these teachers, see Jennings (1996); Spillane (1995); Grant (1994).

associated with the reforms. Even when the most popular and easiest to use materials are excluded, 65 percent still used at least one set of reform-oriented materials.[29] These are impressive results when viewed in light of earlier reports on the retention of traditional instruction in U.S. classrooms.[30]

But the results are not uniformly impressive. While many teachers do use a new language to describe what they are doing, they use that language in remarkably different ways. Many report that they have adopted a "whole language" approach to reading instruction, but some take this to mean that reading is best learned by dealing with real literature and entire texts rather than studying component facts and skills in isolation, while to others it means employing bits of literature and allowing children only superficial acquaintance with texts. A broad drift toward more thoughtful instruction and the use of more demanding and interesting materials has been accompanied by considerable variability in teachers' interpretation of the new policies.

Second, there are large differences of opinion about the extent and significance of change in teaching. Teachers often say that their changes are dramatic, reporting great progress in a short time and often describing the journey as a revolution. But when reformers view such changes in light of their new goals for instruction, they report that teaching has changed little or not at all.

Third, observational studies reveal that changes in math instruction are not as extensive as those in reading and language arts. One reason for this difference is that teachers are much more literate than they are numerate and thus are able to use innovative reading materials much more extensively.[31] Another is that schools and school systems have many more resources to use to help teachers improve reading instruction than to help them in math. Although state and national reformers think that the mathematics reforms are far ahead because the national mathematics frameworks are so impressive, the math reforms also are far behind because the

---

29. The full list of curriculum materials was Elementary Mathematician, Family Math, AIMS, Math Their Way, Math in Stride, Logo Geometry, Beyond Activities (such as Polyhedraville), Mathematics Replacement Unit Projects (including Math by All Means, Math Excursions 2, Seeing Fractions, Used Numbers, and My Travels with Gulliver), Arithmetic Teacher, and Mathematics Teacher. In the second case, Math Their Way and AIMS were the excluded items.

30. For example, see Welch (1979).

31. See Price, Ball, and Luks (1995); Ball and Cohen (1996); Spillane (1995).

state and local capacity to improve mathematics instruction is so much thinner than in reading.

There are several explanations for the variability in teachers' response to the reforms. Some echo the issues in state and local guidance for instruction, for teachers work in the same fragmented system of schooling that I described earlier, and their knowledge of reform is partly mediated through those organizations. In the city school system discussed above, for instance, the central office subunits—curriculum staff, reading coordinator, chapter 1 office—issued conflicting messages about state reforms to teachers in the district. Teachers who worked with the reading coordinator got time to hear and read about the new policy, including the state documents that were used to promote it. Chapter 1 teachers got much more extensive professional development as well as reading about the new state policy. But regular teachers in the schools eventually got only brief after-school workshops at their home schools at the year's end, in which only a few of the policy ideas could be summarized. Moreover, regular classroom teachers also heard constantly from the district's carefully coordinated system to promote basic skills instruction in all schools, in which all teachers used the same texts and the same tests, and in which teachers were required to test students, to record scores on monitoring sheets, and to report students' progress regularly to their principal. Principals also were required to discuss these with each teacher and to report on the sheets to central administrators.[32]

Teachers' learning about the new state policy also was influenced by managers in individual schools, whose stance toward reform differs quite dramatically. In the same city school system, for example, one elementary principal shielded teachers from the system's basic skills–oriented instructional guidance system so they could teach in a less rigid fashion. He encouraged teachers to use more literature and in the late 1980s helped one to write a grant proposal to use more literature, which she won and proceeded to implement. (Significantly, the proposal went to the reading coordinator in the central office.) In 1990 the principal successfully lobbied the central office to let the entire school faculty try out a new "literature-based" reading text series, which encouraged many teachers toward the reforms.[33] In sharp contrast, other principals in the same system continued to push basic skills instruction. Similarly, while several elementary school principals in an affluent and progressive suburban district in the same state

32. See Spillane (1993).
33. Grant (1994).

resisted pressures from top district administrators to reform reading instruction, other principals in the same district supported the reforms. Despite powerful leadership for reform in the central office, the resisting principals allowed teachers to continue in the established, basic-skills approach to instruction, or they allowed school reading coordinators to do similar things. In the United States, many teachers can find ways to work their will in classrooms despite formal subordination to higher-level authorities, in part because there is so little local infrastructure to support higher-level guidance.

Teachers' learning about policy is also shaped by the social circumstances in which they work, and those vary amazingly in America. Compared with France, Japan, or most other developed nations, the United States is a remarkably diverse society with extraordinarily unequal schools. Schools that enroll the children of extremely poor immigrants from Latin America or Asia—in which more than two dozen languages are spoken, in which many students speak little or no English, and in which families are desperately poor—often sit near schools that enroll students from well-to-do and educationally advantaged families. Educators in the disadvantaged schools see state systemic reforms as another complicating element in their struggles with the problems of an extraordinarily diverse and needy student body, while educators in more privileged schools see the same state policies as a minor element in their efforts to keep up with parents' elevated expectations.

These circumstances help to explain school-to-school differences in teachers' responses to the reforms. But S. G. Grant has shown that teachers' responses often vary as much within schools as among them. Even teachers who work in the same school and have access to the same view of the policy from local central offices and principals often respond rather differently.[34] For example, a relatively unconventional fifth grade teacher in a city school, who had long used literature in her classes and felt quite comfortable with it, viewed the state's new reading policy as confirmation of what she had done all along and reported little change in her approach to reading instruction. Although she accepted the district's basic skills orientation, she said that it did not get in the way of using literature. But a third grade teacher in the same school, with the same amount of teaching experience as the fifth grade teacher, reported that the district's basic skills orientation kept her from using literature as the new policies proposed.

34. Grant (1994).

Teachers' varying experience, knowledge, and sense of efficacy influence what they notice about policy, how they interpret it, and what they do.[35]

But another explanation for differences within schools in teachers' response to reform is that teachers' opportunities to learn vary. Teachers in one elementary school had the same officially sponsored professional development, but responded entirely differently. One aggressively sought out additional privately sponsored summer and weekend workshops on reading reform, read books and articles about whole language, and used the experiences and materials to turn her reading curriculum into a remarkably lively and challenging experience for students. Another learned to pay more attention to students' understanding of text, but otherwise adopted little of the reading reforms. A third argued that he was already doing everything that the reforms suggested—although observers saw a very traditional approach to reading—and concentrated his search outside the school on ideas about "affective" education. A fourth, who already had been using literature extensively for years, interpreted the reform as an opportunity to learn process writing, found suitable materials, and used them to revamp her writing curriculum; her reading instruction changed little or not at all.[36] These teachers not only brought very different knowledge and professional experience to the reforms, but they also made very different use of official and unofficial opportunities to learn. In the United States, governments have no monopoly on the discourse of reform, and official policy is only one among many sources of new ideas.

Classroom instruction has begun to change as teachers respond to systemic reform, but systemic reform has begun to change as ambitious new guidance for instruction has filtered through teachers' knowledge, beliefs, and practices. American public education contains few social and professional structures that would help teachers to continue to learn about teaching and learning, and most teachers' professional education does not prepare them to deal in a polished way with this kind of intellectually challenging content. Teachers thus approach the reforms with little knowledge of the sorts of instruction that reformers desire, and have few of the personal and professional resources with which to monitor their own activity, to notice inappropriate work, and take corrective action. As a result, initial differences of interpretation tend to float free, and teachers' varied knowledge persists as a relatively unexamined influence on instruction. The combination of weakly specified policies, decentralized decisionmak-

35. Cohen and others (forthcoming, chap. 6).
36. See Grant (1994).

ing, and little systematic and sustained professional work on instruction leaves teachers great latitude to assign different meanings to new policies and to respond idiosyncratically. American teachers have moved toward systemic reform, but in a distinctively disjointed and individualistic fashion.

Politics and Performance

Standards-based reform is notable for the notion that schools should be made responsible for student performance. California officials, like many others around the country, declared that a revised state assessment program would "drive" instruction toward intellectually ambitious work in mathematics by focusing attention on results. Many states set about devising ways to keep track of which schools were boosting achievement, in order to reward those that did well and penalize those that did not.[37]

The idea of accountability for performance has broad appeal, but designing and implementing such schemes turns out to be a rich stew of politics, technical and ethical problems, and ideological conflict. As a result, in practice accountability often turns out to be less clear and more complex than it seems to be in theory. Kentucky is one of the few states in which explicit rewards and punishments for professionals have been attached to students' performance, probably because the reform there was ordered by a court rather than devised through political bargaining in the legislature or executive branch. Such bargaining has been central to reform in Vermont, where complex negotiations among the chief state school officer, teachers, parents, local officials, and legislators have been a continuing element in reform. Early ideas about holding teachers accountable for students' test results were soft-pedaled as teachers and others began to realize how novel and demanding the new assessments would be, how much teachers and others had to learn, and how difficult it could be to make teachers accountable for teaching things they had not had time to learn. In Vermont, as elsewhere, it has not been easy to balance teachers' concerns about stiff accountability requirements against pressures for performance.

37. Rather than substituting markets and consumer choice for state-administered schooling, these schemes would augment the state administration of schooling with scientific assessments of educational effectiveness and schedules of rewards and sanctions. Accountability is seen as an effort to improve the operation of schools within a state-maintained framework, not as a way to change the framework.

The political difficulties of settling on a version of accountability were plainly on view in Michigan. In the late 1980s and early 1990s, state education officials revised their reading and math assessments but initially attached no specific rewards or sanctions to results. They did leave in place an earlier system for publishing test scores for districts and schools, on the apparent assumption that public opinion would be a sufficient agent to correct poor performance. Within a few years, however, the legislature mandated a high school–leaving exam that would preclude graduation if students failed. But that did not command enough political support to last, perhaps because the prospect of high failure rates was unsettling. In its place the state created several different sorts of high school degrees depending on test scores, a more forgiving approach than no degrees for those who failed. But shortly thereafter the legislature and governor adopted new school accreditation procedures, which—after the state education department wrote regulations—threatened local school systems with the loss of 5 percent of their state funds for any school in which fewer than 65 percent of students performed satisfactorily on the state tests. This requirement seemed to catch educators' attention, and many schools and districts scrambled to boost students' scores. But after a few years it seems that this modest performance reward program may be thrown overboard by a more conservative state legislature and state school board in favor of ideas about accountability that focus on local control, charter schools, and parental choice.[38] This sort of signal switching has become common in state education policy.

One reason states change course so often is shifts in fashion and response to changing pressures. But another reason is that it is very difficult to design and enact accountability schemes. It is, for instance, difficult to devise new standards, tests, and information systems that are usable, effective, and professionally defensible. And even if design and implementation problems can be solved, it is not guaranteed that school systems, businesses, and universities will take the new accountability systems seriously.[39] The chapter by Richard Elmore, Susan Fuhrman, and Charles Ablemann in this volume reveals that when analysts in Kentucky and Mississippi sought to create professionally defensible schemes they created such complexity that teachers and parents found the schemes extremely difficult to understand and use. If parents and teachers cannot make sense

38. Cohen and others (forthcoming, chap. 7).
39. See Cohen and Spillane (1992).

of the evidence about accountability, it is difficult to see how the schemes could have the desired effects.[40]

But even if defensible and usable state accountability schemes were created tomorrow, the critical question would be how local schools, teachers, and students would respond. Local response to the accountability requirements associated with California's new tests has so far been modest, and many teachers are not well informed about them. In the 1994 survey that I discussed earlier, only 37 percent of elementary teachers reported that they "have had adequate opportunities to learn about the mathematics" test. Only 24 percent reported that they knew enough about the new assessment to explain it to another teacher or parent. One reason may be that the state tests are administered in only three of twelve grades. Although students' performance in any grade is influenced by their work in the preceding grades, the state's scheme contains no incentives for teachers in those preceding or following grades to pay specific attention to the new tests. The incentives to improve performance based on such scores seem likely to remain diffuse and relatively weak unless all teachers in a school are somehow made to feel responsible for what students do on the tests.[41]

That would entail quite an unusual degree of professional interdependence in American public schools. One elementary principal in a southern California district tried. She used test scores to call her teachers' attention to weaknesses in students' performance in a school whose enrollment is about 40 percent eligible for title 1. She collected the faculty in small groups to discuss the scores and formulate strategies for improving them. She then organized faculty members to look for helpful materials and instructional strategies and followed up with meetings to check on implementation. Similarly, one principal of an elementary school in a middle-class section of a Rust Belt city organized his faculty to move its reading program in the direction of the reforms when parents began to complain because test

40. For a fuller discussion of this point, see Cohen (1996).

41. Evidence on the effects of new accountability measures on learning is thin and inconclusive. Reading scores went down in Michigan when more demanding new assessments were phased in, as did mathematics scores in California. Both results were expected because the new assessments held students to higher standards of performance than had been common in their schoolwork. But when Michigan recently added a new mathematics assessment, scores seemed to improve, though no explanations were forthcoming. Kentucky presents a mixed picture: some schools have improved on the new assessments but others have not, and observers reported that the improved schools tend to be in more cosmopolitan and advantaged areas. Without more substantial trend data and evidence on test security and instruction, it would be unwise to interpret these results.

scores on the first new state reading assessment showed that reading comprehension scores had slipped.

But these cases are unusual. Many other principals in these districts and states made no such move. In some cases the lack of action is due to the lack of pressure for action: although most Americans report deep dissatisfaction with public education, most also express deep satisfaction with the public school in their neighborhood. Neighborhoods with worse schools and greater dissatisfaction tend to have parents who are less able to organize to seek school improvement. Finally, schools that are in trouble often lack the leadership that would enable them to respond constructively to accountability requirements.

The most critical problems in the local response to new accountability requirements go far beyond the creation of usable and professionally defensible state systems. Adequate local response to such systems is likely to include helping principals to learn how to understand and attend to both assessment results and parent concerns, improving teachers' and principals' capacity to respond to more demanding assessments, removing those who cannot improve, and mobilizing parents to help students. Solving such problems would bring reformers to the very core of public schools—personnel policy, the management of instruction, and the enhancement of professional capacity. Few accountability schemes make provision for such things.

Incentives are not automatic; they can only work if they work through professionals and schools. All of the relevant evidence suggests that American schools' educational capabilities to respond constructively are seriously limited and would have to be greatly enhanced if professionals in failing schools were to acquire the wherewithal for a constructive response to performance rewards. Of course, some state accountability schemes may never reach the point at which local response would become an issue, because they will explode or peter out before then. American schools already are quite accountable, for local officials in the United States are elected to preside over schools and can be turned out of office if they fail to satisfy voters, something that is quite unusual elsewhere in the world. Systemic reform would graft technical designs intended to hold school professionals accountable for student performance onto existing democratic political designs for holding citizen-legislators more broadly accountable, but many policymakers and politicians prefer political to performance accountability. Members of the new Republican majority in Congress and many statehouses seem much less interested in versions of accountability that are related to academic performance and much more interested in versions that are related to local control, choice, and charter schools.

A version of that problem recently erupted over California's accountability scheme, where a radical revision of the California assessment program (CAP) provoked a political firestorm. State officials had been trying to revise the state assessment since the late 1980s, and had an unusually capable state agency staff to help, but the assessment budget was limited and officials had committed themselves to very ambitious revisions and a tight schedule. As a result, when the state went ahead with a dramatic new math assessment program in the early 1990s, officials lacked many elements of a sensible plan. They were not able to familiarize most local practitioners with the revised assessment; they were not able to help many teachers learn more about the material assessed; nor were they able to inform many parents and other concerned citizens about the assessment. Indeed, the state was not able to score more than a sample of student responses or analyze and report on more than a fraction of students' performances, let alone work with local practitioners to improve their understanding of the results and what they might entail for instruction.

These constraints might not have been so troublesome if Americans were not deeply divided about instruction and poorly informed about mathematics, if schools were not locally controlled, if teachers were not poorly educated, and if most students had done better on the new math assessment. But given those conditions, the new test only inflamed a difficult situation and gave conservative political organizers a made-to-order issue. After heated political debate, Governor Pete Wilson canceled the state testing program. Rather than "driving" the process of reform ahead as reformers had confidently predicted, the new assessment drove it backward, or into the ground.

Systemic reform has given new prominence to the idea that schools should be responsible for students' performance, and many states have adopted some sort of accountability scheme. But only a few states have mobilized penalties and rewards for school professionals that are more potent than the publication of test scores.[42] And no state so far seems to have devised a scheme that meets modest standards—intelligibility, technical feasibility, and professional defensibility—and that has boosted performance.

---

42. No other school system in the world holds professionals responsible; students are instead held accountable for their performance. See Noah (1994).

States have only recently begun this complex undertaking, and more encouraging results may be forthcoming. However, such results would be possible only if states stayed the course, and that will be difficult. Efforts to hold professionals accountable for students' performance will work only if they can be grafted onto an older and more deeply rooted form of accountability in which voters hold elected officials accountable for schools' performance. Such a graft could only work if the elected politicians who govern public education were able to give money, attention, and other resources to a complex professional and technical development process over a long time, to abstain from their long-established habits of frequent legislative and executive action, and to resist responding to many constituency pressures in the meantime. It will be no less difficult for policymakers to mobilize the resources than to adopt political abstinence.

The Goals of School Reform

My report thus far covers the period that ended on November 7, 1994, the date on which Republicans took control of the U.S. Congress, as well as many governorships and state legislatures. These electoral victories capped several years of conservative political organizing—including organizing against systemic reform. Congressional Republicans decided to do away with the National Education Standards and Improvement Council (title 2 of Goals 2000), and the relevant House appropriations subcommittee then proposed to eliminate entirely funding for all of Goals 2000 and to slash spending for title 1. More than a dozen Republican governors and state legislatures have begun major deregulation efforts—including efforts to repeal or cut back dramatically state education codes and to disestablish state education departments—that would partly or entirely dismantle the systemic reforms that states had been constructing.

It is much too soon to know how much success these efforts will have, but it would be surprising if the wars about instruction did not continue. Americans have thrown themselves into pitched battles over their schools' purposes since at least the 1830s; in fact, American education can be read as an intermittent argument between progressive and conservative views of knowledge, teaching, and authority. In one tradition schools have been portrayed as agencies that could sustain democracy and eliminate poverty by cultivating critical thinking, intellectual independence, mutual understanding, and respect among students. In the other, schools have been portrayed as agencies that should preserve political order by cultivating obedience and respect for authority in a curriculum that centered on accepting academic and divine authority and memorizing facts and skills. These two traditions took shape at the very beginning of public education and they differ on virtually every point, from the nature of democracy to the character of cognition. Progress toward one vision of instruction has tended to incite reactions from the other.

Systemic reformers have acted as though government could create new standards and pedagogy oriented to critical thinking and intellectual independence without making allowances either for the historic divisions in American opinion or for Americans' appetite for mortal combat about these issues. Like the curriculum reforms of the late 1950s and early 1960s, systemic reform was advocated mostly by education professionals and members of political elites. As many observers noted, it had no "popular roots." Systemic reformers did not seriously try either to mobilize broad popular support or to frame their program in ways that might avoid the most crippling attacks. Inattention to such matters might be less troublesome in nations with centralized systems that are dominated by education ministries and professionals, but it was a critical weakness in a nation with decentralized government, traditions of local control of schools, weak professionalism, and persistent, popular ideological polarization around education. Reformers are learning once again that schools are political theaters for playing out contrary visions of childhood, culture, history, and identity, as well as places for studying subjects and learning lessons.

Conclusion

Standards-based reform has nudged educators toward more ambitious goals, higher standards, new assessments, and more substantial curriculum. Many states have begun to develop new accountability arrangements. But American education also has begun to change standards-based reforms. This country's unusually fragmented organization of schooling has helped to turn proposals to make education more lean, focused, coherent, and demanding into an astonishing profusion of ideas and practices. Moreover, efforts to devise new systems of professional accountability have run into serious technical problems and hostile political reactions from the inherited system of electoral accountability.

Readers may wish for a report on whether systemic reform is a success, but the jury is still out. This effort at root-and-branch change is less than a decade old—just a beginning for such an ambitious endeavor. Much more experience would be required before any fair judgment could be made about the implementation and effects of standards-based reform, and it remains to be seen if systemic reform will endure.

My account does suggest two central problems that would face continued enactment of systemic reform and widespread adoption of schemes that reward performance, should they endure. One is an appreciable lack of professional capacity to respond constructively to serious efforts of any sort to improve instruction. That is broadly true in public education, and it is especially true for the schools in which improvement is most needed—many of which chiefly enroll disadvantaged students.[43] Standards-based reform is unlikely to succeed unless reformers are able to augment or supplant a standards-and-accountability approach with one that offers educators and others concerned with schooling many more incentives and opportunities to learn. It would take much sustained and sophisticated work to devise and enact the arrangements required to accomplish this goal.

Roughly the same thing could be said of performance rewards. The success of such schemes depends heavily on whether state or local school systems could enhance the capacity of the worst schools to respond constructively to more powerful incentives, for those would be the schools least likely to be able to respond well on their own. But precisely because of the educational weaknesses that reformers wish to correct, state and local systems have at best only modest professional capacity to solve this problem.[44]

Politics is a second problem that faces these reforms. Standards-based reform has been promoted as though it was chiefly a matter of policy, but policy cannot work unless it is situated in an enabling politics. That is especially true in the United States, where fragmented government and contentious politics create many opportunities to oppose policies, and where cultural and political divisions create fertile ground for oppositional movements. Such opportunities and divisions are much less common in more centralized political systems with more deferential political cultures. As a

43. For instance, though most teachers appear to believe that their students can learn, those who teach students from disadvantaged circumstances tend to believe that their charges are less able to learn than other students. See U.S. Department of Education (1993, pp. 235–40).
44. See Cohen (1996) for the development of this point.

result, America displays few signs of the political patience, trust of professionals, and willingness to learn that standards based reform would require from politics, politicians, and the public. The picture for reform is not entirely bleak: some states have retained much of the structure of standards-based reform even as others have begun to retreat, and some business groups have begun to rally to support standards-based reform.[45]But sustained conflict impedes development of the patience, improved professionalism, and capacity to learn that reform would require.

Political turbulence has been an intermittent hallmark of American education. If a movement to promote performance rewards somehow gathered the momentum that systemic reform did in the decade just past, it probably would provoke much the same sorts of passionate political controversy and opposition that has marked standards-based reform, though for somewhat different reasons. There is no way to know how things would turn out for such a movement, but it seems likely that no movement for fundamental change can make dramatic progress unless reformers find ways to depoliticize education while building a broader constituency for their ideas. That would take sustained and sophisticated work, which is unfortunately rare in public education.

45. "Business Backs School Standards," *Ann Arbor News,* September 6, 1995, p. 1.

References

Ball, Deborah, and David K. Cohen. 1995. "What Does the Educational System Bring to Learning: A New Pedagogy of Reading or Mathematics?" Working Paper. Michigan State University.

Clune, William H. 1993. "The Best Path to Systemic Educational Policy: Standard/Centralized or Differentiated/Decentralized." *Education Evaluation and Policy Analysis* 15 (Fall): 233–54.

Cohen, David K. 1982. "Policy and Organization: The Impact of State and Federal Educational Policy on School Governance." *Harvard Educational Review* 52 (November): 474–99.

———. 1996. "Rewarding Teachers for Students' Performance." In *Incentives and Systemic Reform,* edited by Susan Fuhrman and Jennifer O'Day. San Francisco: Jossey-Bass.

Cohen, David K., and James P. Spillane. 1992. "Policy and Practice: The Relations between Governance and Instruction." *Review of Research in Education* 18: 3–49.

Cohen, David K., and others. Forthcoming. "Reading Policy: Reading Reform in Michigan."

Darling-Hammond, Linda. 1996. "Beyond Bureaucracy: Restructuring Schools for High Performance." In *Incentives and Systemic Reform,* edited by Susan Fuhrman and Jennifer O'Day. San Francisco: Jossey-Bass.

Education Funding Research Council. 1995. *Title I Update* 26 (August): B-319–20.

Fuhrman, Susan, William H. Clune, and Richard F. Elmore. 1988. "Research on Education Reform: Lessons on the Implementation of Policy." *Teachers College Record* 90 (Winter): 237–57.

Fuhrman, Susan H., and Richard F. Elmore. 1990. "Understanding Local Control in the Wake of State Educational Reform." *Educational Evaluation and Policy Analysis* 12 (Spring): 82–96.

Grant, Scott Geoffrey. 1994. "The Variation in Teachers' Responses to Reading, Writing, and Mathematics Reforms." Ph.D. dissertation, Michigan State University.

Jennings, Nancy. 1996. *Interpreting Policy in Real Classrooms.* New York: Teachers College Press.

Jennings, Nancy, and James P. Spillane. 1995. "State Reform and Local Capacity: Encouraging Ambitious Instruction for All through Local Decision-Making." Paper prepared for annual meeting of American Educational Research Association.

Jennings, Nancy, James P. Spillane, and Jennifer Borman. 1995. "Basic Skills to Ambitious Teaching: One District's Efforts at Structural and Instructional Reform." Paper prepared for annual meeting of American Educational Research Association.

Noah, Harold. 1994. "Setting Standards in Other Countries." Washington: National Education Goals Panel.

O'Day, Jennifer A., and Marshall S. Smith. 1993. "Systemic Reform and Educational Opportunity." In *Designing Coherent Education Policy: Improving the System,* edited by Susan Fuhrman, 250–312. San Francisco: Jossey-Bass.

Price, Jeremy, Deborah L. Ball, and Susan Luks. 1995. "Marshaling Resources for Reform: District Administrators and the Case of Mathematics." Research Report 95-2. Michigan State University, National Center for Research on Teacher Learning.

Schwille, John, and others. 1983. "Teachers as Policybrokers in the Content of Elementary School Mathematics." In *Handbook of Teaching and Policy,* edited by Lee S. Shulman and Gary Sykes, 370–91. New York: Longmans.

Scott, W. Richard, and John W. Meyer. 1983. "The Organization of Societal Sectors." In *Organizational Environments: Ritual and Rationality,* edited by John W. Meyer and W. Richard Scott, 129–53. Beverly Hills, Calif.: Sage.

Spillane, James P. 1993. "Interactive Policy-Making: State Instructional Policy and the Role of the School District." Ph.D. dissertation, Michigan State University.

_____. 1995. "Constructing an Ambitious Pedagogy in Fifth Grade: The Mathematics and Literacy Divide." Paper prepared for the annual meeting of the American Educational Research Association.

_____. 1996a. "Districts Matter: Local Educational Authorities and State Instructional Policy." *Educational Policy* 10 (1).

_____. 1996b. "School Reform: Implementing Standards-Based Reform and the Non-Monolithic Character of the Local School District." Michigan State University, College of Education.

Thompson, Charles, James P. Spillane, and David K. Cohen. 1994. "The State Policy System Affecting Science and Mathematics Education in Michigan." Michigan State University, College of Education.

U.S. Department of Education. 1993. *Prospects: The Congressionally Mandated Study of Educational Growth and Opportunity, The Interim Report.*

Welch, Wayne W. 1979. "Twenty Years of Science Curriculum Development: A Look Back." *Review of Research in Education* 7: 282–306.

Comments on Chapters Two, Three, and Four

Eric A. Hanushek

THE CHAPTERS in this volume mark a new phase in educational reform. For some time, one significant thrust of the discussion of improving education has centered on developing stronger incentives based on student performance.[1] At the same time, simply saying "use incentives" is not very useful or satisfying. Incentives come in many forms, and as the papers in this volume richly illustrate, there is mounting evidence that the details matter a lot. The question is not whether to have incentives or not. Everyone is always faced with a variety of incentives—whether we make them explicit, whether we attempt to design them consciously, or whether we just let those in existence continue. Thus the real question is whether the incentive structure points us toward the outcomes we desire.

The chapters in this volume consider what can be learned from some initial efforts to design explicit performance incentives for schools. Only by extracting some general lessons will we be able to move forward. School personnel, legislators, and state education administrators are not, as pointed out by the chapters, generally prepared to think about incentives, and they must rely on others to provide guidance in developing sound structures. What they do not realize is that the academic community, which might be thought of as the logical source of information for such design work, also is pretty much in the dark about the precise ways to proceed. My comments begin with some observations about the difficulties in learning about incentives and drawing conclusions about how to move forward. Then I move to the contributions of the specific papers.

At least forty-three states are in the throes of developing and revising their policies to increase the emphasis on performance and accountability,

1. See, for example, Hanushek with Benson and others (1994).

as Elmore, Abelmann, and Fuhrman note. The common pattern is to develop new structures that spring from the earth fully formed. They are not based on accumulated experience, because we do not have much of that. Instead, they take a conceptual model of how to introduce performance incentives and simply legislate it.

The problems with this approach from a policy view are obvious: We do not have sufficient information to have much faith in the incentives that emerge from this process. The problems from the viewpoint of policy development and learning have, however, received less attention. Programs put into existence by states are more like demonstration programs than like experiments. Everybody in the state receives the same "treatment," making it exceedingly difficult or impossible to understand the effects of the treatment. One cannot readily observe how individuals faced with the program differ from those not faced with the program. One can observe that some districts, for example, are slow in reacting to any state program and then compare slow- and fast-reacting districts, but such analysis is really getting at a different question from one of how the incentive structure changes performance.

With the emphasis on demonstration programs that are instituted as operational activities, little attention is given to evaluation efforts. This missing element is especially harmful in the case of demonstration programs, because the clearest hope for evaluating the effectiveness of such a new scheme comes from comparing preadoption to postadoption outcomes, so that district operations before any new program would serve as the control for what happens after adoption. This kind of evaluation requires systematic activities early in the policy cycle. The chapter by Clotfelter and Ladd demonstrates that although it is possible to make inferences about programs by ex post analysis, such evaluation is difficult and prone to considerable uncertainty, because it relies on being able to reconstruct relevant information. Part of the reason for difficulties is a general lack of concern about evaluation and knowledge development throughout the education system. Moreover, when large-scale incentive structures are put into place, it is often done in an atmosphere of knowing what will work—thus obviating the need for analysis and evaluation. The alternative approach is beginning with the view that the best way to proceed is not known and that a combination of experimentation and evaluation is needed. From this approach, it would be natural to think of introducing variation in incentive structures so that evaluation would be possible.

It has been long recognized that education is driven by fads. "The" way to improve things becomes commonly accepted, and schools rush to introduce today's new idea. Are performance incentives just another fad, soon to be replaced by a different model of how to proceed? Those of us who believe in the necessity of better incentives hope that this interest is not just the latest fad, but the development of incentives against a backdrop of fads seriously compromises the ability to learn.

School personnel themselves recognize the existence of short-lived waves of enthusiasm for projects that are soon replaced with others. This recognition must affect their behavior, because whether they take the new program seriously and undertake major changes will be conditioned by their expectations of the program's survivability. How, then, should any data generated by a new program be interpreted? Should any long-run effects be expected? Is the rate of adoption of new programs also affected by different preferences and views of local personnel, thus confusing program effects with other factors? Embedding new incentive structures in a system that has previously not shown any long-run commitment to programs will obviously compromise the ability of the incentives to affect long-run behavior, as well as affecting evaluation possibilities. The importance of commitment is an underlying theme in the chapters by Cohen and by Elmore, Abelmann, and Fuhrman.

There is large uncertainty about what components of programs will be most effective and even larger uncertainty about when one should expect to see any results. Many new programs are introduced with a sense of urgency that derives from a crisis mentality. In such a circumstance, part of the development of the programs is convincing policymakers, parents, taxpayers, and school personnel that "program X" will turn the situation around. Expectations are increased, frequently too much. The magnitude of any expected improvement is generally unstated, but at times just oversold. Moreover, little attention is given to the time path of any increase. A moment's reflection leads to the conclusion that programs—even when fully functioning—will take a number of years before they have large effects on the performance of twelfth graders, whose performance represents the cumulative past history of schools and other inputs. Many incentives require some adjustment time before having their impact. Yet evaluation tends to begin looking for noticeable change almost immediately.

When we begin talking about incentive structures and their potential effects, we frequently do not have very good notions of how incentives will operate or even where to look for their effects. This situation is far different from other areas, such as school finance. In school finance discussions, we would naturally begin to look at how the local "price" of raising funds varies across districts and how districts altered their spending policies as a result. We might also look at how Tiebout selection affects both household location and school finance choices. Moreover, we have characterizations of basic finance plans—for example, foundation, variable matching, flat grant, and categorical—and can fit these into basic demand models. But in discussing incentives, we lack a coherent and widely accepted characterization of different approaches. We even have difficulties with the appropriate language for characterizing differences in approaches.

The preceding discussion describes the difficulties we have in developing new knowledge from existing attempts to use various incentives. These are important issues that must be dealt with if we are to convert performance incentives from just a fad of the 1990s into an operating and ongoing reform principle.

To cement these ideas, let me consider an example that has puzzled me for some time. It is now broadly accepted that merit pay that leads to differential rewards to teachers doing similar tasks in the same school (or system) will not work.[2] The common story is that merit pay has been tried, it does not and cannot work, and that any direct pay incentives for teachers must go to an entire school instead of to individual teachers. These conclusions come largely from reviews of the staying power of merit pay systems that have been introduced into schools and from popular conceptual ideas about the difficulty in measuring individual teacher performance and about potential destructive competition among teachers. But the number of evaluations of specific merit pay schemes is limited. School systems are frequently not committed to maintaining these systems and will jettison them when there is any fiscal pressure. Most people outside schools find ideas of merit pay for teachers appealing, perhaps because the vast majority of other workers in the economy face some sort of merit determination of pay even in situations where measurement of individual performance appears much more difficult than in schools. The reaction of people outside schools is frequently to question what is different about schools and why should we expect less value of performance evaluation there. This incredulity is reinforced by the absolute agreement of teachers that evaluation and differential reward of individual students is essential to the entire educational process.

Part of the difficulty in the consideration of merit pay is that we do not even have a good idea of how to characterize different schemes. Do we

2. This is based on the fundamental work by David Cohen and Richard Murnane (1986). In this volume, Clotfelter and Ladd discuss this point.

look at the absolute size of any bonus payments? Relative to base pay? Relative to outside opportunities? What about the distinction between intrinsic and extrinsic rewards? And, where should we look for results? Merit pay could have two distinct effects. First, it could induce current teachers to work harder (or better). This effect relies on a view that teachers are not conscientious and hard working, which I do not believe. Second, the potential effect could come from changing the pool of teachers by inducing poor teachers to seek more rewarding places to work and by encouraging good teachers to remain in schools for longer careers. This latter source of effects, which I personally believe to be the more significant reasons for considering merit pay schemes, suggests that short-term evaluations that concentrate just on the set of current teachers are unlikely to uncover the true effects of a well-functioning merit pay system. Moreover, there is imperfect understanding of what lessons are to be taken from related situations. For example, many colleges and universities have merit pay determinations within individual departments without creating unproductive competition and lack of cooperation. Many businesses employ combinations of individual and group rewards based upon a wide variety of evaluation systems. Can we apply any lessons from these to our public schools?

This discussion of merit pay is not meant as an appeal for introducing such schemes. Instead it is meant to illustrate some of the shortcomings of existing knowledge, even in areas where we might think that we know the answers.

The seriousness of the existing evaluation issues leads me to think about trying more systematic experimentation with evaluation. Specifically, I believe there is a very strong case for states to develop true experiments complete with careful consideration of varying the incentives across districts in ways that will permit better evaluation of the effects.[3] Natural experiments are frequently difficult to interpret because they tend to confuse incentive effects with a variety of other potential influences on outcomes. Demonstration programs of the type undertaken when a state simply changes the structure for all schools simultaneously likewise poses extremely serious inferential problems.

That all having been said, the chapters in this volume make very useful contributions to our understanding of incentives. The authors, all accomplished observers of schools and their outcomes, have provided us with

3. This idea is central to the policy conclusions of Hanushek with Benson and others (1994).

many insights. They are each faced with the evaluation problems discussed above, and each tends to reinforce parts of the general observations about what it takes to learn from current experience. Each also provides us with knowledge about where things might go in the future. I will attempt to underscore what I think are the key things to take away from the chapters by Clotfelter and Ladd, by Cohen, and by Elmore, Abelmann, and Fuhrman.

The excellent chapter by Clotfelter and Ladd represents one of the first attempt to add empirical content to many assertions about test-based incentive schemes that have actually been applied. The literature is full of assertions and conceptual arguments and short on actual investigations.

The most important part of their chapter is the comparison of alternative approaches for evaluating school performance. The authors tend to emphasize differences among the various approaches to judging school performance, but I have a slightly different reading of this. When I look at the results of different standardizations of test scores, I conclude that all of the approaches that rely on some variant of growth in individual performance yield very similar rankings. Approaches that do not concentrate on individual gains give very different, and inferior, estimates of school performance. This finding has important implications for the design of indicator and incentive systems.

A second important aspect of this chapter is a particularly lucid discussion of some of the key conceptual issues. The discussion of intended and unintended incentive effects is important, but it also illustrates the difficulties of ex post evaluation. Some of these issues could be addressed more directly with a research design instituted before the introduction of the incentive scheme.

That having been said, I have two quibbles with their discussion. First, I am unsure how to think about "comprehensibility" as a criterion. One cannot deny that comprehensibility is better than incomprehensibility, but the real implications in a complicated world are not obvious. Many things in the world are complicated, and many programs are difficult to understand—but few are as concerned about the nitty-gritty of construction as they are about the implications. A part of this issue also seems to relate to how the program is marketed. In any event, at its current level of discussion this consideration largely rests on the general difficulty of communicating regression analysis to people untrained in statistics—which does not have much bite. Second, and more important, is the discussion of fairness. They choose a particular empirical meaning of fairness that strikes me as odd.

They test whether the estimated measure of school performance is correlated with race or poverty. Apparently, if the correlations are zero, the evaluation is fair. But, what if the schools actually differ in quality by race of the student body? In such a case, one would not want to produce a performance measure that was uncorrelated with student body characteristics. For me, fairness can only be discussed in relation to "truth" about relative performances of schools, and truth is unknown for Dallas.

The final section of the chapter considers differences in the performance of the largest city school districts in Texas. This part addresses the fundamental policy question of whether or not the reform program improved the performance of the system. Unfortunately, it is very difficult to sort out the program effects from other factors that influence student performance. This difficulty of interpretation corresponds directly to the interpretative difficulties of "natural experiments."[4] The analytical problems are significant and true uncertainty remains about the effects of the Dallas experiment.

Elmore, Abelmann, and Fuhrman document the rush to implement systems of performance-based accountability. The authors use the examples of Mississippi and Kentucky to make a series of important observations about new systems of accountability.

These perceptive authors range over several very important aspects of new movements toward performance-based reform. Three specifically stand out in my mind as requiring attention. First, they discuss in detail the measurement of performance and its use in accountability. They introduce questions about the ability to design fair, widely accepted tests of desired content. This discussion, highlighting a key element of much of the reform debate, presages the report of the technical review panel commissioned to investigate the Kentucky situation.[5] That group of distinguished test experts concludes that the assessment system is simply not up to the tasks it is given. My interpretation here is that testing faces fads similar to more general reform, so that the combination can have very important implications.

Second, and following the first, Mississippi and Kentucky each go the prevailing route: institute an entirely new system and then fill in the details. By mandating a specific approach for the entire state without having a good idea of the details, they are likely to make mistakes. Moreover, we are likely

---

4. For a discussion of natural experiements with regard to the minimum wage, see Hamermesh (1995).
5. Hambleton and others (1995).

to learn very little, because there is no way of comparing the mandated approach with alternative ones.

Third, these authors underscore the central role of politics in the course of educational reform. Because the entire structure of reform comes as a regulatory system, the arbiters of the regulations have enormous influence. And, because reform changes the rules of operations and the relative advantages of different actors, some group always finds it in their interest to push for different rules. The result is a potential instability of the political environment and a tendency for reform to cycle across different options. The instability of the political environment clearly affects the course of reform, a point made vividly in this chapter.

The chapter by Cohen also highlights the importance of politics and the changing environment for determining the outcomes of reform. But Cohen also goes to another level of consideration of reform. The heterogeneity of schools and even classrooms enters into the determination of how the system reacts to reforms. This heterogeneity is not, however, a central design parameter in much of the discussion of systemic reform. Therefore the movement toward new reform approaches may hit on another stumbling block, one that may quite seriously complicate any efforts at evaluation of reform efforts. Heterogeneity and politics are particularly important at the local level, but reform discussions seldom consider these. The importance of heterogeneity suggests that decentralization of decisions is almost certainly necessary. Nonetheless, decentralization requires faith in the local district, a faith that Cohen suggests may not be uniformly warranted.

This strong set of chapters moves us one step farther in understanding reform. Each is cast in terms of the difficulties facing reform, but each also starts to unravel the next level of concerns that must be addressed.

References

Cohen, David K., and Richard J. Murnane. 1986. "Merit Pay and the Evaluation Problem: Why Most Merit Pay Plans Fail and a Few Survive." *Harvard Educational Review* 56 (February): 1–17.

Hambleton, Ronald K., and others. 1995. "Review of the Measurement Quality of the Kentucky Instructional Results Information System, 1991–1994." Final Report, Technical Review Panel, Office of Educational Accountability, Kentucky Legislature.

Hamermesh, Daniel S. 1995. "What a Wonderful World This Would Be." *Industrial and Labor Relations Review* 48 (July): 835–38.

Hanushek, Eric A., with Charles S. Benson and others. 1994. *Making Schools Work: Improving Performance and Controlling Costs.* Brookings.

Comments on Chapters Two, Three, and Four

Robert H. Meyer

THE CHAPTERS by Clotfelter and Ladd, Cohen, and Elmore, Abelmann, and Fuhrman provide informative and stimulating analyses of a number of innovative state and district educational accountability systems. One of the things that interests me most about the accountability systems studied by the authors is that measurement of school performance is a central feature of all of the systems. It is therefore intriguing that the systems fail to use a common approach for measuring school performance. For example, Dallas and South Carolina measure school performance using a sophisticated value-added system based on traditional multiple-choice tests administered at every grade level. At the other extreme, Kentucky measures school performance in terms of a set of innovative assessments, including performance-based tasks and portfolios, that are administered only in selected grades. To evaluate these (and other) accountability systems, I believe it is important to have some agreed-on criteria that define a fair and valid performance indicator system.

In my previous research, I have proposed three such criteria:[1] Are the outcomes included in the indicator system valid and reliable? Do the indicators accurately measure school performance with respect to the specified student outcomes? Are the indicators resistant to corruption?[2] The first two criteria are particularly relevant for analyzing the indicator and accountability systems discussed by the authors.

First, the set of tests and other outcomes that underlie a performance indicator system should measure the types of skills that are demanded by

1. Meyer (1994, forthcoming).
2. The second criterion is in many respects similar to the fairness criterion discussed by Clotfelter and Ladd. I prefer to anchor the evaluation of alternative indictors in terms of whether the indicators accurately measure school performance. As indicated below, one of the primary benefits of an accurate (valid) school performance indicator is that it is fair.

society. If they fail to do this, a high-stakes accountability system could drive educators to implement a curriculum that emphasizes skills of minimal value to society. As is well known, many educators believe that standardized, multiple choice tests are flawed because they focus almost exclusively on low-level academic content and are deliberately designed to be curriculum-free, that is, not tied to specific curriculum objectives.[3] As a result, many school districts, states, and professional test developers are currently experimenting with new types of tests and assessments—for example, tests with open-ended questions, performance-based assessments, graded portfolios, and curriculum-based multiple choice tests—that offer the promise of being more highly related to educational objectives than prior tests.[4] As indicated by Elmore, Abelmann, and Fuhrman, Kentucky is one of the prime innovators in this area. The other accountability systems, with the exception of California, tend to use more traditional tests.

What is the evidence on the reliability of traditional standardized tests and performance-based assessments? In general, standardized tests have tended to be very reliable. In contrast, performance-based tests, like the ones developed in Kentucky and Vermont, have tended not to be very reliable.[5] This suggests that in order to develop assessments that are both valid and reliable, test developers may want to focus on developing new "hybrid" assessments that combine the best features of both standardized and performance-based assessments.

Second, a performance indicator must measure school performance accurately and reliably, where school performance with respect to a particular test or other student outcome is defined as the contribution of the school to that outcome. Many district and state indicator systems fail to satisfy this criterion.

The question of how to measure school performance is, fundamentally, a technical, statistical problem. Fortunately, this task is essentially identical to the task of measuring the efficacy of school policies and inputs, a research problem that has been addressed in the evaluation literature for well over three decades and continues to be an active area of research.[6] The

3. See, for example, Smith and O'Day (1991) and Clune (1994).

4. See, for example, Wiggins (1989), Darling-Hammond (1991), Shepard (1991), and Koretz and others (1994).

5. See, for example, Koretz and others (1994).

6. See, for example, Coleman (1966); Hanushek (1972); Murnane (1975); Boardman and Murnane (1979); Raudenbush and Bryk (1986); and Meyer (1992). For studies explicitly focused on school performance indicators, see Dyer, Linn, and Patton (1969); Willms and Raudenbush (1989); Hanushek and Taylor (1990); Meyer (1994); and Meyer (forthcoming).

common characteristic of the models used in this literature—referred to as value-added models—is that they measure school performance or the effect of school policies and inputs using a statistical regression model that includes, to the extent possible, all of the factors that contribute to growth in student achievement, in particular, prior achievement and student, family, and neighborhood characteristics. The key idea, as discussed by Clotfelter and Ladd, is to isolate statistically the contribution of schools to student achievement. This is particularly important because differences in prior achievement and student and family characteristics account for far more of the variation in student achievement than school-related factors. Failure to account for differences across schools in these characteristics could result in highly biased indicators of school performance.

In fact, Clotfelter and Ladd present evidence based on South Carolina data that non-value-added indicators (particularly the average test score and the North Carolina "par" indicator) are very poorly correlated with value-added indicators of the type used in Dallas or South Carolina. I have obtained very similar results in my own research.[7]

Given the fact that average test scores and other traditional educational indicators tend to differ substantially from value-added indicators, what are the possible consequences of failing to use value-added indicators? In other words, why does it matter whether a school performance indicator accurately measures school performance?

Making policy on the basis of non-value-added indicators could lead to the expansion of programs that do not work and to the cancellation of programs that are truly effective. Similarly, non-value-added indicators are likely to give students the wrong signals. In practice, this means that prospective students, both academically advantaged and disadvantaged, could be fooled into abandoning an excellent neighborhood school simply because the school served students that were disproportionately academically disadvantaged. At the other extreme, these indicators could contribute to complacency on the part of families whose children attend schools that disproportionately serve academically advantaged students. In fact, these schools could be adding relatively little to the achievement growth of their students. In short, indicators other than the value-added performance indicator convey potentially inaccurate information about school quality and therefore could severely harm the policymaking process and distort the school choices of students and families. As a result, student achievement is apt to be lower than it would otherwise be.

7. Meyer (1994).

The consequences of using average test scores or other non-value-added indicators for purposes of public accountability are, if anything, potentially much worse than in the cases discussed above. These indicators could severely distort the behavior of teachers and administrators. Moreover, these indicators are biased against schools that disproportionately serve academically disadvantaged students and communities and thus are undesirable from the standpoint of fairness, a point that is stressed by Clotfelter and Ladd.

The first effect—distorting the behavior of teachers and administrators—is likely to be particularly acute if teachers and administrators are rewarded or penalized on the basis of their performance with respect to a given indicator, as is the case, for example, in Dallas, South Carolina, and Kentucky. In a high-stakes accountability system, teachers and administrators are likely to exploit all avenues to improve measured performance. For example, teachers may "teach narrowly to the test." For tests that are relatively immune to this type of corruption, teaching to the test could induce teachers and administrators to adopt new curriculums and teaching techniques much more rapidly than they otherwise would. On the other hand, if school performance is measured using a non-value-added indicator, teachers and administrators have the incentive to raise measured school performance by "creaming," that is, teaching only those students who rate highly in terms of average student and family characteristics, average prior achievement, and community characteristics.

The potential for creaming is apt to be particularly strong in environments where schools have the authority to admit or reject prospective students and to expel already enrolled students. However, the problem could also exist in more subtle, but no less harmful, forms. For example, schools could create an environment that is relatively inhospitable to academically disadvantaged students, provide course offerings that predominantly address the needs of academically advantaged students, fail to work aggressively to prevent students from dropping out of high school, err on the side of referring "problem" students to alternative schools, err on the side of classifying students as special education students (if these students are exempted from statewide testing, and make it difficult for low-scoring students to participate in statewide examinations. These activities are all designed to improve average test scores in a school, not by improving school quality, but rather by catering to high-scoring students while ignoring or alienating low-scoring students.

Similarly, high-quality teachers and administrators may find that the easiest way to obtain high student test scores is to move to neighborhood schools that predominantly serve high-scoring students. Hence, using the average test score as a high-stakes performance indicator could trigger an exodus of highly skilled educators from schools that disproportionately serve academically disadvantaged students. Clearly, accountability systems that fail to use value-added indicators as the basis for their systems could severely distort the behavior of educators and students.

Any value-added system will have two basic data requirements. First, annual testing at each grade level is highly recommended. It maximizes accountability by localizing school performance to the most natural unit of accountability, the grade level or classroom. It yields up-to-date information on school performance. It limits the amount of data that is lost due to student mobility.

As the time interval between tests increases, these problems become much more acute. In fact, for time intervals of more than two years it could prove difficult, if not impossible, to construct valid and reliable value-added (or gain) indicators for schools with high mobility rates. Mobile students generally must be excluded from the data used to construct value-added and gain indicators, since both indicators require pre- and post-test data. In schools with high student mobility, infrequent testing diminishes the likelihood of ending up with student data that are both representative of the school population as a whole and large enough to yield statistically reliable school performance estimates. Less frequent testing—say at grades kindergarten, 4, 8, and 12—might be acceptable for national purposes, since student mobility is not really an issue at the national level. For purposes of evaluating local school performance, however, the problems created by student mobility argue strongly for frequent testing, at least for schools and school districts where student mobility is high.

Thus it is clear that one of the problems with the Kentucky assessment system is that the assessments are not administered at every grade level. In contrast, Dallas and South Carolina administer tests in most grades. Even if Kentucky decided to adopt a value-added indicator system, it would need to expand its assessment program to additional grades. In fact, it might not be too difficult for Kentucky to do this, because the state already has already developed "practice" examinations for grades that are not covered by the required assessments.

The second requirement for a sound value-added system is that to control for differences across schools in student, family, and community characteristics, it is necessary to collect data on these characteristics for all students. One of the primary obstacles to developing a high-quality indicator system is the difficulty of collecting this type of data.

This issue is potentially quite important because value-added indicators are often implemented—as in South Carolina and Dallas—using the rather limited administrative data that are commonly available in schools: for example, race and ethnicity, gender, special education status, limited English proficiency (LEP) status, eligibility for free or reduced-price lunches, and receipt of welfare benefits. Researchers equipped with more extensive data have demonstrated that parental education and income, family attitudes toward education, and other variables are also powerful determinants of student achievement growth. The consequence of failing to control adequately for these and other student, family, and community characteristics is that feasible real-world value-added indicators are apt to be biased, if only slightly, because they absorb differences across schools in average unmeasured student, family, and community characteristics. The bottom line is that value-added models can control for differences across schools in student, family, and community characteristics only if the models include explicit measures of these characteristics.

It would be useful for school districts and states to experiment with some alternative approaches for collecting the types of data that are frequently missing from administrative data. As one possibility, I am currently experimenting with using census block-group data—for example, average adult educational attainment in the block-group—as a substitute for unobserved student-level data.

Given the above framework, it is apparent that Dallas and South Carolina have indicator systems that should be rated quite highly in terms of the second criterion—that is, accurate measurement of school performance. These systems, however, could conceivably be improved, either by improving the control variables used to adjust for differences across schools in student, family, and community, or by improving the tests so that they are less dependent on traditional multiple choice test items.

I am less enthusiastic about the systems in Kentucky and Mississippi because they are not based on value-added indicators.[8] In addition, the new assessment system developed in Kentucky, although highly ambitious, apparently fails to satisfy minimum requirements for test reliability. As a re-

8. The indicator used in Kentucky is similar, in some respects, to the change in average test scores over time for students in the same grade. (The additional wrinkle is that schools with low average test scores are expected to improve their average test scores at a faster rate than other schools.) As discussed in Meyer (1994), this indicator is likely to be highly contaminated (biased) by student mobility, changes over time in true school performance, and changes over time in student, family, and community characteristics.

sult, it probably should not be too surprising that support for the Kentucky accountability system has been mixed.

Given that there are compelling technical reasons to prefer value-added indicators over non-value-added indicators, it is interesting to consider why many districts and states, including Kentucky and Mississippi, have failed to adopt value-added indicators. One answer is that these systems are relatively new and complicated. Clotfelter and Ladd, for example, note that the Dallas system is very difficult to understand. I do not believe that this is inherent in the approach, though. I have been working with the Minneapolis public schools over the past several years to develop a value-added indicator system that promises to be much easier to understand than previous indicator systems.[9]

Another reason, pointed out by Elmore, Abelmann, and Fuhrman, is that some districts believe that controlling for differences across schools in prior achievement and student, family, and community characteristics "institutionalizes low expectations for poor, minority, low-achieving students," Elmore, Abelmann, and Fuhrman quote a member of the Department of Education in Mississippi: "We pushed very hard to have an SES factor, but the State Board cut it off at the gap . . . as some members said it would present a double standard." This concern is obviously very important. My own belief is that it is quite possible to design a value-added indicator system that provides both accurate measurements of school performance and high performance expectations for all schools and all students.

The key idea is that the process of evaluating school performance and the process of setting student achievement expectations must be viewed as separate activities. There is nothing in the value-added method that prevents a district or state from establishing high performance expectations for all students, particularly disadvantaged students. To avoid creating an incentive for schools to engage in creaming, however, it is essential to translate student performance expectations into the corresponding school performance goals, defined in value-added terms.[10] If this is done, it turns out that, for a given student achievement goal, the corresponding school performance goal will always be higher, not lower, for schools that disproportionately serve disadvantaged students. The reason is straightforward: to achieve a given student achievement goal, it is necessary for schools that disproportionately serve disadvantaged students to outperform other schools. If student achievement expectations are sufficiently high, the

9. The basic elements of this system are described in Meyer (forthcoming).
10. See Meyer (forthcoming).

above procedure will almost certainly produce school performance goals that are extremely ambitious for schools that disproportionately serve disadvantaged students. This is a strength, not a weakness, of the value-added approach. If our society is serious about setting high expectations for all students, it is important to translate these performance expectations into school performance goals. Given concrete school performance goals, we can then act accordingly to do whatever is necessary and appropriate to assist schools in attaining these goals.

In summary, if one is interested in having indicators that are appropriate for accountability purposes, I believe that it is necessary to design an indicator system that satisfies the three criteria listed above. There are reasons to be optimistic that it is possible to do this. A number of states, including Kentucky, have recently set out to develop new tests and assessments that are intended to be aligned with state educational goals and further intended to represent the types of skills that are demanded by society. The value-added indicator systems implemented in South Carolina, Dallas, and, more recently, in Tennessee appear to be particularly promising.

The other option is to give up the idea of using outcome indicators to hold schools accountable for their performance. This option could very well dominate the option of implementing an indicator system that was not appropriately designed to drive a high-stakes accountability system. If policymakers are serious about holding schools and districts accountable for their contribution to growth in student achievement, it is crucial to quantify that contribution in a valid and accurate manner using student outcome measures that accurately reflect educational goals.

References

Boardman, Anthony E., and Richard J. Murnane. 1979. "Using Panel Data to Improve Estimates of the Determinants of Educational Achievement." *Sociology of Education* 52 (April): 113–21.

Coleman, James S., and others. 1966. *Equality of Educational Opportunity.* U.S. Department of Health, Education, and Welfare.

Clune, William H. 1994. "Systemic Educational Policy: A Conceptual Framework." In *Designing Coherent Education Policy,* edited by Susan Furhman, 125–40. San Francisco: Jossey-Bass.

Darling-Hammond, Linda. 1991. "The Implications of Testing Policy for Quality and Equality." *Phi Delta Kappan* 73 (November): 220–25.

Dyer, Henry S., Robert L. Linn, and Michael J. Patton. 1969. "A Comparison of Four Methods of Obtaining Discrepancy Measures Based on Observed and Predicted School System Means on Achievement Tests." *American Educational Research Journal* 6 (November): 591–605.

Hanushek, Eric A. 1972. *Education and Race: An Analysis of the Educational Production Process.* Lexington, Mass.: Lexington Books.

Hanushek, Eric A., and Lori L. Taylor. 1990. "Alternative Assessments of the Performance of Schools: Measurement of State Variations in Achievement." *Journal of Human Resources* 25 (Spring): 179–201.

Koretz, Daniel, and others. 1994. "The Vermont Portfolio Assessment Program: Findings and Implications." *Educational Measurement: Issues and Practice* 13 (Fall): 5–16.

Meyer, Robert H. 1992. "Applied versus Traditional Mathematics: New Econometric Models of the Contribution of High School Courses to Mathematics Proficiency." Discussion Paper 966-92. University of Wisconsin-Madison, Institute for Research on Poverty.

————. 1994. "Educational Performance Indicators: A Critique." Discussion Paper 1052-94. University of Wisconsin-Madison, Institute for Research on Poverty.

————. Forthcoming. "Value-Added Indicators of School Performance." In *Improving America's Schools: The Role of Incentives,* edited by Eric A. Hanushek and Dale Jorgenson. Washington: National Academy Press.

Murnane, Richard J. 1975. *The Impact of School Resources on the Learning of Inner City Children.* Cambridge, Mass.: Ballinger.

Raudenbush, Stephen W., and Anthony S. Bryk. 1986. "A Hierarchical Model for Studying School Effects." *Sociology of Education* 59 (January): 1–17.

Shepard, Lorrie A. 1991. "Will National Tests Improve Student Learning?" *Phi Delta Kappan* 73 (November): 232–38.

Smith, Marshall S., and Jennifer O'Day. 1991. "Systemic School Reform." In *The Politics of Curriculum and Testing: The 1990 Yearbook of the Politics of Education Association,* edited by Susan H. Furhman and Betty Malen, 233–67. New York: Falmer Press.

Wiggins, Grant. 1989. "A True Test: Toward More Authentic and Equitable Assessment." *Phi Delta Kappan* 70 (May): 703–13.

Willms, J. Douglas, and Stephen W. Raudenbush. 1989. "A Longitudinal Hierarchical Linear Model for Estimating School Effects and Their Stability." *Journal of Educational Measurement* 26 (Fall): 209–32.

PART TWO

Choice and Performance

CHAPTER FIVE

School Choice and Student Performance

John F. Witte

Educational choice has been the lightning rod issue of the 1980s and 1990s, yet it is probably the least understood topic in this book. Educational choice comes in many categories and subdivisions, each of which defines different research and policy issues. The purpose of this chapter is to assess how efforts to extend choice in American education may affect educational performance—as measured by achievement on standardized test scores and years of education completed.

Of course, the arguments for and against educational choice involve more than test scores and educational attainment. Major arguments *favoring* choice include the inequity of choices under the current system, in which economically advantaged families have greater choices within both the public and private sectors; taxpayer equity, in that private school users must pay taxes for schools to which they choose not to send their children; and facilitation of diversity in education (including religious instruction). Arguments *against* choice that are not based on achievement include the inequity that could result from a voucher system that may primarily benefit existing private school users (who are considerably better off than the average public school user); first amendment concerns involving the separation of church and state; and the sacrifice of a common school tradition to serve diversity in education. These issues are of obvious importance, but because this essay is confined to trying to assess the effects of choice on educational performance, other factors affecting the choice debate will be discussed only in passing.

The study of educational choice and student performance includes a wide range of research. Studies by economists tend to emphasize the market model or metaphor as the appropriate theoretical and empirical tool for understanding education. Work carried out by sociologists and education specialists often focuses less on competition, and more on the innovative differences that emerge in schooling based on parental choices. While those focusing on competition usually assume schools are black boxes, researchers in the second tradition concentrate on what it is in the box that seems to produce higher levels of student performance. This chapter includes both of these traditions.

Theories of Educational Choice and Educational Performance

The idea that education would be more efficient if it operated through a market system in which parents had broad discretion to select schools was introduced in modern form in a 1955 article by Milton Friedman.[1] The inclusion of that article in his 1962 book, *Capitalism and Freedom*, brought wider attention to the prospect of creating a market system for education.[2] Friedman argued that the public provision of education failed on both the consumer and producer side. Consumer choices were distorted because the difference in marginal costs between public and private schools was extreme (with the marginal cost of public schools at zero). Producers were inefficient because the quasi-monopoly of public schools led to internal surpluses (monies not directly expended on student achievement or quality of education) and excessive bureaucracy.

Although Friedman did not specify the underlying assumptions and the details of the voucher system, the root idea has magnetic appeal, and in recent years it has generated considerable support. The model assumes that parents will seek to maximize the educational achievement of their child, given their resource limitations. In so doing, parents will have accurate knowledge of prices and the expected educational achievement that a school will produce for their child. If anticipated outcomes in any given time period are not satisfactory, parents and students will simply move to another school until they find one that fits their demands. Schools will compete on the quantity of educational performance supplied for a given price. Schools that succeed in attracting and holding students will profit and continue to exist; those that do not will go out of business. Such a system has obvious appeal.

However, educational outcomes are affected by a range of factors apart from the structure of markets and individual choice, as even the most diehard economic theorist will admit. Many of these factors also interact with school choice. Thus, an empirical explanation of how educational choice

1. Friedman (1955).
2. Friedman (1962, chap. 6).

Figure 5-1. *Modeling Achievement Gains with School Choice*

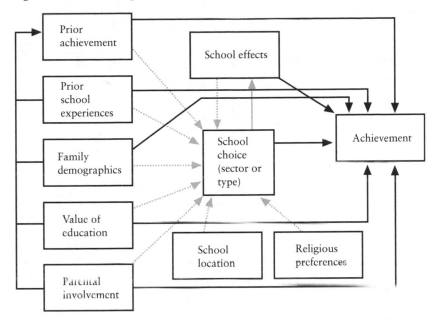

affects performance must take these factors into account. A general version of such a model is presented in figure 5-1. This considers educational choice and achievement as a two-stage process, in which the choice of school is endogenous in the system. I assume that choice is first between a sector or type of school (public or private, magnet or traditional) and second between specific schools within the sector or type. School effects indicate variations by individual school, including such factors as course offerings, pedagogy, and academic orientation. The sector choice is hypothesized as having an independent effect on achievement, apart from the specific school effects. The arrow from "school choice" to "school effects" indicates a dynamic component for the effects of choice as schools respond to choices by families and competition from other schools. Background factors (such as prior achievement or prior school experience) have both an indirect and direct effect on achievement. Religion and school location are assumed to affect school selection but are not related to achievement.[3] The model serves as a guide for describing both studies that attempt

3. Distance has been suggested in a number of studies as a suitable instrumental variable that might be relevant both for public and private school choice. Religion could be an excellent instrument in predicting private school attendance in today's environment in which almost 90 percent of those attending private schools attend religious schools. The

to estimate school choices and those that attempt to understand the effects of choice on student performance.

Empirical Studies of the Market Competition Model of Education

The research analyzed here considers what is known about: why people choose which types of schools; what difference choices seem to make in terms of student performance under existing conditions; and what the effects of educational choice are under dynamic scenarios. Empirical research based on national studies of high schools, evaluations of choice experiments, and various forms of simulations have considerably advanced understanding of these issues over the last decade.[4]

Knowledge about School Selection

If the relationship between student achievement and choice is a two-stage process, as proposed in figure 5-1, the exploration of school choice should begin with what is known about school selection—and that is considerable. Research over the last fifteen years has included analysis of public versus private school enrollment, enrollment in various types of private schools, and enrollment in comprehensive public schools versus public magnet or other choice schools. Some of the research is aggregate in nature, using census tracts or school district data. Data on individual enrollment use either national studies of high schools, such as High School and Beyond (HSB) or the National Education Longitudinal Study (NELS), or general surveys of youths, such as the National Longitudinal Survey of Youth (NLSY). Finally, there are surveys of parents concerning decisions on school choices.

However, much of the research has been restricted to demographic and educational differences between students enrolled in different types of

---

question is whether religion is sufficiently independent of achievement. In chapter 6, Caroline Hoxby finds a correlation between religion and achievement. However, in a major study reviewed below, Catholicism seems to be an effective instrument.

4. There has also been considerable theoretical debate over the applicability of the market model or "market metaphor" since Friedman's article; Henig (1994) offers one of several extended discussions of this topic published in recent years. However, I believe that the theoretical debates quickly reach a standoff (Witte, 1992a), and so I make no attempt to survey this literature here.

schools. Only recently have researchers attempted to model the importance of performance expectations as a factor in school choice, which matters because the assumption that parents will select schools based on
achievement potential is critical to the competitive model of educational
choice. I will first describe the common findings on the differences between
populations in various choice schools. I will then review limited parent
survey data on the rationale given for school selection. Finally, I will discuss the linkages between choice and the achievement prospects for students as developed in several very recent studies.

FAMILY CHARACTERISTICS IN CHOICE AND NONCHOICE SCHOOLS. Several recent studies have shown that enrollment in magnet schools differs
from enrollment in assigned public high schools and private schools. Based
on analyses of NELS, magnet school students are more likely than students
attending assigned schools to be African American or Hispanic and come
from families with lower incomes, and less likely to have parents who attended college.[5] One reason for this pattern is that public magnet schools
increased considerably in large cities in the 1980s, often as one of several
voluntary measures to desegregate school systems. However, magnet
schools have now grown beyond that original purpose.[6]

Private school students, be they in Catholic or nonreligious private
schools, differ considerably from those in traditional public or magnet
schools. Consistently, students attending private schools are more likely
to be white, come from higher-income homes, and have parents with
higher levels of education. Those attending parochial schools (the vast majority of private school students) tend to belong to churches with denominations matching the schools and to report higher levels of religious practice. This has been confirmed across a wide range of studies dating back
to the original work of James Coleman, Thomas Hoffer, and Sally Kilgore,
up through the most recent papers based on NELS data.[7]

5. Plank and others (1993); Gamoran (forthcoming, table 2).
6. Blank (1990).
7. This is reported in numerous HSB studies beginning with Coleman, Hoffer, and
Kilgore (1982, chap. 3). It is also reported in papers based on NELS data, including Plank
and others (1993, pp. 116–17, table 1); Gamoran (forthcoming, table 2); Goldhaber (forthcoming). (Using a structural choice model described below, Goldhaber finds blacks have
a higher probability of attending a private school once estimates of achievement are included
in the choice decision.) Finally, Lankford and Wyckoff find similar results for both elementary and high school students using the 1980 census micro sample. See Lankford and
Wyckoff (1992, especially table 5).

FAMILY CHARACTERISTICS IN VOUCHER PROGRAMS. There have also been several studies of private school voucher programs, which included comparison control groups in the public schools.[8] These have been funded either by the government (the Milwaukee Parental Choice Program, MPCP) or by private sources (the San Antonio Children's Educational Opportunity Program, CEO). Both of the programs have income limitations to qualify: the MPCP is limited to families whose income is 175 percent of the poverty line or less, while the CEO program is similarly limited to families qualifying for free lunch assistance (185 percent of the poverty line).

In one respect, parents in both programs were similar to private school families in general: despite the income limitations, parents in both programs were more educated than their public school counterparts. Parents in the CEO program were also similar to general private school families in having higher levels of employment and two-parent families (61 percent) and smaller numbers receiving public assistance (15 percent) than their public school counterparts. However, MPCP parents were very different on these dimensions. They were much more likely to be single-parent families (75 percent), to be on public assistance (56 percent), and not to have a parent employed full time. The differences between the programs undoubtedly have to do with structure of the programs. The MPCP is limited to prior public school users, the schools must be nonsectarian, and they must select students randomly if they do not have enough slots for applying students. In the CEO program, 50 percent of the slots are set aside for students switching from the public schools, almost all the schools are parochial schools (with Catholic schools enrolling 60 percent of the participating students), and CEO schools did not have to select students at random.

In both programs, parents entering their children in the private schools had less satisfaction with and considerably higher involvement in their prior public schools than the average public school parent. Involvement was measured by contacts with schools, participation in school organizations, and helping students at home. Parents in both programs had higher educational expectations (in terms of years of education) for their children. Finally, despite socioeconomic differences between families in the respective programs, both sets of families had fewer children than public school nonchoosers.

FACTORS PARENTS SAY AFFECT SCHOOL CHOICE. Some parental responses to questions about why they chose their child's current school are

8. The information contained in this section is taken from Witte and others (1994, p. 5 and table 4); Witte and Thorn (1995); Martinez and others (1995, especially tables 2, 3).

Table 5-1. *Factors Influencing Parents' Choice of Child's Current School*
Percent

Item given as "very important"	National private school sample (1983)	Milwaukee private choice (1990–93)	San Antonio private choice (1993)
Staff/teachers	88	. . .	. . .
Discipline	87	76	81
"Academic standards"/ educational quality	84	89	90
General atmosphere	. . .	76	79
"Courses"/special programs	62	68	52
Finances	17	61	73
Location/convenience	25	61	50
Frustration with public schools	. . .	60	63
"Mixes of student backgrounds"/other students in the school	22	30	39
Religion	62	. . .	81
N	(?)	(615)	(956)

Sources: Lankford and Wyckoff (1992, table 1); Witte and Thorn (1995, table 3); Martinez, Godwin, and Kemeyer (forthcoming, table 10).

given in table 5-1. Several patterns are worthy of note. First, staff or teachers and educational quality or academic standards (for the 1983 study) are always important in parents' calculations. School discipline is also important, especially for private school parents. This was consistent for the national sample, the samples in nonsectarian Milwaukee private schools, and the CEO program in San Antonio. Special programs or courses were also high on most people's lists, although there was more variance across samples on that issue. The only other clear pattern is that religion is very important for the private school samples for which the question was asked.[9]

ANTICIPATED ACHIEVEMENT EFFECTS. It is clear that educational quality and academic standards are important aspects of school choice for all parents. But when parents refer to quality and standards, it does not necessarily mean that they are seeking the highest possible achievement for their

9. Lankford and Wyckoff include a table similar to column 2 of table 5-1. However, they also report on public school parents who considered private schools. Religion was "very important" for only 29.5 percent of that sample. In addition, when they indicate the "most important" factor indicated by parents, religion and values are the most important for 29.9 percent of Catholic parents and 42.9 percent of other denominational parents, but most important for only 2 percent of public school parents. See Lankford and Wyckoff (1992, table 2, p. 320).

children. Instead, they may be trying to match their child's achievement to that of students of similar motivation and ability; or they may be searching for an appropriate environmental match in terms of factors such as pedagogy or curriculum. These issues strike at the core of the motivations and expectations of parents who exercise educational choice, and thus at the incentives that choice provides. Two important studies model choice behavior, including anticipated achievement or school quality effects, for public and private schools.

The first study, by Hamilton Lankford and James Wyckoff, employs individual data from the 1980 public use micro sample of the census for New York, combined with New York state public and private school data on schools and school districts. The data allowed them to estimate school choices between public and private schools at both the elementary and high school level and to simulate the effects of tuition vouchers on the proportion of students who would switch to private school if a voucher were available. The inclusion of elementary students is important because national databases have focused on high schools alone, even though more students attend private schools at the elementary than at the high school level.

Their study provides some evidence that parents choose schools based on educational quality, although the findings vary by level of school and whether families are selecting public or private schools. For example, student-teacher ratios (a proxy for quality) have the expected effect for Catholic high schools—smaller classes lead to a higher probability of selecting the school—but the result for public schools is not significant. Similarly, the proportion of students in the area graduating from high school and attending four-year colleges is in the correct direction and close to significant for Catholic high schools, but not for public ones. Their strongest finding of an anticipated achievement effect on school selection is for test scores at the elementary level. The proportion of students in the local area achieving standardized sixth grade test scores at or above the fiftieth percentile is highly significant for both public and Catholic school selection.[10]

Although the Lankford-Wyckoff study provides some assessment of market effects, in one sense the measures remain quite crude. Since precise measures of the variables for each school were not available, "local area"

---

10. Lankford and Wyckoff (1992, tables 5, 6 and pp. 325–30). Interestingly, per pupil operating expenditures have no effect on choices at the elementary level and an inverse effect for high schools; that is, lower operating costs are associated with a positive likelihood of selection. This may make sense for private schools after controlling for other quality variables (because tuition may be lower), but it is counterintuitive for public school choices.

averages for variables were substituted. However, area variables may be more realistic measures for families moving to a school district or region who do not have the time to acquire precise information on particular schools. In any event, their findings provide some rationale for a model that parents do seek out schools of higher quality.

A second study, by Daniel Goldhaber, includes as a major component the estimation of expected achievement differences between public and private sectors as a factor in school selection. One of the ingenious aspects of the study is that he uses individual achievement models recomputed for alternative sectors as a factor in the school selection equation. That provides a direct test of the assumption that families use expected achievement in their selection of schools for their children. The results of the study are complex and will be described in more detail below. In general, it confirms the patterns of private school choice reviewed above. Private school enrollment is related to higher family socioeconomic status, being Catholic or Jewish, higher levels of income set aside for education, and greater educational resources in the home. In addition, private school parents tend to prefer schools with a high proportion of white students. However, when all controls are included, there is also a propensity for blacks and Hispanics to choose a private school. Finally, greater estimated achievement differentials between public and private sectors are related to greater private school choice.[11]

The evidence is far from conclusive, but there are indications that families search for schools based on better anticipated achievement for their children. Private school users seem to select schools with achievement in mind more often than public school families. However, they also place greater value on religious education and the teaching of values. As I will discuss below, several recent studies argue that these two goals are complementary, at least in Catholic high schools.

11. More specifically, the signs are correct for both estimated reading and math, but significant only for math (Goldhaber, forthcoming, table 4). There are several possible problems with this study. The most serious is the estimation of alternative school choices in the absence of any direct data on such choices. If I understand the procedure correctly, a simulated alternative (my term) for each individual is constructed based on estimating the achievement model for the sector not chosen, using an individual model computed with achievement coefficients from the generalized sector model. This may be better than ignoring the alternatives altogether (as in most choice studies), but it remains a far cry from having precise data on the alternatives actually facing each family. The estimation that, with other controls in place, blacks are more likely to attend private schools is in direct contradiction to Gamoran's results, which also use NELS data. See Gamoran (forthcoming, table 2). The difference might be attributable to the fact that Gamoran studied only city high schools, but that seems doubtful.

PRIOR ACHIEVEMENT AND SCHOOL SELECTION. A student's prior achievement can affect both school selection of students and family selection of schools. The policy issue is whether choice schools can "cream off" the best students for their schools and what effect that has on educational outcomes for all students. Relatively few studies allow an assessment of the achievements of students before their enrollment in choice schools. The most important national database in this regard is NELS, although several choice programs in Milwaukee also have data on prior achievement. "Prior" tests in HSB data are actually tenth grade tests taken after students have decided on their respective schools. One can draw only limited inferences from those data, and I will not review them in detail. There is no question in HSB, however, that private school students do considerably better than public school students on all the tenth grade tests in the HSB battery. Several recent studies suggest that different program structures and conditions defining choices have a major effect on the prior achievement characteristics of choice students, but the results are not conclusive.

Analysis of the NELS data indicate that public choice schools, be they stand-alone magnet schools or magnet schools within schools, enroll students who are generally not achieving as well in the eighth grade as students in comprehensive public schools.[12] On the other hand, private school students do much better on their eighth grade test than their public school counterparts.[13]

Stephen Plank and his coauthors report the same findings for private schools, but more complex results for public choice schools. Analyzing NELS data, they categorize public schools as "assigned," "magnet," "choice" (schools allowing student selection or schools with admissions tests), and "vocational-technical" specialty schools. They report:

> Students who had the highest grades and test scores in eighth grade tend to be overrepresented in private schools. Among public schools, students with the lowest grades are overrepresented in assigned schools followed by vocational-technical schools and schools of choice. Magnets appear to have a slight overrepresentation of students who had higher grades in eighth grade. The pattern for test scores among public schools is slightly different than the pattern for grades. Students in the lowest test quartile are the most overrepresented in vocational-technical schools and magnet schools, followed by schools of choice. It is interesting that magnet schools appear to attract stu-

12. Driscoll (1993, pp. 155–56); Plank and others (1993, table 4, p. 122); Gamoran (forthcoming).
13. Evans and Schwab (1993a, table 1).

dents with relatively high grades but low test scores. It may be that students attending magnet high schools tend to be the brightest students in eighth grade schools characterized by low median test scores.[14]

An important book on Catholic schools by Anthony Bryk, Valerie Lee, and Peter Holland has the most detailed study of public and private transition from middle to high schools. They evaluate public school students who remain in public schools and the relatively small number (15 percent) who switch from public to Catholic high school. More important, they evaluate both Catholic school eighth graders who remain in Catholic high schools and the 42 percent who switch to public high schools. Their study is based on HSB data, and the results are quite striking. The authors conclude:

> In general, students who transfer from public into Catholic high schools are more affluent, less religious, better prepared academically, and have higher educational aspirations than students in the other three groups. . . . We know that [Catholic to public] students are moving into less academically competitive environments. They are much less likely to have college plans at the point of high school entry than their Catholic elementary school counterparts . . . remaining in the Catholic sector. . . . In general, the academic profile of the [Catholic to public] transfers is fairly similar to that of the students they are joining in the public sector.[15]

One concrete indicator of selection out of Catholic schools is that 12 percent of those who switched to public schools had repeated an elementary grade, compared with 6.4 percent of those who continued in Catholic school. Of continuing public school students, 12.6 percent had repeated a grade. The net result is:

> Thus, we see a reshaping of the Catholic student population at high school entry into a smaller and more selective group—more academically oriented and somewhat more advantaged—than is characteristic of Catholic elementary school students. This process of transition also involves a recognition of the different academic demands of various schools. Even so, . . . the entry process into Catholic high schools is not especially selective. In most instances, the major element of selectivity consists of self-selection—parents and students choosing to apply first to the sector and then to a particular school.[16]

Finally, studies of choice programs in Milwaukee provide additional evidence on selection effects of choice options. The publicly funded vouch-

14. Plank and others (1993, p. 121).
15. Bryk, Lee, and Holland (1993, pp. 174, 178).
16. Bryk, Lee, and Holland (1993, table 7.4, p. 176, and pp. 179–80).

ers from the Milwaukee Parental Choice Program have consistently attracted families of students not doing well in the public school system. Over four years of data on different cohorts indicate that prior test scores were either at or slightly below the low-income students in the public system and significantly below the average Milwaukee student, even after controlling for a wide range of variables.[17]

A much larger Milwaukee program, known by its statutory number as the Chapter 220 program, allows racial minority students to attend suburban public schools. The program had few constraints on the ability of suburban school districts to select the students they wanted. A 1991 study of this program found that suburban schools had considerable latitude in selecting students from the applicant pool and had full academic and behavioral information on the students. This contrasted sharply with the income limits and random selection requirements of the MPCP. Students enrolled in Chapter 220 were very different from MPCP or other Milwaukee public school students. Students selected into the Chapter 220 program were considerably higher on a number of family socioeconomic indicators (income, two-parent families, employment) than the MPCP students or the average Milwaukee public school student. They also did better on prior achievement tests.[18]

In summary, with the exception of the targeted MPCP, private schools clearly enroll students who are academically more prepared than the average public school student. This is true across a range of national and state data sets. However, the way programs are structured, the population to which they apply, and the latitude of schools make considerable differences. And the implications of these differences go beyond simply better academic preparation. As Bryk and colleagues noted, higher-achieving students may also be better prepared for more challenging academic environments, and more willing to accept higher expectations, a focused academic environment and greater discipline. The issue now is what effect these differences have on achievement gains in choice schools.

Effects of Educational Choice on Student Performance under Existing Conditions

Several previous reviews of the literature have compared the effects of private school choice on achievement.[19] Those studies generally concluded

17. Witte and Thorn (1995, tables 10, 11).
18. Witte and Thorn (1995, tables 5, 6, 8, 12, 13).
19. Jencks (1985); Witte (1992b); Cookson (1994, pp. 80–87). My review of that literature questioned most studies because of measurement errors in achievement tests and

that private schools had a marginally significant effect on achievement, but that the effects were small enough that they may be irrelevant for public policy purposes. Because broad-based voucher programs would undoubtedly create a dynamic process that would alter the current educational environment, comparisons of achievement effects under existing conditions will obviously not answer all questions. However, there is little else to go on, and in any event, incremental change may be the way choice is expanded.[20] I will now update those previous appraisals by discussing new value-added studies that control for prior achievement.

PUBLIC SCHOOL CHOICE AND EDUCATIONAL PERFORMANCE. Public school choice exploded in the 1980s and 1990s. It began with the expansion of magnet schools and programs, followed by interdistrict choice programs and open enrollment. The most recent innovations are quasi-public charter schools. However, almost no reliable studies exist on how public school choice has affected educational performance.

Early studies of magnet schools focused almost exclusively on their initial purpose, voluntary integration and equity, not on outcomes.[21] More recently, Rolf Blank has written an excellent study of the expansion, location, and types of magnet schools in the 1980s, based on detailed data collected in twelve school districts. Although an effort was made to compare outcome measures, only three districts had measures over time and any controls on student characteristics, and only one district had a control group. Blank concluded that "no statistical comparisons of outcomes across the studies, or comparisons with a national standard, would be possible."[22] Other evidence on choice and performance comes from anecdotes, such as the "miracle in East Harlem," or the magnet program in Montclair,

---

inadequate controls for selection effects.

20. Recent legislative initiatives in several states point in the incremental direction. In Wisconsin, the MPCP will be expanded to include religious schools and considerably increase the number of students in the program. Other current restrictions on the program will remain. Ohio has enacted a targeted program for Cleveland, including religious schools. It will be very similar to the Milwaukee program and is slated to begin in 1996. Illinois is considering a small voucher program (2,000 students) for Chicago, but it will also include parochial schools. Statewide vouchers are pending in Pennsylvania, but the amount of money initially caps the program at a relatively modest level.

21. Rossell (1990).

22. Blank (1990, p. 93). In Montgomery County, Maryland, the single district with adequate data and controls, the study of elementary school magnets found positive increases in reading and math achievement for those students who had been in the program the longest. A more extended discussion and analysis of the Montgomery County program is in Henig (1994, pp. 157–59).

New Jersey. However, these successes were almost never carefully analyzed. In the East Harlem case, for example, the schools were changed to
attract students, the student population changed considerably, and thus
the cohort achievement gains claimed by proponents were highly suspect.[23]
In another example, a study of public school choice programs in Minnesota (where many choice programs first appeared), commissioned by the
U.S. Department of Education, studied the size, expansion, participants,
and the reasons given for participating in choice—but made only a bela-
bored and unsuccessful effort to assess minimal outcome effects.[24]

However, several recent studies based on NELS data do provide some
information on achievement gains in public choice schools. A study by
Plank and colleagues includes an analysis of NELS tenth grade test scores
controlling for eighth grade scores, race, family background characteristics, student educational aspirations, and school location.[25] The type of
choice school is then included as a series of dummy variables to distinguish
assigned schools from magnet, choice (schools allowing student selection
or schools with admissions tests), and vocational-technical specialty
schools. With regard to public school choice, in some cases the results are
not significant; in others, the authors fail to discuss significance levels of
coefficients or include the standard deviations of the dependent variables in
the article. Thus the assessment of the size of these variables is not possible.
There are no controls for within-school clustering of similar students nor
for selectivity bias.

Adam Gamoran has completed the most sophisticated study using
NELS data, the only national database that really allows assessment of
magnet and specialty schools, as well as incorporating both public and private school choice. His analysis is limited to urban schools. He estimates
three types of models and incorporates a wide range of variables defining
student background characteristics and school effects. The mean effects
of being in either Catholic, nonreligious private, or magnet schools were
estimated using ordinary least squares regressions, hierarchical linear
models to correct for within-school groupings, and a two-stage instrumental variables model to correct for potential selectivity bias. The results for
magnet schools are striking and very positive for public school choice.

In terms of raw change scores, tenth grade magnet school students, despite having greater economic disadvantages, scored the same as compre-

23. For a critical analysis of these types of programs, see Henig (1994, chap. 6).
24. Funkhouser and Colopy (1994).
25. Plank and others (1993).

hensive high school students in math and science and significantly higher in reading and social studies. When these scores are adjusted for prior achievement on eighth grade tests and student characteristics (sex, race, family composition), the magnet school effects are significant on all tests. Further, the size of the coefficients is only slightly affected by including additional context variables like racial composition, free-lunch percentage, and percentage from single-parent families in the school.

Gamoran makes a very interesting "baseline" estimate in which he estimates test scores for tenth grade dropouts as a basic measure of being in school at all. He calculates that for most tests, the differences between dropping out and being in school are about the same as the additional positive effects of being in a magnet school rather than a comprehensive school.[26]

These results hold up fairly well under alternative modeling strategies. Hierarchial linear modeling estimates allows for more accurate estimates of school-level effects, which may be affected by the clustering of students in schools.[27] Using hierarchical linear modeling reduces the effects for math and science to the point that they are not significant, but the positive effects of being in a magnet school remain for reading and social studies.[28] When Gamoran corrects for selection bias using a set of instrumental variables— Catholic parent, geographic region, and student enrollment in preschool— both the math and social studies coefficients are *higher* than the comparably modeled single-equation regression results. Thus the selectivity effects are actually negative, which is a function of adverse selection into magnet schools, described above.[29]

There are no systematic studies of the effects of magnet schools on the remaining district schools. Do the magnets drain the best students? Do the remaining schools improve as a reaction to the competition? What the expansion of magnet schools and programs suggests is that initial nonmagnet schools lobby for some sort of magnet status. For example, more than half the elementary schools in Milwaukee now have some form of magnet program or school status.[30]

---

26. Gamoran (forthcoming, table 4).
27. This problem was originally described for HSB data in Goldberger and Cain (1982).
28. Gamoran (forthcoming, table 5).
29. Gamoran (forthcoming, table 6).
30. Milwaukee Public Schools (1995). "Magnet schools" are actually broken down into districtwide magnet schools, magnet schools, and magnet school programs. When the program was first created in the late 1970s and 1980s, only districtwide magnet schools existed.

PRIVATE SCHOOL CHOICE AND EDUCATIONAL PERFORMANCE. No one questions that in terms of raw scores, private schools have better test results. This is true of HSB, NELS, and NLSY and tests administered by the National Assessment of Educational Progress (NAEP).[31] The issue has long been whether these higher scores can be explained by controlling for prior achievement, student and family characteristics, school contexts, and any selection effects. Some recent research has illuminated this area. The best summary probably remains the same: if private school users have any significant advantages in achievement gains, the gains are small enough to have little policy importance.

The one exception to this finding might be the study by Plank and colleagues. Their simple regression model, controlling for the variables described above and including dummies for public schools of choice and attendance in a private school (Catholic, religious, non-Catholic, non-religious), produced positive coefficients for both the sophomore composite test score and the math test.[32] But as discussed earlier, their method of analysis has some difficulties.

Goldhaber's research, discussed above, produced very different results from the same NELS data set used by Plank and his colleagues, and Goldhaber's models are more persuasive. He estimated sophomore NELS test scores on math and reading with separate regression models for public, private (non-Catholic), and Catholic school students. His model includes a set of student variables, including religion, a dummy for being learning disabled or being held back a grade, and the number of courses the student had taken in the subject area; the standard family variables; a very complete set of school variables (percentage of students going to college, percentage of teachers with master's degrees, highest teacher salary in the school, average socioeconomic status of students); and a set of classroom-level variables (class size, class track, teacher with master's degree, and teacher certification or degree in the subject matter). The model also controls for unmeasured selection effects (by including an inverse Mill's ratio probit estimate). In short, the model is as complete a set of variables as I have observed in research estimating achievement effects.

Goldhaber's analysis estimates the three sets of achievement equations for public, private, and Catholic students and then computes "what a given student would have achieved in tenth grade had she been attending a school

31. National Center for Education Statistics (1994).

32. Plank and others (1993, app. B, p. 134). For composite test, b = 1.125; standard error = 0.432. For math test, b = 0.668; standard error = 0.217.

Table 5-2. *National Education Longitudinal Study Achievement Test Scores for Tenth Grade Students, by Type of School*[a]

	Math achievement			Reading achievement		
Differential	Full sample	Lowest quartile	Highest quartile	Full sample	Lowest quartile	Highest quartile
Mean differential	7.51	...	...	3.81	...	...
(private versus public)	(0.64)			(0.51)		
Corrected differential	0.60	3.35	−1.16	−0.52	0.49	−1.37
(private versus public)	(0.06)	(0.28)	(−0.10)	(−0.07)	(0.07)	(−0.18)
Mean differential	3.78	...	...	0.88	...	...
(Catholic versus public)	(0.32)			(0.12)		
Corrected differential	−4.88	1.24	8.42	−1.21	2.46	−4.65
(Catholic versus public)	(−0.41)	(0.11)	(0.71)	(−0.16)	(0.32)	(−0.62)

Source: Goldhaber (forthcoming, table 2).
a. Numbers in parentheses are the fraction of public school standard deviations on the respective tests.

in the alternate sector and had she *taken all her schooling characteristics with her.*"[33] The effects of these corrections are extraordinary. Nearly all of the differentials in scores disappear, as shown in table 5-2. The most meaningful statistics are the standard deviations in test score changes, which are given in parentheses in the table. As is apparent in comparing all private school students with public school ones, the difference in math drops from a 0.64 standard deviation advantage for private schools to 0.06. In reading, the differential drops from 0.51 standard deviations to −0.07, making the reading achievement higher for public school students. The results are even more dramatic for Catholic-public comparisons. For math there is a switch of 0.73 standard deviations, from a 0.32 advantage for Catholics before correcting, to a 0.41 disadvantage after the correction. The reading shift is less, from 0.12 to −0.16.

To further illustrate these results, Goldhaber decomposes the raw differentials into school sector effects, student characteristic effects, and selection effects (as measured by the inverse Mill's ratio). The results indicate that the vast majority of the differences are based on student differences; once they are accounted for, there are negative sector effects for private schools. This leads Goldhaber to conclude: "*In no case is there a positive statistically significant sectoral effect favoring private schools.* Hence, the argument that the private sector outperforms the public appears weak."[34]

33. Goldhaber (forthcoming) (emphasis in original).
34. Goldhaber (forthcoming, table 3) (emphasis in original).

One other important result, which adds to the growing evidence on this point, is that results differ considerably for students of different ability levels in the private schools. As shown in table 5-2, private schools apparently do better for students in the lowest achieving quartile and actually disadvantage students at the top.[35]

Gamoran's analysis of NELS data also supports the limited effects of private schools. Controlling for student differences, including prior achievement as measured by eighth grade tests, eliminates almost all raw score differences between public and private schools. Nonreligious private school coefficients drop to close to zero or become negative (for reading and social studies). Catholic schools retain an advantage in math and reading, but the size of the effects are only 0.08 (math) and 0.06 (reading) standard deviations. When school context variables are included, the reading difference disappears and the math difference is only 0.05 standard deviations. When the hierarchical linear model is estimated, all effects between public and private sectors become insignificant. When the instrumental variables model is estimated, the Catholic advantage in math increases slightly (to 0.09 standard deviations).[36] Gamoran summarizes these results:

> If these results stand up to further scrutiny, what implications for policy do they hold? They are not favorable for promoters of private-school choice in cities. The results showed no advantage of secular private schools, and a Catholic-school advantage only in math at best. If public schools could take on a more focused academic climate and promote more coursetaking in math, this difference, too, would disappear.[37]

A different result, however, emerges from a new study of HSB data by William Evans and Robert Schwab. That study focuses not on test scores but on high school completion and subsequent enrollment in college. They first document that students from Catholic schools show considerably higher graduation rates than public school students (97 percent to 79 percent) and higher rates of enrolling in a four-year college (55 percent for

---

35. This general result was also noted in a number of earlier HSB studies and is very striking in a working paper by William Evans and Robert Schwab that is based on both HSB and NELS data. I do not report on that study because it estimates achievement without controls for prior achievement. In essence, their quantile regressions depict the raw score differences between sectors. I disagree with their assessment that that method better captures the long-term effects of schooling in each sector. See Evans and Schwab (1993a).

36. Gamoran (forthcoming, tables 4, 5, 6, and app.).

37. Gamoran (forthcoming).

Catholic students, 32 percent for public).[38] As with all of these studies, the issue is whether these differences remain after controlling for student, family, school characteristics, and unmeasured selectivity effects. In direct contrast to achievement test studies, the answer is yes.

Even after adjusting for gender, race, age, and religious attendance, family income and structure and parents' education, they calculate that a representative student in a Catholic school retains a 0.12 advantage in probabilities of graduating from high school and 0.14 of attending college. These results were impressively robust to the introduction of any or all other variables, including sophomore tests, school peer variables, family education resource variables, and fixed state effects. They used two techniques to check for selection effects. They reestimated their base models for Catholic schools with or without school entrance examinations and waiting lists. These variables had not been studied previously, but they had little effect on the advantage of Catholic schools. They also used several instrumental variables, with the primary instrument being student Catholicism. This slightly diminished the Catholic effect on college entrance, but did not affect the graduation rate difference.[39]

This study is important because it indicates the most significant and robust positive effects to date of Catholic high schools. Other studies have questioned whether Catholic school students do significantly better than public school students on standardized achievement tests.[40] This study, however, indicates a substantial private school advantage in terms of completing high school and enrolling in college, both very important events in predicting future income and well-being. Moroever, as with the Goldhaber results, the effects were most pronounced for students with achievement test scores in the bottom half of the distribution. The Catholic school graduation advantage ranged from 28 percent for the lowest test quartile to just 4 percent for the highest test quartiles.[41]

INSIDE THE BLACK BOX: SCHOOL EFFECTS OF EDUCATIONAL CHOICE. The results on student performance outlined above for public and private schools of choice concentrate on mean effects, with the choice school or sector depicted as dummy, "black box" variables. As intrinsically interest-

---

38. Evans and Schwab (1993b), table 1.
39. Evans and Schwab (1993b, tables 6, 7).
40. Witte (1992b).
41. Evans and Schwab (1993b, tables 2, 3, 4).

ing and important as that may be, it really does little to aid educators who want to know how to improve schools. If schools of choice are doing better than traditional schools, what is it that they are doing to produce those results? If the answer is merely selecting better students, then the question is moot. However, there is evidence that, at least for magnet and Catholic schools, the effects go beyond selection. Fortunately, there is also a growing body of evidence, reinforced across studies, concerning what is happening in that black box.

Over a decade of research indicates that at least two sets of phenomenons may have an impact on educational performance in successful choice schools. The first is establishing a positive and challenging academic climate; the second, creating a set of communal values within a school that reinforce the general climate and provide positive support for students.

The academic climate of schools is measured by a number of factors: the likelihood of students being in academic tracks; the number and scope of academic courses students take; and the aspirations and expectations of students and staff in the schools. Evidence from HSB, from a broad set of studies, clearly indicates that private school students are much more likely to be in an academic track, to take more academically oriented courses, and to have higher educational aspirations that are matched by the expectations of school personnel.[42]

More recent NELS data further confirm the public-private distinction on academic course taking, tracking, and aspirations, although not as much research has as yet been completed as that using HSB data. The results are not as clear-cut for public choice schools. Magnet schools are clearly higher than assignment schools on math course taking, but that does not seem to be the case for other courses (except perhaps science). And there are no differences in aspirations of students.[43]

There is abundant evidence from both HSB data and NELS studies that being in an academic track, taking more academic courses, and having higher educational aspirations predict greater achievement gains after con-

---

42. For a review of these effects through 1991, see Witte (1992b, pp. 376–81). For more recent and more detailed information, see Bryk, Lee, and Holland (1993, especially chap. 4). What is very impressive in their analysis is not only the higher percentage of Catholic students in academic tracks but also the academic course content in general and vocational tracks in Catholic schools. The difference in math and English course taking is considerably higher in comparison with the public schools for general and vocational tracks than for comparable academic tracks.

43. See Gamoran (forthcoming, table 3); Plank and others (1993, tables 5, 6).

trolling for other relevant variables.[44] In one sense this is not surprising: students who are more academically focused and take more courses in the test subject areas do better. However, commonsense results often lead to the best policies, and, given the variation in academic focus across schools, the result is far from trivial.

Perhaps more controversial is the effect of communal values as both a distinguishing mark of private (Catholic) schools and as a factor in improved achievement. Bryk, Lee, and Holland make the idea of school as community the theme of their study of Catholic high schools. They argue that "a constrained academic structure, a communal school organization, and an inspirational ideology are the major forces that shape the operations of individual Catholic schools and contribute to their overall effectiveness."[45] The accumulated evidence on the accuracy of this description is convincing. However, the richness of the communal concept, which was so important in describing the distinctiveness of Catholic schools, has been poorly represented in their models that estimate achievement. Further, it appears to be entangled with measures of academic climate. In addition, the direct paths between student achievement and school characteristics of all kinds are decidedly weak, bordering on nonexistent.[46]

Despite the lack of strong evidence linking school as community with achievement outcomes, I consider the concept important for two reasons. First, it is convincing in arguing that Catholic high schools do differ from most public high schools on this dimension. Second, Catholic schools appear to do better in improving achievement for those students who begin at the lower end of the distribution, they graduate nearly everyone, and they produce many more students who go on to college. These phenomenons could be affected by both academic climate and the ideal of school as community. Students behind in achievement could easily be tracked into

44. See Gamoran (forthcoming, table 4); Plank and others (1993, tables 5, 6, and app. B); Goldhaber (forthcoming, table 1).

45. Bryk, Lee, and Holland (1993, p. 11). This emphasis also appears in Coleman and Hoffer (1987).

46. In an apparent attempt to reach a large audience, they do not clearly describe their path analysis model, and it is unclear what types of variables were finally included in the model. For example, under the heading "school characteristics," they write: "Among the school measures we were able to construct from High School and Beyond, the most important characteristics are the academic and disciplinary climate of the school." This comment, which is not clarified in the sentences that follow it, raises several questions. It is unclear what exactly was included in the analysis: "school characteristics" obviously incorporates and thus entangles the two separate ideas of academic climate and communal values, and "disciplinary climate" is a very poor proxy for the notion of community as they had previously described it. See Bryk, Lee, and Holland (1993, pp. 222–23).

nonacademic tracks or remedial courses. In addition, the community ideal creates empathy for all its members, while a more individualistic and perhaps more competitive organization may have less concern for those likely to do less well.

A remaining issue is whether these practices and characteristics can be realistically transferred to the public sector. Perhaps magnet and Catholic schools simply mold predispositions that arise through the educational aspirations and religious beliefs of students and parents. While the task is difficult, the low level of achievement in some public schools would appear to warrant some experimentation along these lines.

SUMMARY. The most recent and most sophisticated estimates of magnet school effects on achievement, based on national samples, are quite positive, reinforcing earlier but much less systematic studies supporting the positive educational performance of students in magnet schools. Very little is known of the systemwide effects of these programs, especially on students in schools not designated as choice schools. The evidence on private school performance remains uncertain. Raw test scores are higher at nonreligious private and Catholic schools, but this seems to be explained by the charactistics of the students, not the performance of the school. There do appear to be positive effects of attending private schools for students who are not doing as well academically. In addition, Catholic school enrollment appears to have a major effect on the probability a student will graduate from high school and enter college. Finally, choice schools seem to have more academic focus and a stronger academic climate than nonchoice schools, and they are characterized by communal and common values.

Effects of Educational Choice on Student Performance under Dynamic Scenarios

Nearly all quantitative estimates of school selection and the effects of school choice on performance are based on extrapolations from the current system of education. However, a broad-based voucher system such as that proposed by either John Chubb and Terry Moe or by John Coons and Stephen Sugarman might create such a different market for education that estimates based on the current arrangements would be meaningless.[47]

47. Chubb and Moe (1990, chap. 6); Coons and Sugarman (1992).

SWITCHING BETWEEN PUBLIC AND PRIVATE SCHOOLS. Very few studies address this basic question: who might switch to private schools under a voucher program? Many parents are concerned about the educational quality, but given an inevitable confusion over the estimated performance effects of different sectors, it is not clear how they would react.

Fragments of information do exist. Lankford and Wyckoff simulate a voucher program in their study of school choice, and estimate that a voucher covering full costs of private education in New York would cause approximately 15 percent of current public school users to switch to private schools.[48] Goldhaber's models find that changes in quality of schools could cause significant switching to private schools.[49] However, these studies beg the critical question of whether schools—public or private—would improve under extended conditions of choice.

Charles Manski has created an equilibrium model and simulation of educational choice. It includes public and private schools under different assumptions concerning community characteristics, voucher levels, and public school behavior (surplus maximization or competitive).[50] This innovative study is the first attempt to provide a model that attempts to determine if an equilibrium condition could be achieved under varying conditions of educational choice. Interestingly enough, even Manski's fairly simple set of behavioral equations could not be definitively solved and had to be simulated to determine outcomes.

I am not sure how to interpret Manski's results. Certain crucial assumptions that he makes can be questioned. For example, he assumes that parents and students will base assessments of educational quality, and hence choice, on per pupil expenditures, although the empirical findings of Lankford and Wyckoff indicate that per pupil expenditures seem to be irrelevant to school choice. Another assumption is that families will select schools that match the educational motivation of the student, which violates the competitive market assumption that parents and students attempt to maximize expected achievement, rather than seeking a good fit. However, several of Manski's results are quite consistent under varying simulation conditions and parameter values and thus are suggestive for trying to understand the dynamic aspects of choice.[51]

48. Lankford and Wyckoff (1992, p. 333).
49. Goldhaber (forthcoming).
50. Manski (1993).
51. Manski has made available the simulation model for wider experimentation with model assumptions.

One of Manski's most crucial results is that public school behavior has an enormous effect on choice for everyone: the poor, middle class, and wealthy. Every relevant parameter is affected by whether public schools react to vouchers by internalizing surplus value in consuming resources on nonachievement-targeted expenditures or by acting competitively and expending resources on educational quality. In the poor community, given substantial voucher levels, more than twice as many students would enroll in public as in private schools if public schools behave competitively. Among the wealthy, this increase shrinks to about 30 percent, but that number is still substantial. Similarly, per pupil expenditures are estimated to double, and the percentage of highly motivated students in all schools would rise substantially under competitive conditions.[52]

The other set of persistent findings is that improvements in social mobility are doubtful under choice. In Manski's model, per pupil expenditures are always higher in the private sector. In addition, the concentration of highly motivated students is also higher in the private sector and always higher in wealthier communities. These results lead Manski to conclude: "These findings alone suffice for me to conclude that our nation should not rush to implement voucher programs. . . ."[53]

OTHER DYNAMIC EFFECTS. As suggested by Manski's results, changes in the behavior of schools are critical. Choice proponents consistently assume that competition would alter the behavior of public schools, breaking them out of traditional patterns of operation that have been insulated by decades of quasi-monopoly. Would this occur? There is little evidence either way on that hypothesis. Current experiments with vouchers, be they publicly (MPCP) or privately funded (CEO), are simply too small to provide evidence of market reactions by either the public or private sectors. And, unfortunately, even if some state finally passes a voucher initiative, it is unclear if the baseline data will be available to assess anything other than crude changes in enrollment and school numbers.

What of private schools? Private schools currently operate under minimal regulations.[54] If private schools receive public subsidies, will they be

52. Manski (1993, tables 1, 2, 3).
53. Manski (1993, p. 368).
54. For example, Wisconsin statutes governing private schools take up less than ten pages. They require minimum instructional time per year, a sequentially progressive curriculum, health and safety regulations, and provisions preventing abuse of students. Public school statutes are several inches thick. This is common in all states because most private schools are religiously affiliated. The First Amendment to the U.S. Constitution prohibits both the "establishment" of a state religion and the "entanglement" of the state in religious practice. It is the latter clause that prevents states from excessively regulating private schools.

forced to conform moderately to standards of public accountability, or, in the extreme, will they be "swallowed" by the public sector? Again, there is little more than speculation to go on. In this case the speculation involves political reactions: if private schools get the money, will strings follow? But it also involves legal interpretations: if the establishment clause barrier is dropped to allow vouchers, can the entanglement clause, protecting private schools from regulations, remain in place?

Finally, what does choice imply for the cost of the education? In the short term, if widespread voucher programs are enacted without limits, because of the religious factor, it must be assumed that the primary beneficiaries will be current private school users and families who would have sent their children to private schools anyway. The longer-term prospects are less certain. Private schools currently spend less than their public school counterparts. Would spending eventually equalize between sectors? Public schools might become more efficient because of the increasing competition. Private schools might increase their costs either because their wage rates will have to more closely match public schools', or because they will become the targets of unionization. Very few private schools are now unionized, but that might change with a major infusion of voucher monies.

Conclusion

This chapter has summarized the considerable progress that has been made during the last decade in understanding the market theory of education and its possible shortcomings and in learning who selects which schools and for what reasons. Clearly, more research is needed on a number of important issues, however.

One area is parent and student motivation about school selection. Families are clearly concerned about educational quality and discipline, but they also seek to fit other needs of their children. Studies of emerging charter schools might be useful in understanding these complex motivations.

A second area is the internal dynamics of both public and private schools. Manski's simulation study produced dramatically diverse results depending on whether public schools behave as surplus-maximizing bureaucracies or competitive market participants. The Bryk, Lee, and Holland study, which lauded Catholic schools, ironically argued that their success was dependent on them acting as a caring community, in exactly the opposite manner most people associate with competitive, individualistic, market-oriented behavior.

More attention must also be directed at the outcome effects of public school choice, which is probably now accounting for more choice than the private-sector alternative. There is a need for better models of public school selection and much more systematic information on the achievement effects of various choice alternatives.

Finally, little is known about the dynamic aspects of educational choice systems. The crucial evidence here will arrive when a large-scale voucher program is enacted in some state. Without such a study, it is difficult to anticipate market entry of new schools, competitive reactions of existing schools, union bargaining efforts, or the reactions of families to greater opportunities for choice. When that happens, social scientists must hope that adequate lead time and baseline data will be available to study at least some of these dynamic issues.

References

Blank, Rolf K. 1990. "Educational Effects of Magnet High Schools." In *Choice and Control in American Education*, edited by William H. Clune and John F. Witte, vol. 2: *The Practice of Choice, Decentralization and School Restructuring*, 77–123. New York: Falmer Press.

Bryk, Anthony S., Valerie E. Lee, and Peter B. Holland. 1993. *Catholic Schools and the Common Good*. Harvard University Press.

Chubb, John E., and Terry M. Moe. 1990. *Politics, Markets, and America's Schools*. Brookings.

Coleman, James S., Thomas Hoffer, and Sally Kilgore. 1982. *High School Achievement: Public, Catholic, and Private Schools Compared*. Basic Books.

Coleman, James S., and Thomas Hoffer. 1987. *Public and Private High Schools: The Impact of Communities*. Basic Books.

Cookson, Peter W., Jr. 1994. *School Choice: The Struggle for the Soul of American Education*. Yale University Press.

Coons, John E., and Stephen D. Sugarman. 1992. *Scholarships for Children*. University of California, Berkeley: Institute of Governmental Studies Press.

Driscoll, Mary Erina. 1993. "Choice, Achievement and School Community." In *School Choice: Examining the Evidence,* edited by Edith Rasell and Richard Rothstein, 155–56. Washington: Economic Policy Institute.

Evans, William N., and Robert M. Schwab. 1993a. "Who Benefits from Private Education? Evidence from Quantile Regressions." University of Maryland, Department of Economics.

_____. 1993b. "Finishing High School and Starting College: Do Catholic Schools Make a Difference?" University of Maryland, Department of Economics.

Friedman, Milton. 1955. "The Role of Government in Education." In *Economics and the Public Interest,* edited by Robert A. Solo, 123–44. Rutgers University Press.

_____. 1962. *Capitalism and Freedom.* University of Chicago Press.

Funkhouser, Janie E., and Kelly W. Colopy. 1994. "Minnesota's Open Enrollment Option: Impact on School Districts." Washington: Policy Studies Associates.

Gamoran, Adam. Forthcoming. "Student Achievement in Public Magnet, Public Comprehensive, and Private City High Schools." *Educational Evaluation and Policy Analysis.*

Goldberger, Arthur S., and Glen G. Cain. 1982. "The Causal Analysis of Cognitive Outcomes in the Coleman, Hoffer, and Kilgore Report." *Sociology of Education* 55 (April–July): 103–22.

Goldhaber, Daniel. Forthcoming. "Public and Private High Schools: Is School Choice an Answer to the Productivity Problem?" *Economics of Education Review.*

Henig, Jeffrey R. 1994. *Rethinking School Choice: Limits of the Market Metaphor.* Princeton University Press.

Jencks, Christopher. 1985. "How Much Do High School Students Learn?" *Sociology of Education* 58 (April): 128–35.

Lankford, Hamilton, and James Wyckoff. 1992. "Primary and Secondary School Choice among Public and Religious Alternatives." *Economics of Education Review* 11 (December): 317–37.

Manski, Charles F. 1993. "Educational *Choice* (Vouchers) and Social Mobility." *Economics of Education Review* 11 (December): 351–69.

Martinez, Valerie, Kenneth R. Godwin, and Frank R. Kemerer. 1995. "Private School Choice in San Antonio." In *Private Vouchers,* edited by Terry M. Moe. Hoover Institution Press.

Martinez, Valerie, and others. 1995. "The Consequences of School Choice: Who Leaves and Who Stays in the Inner City." *Social Science Quarterly* 76 (September): 485–501.

Milwaukee Public Schools. 1995. *Directions: Three-Choice School Selection Process, 1995–96.*

National Center for Education Statistics. 1994. *NAEP 1992 Trends in Academic Progress.* Government Printing Office.

Plank, Stephen, and others. 1993. "Effects of Choice in Education." In *School Choice: Examining the Evidence,* edited by Edith Rasell and Richard Rothstein, 115–18. Washington: Economic Policy Institute.

Rossell, Christine H. 1990. *The Carrot or the Stick for School Desegregation Policy: Magnet Schools or Forced Busing.* Temple University Press.

Witte, John F. 1992a. "Public Subsidies for Private Schools: What We Know and How to Proceed." *Educational Policy* 6 (June): 206–27.

————. 1992b. "Private School versus Public School Achievement: Are There Findings That Should Affect the Educational Choice Debate?" *Economics of Education Review* 11 (December): 371–94.

Witte, John, and others. 1994. *Fourth Year Report: The Milwaukee Parental Choice Program.* Madison: Report to the Wisconsin State Legislature.

Witte, John, and Chris A. Thorn. 1995. "Who Chooses? Voucher and Interdistrict Choice Programs in Milwaukee." Federal Reserve Bank of Chicago.

CHAPTER SIX

The Effects of Private School Vouchers on Schools and Students

Caroline Minter Hoxby

Vouchers for private schools are a widely debated reform, and much of the contention stems from the fact that mutually consistent theoretical arguments can support either side of the debate, depending on which predicted effects dominate. Thus there is a strong need for empirical evidence on the size of the predicted effects. In this chapter I attempt to predict empirically how vouchers for private schools would affect the number of students who attend private schools, the sorting or self-segregation of students among schools, spending in public schools, and outcomes for both public and private school students.

The ideal experiment for this purpose would be one in which metropolitan areas of the United States were randomly assigned different levels of private school vouchers (including no vouchers) and allowed to reach new long-run equilibria. Of course, such an ideal experiment does not exist. My approach is to analyze tuition subsidies for private schools, which vary across metropolitan areas. The advantage of this experimental strategy is that it handles issues that analyses of short-term experimental voucher programs cannot address.[1] In particular, the strategy allows me to estimate effects predicted to occur in the long term, such as improvements in student performance, as well as effects predicted to occur in the short to medium term, such as changes in public school spending and the distribution of students across public and private schools. The strategy also allows me to measure student performance by educational attainment and wages as well as by test scores.

Most important, the strategy allows for the fact that the regime currently in existence—containing an experimental voucher program or

---

1. See, for example, John Witte's chapter in this volume; Witte and Ridgon (1993); Clune and Witte (1990); Kirkpatrick (1990); Chubb and Moe (1990).

tuition subsidies—is a function of variables that also determine student performance. For instance, the availability of high-quality public schools may reduce the population's willingness to experiment with vouchers for private schools. Thus one could falsely attribute good public school student performance to the absence of vouchers. As another example, suppose that donations are such that per pupil subsidies in private schools are high where a large share of students come from poor families. An abundance of students from poor families is likely to be negatively correlated with average student performance. In this case, one could falsely attribute poor student performance to high per pupil subsidies. This chapter's strategy is to use only variation in tuition subsidies that is not correlated with public school quality or other determinants of student performance.

Since Catholic adherents subsidize Catholic schools and Catholic schools accounted for about 80 percent of private school students in 1980, differences among the historical Catholic population densities in various metropolitan areas can provide the variation in tuition subsidies needed for this approach to be fruitful.[2] In fact, historical Catholic population densities prove to be good instrumental variables for tuition subsidies, both econometrically and also in the sense that a simple model logically explains their relevance.

Finally, it is worth noting that the strategy of this paper uses existing tuition subsidies in existing private schools. This means that the results should be interpreted as the effects of a tuition voucher, assuming that vouchers are distributed as subsidies are distributed (partly means-tested, disproportionately to Catholic students) and that private schools retain their current character. This interpretation is both an advantage and a limitation. It is an advantage because the results are grounded on actual private schools. It is a limitation because vouchers may be distributed more or less evenly across families of different means than subsidies are distributed, and because responses to vouchers possibly include fundamental changes in private schooling, such as the widespread entry of for-profit private schools.

Predicted Effects of Vouchers for Private Schools

The possible effects of vouchers for private schools fall into two categories. Short- to medium-term effects result from students' use of the vouchers,

---

2. I used 1980 as the reference year because the data used in this paper are from 1980. More recent data on subsidies for all U.S. private schools are not available.

which will affect the sorting of students between public and private schools and the effect on public school spending. Long-term effects result when schools adjust their conduct in response to the new environment.

A voucher that lowers the price parents pay for private schools would tend to increase the share of students who attend private schools. The probability that a student switches from public to private school as a result of a given voucher increases with the marginal utility his or her household derives from the switch. Thus vouchers are expected to increase private school enrollment among students from low-income households, from households located near low-quality public schools, and from households with a preference for private schooling.[3] Private school enrollment is also expected to increase among students whose peculiar abilities enable them to benefit disproportionately from private school curriculum or disciplinary atmosphere. Note that the often-foretold "cream-skimming," in which very able or advantaged children enroll disproportionately in private schools in response to vouchers, is simply a particular form of sorting.

Thus vouchers not only have the potential to increase the share of students who attend private school, they also have the potential to change the composition of the student body in private and public schools because they differentially affect students with different characteristics. Increased sorting can affect student outcomes either because the same student will perform differently in private versus public schools or because a student will have different peers in a voucher regime.

In the short to medium term, vouchers are also expected to affect public school spending. Typically, vouchers can be characterized as a dollar amount that accompanies the student. Consequently, each student who attends private school reduces the spending of the public school that that student would otherwise have attended by the amount of the voucher.[4] I will call this the *direct* effect of vouchers on public school spending.

Although the direct effect of vouchers on total public school spending is unambiguously negative, the direct effect on per pupil spending can be set by policymakers to be positive, zero, or negative. The sign of the direct effect depends on what share of a school's potential students are induced

---

3. Given that the empirical strategy requires Catholic school subsidies to be used in place of vouchers, parents with a "preference for private schooling" will be disproportionately Catholic. This is because subsidies are like vouchers that can be used only in Catholic private schools, and Catholics presumably have a greater preference for Catholic schools.

4. Note that public school spending decreases not just for each student whom the voucher induces to attend private school but also for each student who would attend private school regardless of the voucher.

to attend private school by the voucher, the size of the voucher relative to a school's per pupil spending, the share of a school's potential students who attended private school before the voucher, and the degree to which the voucher is means-tested. For instance, suppose one student who would otherwise have attended a public school with per pupil spending of $5,000 is induced to attend private school by a $1,000 voucher. Suppose also that the voucher is means-tested and all students who attended private school before the voucher come from families whose income exceeds the cutoff for receiving the voucher. Then the direct effect of the voucher is to decrease total spending by $1,000 in the public school the student would have attended but to increase per pupil spending by $4,000 divided by the number of students in the school. However, if there were four other students who attended private school before the voucher and come from families with incomes below the cutoff, total spending would decrease by $5,000 and per pupil spending would be unchanged.

Except for the elasticity of private school attendance with respect to the size of the voucher, all of these parameters are known or can be set by law. Thus the direct effect is a matter of *choice* for any given elasticity. I estimate the elasticity of private school attendance with respect to the size of private school subsidies, but I otherwise set aside the direct effect until the end of the chapter, where I simulate the full effects of vouchers.

In the short to medium term, vouchers also have an indirect effect on public school spending that operates through the amount of tax revenue collected for public schools. As more parents in a school district send their children to private schools, property values fall to reflect the fact that a larger proportion of potential home buyers derive no marginal utility from per pupil spending that exceeds the value of the voucher. When parents who send their children to private schools and others who prefer lower public school spending actually form a majority of voters, tax rates are likely to fall.[5] Given that a large share of voters must move their children to private schools before tax rates can adjust through the political process, and given that tax rates are constrained in many states, property values will be the primary means through which vouchers affect tax revenue and thus indirectly affect public school spending. The indirect effect on total public school spending is unambiguously negative, but the indirect effect

5. The median-voter model applies to school districts where the school budget is determined by a majority vote. Many districts determine the budget by a more complex process that may require a supermajority or only a minority of a certain size.

on per pupil spending is again ambiguous. I estimate both effects using private school subsidies.[6]

In the long term, schools would adjust to a voucher regime in which dissatisfied parents are more likely to send their children to private schools and thus affect public school spending. In this regime, school administrators may have stronger incentives to improve school productivity, as measured by student outcomes per unit of school inputs.[7] My goal is to estimate the size of this effect using private school subsidies.

Adjustment to a new equilibrium with vouchers is likely to be slow. In the short term, relatively few parents will switch from public to private schools because the disadvantages of moving an acclimatized child may outweigh advantages of private school attendance. Switchers will be concentrated among those who are moving their residence for other reasons and those for whom a private school is particularly convenient. In the medium term, parents will take the voucher into account when planning their children's schooling, and effects on public school spending will be greater. Any short- to medium-term productivity effects are likely to derive from increased sorting rather than improved incentives. The performance of students who end up with peers who are a better match or of higher quality may improve, while that of students who end up with worse peers may deteriorate. Long-term adjustment to a new general equilibrium will require schools to change employees, wages, work requirements, hiring practices, and ownership of buildings and other capital. Notice that studies of experimental voucher programs must necessarily emphasize short-term effects and exclude long-term effects, especially when the terms of the ex-

---

6. The indirect effects depend on the elasticity of private school attendance with respect to the size of the voucher, the political process, and the distribution of preferences among residents with respect to per pupil spending and private schooling. Of course, estimates based on private school subsidies incorporate all these factors.

7. This statement can be supported by a variety of models. One simple model notes that the elasticity of *total* school spending with respect to school productivity is higher under a voucher regime, so that vouchers automatically generate higher productivity if there is decreasing marginal productivity of inputs. A variation of this model can be constructed for the case in which the elasticity of *per pupil* spending with respect to school productivity is higher under a voucher regime. More complex models postulate objective functions for school administrators. Administrators may dislike cutting total budgets because they require decisions that are unpopular with staff. Administrators may dislike shrinking enrollment simply because they lose prestige. Finally, administrators may not dislike shrinking enrollment per se but may dislike losing the type of student who is most likely to be induced to attend private school in a voucher regime. See Hoxby (1994a) for details.

periment explicitly constrain changes necessary for long-term adjustment, including changes in teacher employment and wages.

Empirical Strategy

With two exceptions, tuition subsidies and vouchers are identical in nature, if not in name. The first exception is that the amount of the voucher is drawn from public school spending, while the amount of the subsidy is drawn from donations or an endowment.[8] The second exception is that tuition subsidies are not uniform across private schools. This second exception requires one to think of subsidies as proxies for vouchers, rather than vouchers by another name, and to consider the appropriate measure of tuition subsidies.

Ideally, data would be organized by local educational market, defined as the set of all localities considered by a household as places of residence and schooling, given its employment situation. Tuition subsidies would vary between local educational markets, but not within them.[9] This would be ideal if the decision model that households follow is, approximately, to accept an employment situation and then choose residence and school based on the full menu of house quality, house prices, commuting distances, school quality, tax rates, local public goods, and private school tuitions, taking account of the locally prevailing tuition subsidy.[10] Then the variation in the subsidy among local educational markets would identify the effects of different-sized vouchers, including vouchers equal to zero. I use metropolitan statistical areas (MSAs) as the best available approximations of local educational markets.[11]

A tuition subsidy is the difference between the cost of educating a student in private school and the tuition paid by the student's household.

8. This difference does not interfere with estimating the direct effect of vouchers on public school spending, since the factors for that calculation are known except for the elasticity of private school attendance with respect to the size of the voucher. This last quantity can be estimated using tuition subsidies.

9. However, tuition subsidies might be means-tested or otherwise vary systemically with family income, number of students in the family, or student disabilities.

10. The definition of a local education market and the choice model can be greatly relaxed, with the exception of one assumption: that households do not choose their employment situations based on the local tuition subsidies.

11. I consistently use the 1980 definitions of MSAs, except in New England where I consistently use the 1980 definitions of county metropolitan areas (NECMAs). Variables that are measured at the metropolitan area level, regardless of the data's original level of aggregation, are always calculated properly for these 1980 definitions.

Most private schools in the United States give tuition subsidies, which is to say that most private schools do not entirely cover their costs with income from tuition and fees. Catholic and other religiously affiliated schools fund tuition subsidies through church offerings and endowment income. Subsidies and fund raising accounted for 56 percent of the income of elementary Catholic schools and 19 percent of the income of Catholic secondary schools in 1980.[12] Church offerings are solicited from all Catholic adherents, and adherents can easily direct their offerings to Catholic schools because the intended use of the funds is typically announced. Except in a small number of Catholic schools, endowments are a minor source of subsidy funds relative to current offerings. Offerings for Catholic schools are redistributed among richer and poorer parishes within a diocese, but virtually all of this redistribution takes place within MSAs. Thus the funds available for tuition subsidies in an MSA are largely determined by church offerings in that MSA. I can measure the locally prevailing subsidy as the average subsidy offered by MSA private schools, weighted by the enrollment in each school. This is the average subsidy considered by an MSA household in its choice among schools.[13]

I calculated the per pupil subsidy in a school as follows. Per pupil income is the sum of per pupil tuition income and per pupil "other source" income.

12. See Bredeweg (1982). A larger percentage of income was derived from subsidies and fundraising in Catholic secondary schools that were parochial (34 percent) or diocesan (22 percent).

13. Since the price of private school is tuition, one might ask whether it would be preferable to use the variation in tuition (or the variation in the ratio of subsidy to tuition), rather than the variation in the subsidy, to identify the effects of a voucher. This would be undesirable because the only "useful" variation in the tuition would come from the subsidy. All other variation in tuition would come from variation in the cost of private schooling. Most of the variation in this cost comes not from differences in the cost of living but from the type of private schooling offered: the teacher-student ratio, whether the curriculum is college preparatory, and the generosity of school inputs, like computers, meals, classroom materials and comforts, sports facilities, and extracurricular resources. Clearly, all of this variation in cost is highly correlated with MSA and student characteristics, such as income and taste for education. This high correlation would mean that estimated effects of differences in tuition would certainly suffer from omitted-variable bias. Managing the omitted-variable bias by using historical Catholic population densities as instruments for tuition would be strictly inferior to using the densities as instruments for subsidies. The first reason is that the instruments are more weakly correlated with tuition than with subsidies since tuition varies with all the elements of cost named above (which are irrelevant to the empirical strategy). Unlike strongly correlated instruments, weakly correlated instrumental variables produce estimates that suffer from bias and problematic hypothesis testing. See Bound, Baker, and Jaeger (1993); Staiger and Stock (1993). The second reason is that the goal of this chapter is to simulate the effects of vouchers, and using tuition rather than subsidy as the variable of interest unnecessarily complicates the simulation.

Table 6-1. *Tuition and Subsidies in Private Elementary and Secondary Schools for Eight Denominations*[a]
1994 dollars

	Tuition paid per pupil[b]		Subsidy per pupil[c]	
Denomination	Elementary	Secondary	Elementary	Secondary
Catholic	543	1,777	611	496
Lutheran	646	1,767	879	1,128
Episcopalian	2,019	7,522	280	2,738
Jewish	2,171	3,252	787	1,633
Methodist	2,475	6,540	172	1,302
Friends	2,858	7,844	559	2,054
Presbyterian	2,024	6,573	280	3,353
Baptist	1,776	2,898	186	818

Source: Author's calculations based on U.S. Department of Education (1980).
a. Tuititions and subsidies are 1979 values inflated to 1994 dollars using urban services (excluding medical care) CPI. Schools are weighted by enrollment. Includes only regular secondary and elementary schools; excludes schools with combined elementary and secondary education, middle schools, schools devoted to nonregular instruction, and schools with fewer than ten pupils.
b. School's income from tuition and fees, divided by number of students.
c. Difference between school's per pupil expenditure and per pupil tuition paid. Excludes capital costs and other noncurrent operating expenses.

The "other source" income includes offerings, other donations, diocesan redistributions, and endowment income. Since per pupil income is equal to per pupil spending,[14] per pupil subsidy is equal to per pupil "other source" income. Recall the MSA average subsidies are weighted by school enrollments. Also note that individual Catholic schools typically give larger subsidies to students from needier households. (I will discuss this informal means-testing later when interpreting the simulated effects of vouchers.) Finally, Catholic school tuition is implicitly subsidized through the contribution of teaching and other services by members of religious orders. The value of these services was estimated to be 12 percent of Catholic secondary school revenue in 1980.[15] I will later find it useful to inflate the explicit subsidies by 30 percent of costs to show the range of plausible dollar-for-dollar translations between subsidies and vouchers.

The per pupil tuition paid and per pupil subsidy for private schools affiliated with eight major denominations are shown in table 6-1. These eight denominations accounted for 89 percent of regular elementary and 86 per-

14. This is both a theoretical identity and an observation from the data.
15. See Bredeweg (1982). The value of contributed services was probably a somewhat higher percentage of Catholic elementary school revenue, based on elementary schools' greater dependence on teachers in religious orders.

cent of regular secondary private enrollment in 1980.[16] In line with previous quoted estimates, subsidies accounted for 53 percent of the Catholic elementary school per pupil costs and about 22 percent of the Catholic secondary school per pupil costs. Contributed teaching services are indicated by the fact that 26 percent of Catholic elementary teachers and 29 percent of Catholic secondary teachers were members of religious orders.

The purpose of this study is to uncover the effect of tuition subsidies by comparing different subsidies in different metropolitan areas and adjusting for other factors as needed. The analysis can be divided into several areas: how tuition subsidies will affect the quantity of students attending private schools, the composition of students attending private schools, spending in public schools, and student performance. The empirical strategy described in this chapter requires financial information and enrollment information on both private and public schools in the United States. It requires information about religious populations and other MSA characteristics, and, finally, about the schooling choice and performance of individual students. To meet these requirements, I geographically matched five data sets that center on the year 1980. The interested reader will find a fuller discussion of the sources of data and more complete presentation of regression results in appendix A.

Effects of Tuition Subsidies on Private School Attendance

I begin by seeking a straightforward connection between the effect of tuition subsidies and the percentage of students who attend private schools by using a basic regression equation. The dependent variable $PctPrv_j$ will measure the percentage of enrollment in an MSA that takes place in private schools. The independent variables include the average tuition subsidy in private schools, denoted by $Subs_j$ (enrollment weighted, as discussed in the previous section), a vector X_j of characteristics that might potentially affect the percentage of students who attend private school, and an error term.

16. Catholics make up 78.3 percent of private elementary school enrollment in the United States and 80.2 percent of private secondary school enrollment. Lutherans are 6.1 percent of elementary enrollment and 2.2 percent of secondary; Jews are 1.9 percent of elementary and 1.1 percent of secondary; Episcopalians are 1.3 percent of elementary and 1.1 percent of secondary; Baptists are 1.3 percent of elementary and 1.0 percent of secondary; and nonsectarians are 6.1 percent of elementary and 9.4 percent of secondary. Author's calculations based on Roper Center (1980).

For each variable, j indexes the different MSAs. Thus we have the regression:

(1) $$PctPrv_j = \beta_1 Subs_j + X_j \beta_2 + \epsilon 1_j.$$

What variables need to be included in the X_j vector? It should include all available determinants of private school attendance. A list of the variables appears in table 6-2; most are straightforward measures such as various population groups, prior education levels, and economic status. One variable that may need a bit of explanation acts as a measure of the ease with which parents can choose among public schools in their MSAs. I have shown in other work that parents who can choose among public schools more easily are less likely to enroll their children in private schools. I have also shown that easier choice of public schools depresses per pupil spending and improves student performance. A Herfindahl index of public school enrollment concentration for each MSA has been found to be a succinct measure of the ease of choice among public schools.[17]

This regression is straightforward enough, if one is willing to assume that the tuition subsidy is uncorrelated with determinants of school and student performance not yet included in X. Unfortunately, observed tuition subsidies are likely to be correlated with unobserved determinants of private school attendance. To illustrate the problem, suppose that an MSA's public schools are of idiosyncratically low quality. In that case, demand for private schools is high and student performance is poor. The high demand for private schools strains the sources of subsidy funds, so that per pupil subsidies are low, and it will appear that lower subsidies lead to higher demand for private schools. In short, to the extent that public school quality is not perfectly observed, the effects of subsidies on private school attendance and on student performance are biased downward by omitted-variables bias. As another example, suppose that an MSA has a very heterogeneous population living in close proximity. In that case, demand for private schools is high: students who would otherwise attend public school might attend private school instead because their parents prefer them to have somewhat homogeneous peers. The high demand for private schools keeps per pupil subsidies low, all else being equal. Again, to the extent that

---

17. See Hoxby (1994b); Borland and Howsen (1992). A Herfindahl index of public school enrollment concentration has the same qualities as the familiar Herfindahl index of market concentration. It varies between zero and one. An index equal to one indicates maximum concentration since it indicates that there is only one school district in the MSA. Calculate each school district i's share of total SMSA enrollment: s_i where $i = 1, \ldots, n$. Then the Herfindahl index of public school enrollment concentration is: $H = \Sigma_i s_i^2$.

Table 6-2. *Effect of Tuition Subsidies and Other Variables on Enrollment in Catholic Schools*[a]

Variable	Enrollment in Catholic schools[b]	
	Ordinary least squares	Instrumental variables
MSA tuition subsidy in Catholic schools (hundreds of 1994 dollars)	−0.23 (0.15)	0.41 (0.19)
Percentage of 1980 MSA population who are Catholic adherents	0.57 (0.09)	0.59 (0.09)
Square of Catholic adherents	−0.007 (0.002)	−0.007 (0.002)
MSA Herfindahl index of public school enrollment concentration	2 (1)	2 (1)
MSA land area (hundreds of square miles)	−0.0007 (0.0003)	−0.0006 (0.0003)
Square of land area	2.1e-8 (1.5e-8)	2.0e-8 (1.9e-8)
MSA population (millions)	3.1 (1.1)	2.5 (2.3)
Square of population	−0.32 (0.14)	−0.42 (0.30)
MSA per capita income (thousands of 1994 dollars)	0.04 (0.22)	0.04 (0.23)
Percentage of MSA population in poverty	0.13 (0.22)	−0.31 (0.25)
African American percentage of MSA population	−0.01 (0.06)	−0.76 (0.31)
Hispanic percentage of MSA population	−0.17 (0.05)	−0.72 (0.21)
Percentage of MSA population with at least twelve years of education	−0.12 (0.10)	−0.14 (0.09)
Percentage of MSA population with at least sixteen years of education	0.13 (0.05)	0.14 (0.09)
Census division indicator variables	yes	yes
Asymptotic chi-squared statistic[c]	. . .	0.16 (0.31)

a. Numbers in parentheses are standard errors. $N = 235$ in elementary school equation, 202 in secondary school equation. All covariates are listed (constant and indicator variable coefficients not shown).
b. Percentage of MSA enrollment in Catholic schools (mean 6.0, standard deviation 6.5).
c. For a Hausman Lagrange multiplier test of identifying restrictions with one degree of freedom. The number in parentheses is 1 minus the cumulative probability.

population heterogeneity matters, the effects of subsidies on private school attendance are biased downward by omitted-variables bias.

Useful instrumental variables must fulfill two conditions. They must be correlated with MSA average per pupil subsidies, and they must be uncorrelated with the portions of private school enrollment that are not explained by the other dependent variables. I use the change from 1950 to 1980 in the percentage of an MSA's population who are Catholic adherents as an instrumental variable for subsidies. Appendix B presents the empirical evidence that these do serve as useful instrumental variables.

The logic is that Catholic school capacity increases with increased demand for Catholic schools by Catholic parents, but only slowly adjusts downward when there is insufficient demand from Catholic parents. Therefore, in MSAs that have experienced declining Catholic population densities, there is likely to be excess capacity in the Catholic schools for reasons exogenous to school quality. Conversely, in MSAs that have experienced increasing Catholic population densities, excess capacity is unlikely. If Catholic schools are more likely to accept non-Catholics when they have excess capacity, then MSAs with declining Catholic population densities have a larger percentage of students drawn from the non-Catholic population, which has a lower propensity to donate money for Catholic schools than the Catholic population. Given these conditions, MSAs that have experienced declining Catholic population densities will have lower per pupil subsidies, all else being equal.[18]

I choose the 1950–80 change because data on Catholic adherence are available for both years, and 1950 falls during a stable period for the Catholic schools, when school capacity was probably roughly in line with demand from Catholic parents. I also use the square of the change because the relationship between the change and subsidies is expected to be nonlinear. This is because school capacity moves in large, discrete steps when a school opens or closes. In addition, parents' propensities to send their children to Catholic schools can move discretely because these propensities often depend on whether the percentage of neighborhood children who attend Catholic schools is above or below some threshold. This identification strategy allows me to control for the 1980 Catholic population density of an MSA, which independently affects the demand for Catholic schools.

In estimations that do not use instrumental variables, I use the private school subsidy both for Catholic and non-Catholic private schools. However, if one suspects that the subsidy is correlated with other determinants,

---

18. A formal version of this model is available as a technical appendix from the author.

then it is necessary to use an instrumental variables strategy and, in practice, good instrumental variables exist only for Catholic school subsidies. This is because Catholicism is the only denomination that supports private schools in every MSA in the United States. All other denominations support private schools in only a minority of MSAs.[19]

The effects of Catholic school tuition subsidies on Catholic school attendance are shown in table 6-3. I estimate equation 1 using both ordinary least squares (OLS) and instrumental variables (IV), as described above. The IV estimates indicate that a $1,000 increase in the tuition subsidy induces a 4.1 percentage point increase in Catholic school enrollment.[20] The ordinary least squares estimates indicate the presence of negative bias when tuition subsidies are assumed to be uncorrelated with the unexplained portion of Catholic school enrollment, although the estimate is statistically insignificant. The contrast between the IV and OLS results indicates that increased demand for private schools, motivated by factors such as low public school quality, lowers tuition subsidies.[21]

Certain other coefficient estimates are worth noting. A 10 percentage point increase in 1980 Catholic adherence raises Catholic school enrollment by about 2.6 percentage points (evaluated at mean Catholic adherence of 19 percent). Private school enrollment is also significantly increased by public school enrollment concentration, as indicated by the estimated coefficient on the Herfindahl index.[22]

19. In theory, historical population densities for each denomination could be used as instrumental variables for tuition subsidies in that denomination's schools. The predicted subsidies, based on these instruments, could be used to calculate a weighted average subsidy with each denomination's enrollment as its weight. This is not a successful strategy in practice for two reasons that demonstrate why it is important to have Catholic schools in every MSA. First, for every non-Catholic denomination, some assumption must be made for the MSAs that have no denominational schools and therefore no subsidies. Since the nonexistence of a school does not imply that the school would have subsidies equal to zero if it were to exist, such assumptions introduce random error at the best and serious bias at the worst. Second, the weights needed to form the weighted average over denominations need to be instrumented just as much as the subsidies. There are not enough instrumental variables available to identify both the weights and the subsidies.

20. In addition to this specification where subsidies enter linearly, quadratic and other specifications were estimated to identify nonlinearities. Nonlinearities did not appear in the existing range of tuition subsidies.

21. If all private school enrollment is used rather than Catholic school enrollment and tuition subsidies are measured across all MSA schools rather than just Catholic schools, the results are as follows. The IV estimated coefficient on the subsidy is 0.37 (standard error of 0.20), and the OLS estimated coefficient on the subsidy is −0.27 (standard error of 0.19).

22. The asymptotic chi-squared statistic for the Hausman LaGrange multiplier test indicates that one cannot reject, at conventional levels of significance, the identifying restric-

Table 6-3. *Effect of Tuition Subsidies and Other Variables on the Probability of Attending Private School*[a]

Variable	Probability of attending private school[b]	
	Probit[c]	Instrumental variables probit[d]
MSA tuition subsidy in Catholic schools (hundreds of 1994 dollars)	−0.00057 (0.00027)	0.00284 (0.00137)
Subsidy × raised in Catholic household	0.00000 (0.00027)	0.00329 (0.00124)
Subsidy × raised in Catholic household × Hispanic	0.00032 (0.00090)	−0.00584 (0.00465)
Subsidy × African American	0.00038 (0.00087)	0.01045 (0.00414)
Subsidy × at least one parent is college graduate	−0.00052 (0.00028)	0.00036 (0.00148)
Raised in Catholic household	0.06 (0.02)	0.07 (0.02)
Hispanic	−0.0009 (0.0236)	−0.05 (0.02)
African American	−0.01 (0.02)	−0.05 (0.02)
Female	0.013 (0.004)	0.013 (0.005)
Parents' highest grade completed	0.009 (0.001)	0.008 (0.001)
Indicator variables for denomination of household (other than Catholic)	yes	yes
Census division indicator variables	yes	yes

a. Level of observation is a student who lives in an MSA at age 14; $N = 7,859$. Covariates not listed are percentage of MSA population who are Catholic adherents (and its square); MSA Herfindahl index of public school enrollment concentration; MSA land area and its square; MSA population and its square; MSA per capita income; MSA poverty rate; percentage of MSA population who are African American and who are Hispanic; percentage of adult MSA population with at least twelve years of education and with at least sixteen years of education. Numbers in parentheses are standard errors.
b. Indicator variable for whether a student attends private school (mean 0.6, standard deviation 0.23).
c. Change in probability at mean of explanatory variables (or change in probability as indicator variable switches from zero to one).
d. Estimation based on Newey (1987, 1990).

Tuition Vouchers and the Composition of the Student Body

Another goal of this analysis is to learn how vouchers affect the composition of students who attend private school and the composition of students

tion that the 1950-80 change in Catholic adherence is uncorrelated with unobserved determinants of the private school enrollment share. See Hausman (1983).

whose performance changes. This goal requires equations at the level of individual student data, rather than the metropolitan-area data in the previous section, and a subscript *i* is used to index individuals. In individual-level equations, I interact the subsidy with indicators for differences in family background. This allows the effect of a given subsidy to vary by whether a student has college-educated parents, for instance. Differences can be expected based on race, family income, and parental education. Also, simply because so many existing private schools are Catholic and I employ variation in Catholic school subsidies, differences can be expected based on being Catholic.[23]

The second equation allows the effect of tuition subsidies on private school attendance to vary with a student's family background. The dependent variable is $AttPrv_{ij}$, an indicator for whether a student attends private secondary school. The subsidy variable is the same as previously, and the vector of background characteristics X_{ij} that potentially determine whether a student attends private school is listed in table 6-3. Standard error estimation must take into account the fact that subsidies vary at the MSA level, though some equations are based on individual-level data. Essentially, an individual-level equation needs both an MSA-level error term and an individual-level error term, which are $\epsilon2_j$ and $\epsilon2_{ij}$, respectively.[24] This provides a regression equation:

$$(2) \quad AttPrv_{ij} = \delta_1 Subs_j + X_{ij} \cdot Subs_j \delta_2 + X_{ij}\delta_3 + X_j\delta_4 + \epsilon2_j + \epsilon2_{ij},$$

which attempts to explain the individual student's choice between public and private schools. Because of the yes-or-no nature of the dependent variable, the equation is first estimated by probit. Then, because of the fear that the subsidy measure may be correlated with other explanatory variables, it is estimated with a technique for instrumental variables in binary-choice equations based on Newey.[25]

Table 6-4 presents the results. The base student is a white non-Catholic, neither of whose parents is a college graduate, who lives in an MSA with no tuition subsidies. The IV estimates indicate that, in response to a $1,000

23. The differential effects of a *subsidy* on Catholics overstates the expected differential effects of a *voucher* on Catholics. This is because vouchers would not exclusively apply to Catholic schools, whereas the exploited variation in tuition subsidies does.

24. The correct standard errors are based on Moulton (1986) and, for nonlinear equations, also on Newey (1990). I denote linear estimates that are corrected as "feasible generalized least squares" (FGLS) estimates. I denote probit estimates that are corrected as "corrected probit" estimates.

25. Newey (1987, 1990).

Table 6-4. *Effect of Tuition Subsidies and Other Variables on Total and Per Pupil Public School Spending*[a]

Variable	Total public spending[b]		Per pupil spending[c]	
	Ordinary least squares	Instrumental variables	Ordinary least squares	Instrumental variables
MSA tuition subsidy in Catholic secondary schools (hundreds of 1994 dollars)	0.0003 (6.7716)	−0.1 (39.0)	14 (6)	42 (34)
Square of tuition subsidy	0.10 (0.47)	−1.8 (1.3)	−0.7 (0.4)	−0.5 (1.1)
Percentage of 1980 MSA population who are Catholic adherents	2.5 (1.2)	2.8 (1.2)	−2.0 (11.3)	−1.0 (10.8)
Square of Catholic adherents	−0.02 (0.02)	−0.02 (0.02)	0.3 (0.2)	0.3 (0.2)
MSA Herfindahl index of public school enrollment concentration	69 (22)	92 (51)	1,140 (211)	2,138 (806)
MSA land area (hundreds of square miles)	0.010 (0.004)	0.010 (0.004)	0.12 (0.04)	0.09 (0.03)
Square of land area	−3.6e-7 (1.8e-7)	−3.4e-7 (2.7e-7)	−2.7e-6 (1.7e-6)	1.9e-6 (2.4e-6)
MSA population (millions)	−36 (14)	−41 (32)	185 (130)	215 (284)
Square of population	3 (2)	4 (4)	−19 (16)	−33 (37)
MSA per capita income (thousands of 1994 dollars)	3 (3)	2 (3)	44 (25)	69 (29)
Percentage of MSA population in poverty	−5 (2)	−5 (3)	−12 (26)	11 (30)
African American percentage of MSA population	1.4 (0.8)	0.4 (4.3)	−0.8 (7.5)	5.1 (8.7)
Hispanic percentage of MSA population	2.8 (0.7)	1.9 (2.9)	−0.1 (6.2)	3.7 (6.9)

Table 6-4 *(continued)*

Variable	Total public spending[b]		Per pupil spending[c]	
	Ordinary least squares	Instrumental variables	Ordinary least squares	Instrumental variables
Percentage of MSA population with at least twelve years of education	−1.0 (1.6)	−1.5 (2.6)	−16 (11)	−17 (11)
Percentage of MSA population with at least sixteen years of education	1.8 (0.8)	−1.8 (1.2)	58 (15)	87 (23)
Census division indicator variables	yes	yes	yes	yes
Asymptotic chi-squared statistic[d]	. . .	0.61 (0.56)	. . .	0.11 (0.26)

a. Level of observation is an MSA; $N = 235$. All covariates are listed (constant and indicator variable coefficients not shown). Numbers in parentheses are standard errors.
b. Per resident spending on public schools (1982 value inflated to 1994 dollars) (mean $730, standard deviation $138).
c. Per pupil spending on public schools (1982 value inflated to 1994 dollars) (mean $3,508, standard deviation $718).
d. For a Hausman Lagrange multiplier test of identifying restrictions with one degree of freedom. The number in parentheses is 1 minus the cumulative probability.

tuition subsidy, the probability of attending private school rises by 2.8 percentage points for the base group. This is a sizable increase since the mean probability of attending private school is 6 percentage points. Adding the estimated coefficients on the interaction terms to the coefficient for the base groups indicates that the increase in the probability of private school attendance is 6 percentage points for non-Hispanic Catholic students and 13 percentage points for African American students. Students with a college graduate parent experience the same probability increase as the base group. The estimated coefficient on the Hispanic interaction is insignificantly different from zero, but the sign suggests that Hispanic Catholics do not experience as large an increase in the probability of private school attendance as do other Catholics. Like the ordinary least squares estimates in table 6-2, the probit estimates suggest that the estimated coefficient on subsidies is negatively biased when subsidies are treated as though they were uncorrelated with the unexplained portion of the private school attendance decision.[26]

26. Overall, the results of tables 6-2 and 6-3 are consistent because when the coefficients on the subsidy terms in table 6-3 are weighted by the relevant population shares, they add up to about 4 percent, which is the estimate in table 6-2.

In summary, the results of these first two equations demonstrate that a $1,000 tuition subsidy would induce an overall increase of about 4 percentage points in private school enrollment. This is a sizable increase relative to the private schools' current 10 percent of enrollment, but it is not explosive. The increased enrollment would contain a disproportionately large share of African Americans and non-Hispanic Catholics. The result that Catholics are more likely to attend than others derives partly from the facts that private schools are disproportionately Catholic and that the empirical strategy employs variation in only the Catholic school subsidy. The result that students with college-educated parents are no more likely to attend than the base group but that African Americans *are* more likely to attend supports the prediction that the students most likely to move from public to private schools are those whose local public schools are low quality, those who live close to private schools, and those who come from lower-income families. Urban African Americans disproportionately fit into this group, and this fact may account for the dramatic increase in their probability of attending private school in response to a $1,000 subsidy.

Tuition Subsidies and Public School Spending

How does the level of tuition subsidy affect public school spending, either on a per resident or a per pupil basis? In asking this question, I return from individual to MSA-level data. The dependent variable will be either per resident spending on public schools in the MSA, $PerResSpend_j$, or per pupil spending on public schools in the MSA, $PerPupSpend_j$. Per resident spending is the measure of total public school spending because it is necessary to account for the fact that larger MSAs will have higher spending simply because they are larger. The first independent explanatory variable is the average level of tuition subsidy, as already explained. But in this case, the square of the subsidy is included as a second explanatory variable to allow for nonlinear effects that are expected because the tax rate is determined through voting, and voting models suggest that the relationship between spending and the subsidy is nonlinear. For instance, a median-voter model would suggest that the relationship differs below and above the point where the subsidy has induced the median voter to enroll his or her children in private school. A variety of other possible explanatory variables are included in the X vector, appearing in table 6-4. The regression equations are:

(3) $PerResSpend_j = \gamma_1 Subs_j + \gamma_2 Subs_j^2 + X_j\gamma_3 + \epsilon 3_j$

(4) $PerPupSpend_j = \eta_1 Subs_j + \eta_2 Subs_j^2 + X_j\eta_3 + \epsilon 4_j.$

Again, it is necessary to estimate both by ordinary least squares and by an instrumental variables technique. Table 6-4 presents estimates of the effects of tuition subsidies on *per resident* spending on public schools and on *per pupil* spending on public schools, using both estimation methods. Recall that these estimated effects are the same as the indirect effects of a voucher on public school spending. However, per pupil spending decreases as total public school budgets decrease, but increases for every student who leaves the public schools.

The estimated coefficients in table 6-4 show no significant evidence that tuition subsidies decrease per resident spending on the public schools. None of the estimated coefficients on subsidy variables is significantly different from zero at conventional levels of significance. This is an indication that the share of people influenced to change their behavior by current subsidies, a small percentage of the households who have school-age children, is insufficient to affect property values or the political process that determines property tax rates. However, a very large subsidy or voucher, such as $6,000, might have significant effects. The point estimate on the square of the tuition subsidy hints that the negative effect of a subsidy on total public school spending accelerates as the size of the subsidy increases.

Consistent with insignificant decreases in total school budgets and significant decreases in the share of enrollment in public schools, the IV estimates in table 6-4 suggest that higher Catholic tuition subsidies might generate increases in per pupil spending. The estimated coefficients are not significantly different from zero, but the size of the standard errors would preclude most plausible estimates from being significant. The positive point estimates are consistent with a model in which total public school budgets fall very slightly through indirect effects of tuition subsidies on tax revenue, so that the dominant effect is to redistribute the spending for students who switch to private schools over the remaining public school students. I conclude that the effect of a $1,000 subsidy (or the *indirect* effect of a $1,000 voucher) is negligible on total public school spending and is either zero or slightly positive on per pupil spending.

Tuition Subsidies and Student Performance

The final issue to address is the effect of tuition subsidies on student performance.[27] Again, these are regressions where the subsidies are interacted with individual students' background characteristics, so the equations employ individual-level data. The general form of the regression is to have a measure of student performance on the left-hand side as the dependent variable. I actually estimated three different sets of regressions with different measures of student performance: the student's highest grade completed by age 24; the student's percentile score on the Armed Forces Qualifications Test; and the student's hourly wage in his or her most recent job. The vector X of other explanatory variables is much the same. The effect of tuition subsidies on student performance are allowed to vary with the student's family background, through the use of interaction terms. The base student is a white non-Catholic, neither of whose parents is a college graduate, who lives in an MSA with no tuition subsidies. There is again both an MSA-level error term and an individual-level error term. The form of the regression equation is:

$$(5) \quad StudPerf_{ij} = \mu_1 Subs_j + X_{ij} Subs_j \mu_2 + X_{ij}\mu_3 + X_j\mu_4 + \epsilon 5_j + \epsilon 5_{ij}.$$

Table 6-5 summarizes the coefficients of particular interest: the coefficients on subsidy and the interactions between subsidy and student characteristics. Three regression equations, one for each separate measure of student performance, are estimated by FGLS and then, to correct for the likelihood that the subsidy measure is correlated with other explanatory variables, by an instrumental variables approach with corrected standard errors.[28]

Table 6-5 shows that tuition subsidies improve student performance overall, regardless of whether performance is measured by educational attainment, AFQT test scores, or wages. The instrumental variables estimates indicate that greater tuition subsidies significantly improve the performance of all students. Disproportionate improvement is enjoyed by non-Hispanic Catholic students, African American students, and students who have at least one parent who is a college graduate. These improvements in performance are driven by improvements in the performance of *public*

---

27. Both public and private school students are included in these equations. Since selection into private school is potentially affected by the subsidy, I would introduce selection bias if I excluded either type of student from the equation. However, I examine below whether the effect of subsidies varies between public and private school students.

28. Full results from estimating these equations are available on request from the author.

Table 6-5. *Effect of Tuition Subsidies and Family Background on Student Performance*[a]

Dependent variable and estimation method	Variables					
	Tuition subsidy	Tuition subsidy × Catholic	Tuition subsidy × Catholic × Hispanic	Tuition subsidy × African American	Tuition subsidy × college parent	Tuition subsidy × private school attendance
Highest grade completed[b]						
FGLS	0.02	0.04	−0.09	−0.03	0.08	−0.10
	(0.02)	(0.03)	(0.04)	(0.03)	(0.03)	(0.04)
IV	0.21	0.05	−0.09)	0.06	0.10	−0.09
	(0.07)	(0.03)	(0.05)	(0.03)	(0.04)	(0.05)
AFQT score[c]						
FGLS	−0.03	0.94	−0.88	−0.08	0.60	−1.39
	(0.27)	(0.31)	(0.50)	(0.37)	(0.34)	(0.55)
IV	0.79	1.00	−0.28	1.01	0.63	−1.20
	(0.35)	(0.40)	(0.62)	(0.46)	(0.46)	(0.64)
Ln (wage) most recent job[d]						
FGLS	0.003	0.008	−0.21	0.002	0.003	−0.010
	(0.005)	(0.006)	(0.010)	(0.008)	(0.007)	(0.012)
IV	0.012	0.011	−0.004	0.013	0.015	−0.008
	(0.006)	(0.008)	(0.013)	(0.010)	(0.010)	(0.014)

a. Complete regression estimates available from author. Level of observation is a student who lived in an MSA at age 14. Subsidies per pupil are 1979 values inflated to 1994 dollars. Numbers in parentheses are standard errors.
b. By age 24 (mean 12.4, standard deviation 2.2).
c. Equation includes indicator variables for age at test taking (mean 41.0, standard deviation 28.8.).
d. Equation includes number of years since actual completion of school and its square (mean 2.13, standard deviation 0.48).

school students. If the equations are estimated using just the sample of public school students, the results are almost identical.[29] In fact, I find that private school students perform worse as tuition subsidies increase, probably because the marginal student induced to attend private school by the subsidy performs more poorly than the present average private school student. It is entirely consistent for the marginal student induced to attend private school to be better than the average public school student but worse than the average private school student.

29. Private school students are not excluded from the estimates because exclusion might introduce selection bias. For example, if tuition subsidies induced students who performed badly in public schools to switch to private schools, then public school students' performance would improve with the subsidy merely through selection.

For the base group, a $1,000 increase in the Catholic school subsidy improves educational attainment by 2.1 years, AFQT scores by 7.9 percentile points, and wages by 12 percent. For white, non-Hispanic, Catholic, public school students without a college-graduate parent, the improvements are greater: 2.6 years and 17.9 points.[30] The same student who is *Hispanic,* however, enjoys an improvement in performance that is positive but worse than the base group. For instance, the improvement in educational attainment is only 1.2 years. African American, non-Catholic public school students without a college-graduate parent enjoy greater improvements than the base group: 2.7 years in educational attainment and 18.0 points in AFQT scores.[31] Students with a college-graduate parent also enjoy greater improvements. A white, non-Catholic, public school student with a college-graduate parent improves educational attainment by 3.1 years and AFQT scores by 14.2 points.[32] The same student (white, non-Catholic, college-graduate parent) who attends private school earns smaller improvements: 2.2 years and 2.2 points.

The estimates in table 6-5 show that omitted-variable bias is present when one assumes that tuition subsidies are uncorrelated with the unexplained portion of student performance. Generally, the FGLS coefficient estimates on subsidy and its interaction are negatively biased. This direction of the bias supports the hypothesis that public school quality is an important omitted variable because low quality impairs student performance and increases the demand for private schools, thus lowering per pupil subsidies.[33]

These results show that students perform substantially better as tuition subsidies rise. All students with a college-educated parent improve disproportionately, but the most striking result is that African American students improve greatly, all else being equal.

How does one interpret these results? First, the fact that increased subsidies generate negligible changes in public school spending can be used to eliminate the hypothesis that the improvements in student performance

30. The point estimate for the improvement in wages is 23 percent, but the coefficient is poorly estimated, as the standard error is 8 percent.
31. The point estimate for the improvement in wages is 25 percent, but the coefficient is poorly estimated, as the standard error is 10 percent.
32. The point estimate for the improvement in wages is 27 percent, but the coefficient is poorly estimated, as the standard error is 10 percent.
33. Hausman test statistics indicate that one cannot reject the identifying restrictions that the 1950–80 change in Catholic adherence and its square are uncorrelated with unobserved determinants of student performance.

stem from increased inputs. Rather, one must explain why schools—especially public schools, which drive the results—have higher student performance for the same level of inputs. It is unlikely that the results simply reflect an omitted but important MSA characteristic that is related to changes in tuition subsidies *driven* by the change in Catholic adherence from 1950 to 1980. The equations control for MSA characteristics that are likely determinants of school and student performance.[34] Therefore the reasonable conclusion is that private school tuition subsidies force public schools into higher productivity.

Conclusions

Now I will draw on the estimates of previous sections to translate the results into terms that may be more useful for policy decisions. Consider a tuition voucher that averages $1,000 but is about as means-tested as the current system of Catholic school subsidies. My results indicate that the voucher would induce private school enrollment to grow from approximately 10 percent of U.S. enrollment to 14 percent. Note that this increase in private school attendance partly reflects the fact that public schools respond by improving, thus keeping some students who would leave in the absence of such improvements.

Overall, the effect of a $1,000 voucher on the composition of students who attend private school would be to increase private school access across both well-educated and more poorly educated families. The voucher would particularly induce Catholic and African American students to attend private school. The disproportionate inducement for African American students is predicted by the fact that they disproportionately live close to Catholic schools in districts with poor public schools and come from low-income families for whom $1,000 of additional tuition can make a substantial difference. The disproportionate inducement for Catholic students is probably due to the fact that private schools are disproportionately Catholic-affiliated.[35] There does not appear to be a disproportionate in-

34. Also, Hausman tests consistently fail to reject the hypothesis that the only route by which the 1950–80 change affects school and student performance is through tuition subsidies, once one controls for other MSA characteristics such as current Catholic adherence.

35. However, this Catholic student inducement is probably overstated because using variation in Catholic school subsidies overstates the importance of variation in Catholic school attendance relative to non-Catholic private school attendance.

ducement for students with college-educated parents to attend private school compared with students with parents who are only high school graduates, probably because students from better-educated households are already more likely to attend private school or a desirable public school in the absence of a voucher. It is important to remember that high-income parents or parents with strong preferences for high-quality schooling may be pleased to receive a voucher if they already send their children to private school, but they are unlikely to change their choice between public and private schools for a voucher of $1,000. This is an argument for means-testing.

A $1,000 voucher would have negligible *indirect* effects on total public school spending, probably because the number of households who would switch between public and private schools is small relative to the total number of households. These relative numbers are important for the determination of public school spending, because they limit the effect on both property values and the political process. A $1,000 voucher would have negligible or slightly positive *indirect* effects on per pupil public school spending. This is because total public school spending does not decrease, although the number of public school students falls as some switch to the private schools.

One must also examine the *direct* effects of a $1,000 voucher on public school spending. Remember that for any given increase in private school attendance caused by the voucher, the direct effects can be set by policymakers. Since the direct costs of a voucher to the public school system depend heavily on how much money is given to parents whose children already attend private schools, policymakers should use the degree to which the voucher is means-tested as an instrument for regulating the direct effects of a voucher on public school spending. As an extreme example, suppose that a $1,000 voucher was introduced that was not means-tested, so that all students who already attended private school received $1,000 for their education. This is 10 percent of students. The results indicate that an additional 4 percent of students will be induced to attend private school. Suppose the students attend public schools that have the average 1982 per pupil spending of $3,508.[36] If $1,000 were removed from public school budgets for every student who attends private schools (14 percent of students), per pupil spending on the remaining public school students would

36. This is 1982 average per pupil spending inflated to 1994 dollars. It does *not* reflect real increases in per pupil spending between 1982 and 1994 and thus is less than 1994 per pupil spending.

increase by $30.[37] The fact that the voucher is less than the per pupil spending outweighs the fact that the voucher must be given to some students who did not attend public school before.

The combination of direct and indirect effects of a voucher on public school spending points to the fact that it may be practicable for vouchers to discipline "bad" public schools without disciplining their students. The discipline for "bad" schools takes the form of administrators facing smaller total budgets, forcing them to shrink their staff and buildings, although they would not be shrinking their staff and buildings relative to the number of pupils. If administrators dislike making unpopular decisions about eliminating staff and schools, they will have an incentive to improve their productivity.

A $1,000 voucher would improve student performance across the board: both public and private school students would increase their educational attainment (about two years), test scores (about 10 percent), and wages (about 14 percent). The improvements would be greater for Catholic students, African American students, and all students with college-educated parents. These improvements are almost entirely among public school students. The consistency between the groups more likely to attend private school and the groups more likely to improve their performance in public school derives from the fact that public schools that face a disproportionate increase in competition because of the voucher will disproportionately improve their productivity. (The disproportionate improvement for Catholic students is probably overstated.)

These results need a few qualifications. First, this study is not able to estimate the effects of vouchers that are outside the range of existing tuition subsidies. The results presented only allow speculation about the effects of a voucher equal to, say, $6,000. Second, the effects of a $1,000 voucher may be overstated because explicit Catholic tuition subsidies understate true tuition subsidies owing to contributed services. One might deflate the

---

37. The typical school district with above-average per pupil spending also has an above-average share of its students in private schools in the absence of a voucher, so it is not clear whether its per pupil spending would increase by more or less than $30. A school district with per pupil spending of $6,000 would increase its per pupil spending by $176 if only 10 percent of its students attended private schools before the voucher, but by only $67 if 20 percent of its students attended private schools before the voucher. Correspondingly, the typical school district with below average per pupil spending also has a below average share of its students in private schools. A school district with per pupil spending of $2,500 would decrease its per pupil spending by $29 if 10 percent of its students attended private schools before the voucher, but by $28 if only 5 percent of its students attended private schools before the voucher.

202 / Caroline Minter Hoxby

effects of the voucher by 30 percent on the grounds that a $1,000 subsidy is truly equal to a $1,300 subsidy when one takes account of contributed teaching. Substantial improvements in student performance still result: 1.4 additional years of educational attainment, a 7 percent improvement in AFQT scores, and a 10 percent improvement in wages.

A third qualification is that a $1,000 voucher that is not means-tested may have somewhat different sorting and student performance effects. However, it is clearly possible to design a voucher that is as means-tested as existing Catholic school subsidies. A fourth qualification is that a $1,000 voucher restricted to use in nonreligious private schools would have different effects on the composition of students who attend private school. In fact, because secular private schools disproportionately enroll students from high-income families and charge high tuitions, such a restricted voucher might have the undesirable effect of changing the behavior of almost no one while benefiting high-income parents who already send their children to secular private schools.[38] However, the availability of such a voucher might also make some schools give up their religious affiliations, as religious education is not uniformly a major part of curriculum in religiously affiliated schools.

Appendix A: Data Sources and Full Regression Results

The empirical strategy described in this chapter requires financial information and enrollment information on both private and public schools in the United States, on religious populations and other MSA characteristics, and about the schooling choice and performance of individual students. To meet these requirements, I geographically matched five data sets that center on the year 1980.

I drew data for calculating tuition subsidies from the National Center for Education Statistics (NCES) Private Schools in America survey for 1980.[39] This survey comprises 20,050 private schools in the United States, which represent 95 percent of all private schools and a higher percentage of private enrollment. These data are unique because they give information about expenses and sources of income for a very large share of all U.S. private schools. Key variables include geographic location, enrollment in

38. See Hoxby (1994a).
39. U.S. Department of Education (1980). A version of this survey is currently released by the NCES as the "Private Schools Survey."

each grade, the number of teachers (lay and religious), the type of schooling offered, total current expenses, total current income, current income from tuition and fees, and current income from other sources. I use enrollment information from this survey to calculate subsidies per pupil. However, MSA-level information on total private school enrollment comes from the 1980 Census of Population. Data on public schools are drawn from the 1982 Census of Governments, which includes all 16,270 public school districts in the United States (containing more than 85,000 schools). This census is the source of per pupil spending and public school enrollment. I also used Census of Governments data to calculate the Herfindahl index variable discussed in the text.

Religious data are needed both because current religious populations determine private school attendance and because I use historical religious populations as instrumental variables. Since the empirical strategy relies on a measure of the population of potential donors to private schools with religious affiliations, I require data on religious adherence, where adherents are defined as congregation members and other regular participants (a more strict definition than mere denomination preference). Adherence data by MSA come from the 1950 and 1980 surveys of Churches and Church Membership in the United States.[40] These surveys are an attempted census of all Judaeo-Christian congregations in the United States, including 231,708 congregations of 469 denominations in 1980.

From the 1980 Census of Population, I derive other MSA characteristics that are potential determinants of private school attendance, public school spending, or student performance. These include the land area, per capita income, poverty rate, total population, African American population, Hispanic population, adult population with at least twelve years of school, adult population with at least sixteen years of school, and census division (1–9).

Finally, the empirical strategy requires data on individual students' performance and background characteristics. I draw student data from the National Longitudinal Survey of Youth (NLSY), a panel of 12,686 young men and women surveyed every year since 1979 (when they ranged in age from 14 to 22). Each student was matched with the MSA in which he or she was a student at age 14.[41] The NLSY indicates whether the student

40. National Council of Churches of Christ in the United States of America (1952); Roper Center (1980).
41. Because some students are over age 18 at the start of the survey, this is only way to measure the geographic location of a student's schooling that is consistent across all respondents.

attended public or private secondary school and includes three valuable measures of student performance: the student's highest grade completed by age 24, the student's score on the Armed Forces Qualifications Test and the student's wage in his or her most recent job.[42] The NLSY is also the source of background characteristics that are potential determinants of private school attendance and student performance, including a student's race, sex, parents' highest grade completed, and the religion in which the student was raised. The last variable is particularly important because it is necessary to separate the effect of living in an area with generous Catholic school tuition subsidies from the effect of being raised in a Catholic household. Table 6A-1 shows descriptive statistics for the variables used in this study.

Appendix B: Change in Catholic Population Density as an Instrumental Variable

The chapter explains why I expect the change in the Catholic population density from 1950 to 1980 to be positively correlated with tuition subsidies. I demonstrate the correlation concretely in table 6B-1. Formally, the first stage of the instrumental variables strategy is:

(B1) $\quad Subs_j = \alpha_1 \Delta PctCth_j + \alpha_2 (\Delta PctCth_j)^2 + X_j \alpha_3 + \gamma PctPrv_j + \epsilon 8_j,$

In addition to the variables defined in the chapter above, $\Delta PctCth_j$ is the 1950–80 change in the percentage of MSA population who are Catholic adherents, and $\epsilon 8_j$ is the MSA-specific disturbance. The vector X_j includes the 1980 percentage of the MSA population who are Catholic adherents and its square. Recall that the percentage of students who are enrolled in private schools is a dependent variable because increased demand for private schools, motivated perhaps by low-quality public schools, lowers the per pupil subsidy.

The estimates of equation B1 demonstrate that the 1950–80 change in Catholic adherence and its square are significant determinants of per pupil subsidies. A 10 percentage point increase in an MSA's Catholic adherence generates a $50 increase in the subsidy (estimated at zero, close to the mean change in MSA Catholic adherence). This amount represents an 8.4 percent increase in the subsidy. Partial F-tests on the joint significance of the two identifying variables produce a result that is significant at the 0.005

---

42. The NLSY attempted to administer the AFQT to all survey participants.

Table 6A-1. *Descriptive Statistics for Variables*

Variable	Mean	Standard deviation
MSA-level variables		
Per pupil subsidy in Catholic elementary schools (dollars)	596	288
1950–80 change in percentage of MSA population who are Catholic adherents	1	8
Herfindahl index of public school district enrollment concentration	0.31	0.25
MSA land area (hundreds of square miles)	19.54	22.25
Total MSA population (millions)	0.61	1.04
MSA per capita income[a]	20.90	3.35
Percentage of MSA population in poverty	12	4
Percentage of MSA adult population with at least twelve years of education	68	8
Percentage of MSA adult population with at least sixteen years of education	16	5
Per pupil spending in public schools[b]	3,507	717
Per resident spending on public schools[b]	729	137
Percentage of MSA enrollment in private schools	10	7
Percentage of MSA population who are African American	10	10
Percentage of MSA population who are Hispanic	6	12
Percentage of MSA population who are Catholic adherents	19	15
Individual-level variables		
Attended private secondary school (percent)	6	23
Highest grade completed by age 24	12.36	2.17
AFQT percentile score (1989 standard)	41.03	28.58
Hourly wage at most recent job (dollars)	2.12	0.47
Parents' highest grade completed[c]	11.68	3.24
African American (percent)	24	43
Hispanic (percent)	14	34
Female (percent)	49	50
Raised in Catholic household (percent)	32	47
Raised in Lutheran household (percent)	6	23
Raised in Jewish household (percent)	1	10
Raised in Episcopalian household (percent)	2	12
Raised in Methodist household (percent)	8	28
Raised in Presbyterian household (percent)	3	16
Raised in Baptist household (percent)	29	45
Raised in other denomination household (percent)	10	31
Raised in no denomination household (percent)	4	20

a. 1980 value in thousands of 1994 dollars for population aged over 16.
b. 1982 value in 1994 dollars.
c. Maximum of mother's and father's.

Table 6B-1. *Correlation between 1950–80 Change in Percentage of MSA Population Who are Catholic and Other Variables and Correlation between Tuition Subsidies and Other Variables*[a]

MSA characteristic	1950–80 change in percentage of MSA population who are Catholic adherents	Tuition subsidy
MSA per capita income	0.15 (0.21)	−0.06 (0.73)
MSA population	0.17 (0.28)	−0.09 (0.15)
Percentage of MSA population in poverty	−0.02 (0.44)	−0.38 (0.00)
African American percentage of MSA population	0.07 (0.24)	−0.44 (0.00)
Hispanic percentage of MSA population	−0.48 (0.00)	−0.28 (0.00)
Percentage of MSA population with at least twelve years of education	0.06 (0.33)	0.11 (0.07)
Percentage of MSA population with at least sixteen years of education	−0.07 (0.27)	−0.17 (0.01)

a. Numbers in parentheses are significance levels.

level and confirms that the MSA change in adherence and its square are strongly correlated instrumental variables. (The number of observations is small since it is equal to the number of MSAs in 1980.)

One would suspect that the MSA change in Catholic adherence was not a legitimate instrumental variable if it were highly correlated with observed MSA characteristics that are likely determinants of school and student performance. Table 6B-1 shows the correlations between the 1950–80 change in the Catholic population density and MSA characteristics in the vector X. For comparison, this table also shows the correlations between the MSA average tuition subsidy and MSA characteristics in the vector X. The 1950–80 change is not correlated with other MSA characteristics at standard levels of significance, with the exception of the Hispanic population density.[43] The correlations in table 6B-1 provide an intuitive partial test of the second condition that instrumental variables must fulfill.[44]

43. The negative correlation between the 1950-80 change in an MSA's percentage of population who are Catholics and the percentage of an MSA's population who are Hispanics supports common anecdotes claiming that Hispanics have a lower rate of church attendance than other traditionally Catholic ethnic groups. That is, if Hispanics are a large share of the population and only a small proportion of Hispanics adherents even though a large proportion identifies itself as Catholic, the population density of Catholic adherents will be low. This is an example of why it is useful to have adherence data to measure the potential donor population.

44. In contrast to the 1950-80 change, subsidies are significantly correlated with several

MSA characteristics. Subsidies appear to be higher in MSAs that are richer and that have higher population densities of non-Hispanic, traditionally Catholic ethnicities since there are negative correlations between subsidies and the poverty rate, African American population density, and Hispanic population density. Evidence that Catholic schools mainly serve communities where most parents are high school but not college graduates is supported by the combination of a positive correlation between subsidies and the population density of high school graduates and a negative correlation between subsidies and the population density of college graduates. See Coleman and Hoffer (1987); Evans and Schwab (1993a, 1993b).

References

Borland, Melvin V., and Roy M. Howsen. 1992. "Student Academic Achievement and the Degree of Market Concentration in Education." *Economics of Education Review* 11 (March): 31–39.

Bound, John, Regina Baker, and David A. Jaeger. 1993. "The Cure Can Be Worse than the Disease: A Cautionary Tale Regarding Instrumental Variables." Technical Paper 137. Cambridge, Mass.: National Bureau of Economic Research.

Bredeweg, Frank H. 1982. *United States Catholic Elementary and Secondary Schools, 1981–1982.* Washington: National Catholic Educational Association.

Chubb, John E., and Terry M. Moe. 1990. *Politics, Markets, and America's Schools.* Brookings.

Clune, William H., and John F. Witte, eds. 1990. *Choice and Control in American Education.* Vol. 2: *The Practice of Choice, Decentralization, and School Restructuring.* New York: Falmer Press.

Coleman, James S., and Thomas Hoffer. 1987. *Public and Private High Schools: The Impact of Communities.* Basic Books.

Evans, William N., and Robert M. Schwab. 1993a. "Finishing High School and Starting College: Do Catholic Schools Make a Difference?" University of Maryland, Department of Economics.

————. 1993b. "Who Benefits from Private Education? Evidence from Quantile Regressions." University of Maryland, Department of Economics.

Hausman, Jerry A. 1983. "Specification and Estimation of Simultaneous Equation Models." In *Handbook of Econometrics,* edited by Zvi Griliches and Michael D. Intriligator. New York: North Holland.

Hoxby, Caroline Minter. 1994a. "Do Private Schools Provide Competition for Public Schools?" Working Paper 4978. Cambridge, Mass.: National Bureau of Economic Research.

————. 1994b. "Does Competition among Public Schools Benefit Students and Taxpayers." Working Paper 4979. Cambridge, Mass.: National Bureau of Economic Research.

Kirkpatrick, David W. 1990. *Choice in Schooling: A Case for Tuition Vouchers.* Chicago: Loyola University Press.

Moulton, Brent R. 1986. "Random Group Effects and the Precision of Regression Estimates." *Journal of Econometrics* 32 (August): 385–97.

National Council of Churches of Christ in the United States of America. 1952. Churches and Church Membership in the United States, 1950. Database.

Newey, Whitney K. 1987. "Efficient Estimation of Limited Dependent Variable Models with Endogenous Explanatory Variables." *Journal of Econometrics* 36 (November): 231–50.

—————. 1990. "Efficient Instrumental Variables Estimation of Nonlinear Models." *Econometrica* 58 (July): 809–37.

Roper Center. 1980. Churches and Church Membership in the United States, 1980. Database.

Staiger, Douglas, and James H. Stock. 1993. "Instrumental Variables Regression with Weak Instruments." Working Paper 151. Cambridge, Mass.: National Bureau of Economic Research.

U.S. Department of Education, National Center for Education Statistics. 1980. Private Schools in America, 1980. Database.

Witte, John F., and Mark E. Rigdon. 1993. "Education Choice Reforms: Will They Change American Schools?" *Publius* 23 (Summer): 95–104.

Comments on Chapters Five and Six

Thomas J. Kane

THE GOAL of this volume is to assess alternative mechanisms for improving accountability in schools. One such incentive mechanism, school choice, has captured the imagination of many in the popular debate. Although choice can take many forms—magnet schools, public school choice, vouchers—all choice plans rely upon exit, or the threat of exit, as the primary means of sending the message to schools to improve. The "market" is a familiar metaphor, and references to "consumer sovereignty" always sell well to consumers. The chapters by John Witte and Caroline Minter Hoxby get beyond the symbolism to anticipate the likely effects of school choice on a range of outcomes, such as student test scores and public school spending.

Refreshingly, the two chapters take very different approaches to the problem. John Witte takes a "partial equilibrium" approach, surveying the literature on each of a number of the relevant changes that may accompany school choice to anticipate the full impact. In contrast, Caroline Minter Hoxby ignores many of these transitional issues and asks what the new equilibrium might look like under a voucher program, using variation in private school subsidies associated with demographic change at the MSA level, which she takes to be a "natural experiment" in school vouchers.

Witte first reviews the evidence on which parents are most likely to take advantage of a voucher scheme and on what basis they make their decisions. Citing a number of different studies, he reports that those already choosing private schools are more likely to be high income, have more educated parents, and to be Catholic or Jewish. At the transition between elementary and secondary schools, the more academically inclined students in Catholic elementary schools were more likely to continue in Catholic high schools; similarly, those transferring from public elementary schools to Catholic high schools came from more advantaged backgrounds than those who remained.[1]

Witte notes that parents do at least claim to be seeking improved academic performance when they choose private schools. However, they are pursuing other goals as well, such as seeking a stronger disciplinary environment. Religiosity also seems to matter for many parents choosing private schools.

Witte then evaluates the evidence on whether magnet schools, private schools, or Catholic schools actually improve student performance for the youth who choose them. The biggest obstacle to overcome in such empirical work is caused by the point made above: the most advantaged students—those who were most likely to do well wherever they attended school—are most likely to take advantage of choice programs.[2]

Witte offers a provocative summary of the research evaluating private schools: "If private school users have any significant advantages in achievement gains, the gains are small enough to have little policy importance." He later backs off from that strong statement, allowing that private and Catholic schools may improve the performance of the students in the lowest test quartiles. Further, he cites recent work by Evans and Schwab finding large positive effects of Catholic schools on high school graduation and college entry.

Finally, Witte wonders about the likely effects of a school choice program on the behavior of public schools. It is one thing to ask how large a gain the students who switch from public to private schools might expect; it is another to ask whether exit is likely to have any positive effect on the performance of the students left behind. Unfortunately, we are left with little here beyond speculation. Ongoing experiments with voucher programs in Milwaukee and San Antonio are small pilot programs and, as such, would be expected to have little impact on the school system as a whole.

1. The one exception was the Milwaukee Parental Choice Program (MPCP), in which those taking advantage of the vouchers had poorer test scores than the average Milwaukee public school student. However, it was not clear from Witte's description whether this was simply due to the income limitations in the program or some other program characteristic.

2. Much of the research relies upon one of two data sets—the High School and Beyond (HSB) survey of high school sophomores in 1980 and the National Educational Longitudinal Study (NELS) of eighth graders beginning in 1988. Because both data sets are panels of individuals, researchers often study changes in test scores between tenth and twelfth grade or between eighth and tenth grade for students attending different types of schools, attempting to control for observed student characteristics.

Before moving to Hoxby's chapter and a synthesis of the two results, I want to make a few points. Witte's initial observation—that the most advantaged youth choose to attend private schools or public magnet schools—has two important implications that deserve emphasis. First, if we hope to affect behavior, rather than merely subsidize behavior that would have happened in the absence of intervention, any vouchers should be targeted to low-income youth, since they are less likely to choose these schools on their own. Second, to the extent that parental involvement is a resource that is valuable to all students in a school—and not just to the children of the parents who get involved—a voucher program could drain off the most involved parents from the worst schools and actually lead to declines in performance at the original schools. Means-testing is an imperfect, but probably worthwhile, method for slowing the loss of the most valuable parents. (In the worst schools, even the most involved parents are likely to be poor.) A further argument for means-testing is provided by Witte's observation that private schools had the biggest effects for youths with low test scores.

Means-testing would give low-income students the option of enjoying whatever educational advantages private schools offer. However, to the extent that means-testing limits the number of students threatening to exit, it may only marginally improve public schools' incentives to improve.

Witte's point that a poorly designed voucher program may cause public schools to lose high-performing youth with the most involved parents deserves further exploration. We should draw from an earlier literature on the effect of schoolwide socioeconomic status and test scores on individual student test scores. Having smart classmates helps students learn. Therefore, one school's loss may be another's gain. If we knew the characteristics of the parents and children most likely to leave, we could estimate how dramatically the mean characteristics at donor and recipient schools would change. Using the literature on peer effects, we could do a back-of-the-envelope calculation of the likely effect of such movements on both public and private schools. Such "externalities" have long been a primary concern of those critical of school voucher systems. However, the concern is usually not very carefully stated. The presence of externalities by itself does not imply that vouchers would lead to an inefficient outcome. If all students benefit equally from the average characteristics of students in a school, then when talented students exit, their old classmates' loss is exactly equal to their new classmates' gain. Whether the net effect on overall test scores is positive or negative will depend upon whether having well-endowed classmates helps students who previously performed poorly more than good students.

Witte points out that parents at least claim that academic performance is one of their primary goals in choosing private schools. However, the real issue is not what parents *think* they do, but how successful they are at identifying the "best" schools. Parents spend $543 per year to send their children to Catholic elementary schools and $1,777 per pupil for Catholic high schools, as shown in table 6-1 of Hoxby's chapter. Yet, if Witte's summary of the literature is to be believed, we have little evidence that private schools actually increase student performance. Clearly, parents must *think* they are buying something when they spend more to attend private schools or when they pay more to live in a neighborhood with schools that are presumably better. Are these parents merely using the socioeconomic status of the students as an indicator of school quality or can they, in fact, identify the schools with the greatest "value-added"?

If parents cannot identify the schools with the greatest value-added, then we are left with the problem, pursued elsewhere in this volume, of whether a central authority can identify the "best schools" using student test scores and attempting to identify "value-added." Further, if parents must rely upon "school report cards" to identify the best schools, and we are confident that these report cards actually carry useful information, we have to consider why a school choice program would be better than a central administration at rewarding the schools so identified as being effective. If the treatment effect of attending a particular school is fairly uniform, then centralized performance incentive systems are likely to be superior, since they do not have the added problem of hurting the youths who are left behind when students move. On the other hand, the more heterogeneous the treatment effect (that is, "different strokes work for different folks"), the more effective parents may be in matching their youth to the right schools. Therefore, the desirability of "choice" relative to other incentive programs will depend upon just how heterogeneous the treatment effects are and whether the effect of having "good" classmates benefits some students more than others.

While Witte uses the existing literature to piece together an image of what a choice system might produce, Caroline Minter Hoxby believes that hints of a possible future are right under our noses. She first studies differences in private school subsidies that are associated with differences in the historical proportion of Catholic adherents in the area. Taking this variation in subsidies as a natural experiment in vouchers, she then attributes any difference in school performance that is associated with these same demographic differences as being "caused by" the differences in private school subsidies.

Using the metaphor of the randomized controlled experiment, the approach is conceptually appealing. Suppose that tomorrow the federal government paid varying proportions of private school tuition in different MSA's. Such subsidies would be very much like a voucher program. We could then measure student performance in public schools in those cities. If we knew that the subsidies were scattered around randomly, and the vouchers had no effect, we would not expect to find any difference in student test scores. Therefore we could attribute any difference in student test scores that we do observe between cities to the effect of providing vouchers. The critical difference between such a hypothetical experiment and Hoxby's evidence is that we do not *know* that we would have found no difference in student test scores in the districts with large vouchers if there were no effect of the subsidies themselves. Our job as readers is to ask ourselves whether we believe that the differences observed constitute a "natural experiment."

More specifically, Hoxby estimates equations of the following form:

$$Y_{ij} = \delta_1 Subsidy_j + X_{ij}\delta_3 + X_j\delta_4 + \epsilon_{ij},$$

where Y_{ij} represents various outcomes (private school attendance, test scores, highest grade completed and log wage) for person i from MSA j (including those attending both private and public schools); $subsidy_j$ is the average subsidy per pupil at private schools in MSA j; X_j is a vector of MSA characteristics including the proportion of the population that was Catholic in 1980, and X_{ij} measures a number of family background characteristics. She fears that the variable, $subsidy_j$, may be correlated with unobserved characteristics, such as the quality of public schools in the MSA. Therefore, she chooses to pursue an instrumental variables approach, using the change in the percentage of the population that were Catholic adherents between 1950 and 1980 (and that change squared) as instruments:

$$
\begin{aligned}
Subsidy_j &= \gamma_1(\%\,Cath80_j - \%\,Cath50_j) \\
&\quad + \gamma_2(\%\,Cath80_j - \%\,Cath50_j)^2 + X_j\gamma_3 + \epsilon_j \\
&= -\gamma_1\%\,Cath50_j + \gamma_2\%\,Cath50_j^2 \\
&\quad - \gamma_2\%\,Cath80_j\%\,Cath50_j + X_j\phi_3 + \epsilon_j.
\end{aligned}
$$

Since X_j includes the percentage of the population that are Catholic adherents in 1980 and that percentage squared, the source of identification is simply the percentage of the population that were Catholic adherents in 1950, its square, *and* the interaction between the percentage that were Catholic in 1950 with the percentage that were Catholic in 1980.

As Hoxby summarizes her results, she concludes that a $100 increase in subsidies leads to the following outcomes, each defined for non-Catholic, non-Hispanic white youth attending public schools: a 0.28 percentage point increase in private school enrollment; a 0.21 grade-level increase in educational attainment, with even larger effects for Catholics and African Americans; a 1.2 percent increase in wages, with larger effects for Catholics; and a 0.027 standard deviation increase in test scores (as measured by the AFQT).

However, as is always the case with instrumental variables estimates, it is worthwhile spending a few moments unpacking the first and second stages to see how the sausage was made. According to the estimates in the chapter, γ_1 and γ_2 were estimated to be 5.0 and -0.17 respectively, suggesting that those SMSAs with 10 percentage points *more* Catholic adherents in 1950 offered approximately $50 *less* in subsidies per pupil on average (holding the proportion of Catholic adherents in 1980 constant.)[3] As an explanation, one might hypothesize that those areas with a longer-standing Catholic population may simply enroll more students in Catholic schools, leading to lower subsidies per pupil.

Though appealing, this cannot be the explanation: Because the instrumental variables estimate in table 6-2 is positive, the impact of the historical Catholic population in the first stage must have the *same sign* (at the mean) as the effect of the Catholic population on private school enrollment. Using the instrumental variable estimate of the effect of subsidies in table 6-2 (0.41), it is possible to infer the relationship between the instrument and private school enrollment.[4] A 10 percentage point increase in the number of Catholic adherents in 1950 is apparently associated with an approximately 0.20 percentage point decrease in private school enrollment rates. ($0.50 \times 0.41 = 0.20$).

To summarize this "natural experiment" that Hoxby exploits, those areas with more Catholics in 1950 have smaller subsidies today and enroll fewer students in private school. This gives us another way of stating the

3. In making this calculation, I assumed that 20 percent of the population were Catholic adherents on average.
4. If there were only one instrument (Z) for a regressor (X), then the instrumental variables estimate of dY/dX is simply the ratio of the ordinary least squares estimate of dY/dZ over the ordinary least squares estimate of dX/dZ.

results in the paper, which makes the instrumental variables strategy more transparent. Using the results in tables 6-2 and 6-5, a 10 percentage point *increase* in Catholic adherents per capita in 1950 (holding the 1980 Catholic population constant) was associated with the following outcomes, each defined for non-Catholic, non-Hispanic white youth attending public schools: a $50 *decrease* in private school subsidies per pupil; a 0.20 percentage point *decrease* in private school enrollment; a 0.10 grade-level *decrease* in educational attainment, with even larger effects for Catholics and African Americans; a 0.6 percent *decrease* in wages, with larger effects for Catholics; and a 0.013 standard deviation *decrease* in test scores as measured by the AFQT.

To believe the instrumental variable estimates, one must be willing to assume that the effect of the historical Catholic population on all of the outcomes (private school enrollment, educational attainment, wages, and AFQT scores) operated only through the size of the private school subsidies. The standard statistical tests merely allow one to ask whether one would have gotten different results with various subsets of the instruments. However, such tests are only as good as one's best instrument.

While I do not have any strong reasons to doubt the assumption, I do not believe that it is self-evident either. A change in the proportion of the population that are Catholic adherents may simply identify the MSAs with the fastest population growth.[5] If population growth or decline has a direct effect on wages (excess demand?) or educational attainment (overcrowded schools?), then these would violate the assumptions needed to apply these techniques and spoil the experiment. My prior expectation would have been that a larger historical Catholic presence in an area (conditional upon current Catholic population) would have been associated with higher private school attendance, simply due to the effect of parents' attachment to schools. In fact, the opposite was true. I can only guess that most of the action in the change in Catholic adherence happened in the South and the West. In such analyses, even a weak correlation between the instrumental variables and other determinants of student performance could lead to large biases.

But suppose for a minute that the instruments are valid: in other words, that the only effect of the historical Catholic population on the outcomes

5. The source of the variation is not just demographic change, but adherence as well. To the extent that the time trend in adherence conditional upon being Catholic is similar in different regions of the country, this source of variation would simply be absorbed in the constant. Therefore, it is only SMSA-specific levels and changes in adherence that help identify the effect.

of interest operated through the size of private school subsidies per pupil. In that case, the instrumental variable estimates do provide us with some insight into the results of an experiment. But we need to be clear about the rules of the "voucher program" that generated these long-run equilibria. Consider, for a moment, private school subsidy plans A, B, C, and D.

Under plan A, Catholic school administrators are given a fixed pot of money for educating students that does not rise when enrollment rises. Under plan B, Catholic school administrators receive $1,000 for every new student they enroll. Under plan C, Catholic school administrators receive a matching grant for every tuition dollar they collect. Under plan D, Catholic school administrators receive a portion of the public subsidy attached to every public school student they enroll and public school revenues are reduced accordingly.

One might expect that the behavioral responses of private and public schools would be very different under each of these plans. For instance, a plan under which private school funding was based upon enrollment would have stronger implications: it would give private schools incentives to enroll more students and have larger effects on public schools. Moreover, if public schools lose revenue, their incentive to keep students would be stronger. Hoxby interprets the results as if plan D had been implemented. Clearly, that would be the experiment that would be most relevant to the current debate about vouchers. However, we do not know what type of experiment has been run for us. Any of the above plans, and many others, would be consistent with the evidence provided. All we know is that increases in the Catholic population were associated with higher spending per pupil at Catholic schools and higher private school enrollment. Without additional instruments that allowed us to identify both a supply and a demand function for private education—and therefore identify whether the "experiment" meant a shift in the supply curve or a change in slope, and so on—we could not know how the subsidy "experiment" we were evaluating was structured. Therefore, even if we believe that we have an experiment, we do not, in fact, know what type of educational policy was being tested.

As both chapters readily acknowledge, the primary attractiveness of a choice system is the hope that it would provide incentives for existing public schools to improve or perish. Yet we do not yet have sufficient experience with a choice system to know how large these effects might be. While Witte concentrates on identifying the types of parents who are likely to choose to move and on the likely test score effects for those moving, he is the first to admit that we have very little evidence regarding these "systemic effects." Hoxby has attempted to look around our world to seek out variation that mimics such an experiment, but even her evidence does not allow us to be sufficiently specific to anticipate the outcomes of any particular form of school choice. To state the problem plainly, we do not know how public schools would react to a voucher program.

The federal government should be willing to pay for good baseline data and work with those school systems interested in experimenting with various forms of choice to develop an evaluation scheme. Anyone willing to test the waters helps us all. The federal government should play the role of evaluator and clearinghouse. To be sure, this will take time. But there is plenty to be done in the interim. For instance, school systems could be developing some of the prerequisites of a choice system—such as school report cards—that may be valuable by themselves.

Finally, I would note that there may be lessons to be learned from the experience with Pell grants in higher education, an educational voucher program established in 1973. Pell grants—the primary federal means-tested grant program for postsecondary education—give low-income students vouchers they can use at any approved postsecondary institution, public or private. Many of the same issues are involved. For instance, the most able students may be drawn to leave community colleges and are more likely to attend private schools as a result of such vouchers. Private for-profit proprietary schools have sprung up, raising concerns about fraud. Private colleges are not compelled to enroll any low-income student who wants to attend, but can be selective in their admissions decisions. Despite the fact that Pell grants may share some of the pitfalls of a K–12 educational voucher program, few of those who are nervous about K–12 vouchers would argue that we should drop Pell grants and redirect the same money to increase direct funding of public institutions. Clearly, there are differences between the postsecondary and K–12 sectors. But those who support Pell grants but oppose K–12 vouchers should be clear about what those distinctions are.

PART THREE

Allocation of Funds

CHAPTER SEVEN

The Allocation of Resources to Special Education and Regular Instruction

Hamilton Lankford and James Wyckoff

M ANY RESEARCHERS, policymakers, and practitioners believe that despite the expenditure of substantial additional resources, today's public
elementary and secondary students are performing only modestly better
than students ten or twenty years ago.[1] They often argue that too few re
sources are reaching the classroom, and that when money is spent on class
room uses, it is not spent productively to increase achievement. To evaluate
this argument, it is necessary to examine how school districts spend their
money. But despite hundreds of production function studies exploring the
relationships between overall inputs and outcomes, there is little understanding of the forces behind the allocation of school district expenditures.
Few of the production function studies employ detailed data on inputs,
and virtually none take account of the entire range of expenditures made
by school districts.

However, researchers have recently begun using state databases to examine how districts allocate expenditures.[2] This chapter will focus most
heavily on expenditure data from New York State, which provide some
support for the notion that an increasing portion of the budget went to
administrative and educational support uses at the expense of classroom

We have benefited from the comments of Jane Hannaway, Helen Ladd, participants at
the Brookings Institution conference, and seminar participants at the University of Kentucky,
the University of Maryland, and Williams College. The chapter was written while Lankford
was in residence at the Mellon Project on Higher Education Finance at Williams College
and Wyckoff was an NSF/ASA fellow at the U.S. Bureau of the Census.

1. See Hanushek and Rivkin (1994).
2. National data are notably weak in identifying many expenditure categories and do
not provide consistent categorization over time. State data are more detailed. Lankford
and Wyckoff (1995) employ school district data over a thirteen-year period in New York.
Monk and Roellke (1994) examine very detailed school-level data for New York, and
Nakib (1994) examines school-level data from Florida. Also see Picus and Nakib (1993).

instruction. For example, the share of resources spent on regular teaching in New York State fell from 53.1 percent in the 1979–80 school year to 48.8 percent in the 1992–93 year; over the same time period, the share of resources spent on special education expanded from 5.0 percent to 11.3 percent. What has driven the large increases in special education expenditures? Have these increases reduced resources going to regular classrooms, or have other factors, such as enrollments and revenues, also changed to mitigate the effect of increased special education allocations?

This chapter addresses these questions, and more generally examines the relationships among regular instructional expenditures, special education spending, spending in other budget areas, school district revenues, and enrollments for regular and disabled students. Although there has been much discussion about these relationships, there has been no systematic research that statistically examines the relationships among various expenditure categories.

Special Education in Public Schools

The education of disabled children became a major concern of school districts in 1975 with the enactment of P.L. 94-142, the Education for All Handicapped Children Act (currently the Individuals with Disabilities Education Act). Although prior legislation had drawn attention to concerns about educating disabled students, P.L. 94-142 initiated a period in which the federal government became much more active in the regulation and financing of special education.[3] For example, the law called for federal reimbursement to the states for each special education student, without regard to the handicapping condition.[4] Although the federal government provides about 8 percent of the average per pupil expenditure for disabled students, the federal presence and regulation have led to substantially increased involvement by state and local governments.[5] On average, states

3. See Verstegen (1994) for a summary of the history surrounding the development and intent of P.L. 94-142.

4. Hartman (1980) has observed that this creates incentives for schools to identify and treat disabled students with the least severe disabilities in order to maximize net revenue. Some have suggested that these incentives lead to overidentification of special education students as a revenue source for school districts. See for example, Parrish (1993) and Parrish and Verstegen (1994) for a discussion and summary of this research. This issue is discussed in more detail below.

5. Parrish and Verstegen (1994, p. 3).

pay for 56 percent and local governments pay 36 percent of special education expenditures. However, there is wide variation in the state portion of special education expenditures, varying from 85 percent in Alabama to 17 percent in Oregon.[6] To some extent, this variation reflects different approaches to financing special education.

State funding formulas for special education basically take one of four formulas: flat-grant, pupil-weighted, resource-based, or cost-based. Flat-grant formulas provide a fixed payment per special education student that may vary by type of disability. Pupil-weighted formulas assign specific weighting factors to various classifications of special education students based on estimates of the cost of providing services to these students. Resource-based formulas reimburse districts for specific resources, such as teachers. Cost-based formulas reimburse districts for some portion of their actual special education costs. These formulas affect the net cost to school districts of classifying students in various special education categories. Recently some states, including Pennsylvania, have moved to reimbursement systems that provide lump-sum payments to districts based on total district enrollment, independent of both the number of students identified as disabled and the actual expenditures for these students. In such a case, a district bears the entire cost of increments in special education expenditures.

The number of students identified as disabled grew at a steady pace between 1980 and 1992, increasing by 24 percent over the period.[7] In contrast, total enrollments increased by less than 1 percent during this period. As a result, special education students rose from 9.6 percent of all students in 1979–80 to 11.8 percent in 1991–92. The composition of special education students changed as well. In 1979–80, 22 percent of special education students were mentally retarded and 32 percent had some specific learning disability. By 1991–92, mental retardation accounted for just 11 percent of the disabled, while 45 percent had some specific learning disability. This shift resulted from a 50 percent reduction in children diagnosed as mentally retarded and a tripling of those diagnosed as learning disabled.

The shifting composition of special education students reflects the fact that the classification of learning disabilities has undergone profound changes over the last twenty years as researchers have learned more about causes and treatment. Advances in diagnostics for learning disabilities have

6. O'Reilly (1993, p. 13).
7. This and the following data on special education enrollments are found in U.S. Department of Education, *Annual Report to Congress on the Implementation of Education of the Handicapped Act,* various years.

resulted in the classification of children as learning disabled who previously would have gone unidentified.[8] Disagreement remains on the definition of what constitutes a learning disability. Consequently, a child diagnosed as learning disabled in one setting could be diagnosed as mildly mentally retarded or as having no handicap somewhere else.[9] Similar imprecision affects the definition of emotionally disturbed special education students.[10] Donald Macmillan suggests that the referral process for identification, which typically begins with teachers, embodies among other things, teacher tolerance for deviant behavior, availability of support for low-achieving students, and the modal achievement level in a given classroom.[11] Naomi Zigmond indicates:

> In a school district (or individual teacher's class) where there is pressure to increase the achievement levels of modal students, and where tolerance of student variance is low, there is an advantage to identifying a student as having learning disabilities *if* it permits that student to access special services reserved only for students with that label *and* removes the student from the responsibility (and accountability mechanisms) of mainstream education. Under these circumstances, many underachievers with *and without* disabilities may be assigned to special education programs for students with learning disabilities.[12]

There is latitude as to which students are identified as special education students. As a result, changes in special education enrollments may reflect changes in the choices made by teachers, administrators, parents and students.

Expenditure data at the national level for special education students are very limited and out of date. As part of its report to Congress on the implementation of P.L. 94-142, the U.S. Department of Education did report special education expenditure data from 1981–82 through 1987–88.[13] However, no national special education expenditure data have been collected since 1988, and the existing data have insufficient detail about how

8. Berninger and Abbott (1994) and Moats and Lyon (1993) describe the lack of a common definition of learning disabilities and the resulting differences in identification rates.

9. Macmillan (1993) describes the relationship between mentally retarded and learning disabled students.

10. Zigmond (1993).

11. Macmillan (1993).

12. Zigmond (1993, pp. 264–65). (Emphasis in original.)

13. In addition, Moore and others (1988) collected data from eighty school districts in eighteen states for the 1985–86 school year. Although well designed and carried out, this analysis is now somewhat dated.

the remainder of school district budgets are allocated across functional categories and over time. Therefore we turn to state data for our analysis. The remaining analysis considers special education enrollment and financial data and detailed budgeting data for school districts of the state of New York.

Enrollment of special education students in New York State mirrored the national trend by growing substantially over the period from 1979–80 to 1992–93. Special education student enrollments increased by 65 percent over this period, while enrollments of regular students decreased by 13 percent. Special education students are classified into a number of categories, including emotionally disturbed, speech-impaired, mentally retarded, and learning disabled. The first three categories have remained fairly constant as a share of total enrollments, but the share of New York students identified as learning disabled rose from less than 1 percent of total enrollment in 1979–80 to more than 7 percent of total enrollment by 1992–93.

Even within many disability categories there is fairly wide variation in the placement setting (and hence cost) to which the student is assigned. For example, New York categorizes its public school placements according to whether students are pulled out of regular classes at least two periods a week, but not more than 20 percent of the time; out of regular classes between 20 and 60 percent of the time; out of regular classes at least 60 percent of the time; or attending special public day schools.[14] The relationship between type of disability and treatment setting is shown in table 7-1.[15] Students with learning disabilities accounted for 59.9 percent of all public nonresidential special education placements during the 1992–93 school year and were fairly evenly divided between the various placement settings. However, most (nonresidential) students with emotional disturbance, mental retardation, or multiple disabilities are placed in higher cost settings, which means either outside regular classes at least 60 percent of the time or in a special public day school.

14. These are the four placement settings defined under the New York regular public excess-cost aid, which accounted for more than 80 percent of all state aid for special education in 1992–93. In addition, there are private day schools, public and private residential schools, and home and hospital living situations. These placements are generally the most expensive, but represented less than 5 percent of the total special education enrollment in New York during the 1992–93 school year.

15. The six disability types not shown in table 7-1 each constitute less than 2 percent of public nonresidential special education students and 4 percent in total.

Table 7-1. *Relationship between Type of Disability and Placement, All Public Nonresidential Special Education Students, New York State, 1992–93*[a]

| Type of disability | Percent of all nonresidential special education students | Placement setting | | |
		Less than 20 percent[b]	20 to 60 percent[c]	More than 60 percent and special public day[d]
Learning disabled	59.9	25.2	36.0	38.8
Speech impaired	13.7	49.1	11.4	39.5
Emotionally disturbed	12.2	10.8	15.4	73.8
Mentally retarded	6.0	7.2	8.0	84.8
Multiple disabilities	3.8	8.1	8.3	83.6
Total, all disabilities	100.0	25.5	26.6	47.9

a. Authors' calculations from the state summary of the PD-4 survey made available to us by the New York State Education Department.
b. Pulled out of regular classes at least two periods a week but not more than 20 percent of the time.
c. Pulled out of regular classes 20–60 percent of the time.
d. Pulled out of regular classes at least 60 percent of the time or attending special day schools.

There appears to be wide variation across districts in the rate of identification of special education students as well as in placement settings. Table 7-2 shows that during the 1992–93 school year, the special education identification rate was about twice as high in districts at the ninetieth percentile as in districts at the tenth percentile (13.7 percent versus 7.3 percent). Large differences in identification rates, in total and for each placement setting, have existed through time, as is shown by comparing the 1979–80 distribution with that for 1992–93. The data behind this table suggest some other connections as well. School districts with a higher incidence of students pulled out at least 60 percent are likely to have fewer of the students pulled out 20 to 60 percent. A similar relationship exists between the students pulled out 20 to 60 percent and the students pulled out less than 20 percent.[16] This suggests the possibility that districts may have discretion to alter the classification of students at the margin. The wide variation in identification rates also suggests this possibility. The issue will be examined later in this chapter.

The policy environment for special education in New York State, like that in most states, is complex and idiosyncratic. New York has four different formulas that specifically provide aid for special education students, and several other formulas—like transportation aid—that reimburse

16. The rate of the first correlation is −0.28; the rate of the second is −0.14. However, there appears to be no relationship between the students pulled out at least 60 percent and the students pulled out less than 20 percent.

Table 7-2. *Rate of Identification of Nonresidential Special Education Students, by Placement Setting as a Percentage of All Students, New York State School Districts, 1979–80 and 1992–93*

	1979–80		1992–93	
Placement setting	10th percentile	90th percentile	10th percentile	90th percentile
20 percent or less	0	3.6	0	3.1
20 to 60 percent	0	3.4	2.4	7.7
60 percent or more	0.7	3.9	1.9	6.8
All placements	2.0	8.5	7.3	13.7

school districts for a portion of certain costs that are often larger on a per pupil basis for special education students than for regular students. As a result of the different formulas, floors and ceilings, adjustments for wealth, save harmless provisions, and so on, there is wide variation in the addi tional state aid that a district receives when it identifies an additional student to receive special education. For most of the aid, districts receive nonmatching reimbursements, although in some limited cases the state matches a school district's allowable expenditures. Given that much of the aid results from something called the "public excess-cost formula," which gives districts additional reimbursements based on the number of students in each special education classification, there may be a financial incentive to categorize students as needing special education.[17] Districts would have such an incentive to the extent that the reimbursement exceeds the cost of providing the services required for that placement. That incentive will tend to be greater for districts with higher aid ratios (lower wealth) and higher approved operating expenditures per pupil, as long as certain ceilings and cutoffs are not reached. A district in the top 10 percent of state aid reim bursement per special education student had twice the financial incentive to classify a student for special education as did a district in the bottom 10 percent. Of course, financial incentive is just one of the reasons that some school districts might have larger special education enrollments than others.

17. Because the definitions employed to determine if a student should be classified as needing special education are open to wide variation in interpretation, the issue of whether school districts are influenced by the potential financial benefits has often been raised. For example, Leo Klagholz, education commissioner for New Jersey, recently was quoted as saying that "he believed the rise in the number of children in some categories (of special education) could be at least partially attributable to efforts on the part of local school districts to increase revenues from the state." Robert J. Braun, "Klagholz Fears Schools Inflate Special Ed Need," *Newark Star-Ledger,* March 19, 1995.

The growth in special education student enrollment and expenditures has led many to assert that special education expenditures have increased at the expense of resources for regular students. During the early 1990s, many school districts were experiencing the fiscal pressures of reduced growth in state aid and mounting resistance to property tax increases. In this climate, large special education budgets became less tolerable,[18] and it has become conventional wisdom that increased spending on special education has crowded out spending on regular students. To explore this issue, we next examine special education spending per pupil over time and its relationship to per pupil spending on regular students.

Per Pupil Expenditures for Regular and Disabled Students

The debate in the education production function literature over whether money matters for educational performance considers the relationship between expenditures and achievement. Invariably, empirical studies make no distinction between resources allocated to regular students and those going to disabled students, who are not tested for achievement. Nor do such studies distinguish between whether resources allocated to regular students are ending up in the classroom, or in administration, transportation, and other uses. If a disproportionate share of increased spending is not arriving in the classrooms of regular students, then researchers who use total per pupil expenditures on education may systematically understate the effect of such expenditures. To understand how resource allocations to regular classrooms have changed over time, it is necessary to isolate expenditures made on behalf of regular students.

There are very few estimates along these lines. Several studies have produced detailed estimates of the cost of special education for particular districts at a point in time, but none appear to have examined these costs or expenditures in a systematic or consistent way over time.[19]

18. For example, Herman Badillo, New York City Mayor Rudolph Giuliani's special advisor on education finance, "says the Board of Education has allowed special education and bilingual programs to develop bloated payrolls, draining money from students in regular classrooms." The board's budget director, Leonard Hellenbrand, "agreed that regular students had suffered as a result of court ordered increases in special-education spending." Sam Dillon, "Badillo Contends That the Cost of Special Education Is Inflated," *New York Times,* August 14, 1994, p. 1.

19. For example, see Chaikind, Danielson, and Brauen (1993); Rossmiller, Hale, and Frohreich (1970); Kakalik and others (1981); Moore and others (1988); and Chambers and Duenas (1994).

Table 7-3. *Allocation of the Real Increase in Education Expenditures in New York State and City between 1979–80 and 1992–93*[a]

Expenditure category	1980 share of total expenditure (percent)	1993 share of total expenditure (percent)	Real change in expenditure (thousands of dollars)	Share of real change (percent)
New York State (excluding New York City)				
Teaching, regular	53.1	48.8	1,073,591	33.3
Teaching, disabilities	5.0	11.3	1,099,305	34.1
Tuition	0.7	1.2	100,513	3.1
Central administration	3.1	3.5	156,423	4.9
Building supervision	4.9	4.5	93,156	2.9
Curriculum development	0.5	0.6	28,338	0.9
Pupil personnel services	3.9	4.1	157,072	4.9
Other educational support	2.0	2.3	102,777	3.2
Operations and maintenance	10.6	8.6	47,043	1.5
Miscellaneous	3.6	4.1	191,114	5.9
Transportation	5.5	5.6	189,990	5.9
Insurance	0.6	0.9	60,117	1.9
Debt	6.1	1.5	78,618	2.3
Total	100.0	100.0	3,223,819	100.0
New York City				
Teaching, regular	54.3	47.7	562,806	28.5
Teaching, disabilities	6.9	18.6	1,045,638	53.0
Tuition	0.6	3.8	263,193	13.3
Central administration	2.2	3.3	132,449	6.7
Building supervision	7.2	3.0	−184,435	−9.3
Curriculum development	0.2	0.2	7,863	0.4
Pupil personnel services	2.7	2.5	35,034	1.8
Other educational support	1.0	0.3	−33,193	−1.7
Operations and maintenance	9.6	8.8	126,957	6.4
Miscellaneous	2.5	1.8	−7,527	−0.4
Transportation	6.0	6.4	148,383	7.5
Insurance	0.0	0.0	−302	0.0
Debt	6.9	3.5	−123,312	−6.2
Total	100.0	100.0	1,973,555	100.0

Source: Authors' calculations based on data from annual financial reports (ST-3) of New York State Department of Education.

a. All dollar amounts have been adjusted to 1993 dollars using the state and local government purchases component of the implicit price deflator for gross domestic product (*Economic Report of the President, 1995*).

Allocation of Resources

As a starting point, consider table 7-3, which divides expenditures in New York State and New York City into thirteen categories. From the 1979–80 school year until 1992–93, total real educational expenditures in New York State (excluding New York City) rose by $3.2 billion.[20] Over that same time, the share of total spending going to regular teaching fell from 53.1 percent to 48.8 percent, while the share going to disabilities teaching rose from 5.0 to 11.3 percent. If regular instruction had maintained its share of total spending, it would have received an additional $700 million in 1992–93. Where did this money go? Some of it may have gone to central administration, pupil personnel services, other educational support, transportation, and curriculum development, all of which slightly increased their share of total educational expenditures over this time frame. However, special education is by far the largest source of new spending. In fact, slightly more of the increase in total spending was allocated to instruction for special education students than to instructional spending for regular students. The importance of special education spending is magnified in New York City, where the increase in regular teaching expenditures was about half of that for special education teaching.[21]

However, table 7-3 does not account for enrollment changes that occurred over the period; it simply indicates the changing share of total dollars. Regular enrollments in districts outside New York City decreased by 20 percent over the 1980–93 period, while special education enrollments increased by 70 percent. As a result, it is necessary to recompute these differences on a per pupil basis.

Estimates of expenditures per pupil for regular and disabled students are presented in table 7-4 for New York City and the remaining school districts in New York State. For the first row, overall expenditure per pupil is simply total expenditures divided by average daily enrollment over the school year (as defined by the State Education Department), regardless of the status of students. However, dividing up expenditures between regular and special education students is not straightforward. Since most special education students spend some portion of their day in regular classrooms, spending on teaching for special education students must include both instruction expenditures for those students in placements outside regular classrooms and a prorated share of the instructional expenditures for regular classrooms and of other educational expenditures.

---

20. Unless otherwise stated, we employ real expenditures measured in 1993 dollars. We deflate nominal expenditures by the state and local component of the GDP implicit price deflator. Ideally, we would like to deflate by a cost of education that takes regional differences into account; however, such a measure is not available.

21. A detailed description of the data and definitions behind these statements is provided in appendix A.

Table 7-4. *Estimated per Pupil Expenditures for Regular and Special Education Students, by Assumptions about Resource Use, New York City and State, 1980 and 1993*
Amounts in 1993 dollars

Resource use assumption	New York State (excluding New York City)			New York City		
	1980	*1993*	*Percent change*	*1980*	*1993*	*Percent change*
Overall expenditure	6,228	9,295	49.2	6,317	7,799	23.5
Resource use assumption 1[a]						
Spending on teaching						
Per regular student	3,427	4,902	43.1	3,631	4,125	13.6
Per special education student	6,909	11,027	59.6	7,376	16,396	122.3
Total spending						
Per regular student	6,015	8,544	42.0	6,060	6,545	8.0
Per special education student	9,497	14,668	54.4	9,805	18,817	91.9
Resource use assumption 2[b]						
Spending on teaching						
Per regular student	3,375	4,734	40.3	554	4,002	12.6
Per special education student	7,708	12,235	58.7	8,414	17,474	107.7
Total spending						
Per regular student	5,757	7,602	32.0	5,781	6,188	7.0
Per special education student	12,490	17,806	42.6	13,588	21,958	61.6
Resource use assumption 3[c]						
Spending on teaching						
Per regular student	3,349	4,653	38.9	3,517	3,943	12.1
Per special education student	8,099	12,809	58.2	8,917	17,989	101.7
Total spending						
Per regular student	5,662	7,388	30.5	5,655	6,028	6.6
Per special education student	13,905	19,408	39.6	15,299	23,361	52.7

a. Assumes that each FTE pupil uses same quantity of resources outside special education classrooms.
b. Assumes that the FTEs of special education students spending less than 20 percent of their time outside regular classes have a weight of 1.1 (10 percent more resources than regular students); those pulled out 20 to 60 percent of the time have a weight of 1.5; and those pulled out 60 percent or more have a weight of 2.5.
c. Assumes that the FTEs of special education students spending less than 20 percent of their time outside regular classes have a weight of 1.15; those pulled out 20 to 60 percent have a weight of 1.75; and those pulled out 60 percent or more have a weight of 3.25.

One assumption is that regular and special education students in a regular classroom each receive the same level of service. In this case, a special education student in a regular classroom would receive 1/nth of the resources, where n is the total class size. A similar assumption could be made with respect to nonteaching resources: regular and special education students share equally in pupil personnel services, administration, operations and maintenance. This assumption is reflected in the estimates of per pupil spending on teaching and overall per pupil spending for both New York State and City, reported in the section of table 7-4 identified as "Resource use assumption 1."

An alternative assumption would be that special education students receive more resources per pupil than regular students, with the difference depending on the severity of the disability. A natural step here is to assign varying weights to students in the three categories of placement settings: that is, those who spend less than 20 percent of their time outside regular class, those who spend 20–60 percent outside regular class, and those who spend more than 60 percent outside regular class. Based on studies that examine the costs of providing special education, we believe that the estimates of spending per pupil in these three categories with weights of 1.1, 1.5, and 2.5, are the most plausible.[22] For example, a special education student who spends 20–60 percent of time outside a regular classroom will use 1.5 times as many regular classroom resources while in a regular class as other students, a multiple that does not count the resources spent directly on special education. In table 7-4, the rows labeled "Resource use assumption 2" use these weights and show that spending on teaching for regular New York State students increased by about 40 percent over the 1980–93 period, while teaching expenditures for special education students increased by 59 percent. Thus spending on teaching for special education students is increasing nearly 50 percent more rapidly than spending for regular students. Total spending per regular student increased from about $5,800 in 1980 to $7,600 in 1993, a 32 percent increase, while total spending per special education student increased from $12,500 to $17,800, a 43 percent increase.

The final portion of table 7-4, "Resource use assumption 3," offers a scenario where the costs of special education students are assumed to be higher. Here, the spending weights for the three categories are 1.15, 1.75, and 3.25.

Expenditures in New York districts outside New York City show substantial increases across all the per pupil measures, regardless of the weigh-

22. In 1980 the New York State Education Department conducted a detailed estimate of special education costs to determine the appropriate weights for each of the three special education classifications (less than 20 percent, between 20 and 60 percent, and greater than 60 percent) used in our analysis. Based on this analysis, the state developed weights of 1.13, 1.80, and 2.70 respectively. Additionally, the ratio of special education expenditures to regular expenditures is about 2.2 in 1980 and 2.3 in 1993. This is consistent with previous cost studies; see note 21. In the case of regular teaching resources going to special education students, these weights are used together with the fraction indicating the portion of the day that these students are in regular classes.

tings employed. However, expenditures reported for New York City suggest that special education per pupil spending has shown dramatic increases, both for teaching and in total, while per pupil expenditures for regular students have barely increased. According to the second resource use assumption (our intermediate case), total spending on regular students increased from $5,800 per pupil in 1980 to $6,200 in 1993, an increase of 7 percent. Special education expenditures grew from $13,600 per pupil in 1980 to $22,000 in 1993, an overall growth of 62 percent. Although regular students in New York City and the rest of the state received about the same resources in 1980, by 1993 regular students in New York City were receiving nearly 20 percent fewer dollars than those residing in districts outside the city. It appears that per pupil expenditures in regular classrooms in New York City have suffered while per pupil special education spending has ballooned.

The rapid increase in special education expenditures in New York City is often attributed to a consent decree filed on behalf of Jose P., a disabled student, which has been in force since 1980. As a result of this decision, virtually every aspect of policy and administration of special education in New York City is protected by the consent decree and subject to negotiation with the plaintiff's legal representation. As a result, the Board of Education for New York City has very little discretion over special education expenditures.[23] Therefore the remainder of the school district budget—the non—special education portion—is subject to the fiscal pressures that face the city. This likely accounts for much of the disparity in the growth of per pupil spending between special education and regular students reported in table 7-4.[24]

These estimates illustrate vividly why measuring educational resources by average expenditure per student, as is often done in policy discussions and production function studies, can be so misleading. Compare overall expenditures per pupil at the top of table 7-4 with total spending for regular students. For districts outside New York City, overall expenditures per pupil in 1993 ($9,295) overstate our best estimate of expenditures per regular student ($7,602) by 22 percent. For New York City, overall expenditures per pupil are too high by 26 percent. Perhaps more important are

23. Information about the circumstances of special education in New York City is based on a conversation with Rebecca Cort, New York City coordinator for special education services, New York State Education Department.

24. For a detailed analysis of special education in New York City, see Fruchter and others (1995).

the overestimates of the growth in expenditures for each type of student. Overall expenditures per pupil grew by 49 percent from 1980 to 1993 in districts outside New York City. However, our intermediate estimate of the growth of total spending per pupil is 32 percent for regular students and 43 percent for special education students.[25] Thus the simple measure of overall expenditure per pupil overstates growth by about 50 percent for regular students and 30 percent for special education students. In New York City, the overall expenditure growth of 23.5 percent overstates actual growth for regular students by 16 percentage points, or 200 percent.[26]

Decomposing the Growth in Special Education Expenditures

Expenditures for special education students in New York State grew 220 percent from 1979–80 to 1992–93, which is an average annual rate of 9.4 percent. What accounted for this extraordinary growth? Some insights are gained by decomposing the total growth into two portions: one attributable to enrollment increases and one resulting from increases in

---

25. That growth for both types of students can be below that for the overall expenditures per pupil may at first seem curious, but it is largely due to declining enrollments of regular students and increasing enrollments of special education students. Only when the mix of regular and special education students is unchanged will the percentage changes in total expenditures for regular and special education students necessarily bound the percentage change in the overall expenditure per pupil. While this is relatively easy to prove, a simple example may be more insightful. Suppose that in time t_1, a school district spends $1,000 on each regular student, of which there are 100, and $2,000 on each special education student, of which there are 10. Average expenditures per pupil for all pupils is $1,091. In t_2, the district again spends $1,000 per pupil for regular students and $2,000 on each special education student. However, in t_2 there are 80 regular students and 17 special education students. Overall spending per pupil is now $1,175. Spending for each type of student remained constant, but overall expenditures per pupil increased by 8 percent due to the enrollment shifts. In this case, the failure to differentiate among types of students overstates the resources available to students in *both* groups.

26. Eleven states had overall enrollments that declined by at least 5 percent during the period from 1980–81 to 1992–93 (New York declined 6 percent). U.S. Department of Education (1994, pp. 52–53). These averages undoubtedly mask much larger enrollment reductions in some districts in these and other states. Special education enrollments have generally been increasing in most districts. As a result, it is likely that many places are experiencing the phenomenons of increasing special education and declining regular enrollments, causing overall per pupil expenditure growth rates to exceed either regular or special education per pupil growth rates. Furthermore, the effect is likely to be larger in many places than indicated here, as our results are for an average of 655 districts.

Table 7-5. *Growth in Total Expenditures for Special Education Students, Decomposed between Changes in Enrollment and Changes in Expenditures per Pupil, Selected Periods, 1980–93*
Percent

Item	1980–85	1985–89	1989–93
New York State (excluding New York City)			
Annual growth in expenditures for disabled students	8.1	7.8	5.1
Decomposition of change in expenditure			
Enrollment	79.2	22.9	89.7
Expenditures per pupil	20.8	77.1	10.3
Decomposition of change in enrollment			
60 percent or more	40.7	109.5	28.6
20–60 percent	53.7	34.3	79.3
20 percent or less	5.6	−43.8	−7.9
New York City			
Annual growth in expenditures for disabled students	12.9	5.2	3.0
Decomposition of change in expenditure			
Enrollment	79.0	−8.3	15.4
Expenditures per pupil	21.0	108.3	84.6
Decomposition of change in enrollment			
60 percent or more	24.8	196.4	−3.1
20–60 percent	24.3	52.2	795.2
20 percent or less	50.9	−148.6	692.1

expenditures per disabled student.[27] The results of this decomposition for New York districts over three subperiods are shown in table 7-5. In general, the three periods are characterized by very different decompositions.

Consider first the top half of table 7-5, describing the New York State districts outside New York City. The 1980–85 period is characterized by relatively large growth in total expenditures for special education stu-

---

27. The basic decomposition formula is $1 = [S_2(E_2 - E_1) + E_1(S_2 - S_1)]/(T_2 - T_1)$, where S denotes expenditures per pupil, E denotes enrollment, T denotes total expenditures, and the subscripts reflect time periods. E can be replaced by its components, the three disability groups, to further decompose the effects due to changes in enrollment. Ideally we would like to have expenditures per pupil by special education classification to identify which group is responsible for increasing per pupil costs. Such data are unavailable in New York.

dents.[28] About 80 percent of the expenditure increase during this period is attributable to increases in overall special education enrollments, and 20 percent results from increases in spending per pupil. This is the period with the highest growth in enrollment of students pulled out at least 60 percent (annual growth rate of 5.6 percent). These students, who are typically the most expensive to treat, accounted for 41 percent of the total increase in disabled enrollment during this period. In contrast, during 1989–93 enrollment changes also accounted for the bulk of the increase in total expenditures, but the annual growth rate in the students pulled out at least 60 percent was half of that in the first period (2.8 percent), accounting for only 29 percent of the total growth in disabled enrollment. The reduction in the overall expenditure growth rate from 8.1 percent in 1980–85 to 5.1 percent in 1989–93 largely reflects the changing mix of special education students. Expenditure growth in the 1985–89 period is driven by increases in expenditure per pupil, which results largely from a growth in the number of students pulled out at least 60 percent (109 percent of total).

In New York City, shown in the bottom half of table 7-5, the pattern is quite different. During 1980–85 the number of special education students exploded at an annual rate of 9.3 percent, with sizable increases occurring in all three disability groups. This enrollment growth accounted for most of the very large (nearly 13 percent) annual increases in spending on special education. In the two later periods, total enrollment did not increase much at all, with annual growth averaging 0.2 percent. This implies that increases in expenditures per pupil drove most of the disabled spending increases over the two more recent periods. Because the number of high-cost students did not increase during these two periods, per pupil spending increases were held down as well.

Explaining Enrollment Growth

Since enrollment increases dominate so much of the increase in total special education expenditures during the 1989–93 period, it is of interest to attempt to understand what accounts for the enrollment growth.

---

28. As described above, the expenditure numbers reflect a prorating of regular classroom expenditures to the three types of special education students based on the portion of the time they are in regular classrooms. We use the weights in table 7-4 under resource assumption 2.

The rates at which students are classified to receive special education can vary among school districts for two general reasons. First, school districts may have student populations with differing likelihoods of having disabilities. For example, there is evidence that students from lower socioeconomic backgrounds and babies born to substance-abusing mothers are more likely to sustain disabilities.[29] Second, the lack of clear, well-accepted definitions and reliable diagnostic methods for determining disabilities in schools creates the opportunity for identification rates to vary.

The reason for varying identification rates may simply be that the existing ambiguities create differences that are specific to the district but unrelated to ulterior motives of administrators, teachers, parents, or students. A more provocative assertion is that district personnel use the latitude in definitions and diagnostics to respond to other pressures they face. For example, many school districts are under pressure to improve academic performance, to raise revenue to meet ever increasing expenditures, or to address student behavioral problems. Pressures regarding academic performance in many public school districts create incentives to classify poorly performing students for special education so that they will not be subject to the same testing and reporting as regular students. Likewise, school districts may see the state special education aid formulas as a means to increase district revenues by classifying students at the margin for special education. Finally, school personnel may employ their identification discretion to move an unruly student from a regular class to a smaller special education class setting where that student can receive more supervision. School personnel do have some ability to pursue other goals through their decisions whether to classify students as needing special education, at least for students at the margin.

There is some weak evidence that school districts do identify students to some special education placements because of increased state aid. Table 7-6 shows the results of regression equations estimated to explain the enrollments in each of the three special education placement settings described above. Explanatory variables reflect the alternative reasons for differences in identification that occur across districts. We hypothesize that districts with larger enrollments, a stronger financial incentive (because of the charactistics of the aid formulas), a larger poor population (proxied by the number of students eligible for free and reduced-price school lunch), a larger population with limited English proficiency, and larger classes will have higher incidence of special education placement. We include dummy

29. Parrish and Verstegen (1994) discuss this literature.

Table 7-6. *Determinants of Special Education Enrollments*[a]

	Special education placement settings		
Variable	60 percent or more	20 to 60 percent	20 percent or less
Total enrollment	0.0108	0.0445**	0.0044
	(1.93)	(5.17)	(0.50)
Special education aid	0.00043*	0.00028	−0.00051
	(2.34)	(1.02)	(−1.79)
School lunch	0.0323**	0.0344**	−0.0064
	(8.32)	(5.77)	(−1.05)
Average class size	−0.161	0.3263	−0.0861
	(−0.85)	(1.12)	(−0.29)
Limited English proficiency	0.0046	−0.0073	−0.0059
	(0.24)	(−0.25)	(−0.20)
1990 year dummy	1.205*	3.477**	0.324
	(2.32)	(4.36)	(0.40)
1991 year dummy	1.623	7.600**	−1.681
	(2.914)	(8.90)	(−1.92)
1992 year dummy	2.048**	12.59**	−3.313**
	(3.49)	(13.98)	(−3.58)
N	2,540	2,540	2,540
Adjusted R^2	0.985	0.936	0.852

*Significant at the 5 percent level.
**Significant at the 1 percent level.
a. Results of fixed-effect, weighted regressions. Variables included in the regressions but not shown include the portion of a district's students who are black or Hispanic, the proportion of a district's teachers in three different experience ranges, and the district dummies. Observations are weighted by the inverse of total enrollment. Numbers in parentheses are *t*-statistics.

variables for 1990, 1991, and 1992.[30] We also include teacher experience, student racial variables, and district "fixed effects" as controls in the regression, although the results are not reported in the table.

The special education aid variable measures the dollar increase in public (excess-cost) aid that results from an additional weighted special education student, holding the number of total students constant. As shown in table 7-6, the effect is statistically significant for students pulled out of class more than 60 percent of the time, but the elasticity, 0.02, is very small. The effect of state aid is not statistically significant for the other two special education classifications. Thus, there is at best weak support for the notion

30. Detailed definitions of variables, along with the means and raw data, are available on request from the authors. The estimation employs a two-way fixed-effects model with each observation weighted by the inverse of its total enrollment to correct for heteroskedasticity.

that New York school districts alter special education classifications in response to the financial incentives of the state aid formula.[31]

A few other results from this regression are worth noting. The year dummy variables are consistently significant and take on higher values with the passage of time (except for the students pulled out 20 percent or less, for which two of the three year dummies are insignificant), suggesting a trend to increase special education enrollments, other things being equal. Finally, the enrollments of students pulled out 20 percent or less appear to be unaffected by any of the policy variables.

This descriptive work summarizes the financial setting that New York school districts face with respect to the funding of special education and regular students, but it does not reveal how districts alter their budget allocations in response to changes in aid or in regular and special education enrollments. To examine these relationships and to explore allocations across budget categories, we now turn to a statistical model of school district finance.

A Model of School District Finance

Several policy issues have been raised in this chapter: Are dollars reaching regular classrooms, or are they being diverted to other uses? Has special education crowded out spending on regular students? Are recent trends in special education enrollments and per pupil expenditures likely to put substantial pressure on school district budgets? We address these questions using information regarding the estimated links between expenditures by category and enrollments for both regular and disabled students. As noted earlier, a large body of empirical research is concerned with the determinants of *total* educational expenditures. In contrast, there is a striking void in research on the factors that affect the allocation of educational resources across expenditure categories and over time. However, in thinking about how to model the allocation of resources, we can draw on the analytical framework developed by those who have worked on total expenditures.

In modeling the determination of total expenditures, researchers typically assume that expenditures are affected by the incomes, tax prices, and

31. It should be noted that we have not examined district responses to public high-cost aid or private excess-cost aid. Although these classifications represent relatively small shares of the total dollars, per pupil reimbursements from the state can be very large. In the case of private excess-cost aid, reimbursements cover the full cost of treatment.

preferences of citizens (voters) in the district; by state and federal aid; and by cost factors, including the prices of educational inputs. The attributes of students and their parents may be reflected in both demand and the cost of attaining any given educational outcome. For example, better-educated parents may have greater demand for educational services, and students from such households may be able to achieve any given level of educational attainment at lower public cost as a result of links between home and school inputs. The standard practice is to specify a structural model of demand and cost that is consistent with an assumed median- or decisive-voter political equilibrium, where the median or decisive voter determines the political outcome. In such a model, total operating expenditures by a public school district are assumed to be a function of the decisive- or median-voter's income and tax price, state and federal aid, tastes for education (as proxied by student and community characteristics), and cost factors. In turn, these cost factors are assumed to be a function of the prices of educational inputs and environmental factors proxied by student body and community characteristics. Such a model is typically estimated using data for a cross-section of school districts.[32]

Two major problems complicate extending such a model to the analysis of how public education expenditures are allocated across a set of education services. First, the idea of a median or decisive voter is generally not applicable when considering a choice among a multidimensional set of alternatives, as in the allocation of resources by a school district between different educational services or different functional categories. There is no broadly recognized public choice model, comparable to the median-voter model, that provides guidance in specifying the allocation of public education expenditures across categories.

A second problem in extending the standard structural model of expenditure determination relates to the specification that holds that expenditures are only a function of contemporaneous variables. This implicitly holds that the pattern of school expenditures in each district is in equilibrium at every point in time. But rather than school districts instantaneously adjusting to changes in the various determinants of expenditures, it is more likely that current expenditures are linked to current and previous values of the exogenous variables, as well as resource choices made by the district in earlier periods. However, political and economic theory provide little guidance regarding the specification of a dynamic structural model linking

32. Examples of this method include the work of Downes and Pogue (1994) as well as Ratcliffe, Riddle, and Yinger (1990).

the allocation of current educational expenditures to current and lagged values of the exogenous variables and lagged values of the predetermined endogenous variables. Developing such a model is a worthy task, but one that would go far beyond the scope of this chapter.

The following empirical analysis is based upon an alternative method that attempts to characterize the empirical regularities relevant to the questions outlined above without estimating a fully specified, structural model of expenditure determination. This is done by estimating the reduced-form linkages between enrollments and expenditures.

To understand this model, share with us the assumption that budgetary decisions are made in two steps. In the first stage, total expenditures are determined on the basis of enrollments, the characteristics of the student population, state and federal aid, households' incomes and tastes, the property tax base, and other factors. In the second stage, the predetermined total expenditure is allocated across the various program and expenditure categories. As an approximation, this two-stage process is consistent with the budgetary process used by public school districts in New York. In the spring before the start of the school year, district officials formulate a tentative budget. The proposed budget is voted on by citizens in a referendum. Defeated budgets are revised and considered in repeat referendums. Since school officials are able to revise the initial budgetary plan over the summer and during the school year, the actual allocation of total expenditures may differ from the budget initially proposed.[33]

Figure 7-1 is a schematic diagram of our model. Notice that attributes of the student population directly affect both total expenditures and the allocation of those expenditures. Financial variables such as household incomes and the property tax base, as well as state and federal aid, directly affect total expenditures, but only indirectly affect the allocation of those expenditures.[34] The diagram also shows that income and the property base in a district, enrollments, and student characteristics all affect state and federal aid. Thus the total effects of enrollments on the allocation of expenditures by category reflect both the direct and indirect links shown in the figure.

33. This description is only a general characterization of the referenda process in New York. Direct voter approval in referendums is not required in 62 of the 693 major districts; budgets in these districts require only the approval of elected school boards. In districts holding referendums, only small portions of their budgets are effectively at stake, as the reversion budgets in the referendums cannot alter teacher contracts and other core expenditure components.

34. Matching or earmarked aid would also affect particular categories of expenditures. However, New York State aid is largely lump-sum.

Figure 7-1. *A Reduced-Form Model of School District Expenditures*

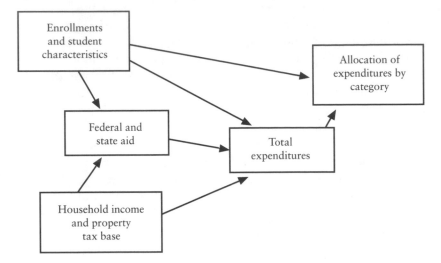

Statistical Model

To account for all these linkages, we have separately estimated models of state and federal aid, total expenditure determination, and the allocation of that total, using both present and lagged values of the explanatory variables.[35] In each equation, we employ a "fixed-effect" linear regression specification:

$$E_{it} = \alpha_t + \beta_0 X_{it} + \beta_1 X_{it} + \ldots + \beta_m X_{it-m} + d_i + \epsilon_{it}.$$

In this formulation, E_{it} is the dependent variable, for example, total expenditure; in the case of the total expenditure regression, it would be for the ith district during period t. α_t is a constant term that can differ across years. X_{it-n} reflects the values of the time-varying explanatory variables for the ith district in period $t - n$. The total number of lags (m) may be large or

35. As the discussion above mentioned, it is also possible that enrollments of both regular and special education students are affected by state and federal aid, total expenditures, and expenditures by category. We have not accounted for these potential relationships in the estimates presented below, largely because the data necessary to incorporate such estimation were not completely available. In Hausman tests for endogeneity of special education enrollments in a more limited version of the model, we found evidence that the number of special education students in the equations for two expenditure categories (special education and building) probably suffer from endogeneity. We believe that not accounting for endogeneity is a potential problem of this analysis and see such modeling as an important item for future research.

small, depending upon the nature of the dynamic process. $\beta_0, \beta_1, \ldots, \beta_m$ are vectors of parameters. d_i is a district-specific constant that captures the net effects of all measured and unmeasured attributes of the district that do not vary over the period.[36] The effects of the exogenous variables that determine expenditures and local taxes and the dynamic linkages in the process will determine the coefficients of the reduced-form model, which reflect the net effect of changes in the exogenous variables on expenditures.

With this framework in mind, the order of analysis works this way. The state and federal aid equations are functions of enrollments, income, property tax base, and student characteristics. Then, total educational expenditures are estimated based on the time-varying variables reflecting enrollments, student characteristics, state and federal aid, income and the district's property tax base. We then divide up total expenditures into three categories: regular teaching, special education, and "other." For each of these categories, we then use a regression in which the time-varying explanatory variables are total expenditures, enrollments, and measures of student characteristics.[37] The specific variables employed and the parameter estimates are presented in appendix B. Here, the discussion will focus on the determinants of instructional expenditures for regular and special education classes.

As already discussed, disabled students when in regular classes receive services associated with expenditures for regular teaching, and although such students undoubtedly have higher than average expenses for administration, educational support, and transportation, we are unable to identify all of these expenditures directly. However, our statistical analysis shows how noninstructional expenditures are affected by enrollment changes in each of the three types of special education students.

36. More properly, $d_i = \gamma W_i + \delta_i$ is the "fixed effect," where the vector W_i represents those exogenous variables that are unchanged over the period analyzed. We use the fixed-effect specification for two reasons. First, our statistical analysis is motivated by an interest in how expenditures vary as a result of changes in enrollments. Fixed-effect estimation avoids statistical problems that arise when the individual effects are correlated with the error term. Second, a major advantage of the fixed-effect estimator is that the effects of the time-varying variables (such as enrollments) can be estimated without specifying or measuring any of the explanatory variables that are time-invariant. In the current case, this is appealing since the selection of a complete set of variables would be somewhat arbitrary in the absence of an explicit theoretical model of expenditure determination, and data would be very difficult to obtain.

37. An instrumental-variables estimator is used in the model of expenditures by category since total expenditures is one of the explanatory variables.

As shown in the earlier decomposition of the growth in total special education expenditures, the periods before and after 1989 differ greatly. In addition, an expanding New York State economy during the mid-1980s afforded large increases in educational expenditures when enrollments were declining. By 1988 the economy had begun to slow, thereby limiting state and local tax increases. For example, state aid to local school districts grew at an annual rate of 4 percent between 1980 and 1989 but fell by 1.3 percent annually over 1989–92. In 1989–90, statewide enrollments began to increase for the first time in eighteen years. These conditions produced a slowdown in the growth of real expenditures per pupil, which actually started to fall in 1991–92. Thus the fiscal and enrollment environments before and after 1988 were quite different. Several studies have provided evidence that school districts respond differently to enrollment increases and declines.[38] These results, along with the possibility that district responses may also be asymmetric with respect to improving and declining fiscal environments, motivated us to analyze the pre- and post-1988 periods separately. Because the latter period mirrors current expenditure and fiscal trends, the following analysis focuses on the period since 1988.

An important debate in educational policy centers around whether schools make "good use" of additional dollars. Other chapters in this volume are in a better position to determine whether additional inputs affect measured outputs. However, our analysis indicates the extent to which additional dollars would be allocated to regular and special education instruction—an important and not well understood piece of the puzzle. The estimated model indicates that, conditional on unchanged enrollments and other student characteristics, school districts are estimated to allocate twenty-eight cents of an additional dollar of expenditure to regular teaching and six cents to special education. Based on average expenditure shares, regular instruction should receive about 40 percent and special education about 10 percent of additional revenue. Without more information, it is difficult to determine whether school districts are making good use of additional revenue, but these estimates certainly indicate that a smaller

38. Freeman and Hannan (1975) examine the differential effect of growth and decline in organizations. In particular, they believe that school districts will behave symmetrically with respect to hiring and firing of teachers (the direct component), but will behave asymmetrically with respect to the hiring and firing of administrators (the supportive component). McKee and Wintrobe (1993) argue that not only do administrators not face symmetrical hiring and firing decisions during time of organizational growth and decline, but, consistent with Parkinson's law, the number of administrators actually expands during periods of organizational decline.

than expected share of new money is allocated to classroom uses. However, it does not seem that special education has a disproportionate claim on new revenue, either. Of course, the question being posed here—how would an additional dollar of expenditure be allocated conditional on unchanged enrollments?—is very different from asking how budget allocations have changed over a given time period. The budget shares presented earlier embody altered enrollments, which have a substantial effect on how budgets are allocated.

We estimate that a dollar of federal or state aid both increase total expenditures by about $0.80. It is surprising that this much of both kinds of aid "stick" in the school budget.[39] After all, the vast majority of state and federal aid is provided in a lump sum as opposed to a matching form, and school districts could readily offset such government aid by reducing local taxes, since local revenues make up over 50 percent of the total.

When school districts have revenue constraints, increases in spending in one area must come at the expense of spending in some other areas—the so-called crowding-out effect. One way of understanding how districts make these trade-offs is to examine the effect of additional enrollments on spending across categories. Table 7-7 indicates how instructional and noninstructional spending would change if enrollments for each type of student were to increase by one student with other enrollments remained unchanged, first if revenues remained unchanged and then if local, state, and federal revenues did change in response to the additional student. For example, an increase of one student in the number of regular students, with no change in revenue, is estimated to increase regular teaching by $1,491, reduce special education by $391, and reduce noninstructional spending by $1,100.

A similar analysis for the addition of a special education student provides no conclusive evidence that spending on regular students is reduced to accommodate the increased costs of that student. However, our expenditure data do not allow for a clear assessment. Although there is a modest ($63) decrease in regular classroom expenditures when the most expensive type of special education student is added (with no revenue increase), this indicates the effect on only this spending category, not the effect on regular students. At least some of these special education students spend a portion of their day in regular classes, requiring additional resources in that setting. To the extent that the additional special education student received some regular education services and regular education spending experienced a

---

39. See Hines and Thaler (1995) for an excellent discussion of "flypaper effects."

Table 7-7. *Effect on School District Expenditures of One Additional Student, by Type of Student, 1989–92*
Dollars

Type of additional student	Expenditure categories			Total added expense
	Regular teaching	Special education	Noninstructional	
Regular				
No revenue change	1,491	−391	−1,110	0
Revenue change[a]	3,339	−18	3,227	6,548
Special education (at least 60 percent)				
No revenue change	−63	8,956	−8,893	0
Revenue change[a]	4,094	9,796	846	14,736
Special education (20–60 percent)				
No revenue change	1,658	1,915	−3,573	0
Revenue change[a]	5,254	2,641	4,851	12,746
Special education (20 percent or less)				
No revenue change	1,361	252	−1,613	0
Revenue change[a]	4,331	852	5,343	10,526

a. Local, state, and federal revenues change in response to enrollment increase.

modest decrease, regular students would be at least somewhat worse off. The extent of crowding out with respect to the other two types of special education students is less clear. Since these students are spending increasing portions of their day in regular classroom settings, it is difficult to determine whether the increased expense associated with regular teaching when enrollments increase is sufficient to compensate for resources going to the additional students. In the absence of significant negative effects on regular teaching, we are unable to draw firm conclusions.

Crowding out ultimately depends upon how local and state revenues respond to changes in enrollments and costs and how managers allocate these across budget categories. The second row in each student category in table 7-7 reflects the effect of enrollment changes if federal, state, and local revenues are allowed to change in response to enrollment changes. In general, the addition of a special education student leads to an increase in expenditures in regular classrooms. Again, our data do not adequately discriminate among the recipients of expenditures, only among the settings in which services are provided. As a result, our estimates do not indicate whether regular students actually receive fewer resources. Without better information on the use of resources by special education students when they are in regular classes, it is not possible to say if crowding out exists.

The total marginal effect of increasing regular enrollments by a student is to increase expenditures by about $6,500. An additional special education student who spends at least 60 percent of the day in a special setting increases total spending by $14,736; between 20 and 60 percent, by $12,746; and less than 20 percent, $10,526. These results are generally consistent with each other, both in absolute and relative levels.[40]

A Simulation of the Effects of Enrollment Projections on Expenditures

What can we say about the increasing expenditures on special education? The growth in special education expenditures reflects both increasing costs of serving individual students of each type and changes in the number of students served, although for the 1989–93 period in New York State (outside of New York City) 90 percent of the increase resulted from increasing enrollments. The econometric analysis does not provide good insights on how expenditures per pupil are changing for disabled children. However, we are able to estimate how changing enrollment patterns will affect the costs of school districts. By using total enrollment projections produced by the New York State Education Department and by making estimates of the changing share of total enrollment for regular students and each of the three types of special education students, we obtain two different enrollment projections by student type.[41] Under a conservative assumption we hold student shares constant based on the 1993 enrollment shares of each student type. Under a more high-cost assumption we project

---

40. We would expect that the increment in expenditure associated with an additional student would be lower than average expenditure. The average total cost for all students during this period is about $9,300. Recall our estimate of average expenditures for a regular student is about $8,500 and $14,500 for the average special education student. Based on a 1979–80 detailed cost analysis of special education, the New York State Education Department sets weights for each of three special education groups relative to regular students of 2.7, 1.9, and 1.13. Based on our estimate of the marginal expenditure for a regular student of about $6,500, this implies expenditures of about $17,500, 12,400, and $7,400 for special education students.

41. New York enrollment projections are from New York State Education Department (1994).

student shares based on trends over the last five years.[42] We use these enrollment changes with the estimated regression model to project changes in expenditures by type of student to the year 2000.

We project sizable growth in expenditures under both assumptions. Both methods suggest that even without any increase in costs per student, school district budgets would increase by at least 10 percent between 1993 and 2000. Increasing enrollments and a shift in the composition of students will put substantially more pressure on school district budgets than has been the case until recently. The assumptions based on recent trends show a substantially larger growth in special education enrollments and thus a larger share of expenditures going to this group. For example, a linear projection of recent special education growth implies that over 50 percent of all expenditure growth between 1993 and 2000 will be spent on special education students.

Will special education expenditures overwhelm school district budgets? We are able to provide only a partial answer. Because of changes in the size and composition of special education enrollments, school districts will feel substantially more financial pressure. We estimate district budgets will increase from 11 to 13 percent as a result of these changes in special education alone. Under current circumstances—increasing general enrollments, very slow growth in state aid, and increasing resistance to higher property taxes—finding this additional money for special education is likely to be very difficult.

Conclusion

Understanding how school districts allocate expenditures across types of students and budget categories is important in evaluating policies to improve educational productivity. This chapter focuses on two questions: What factors account for the large increase in special education expenditures that occurred in school districts in New York between 1980 and 1993? Have these increases reduced resources going to regular students? We believe we now have a better understanding of school district finances, although several issues remain unresolved.

42. Recent trends are incorporated into the share projections by regressing the share of each enrollment type on a time trend and using this trend to project shares. We believe that the shares realized in future years will probably fall somewhere between these two estimates. The proportion of students identified as learning disabled will probably increase, but not as much as would be predicted using a linear projection.

The large growth in special education expenditures over the 1980–93 period in New York results from a combination of increasing expenditures per disabled student and an increasing number of students with disabilities. The growth in expenditures per student reflects both a changing composition of special education students and increases in resources devoted to each type of student. In addition, it appears that institutional factors, such as regulations and court cases, have played a role in increasing special education expenditures. Our analysis clearly indicates that changing student composition and overall growth have played an important role in squeezing school district budgets and will continue to do so. Our regression estimates indicate that special education enrollment increases are driven by increasing total enrollments and a trend over time to classify more students to special education. However, we find little support for the hypothesis that financial incentives systematically encourage school districts to increase special education enrollments.

We have attempted to measure expenditures on regular and disabled students, both descriptively and econometrically. In neither case did we find clear support for the claim that special education expenditures crowd out spending on regular students. However, it is clear that descriptions of per pupil expenditures that do not distinguish between regular and special education students substantially overstate the resources reaching regular students at a given time, as well as changes over time. Thus productivity analyses that do not account for this difference are likely to understate the effect of spending on outcomes of regular students.

Several interesting questions remain. The issue of crowding out is far from decided. Because our data identify resources by the setting in which they are used, not the type of students who receive them, it is difficult to know what regular classroom resources flow to disabled students. This problem of identifying the resource flows will be exacerbated as more special education students are mainstreamed. Moreover, our statistical analysis examined only the effect of increased special education student enrollments and not the effect of increased costs per student. Our estimates do not include costs of inputs. It is likely that cost differences account for some of the differences across districts in total expenditures and expenditures by category.

We believe that the basic approach employed here is potentially applicable in considering a variety of related policy questions in educational finance. Having panel data allows an exploration of dynamic behavior. For example, how do enrollment and aid changes in prior years affect expenditure behavior? In descriptive work, we found that school districts appear to respond asymmetrically to enrollment changes for certain types of expenditures. For example, districts reduce spending on administration less when enrollments fall than they increase it when enrollments rise. If this result is robust to multivariate analysis, it would provide support for the notion that slack resources are consumed by an increasingly bloated administrative structure.

Finally, and perhaps most important to the interpretation of the econometric results, is the development of a structural model of school district economic behavior. Our model is clearly a reduced-form characterization of a more complicated budget determination process. With a structural understanding of this process, we can more comfortably attach behavioral interpretations to the empirical regularities documented here.

Appendix A: Description of the Data

The 693 major school districts in New York in 1992–93 comprise our sample. District-level expenditure data are drawn from the annual financial reports (ST-3) for school years 1979–80 through 1992–93. In estimating the statistical model, we excluded districts that consolidated during the period. All the 693 major districts were included in the descriptive analysis. For each of the districts, we aggregated the approximate 500 expenditure items in the ST-3 into 67 groups that differ by both function (such as curriculum development) and type (such as instructional salaries) for each year analyzed. Each of the 67 groups was initially defined in terms of the 1992–93 ST-3 account codes. Reflecting the evolution of the ST-3, a number of account codes were added, deleted, or changed over the fourteen-year period. For each year analyzed, we modified the specific aggregations of the approximately 500 expenditure items to reflect these changes in order to ensure that the 67 groupings were consistent over time.

Based on a preliminary analysis, the 67 groups are aggregated into the 13 categories shown in table 7-3.[43] Expenditures in each category include all general fund and special fund expenditures under the corresponding ST-3 classifications (such as salaries, payments for BOCES services, equipment, supplies and materials, and contractual and other expenses) and em-

---

43. See Lankford and Wyckoff (1995, p. 199) for documentation regarding the ST-3 expenditure items included in each of the thirteen categories.

ployee fringe benefits.[44] The ST-3 includes information on total general fund expenditures for employee fringe benefits but does not allocate these expenses to the individual ST-3 classifications. All fringe benefits are allocated to the expenditure categories based upon the proportion of total salaries attributable to each category.

Information regarding total student membership comes from the Basic Education Data System (BEDS) database.[45] Disabled student counts are drawn from the NYS suspense file used in the calculation of state aid. The data include the number who are in special classes at least 60 percent of the day, the number who are in special classes at least 20 percent of the week but less than 60 percent of the day, and the number who are in special classes at least two periods per week but less than 20 percent of the day. Starting in 1991 a fourth category is reported for the number of disabled students in regular classes full time who receive the services of a consulting special education teacher. The number of students in this category is very small but increasing. In all our analyses, students in this category are merged with students in the 20 percent category since the pupil weightings used by the state reflect the view that students in these two categories receive comparable special education resources. Data for state aid for special education also come from the suspense file.

Even though the expenditure and student data are quite detailed in many respects, numerous problems arise because the data categories do not match those that would allow straightforward calculation of expenditures for each of the categories of interest in this study. We have dealt with the issue carefully by separating the detailed expenditure categories and defining enrollment categories to be consistent. By accounting for very detailed attributes of the reported expenditure and enrollment data, we have confidence in the comparability of enrollment and expenditure categorizations used in this study. Documentation regarding how the expenditure and enrollment data were linked is available from the authors.

---

44. Tuition payments and prekindergarten expenditures are exceptions to this rule. The former expenditures are shown as a separate category rather than as part of regular and disabilities teaching. Because of our focus on K–12 education, "regular" prekindergarten expenditures are assigned to the undistributed and other category rather than regular teaching, as done in the ST-3.

45. In working with the ST-3 and other data and arriving at decisions about the classification of the data, we benefited greatly from the State Education Department fiscal profiles and conversations with Ron Danforth, Richard Glashen, Ruth Henahan, and Diane Hutchinson, all of the department. Benita Stambler was especially helpful in explaining many of the provisions of state aid for special education.

Table 7B-1. *Description, Means, and Standard Deviations of Variables Used in Regression Analysis*

Variable	Definition	Mean
Total enrollment	Total number of students in district	2,327.1 (2,965.7)
Special education aid	Dummy if not on save harmless × limited approved operating expenditures × aid ratio	2,183.0 (1,320.1)
School lunch	Number of eligible applicants to free and reduced-price school lunch program in district	640.8 (2,017.2)
Average class size	Mean class size for all common branch (K-6) classes in the district	21.7 (1.95)
Regular teaching	Expenditures on regular teaching in district	10,675,000 (13,371,000)
Special education	Expenditures on special education in district	2,200,300 (3,240,800)
Total expenditure	Total expenditures in district	21,554,000 (27,676,000)
State aid	Total state aid for education in district	8,985,100 (14,725,000)
Federal aid	Total federal aid for education in district	475,590 (1,410,900)
Regular students	Number of regular students in district	2,065 (2,544)
Special education >60 percent	Number of special education students out of regular class at least 60 percent of day in district	121 (225)
Special education 20 to 60 percent	Number of special education students out of regular class betweeen 20 percent and 60 percent of day in district	98 (121)
Special education <20 percent	Number of special education students out of regular class less than 20 percent of day in district	43 (146)
Full value	Total full value of taxable property in district	725,200,000 (968,180,000)
Total personal income	Total personal income in county in which district is located	11,133,000 (14,390,000)
Limited English proficiency	Number of students who are categorized as limited English proficient in district	38 (171)
Black	Number of black students in district	208 (1,201)
Hispanic	Number of Hispanic students in district	82 (362)

Table 7B-2. *Fixed-Effects Weighted Regression Results for Aid, Total Expenditures, Regular Teaching, and Special Education*

Independent variable	Federal aid	State aid	Total expenditure	Regular teaching	Special education
Regular students t	257.2** (4.32)	376.7 (0.89)	2,704.6** (6.70)	632.9** (2.97)	570.9** (4.35)
Regular students $t - 1$	279.6** (3.81)	880.3 (1.93)	-300.1 (-0.61)	497.6* (1.98)	-371.2* (-2.40)
Regular students $t - 2$	-238.5** (-4.22)	3,137.1** (8.92)	-78.1 (-0.20)	361.2 (1.94)	-591.0** (-5.14)
Special education > 60 percent t	1,139.7** (5.68)	-642.1 (-0.46)	8,354.9** (6.15)	-795.6 (-1.12)	5,192.2** (11.92)
Special education > 60 percent $t - 1$	417.6 (1.92)	4,138.7** (3.07)	-1,772.9 (-1.21)	424.8 (0.57)	2,565.4** (5.59)
Special education > 60 percent $t - 2$	-185.8 (-0.95)	4,084.2** (3.36)	336.3 (0.25)	307.7 (0.46)	1,199.0** (2.90)
Special education 20 to 60 percent t	624.4** (4.45)	-318.5 (-0.26)	5,419.9** (5.71)	390.4 (0.79)	1,945.5** (6.37)
Special education 20 to 60 percent $t - 1$	307.8 (1.90)	1,372.2 (1.37)	294.6 (0.27)	1,098.3* (1.98)	343.2 (1.01)
Special education 20 to 60 percent $t - 2$	-153.0 (-1.02)	4,517.5** (4.83)	21.22 (0.02)	169.5 (0.33)	-373.4 (-1.17)

Table 7B-2 (continued)

Independent variable	Federal aid	State aid	Total expenditure	Regular teaching	Special education
Special education < 20 percent t	400.5** (2.77)	1,882.7 (1.90)	5,158.0** (5.30)	557.9 (1.10)	1,085.5** (3.49)
Special education < 20 percent $t - 1$	188.5 (1.29)	1,008.9 (1.12)	−478.4 (−0.49)	648.8 (1.31)	−237.0 (−0.78)
Special education < 20 percent $t - 2$	−393.2** (−3.07)	4,096.1** (5.12)	305.9 (0.35)	154.4 (0.36)	−595.6* (−2.23)
Full value ($000) t	0.0726 (1.66)	−1.6839** (−5.58)	2.565** (19.78)	...	...
Full value ($000) $t - 1$	0.000058 (−1.41)	0.00062* (−2.38)	...	...	...
Total personal income t	0.00249 (0.24)	−0.7328* (−2.38)	0.4259** (6.22)	...	...
Total personal income $t - 1$	0.01666* (−2.13)	0.1837** (3.76)	...	...	...
Limited English proficient	435.5** (2.94)	3,583** (3.85)	1,077.1 (1.01)	−1,181.0* (−2.18)	−677.8* (−2.03)
Regular student squared	...	0.1382** (6.29)	...	...	...
Special education > 60 percent squared	...	3.526** (2.69)	...	...	...

Table 7B-2 *(continued)*

Independent variable	Federal aid	State aid	Total expenditure	Regular teaching	Special education
Special education 20 to 60 percent squared	...	12.36** (4.14)	...	...	...
Special education < 20 percent squared	...	-3.169** (4.10)	...	...	...
Black	...	...	1,348.4* (2.02)	112.2 (0.33)	277.1 (1.33)
Hispanic	...	...	-1,103.5 (-1.75)	456.6 (1.47)	-1,242.3** (-6.37)
State aid	...	...	0.8029** (32.97)	...	...
Federal aid	...	...	0.7628** (4.89)	...	...
Total expenditure	...	...	...	0.2822** (19.66)	0.0570** (6.44)
N	2,540	2,540	2,540	2,540	2,540
Adjusted R^2	0.96	0.99	0.99	0.99	0.99

*Significant at the 5 percent level.
**Significant at the 1 percent level.

References

Berninger, Virginia W., and Robert D. Abbott. 1994. "Redefining Learning Disabilities: Moving beyond Aptitude-Achievement Discrepancies to Failure to Respond to Validated Treatment Protocols." In *Frames of Reference for the Assessment of Learning Disabilities: New Views on Measurement Issues,* edited by G. Reid Lyon, 163–83. Baltimore: Paul H. Brookes Publishing.

Chaikind, Stephen, Louis C. Danielson, and Marsha L. Brauen. 1993. "What Do We Know about the Costs of Special Education? A Selected Review." *Journal of Special Education* 26 (Winter): 344–70.

Chambers, Jay G., and Ixtlac E. Duenas. 1994. "Impact of the Kentucky Education Reform Act on the Special Education Costs and Funding." Palo Alto: Center for Special Education Finance, American Institutes for Research.

Downes, Thomas A., and Thomas F. Pogue. 1994. "Adjusting School Aid Formulas for the Higher Cost of Educating Disadvantaged Students." *National Tax Journal* 47 (March): 89–110.

Freeman, John, and Michael T. Hannan. 1975. "Growth and Decline Processes in Organizations." *American Sociological Review* 40 (April): 215–28.

Fruchter, Norm, and others. 1995. *Focus on Learning: A Report on Reorganizing General and Special Education in New York City.* New York University, Institute for Education and Social Policy.

Hanushek, Eric A., and Steven Rivkin. 1994. "Understanding the 20th Century Explosion in U.S. School Costs." Working Paper 388. University of Rochester, Rochester Center for Economic Research.

Hartman, William T. 1980. "Policy Effects of Special Education Funding Formulas." *Journal of Education Finance* 6 (Fall): 135–59.

Hines, James R., and Richard H. Thaler. 1995. "Anomalies: The Flypaper Effect." *Journal of Economic Perspectives* 9 (Fall): 217–26.

Kakalik, J. S., and others. 1981. "The Cost of Special Education." A RAND note. Santa Monica: RAND Corporation.

Lankford, Hamilton, and James Wyckoff. 1995. "Where Has the Money Gone? An Analysis of School District Spending in New York." *Educational Evaluation and Policy Analysis* 17 (Summer): 195–218.

Macmillan, Donald L. 1993. "Development of Operational Definitions in Mental Retardation: Similarities and Differences with the Field of Learning Disabilities." In *Better Understanding Learning Disabilities: New Views from Research and their Implications for Education and Public Policies,* edited by G. Reid Lyon and others, 117–52. Baltimore: Paul H. Brookes Publishing.

McKee, Michael, and Ronald Wintrobe. 1993. "The Decline of Organizations and the Rise of Administrators." *Journal of Public Economics* 51 (July): 309–27.

Moats, Louisa Cook, and G. Reid Lyon. 1993. "Learning Disabilities in the United States: Advocacy, Science, and the Future of the Field." *Journal of Learning Disabilities* 26 (May): 282–94.

Monk, David H., and C. Roellke. 1994. "The Origin, Disposition and Utilization of Resources within New York State Public School Systems: An Update." *Proceedings from NCES Conference on Putting It All Together* (Washington: National Center for Education Statistics).

Moore, M.T., and others. 1988. *Patterns in Special Education Service Delivery and Cost.* Washington: Decision Resources Corporation.

Nakib, Y. 1994. "Allocation and Use of Public K–12 Education in Florida." Wisconsin Center for Education Research, Consortium for Policy Research in Education.

New York State Education Department. 1994. "Projections of Public and Non-public School Enrollment and High School Graduates to 2003–04 New York State." State University of New York, Albany.

O'Reilly, Fran. 1993. "State Special Education Finance Systems, 1992–93." Palo Alto: Center for Special Education Finance, American Institutes for Research.

Parrish, Thomas B. 1993. "Federal Policy Options for Funding Special Education." Policy Brief. Palo Alto: Center for Special Education Finance, American Institutes for Research.

Parrish, Thomas B., and Deborah A. Verstegen. 1994. "Fiscal Provisions of the Individuals with Disabilities Education Act: Policy Issues and Alternatives." Policy Paper. Palo Alto: Center for Special Education Finance, American Institutes for Research.

Picus, L., and Y. Nakib. 1993. "The Allocation and Use of Educational Resources at the District Level in Florida." Working Paper 38. Consortium for Policy Research in Education.

Ratcliffe, Kerri, Bruce Riddle, and John Yinger. 1990. "The Fiscal Condition of School Districts in Nebraska: Is Small Beautiful?" *Economics of Education Review* 9 (1): 617–43.

Rossmiller, Richard A., James A. Hale, and Lloyd E. Frohreich. 1970. *Educational Programs for Exceptional Children: Resource Configurations and Costs.* University of Wisconsin, Department of Educational Administration.

U.S. Department of Education. 1994. *Digest of Education Statistics, 1994.*

Verstegen, Deborah A. 1994. "Fiscal Provisions of the Individuals with Disabilities Education Act: Historical Overview." Palo Alto: Center for Special Education Finance, American Institutes for Research.

Zigmond, Naomi. 1993. "Learning Disabilities from an Educational Perspective." In *Better Understanding Learning Disabilities: New Views from Research and their Implications for Education and Public Policies,* edited by G. Reid Lyon and others, 251–72. Baltimore: Paul H. Brookes Publishing.

Comments on Chapter Seven

Jane Hannaway

THE CHAPTER by Lankford and Wyckoff is different from most of the others in this volume. It focuses on the allocation of resources within school districts, not on performance per se. As such, it makes an important contribution. The chapter is primarily concerned with spending on special education, and it goes a long way in sorting out the implications for regular education of this relatively new and powerful claimant on education resources. Perhaps more important, it also provides us with a general reminder that education is an arena in which competing objectives, subplots, and nonobvious incentives and constraints play out. I first discuss the authors' analysis of special education expenditures and then turn to more general issues associated with the need for a better understanding of the processes that drive education as we attempt to move to a more performance-based system.

A major claim of education critics concerned with reform is that while expenditures for education have increased substantially, performance—as measured by how well students do on standardized tests—has not. Lankford and Wyckoff show that using measures of overall expenditures per student can be misleading, because they overstate expenditures for regular students whose test scores typically provide the performance measures. This does not mean that there is not considerable room for performance improvement, only that less effort (as measured by spending levels) may have gone into improving regular education under the current system than is commonly presumed.

Using data from New York State, the authors show that a substantial fraction of total spending increases since 1980 has gone to special education, not regular education. The pattern is particularly dramatic in New York City, where 53 percent of the increase went to teaching students with disabilities and only 28.5 percent went to teaching regular students. On a per pupil basis, spending in districts outside New York City increased substantially for all students, but the increase for teaching special education students was about 50 percent greater than the increase for regular students, regardless of the assumption about student resource use. In New York City, the increase in spending on teaching special education students was more than eight times greater than the increase for regular students. As a consequence, by 1993 spending on teaching regular students in New York City, where there are serious student performance problems, was about 15 percent lower than spending on similar students in other districts in the state.

Most discussions of special education spending have been anecdotal or nearly so, and politically and emotionally charged. Lankford and Wyckoff bring a welcome analytic eye to the picture and attempt to account for the reasons for the growth in special education spending and, further, to examine whether special education spending is, in fact, "crowding out" regular education spending. Their findings are informative and important, though not fully conclusive for a variety of reasons they carefully identify.

The first and most notable insight provided by their analyses has already been mentioned: attempts to assess the effect of expenditures on student performance will undoubtedly underestimate the effect if spending on special education is not separated out. In fact, any attempt to evaluate policies designed to affect the behavior of school districts should differentiate regular and special education.

Second, they identify enrollment increases in special education and assignment of students to particular treatment categories, as opposed to per pupil expenditure increases, as the primary sources of expenditure increases in special education. This opens questions of the extent to which incentives in the system encourage the identification of students for special education for other advantages. For example, having a larger number of special education students could bring financial gain to a district, raise the district test performance for the remaining students, or ease teacher workload. Lankford and Wyckoff explore these possibilities in a preliminary way and find only modest support for them, but the question still remains largely open.

Third, Lankford and Wyckoff's analysis raises a number of cautionary notes for expenditure-related research in education. They show, for example, that cross-sectional analyses of the expenditure patterns of school districts are highly likely to yield misleading results. In addition, they show that districts allocate resources differently during periods of enrollment growth and enrollment decline: changes in administrative expenditures are less responsive to resource reductions than they are to resource increases.

These results are important not only for studies attempting to explain how districts spend their money, but also for studies relating to performance and expenditures, if any of the dynamic factors affecting expenditure interact with performance.

The Lankford and Wyckoff chapter also has more general implications for designing a performance-based system of education, although there is nothing in the paper explicitly about performance. The examination of special education exemplifies the instability and murkiness of the education process and the way that powerful new demands on the system can shift its focus. The objectives of education systems are multiple and the boundaries are fluid. Objectives change over time and from setting to setting. The means to attain the objectives are also poorly understood and, the chapter suggests, they raise opportunities for gaming the system. A well-designed performance-based system has important advantages under these conditions. In effect, it acknowledges that the process is murky and may not be well understood; but it says if we focus on outputs, the process will sort itself out. Actors in the system will learn and focus their energies on what works in achieving important measurable academic objectives in their situation.

The logic of performance-based reform is compelling precisely because we have a limited understanding of the relationship between means and ends in education. Indeed, if this relationship were perfectly understood and we had good measures of inputs, it would not make any difference if we directed the system by monitoring and rewarding the inputs or the output. But in cases like education where the critical production variables are effort or the exercise of skills involving considerable judgment, like teacher classroom performance, then measuring student outcomes makes good sense. It allows local schools or districts to shape education programs in ways that best fit their contexts and encourages schools to learn ways to be more effective. However, if a performance-based system is not well designed, there is the risk of diverting resources to those areas that are more easily measured.

What might we really have in a performance-based system? The chapters in this volume suggest the best we can hope for is an imperfect system of performance measurement, even when we limit our focus to the academic performance of regular students. Measuring student academic performance is not the same as measuring a car coming off a finishing line with a checklist of inspections and tests to see whether it meets certain performance criteria. We have to infer general learning from the performance of students on a limited number of tasks. Ensuring that measures do measure what we want them to measure is no small feat. In the case of the car, for example, it may be reasonable to infer that the tail lights work well if the headlights do—at least we know the electrical system is functioning—but we would not want to infer that the brakes work well on the basis of the paint job.

In general, the larger the number of tasks examined in any domain, the better we are able to assess learning in that domain. One of the virtues of multiple choice tests is that many items can be examined in a relatively short period of time, so we can have reasonable confidence in our measures. The limitations of multiple choice tests, however, are well known: what they test is restricted. Newer forms of assessment of the type discussed in this volume measure performance on more complex tasks. Their complexity, however, lead to measurement problems: first, because the tasks are time consuming, relatively few tasks are typically assessed; and second, scoring a complicated student performance is difficult and often open to dispute. So while the lack of knowledge in the means-end relationship in education argues for performance-based systems, imperfect measures of performance advise us to move cautiously.

Education, of course, is not the only area of production where performance measurement is difficult. Indeed, agency theorists in organizational economics have considered situations where input and performance are not perfectly measurable and where the relationship between inputs and outputs is not well understood. Under these conditions, all relevant information, both input and performance, should be monitored. Observable elements of the process by which inputs are transformed into outputs should also be monitored, since the action of the system is not well directed by either input controls or output controls. Indeed, perhaps there should be some restrictions on the process.

The Lankford and Wyckoff chapter provides us with an example of a sharp shift in expenditure patterns in New York school districts as a result of increases in special education enrollments. What would have happened if a performance-based system were in place? Perhaps placement of students in the special education programs might have increased because special education students are typically exempted from testing. Or perhaps fewer students might have been placed in the high-cost special education category because they would have drawn resources from the regular students whose performance was being measured. To the extent that the real incidence of special education needs varied by school district, some dis-

262 / Jane Hannaway

tricts would have been held to the same performance standards while operating with lower expenditure levels than other districts. This suggests that equity issues will arise unless corrections are made for the quality of one of the central ingredients to the education process—the students. These possibilities suggest that monitoring certain processes—like the determination of special education enrollments and expenditure patterns— along with input and performance measures may be important for an effective and equitable system.

PART FOUR

Costs of Achieving High Performance

CHAPTER EIGHT

How and Why Money Matters:
An Analysis of Alabama Schools

Ronald F. Ferguson and Helen F. Ladd

O
VER THE LAST THIRTY YEARS, many researchers have investigated the empirical relationship between measurable inputs into schooling and outcomes as measured by student performance. Yet the correct reading of the evidence is not clear. In a series of influential survey articles covering most of the published empirical literature, Eric Hanushek argued that the public inputs into schooling—namely, teacher-pupil ratios, attributes of teachers such as advanced education and years of experience, and expenditures on administration and facilities—exert no consistent effect on student performance on standardized tests.[1] In a reanalysis of essentially the same literature, Larry Hedges, Richard Laine, and Rob Greenwald come to the opposite conclusion: that school inputs not only affect student outcomes, but also that the effects are large enough to be relevant for policy.[2]

To some people, the entire debate about whether school resources affect educational outcomes is frivolous, either because the answer is obvious or because even if systematic relationships are not found, the policy implications are not clear.[3] To others, the empirical studies are not very meaningful because they focus on too narrow a range of educational outcomes (like test scores) and include the wrong explanatory variables.[4] This paper starts from a different observation: none of the literature surveys just mentioned makes an attempt to distinguish the more methodologically sound studies from those with significant weaknesses. For reasons that we spell out be-

The authors would like to thank Anthony Shen for able research assistance. In addition, they are grateful for the thoughtful comments of William Clune, Ronald Ehrenberg, Eric Hanushek, Richard Murnane, and other participants in the Brookings conference.

1. Hanushek (1986, 1989, 1996).
2. Hedges, Laine, and Greenwald (1994).
3. See Murnane (1991).
4. See, for example, Smith, Scoll, and Link (1995).

low, we believe that an additional attempt to quantify the relationship between certain school inputs, such as class size, and outcomes, such as student performance on standardized tests, can be a worthwhile and important endeavor.

This paper reports the results of such an attempt to measure the systematic effects of school inputs on student test scores. The study is based on both district-level and student-level data from Alabama. The district-level analysis allows us to compare results from Alabama with those from Ferguson's widely cited study of Texas school districts that finds systematic relationships between school inputs and student outcomes.[5] The analysis at the student level allows us to compare the district results with those from a more disaggregated analysis that is more methodologically sound. This chapter provides new evidence that schools' inputs affect educational outcomes and that the effects are large enough to be relevant for deliberations about educational spending.

Methodological Considerations

When economists investigate the relationship between educational inputs and outputs, they use a production function approach. In the education context, this usually means a function in which the output is a measure of student achievement, like test scores, and the inputs include measures of purchased school inputs (like the ratio of teachers to pupils) and other inputs like student, family, and community background characteristics. The production function approach immediately raises a number of questions. We will begin by defending the use of test scores as a reasonable measure of educational output. Then, we address three further methodological considerations: specification, aggregation, and measurement of the key school inputs. We believe that empirical work done with attention to these methodological issues, like the work we present, is worthy of greater attention than other studies, because it is more likely to generate accurate results.

Using Test Scores to Measure Educational Outcomes

There is a long tradition of using test scores to measure educational outcomes—and an equally long tradition of researchers and educators who

5. Ferguson (1991a, b).

are skeptical of the practice. In the tradition of human capital models, education is an investment that yields returns primarily in the form of higher income. Hence, to many economists, the more interesting and relevant outcomes are subsequent returns in the labor market. In one well-known study, David Card and Alan Krueger claim that variations in school inputs across states in the 1920s and 1930s influenced the earnings of men in the 1960s and 1970s.[6]

Such work is thought-provoking and worthwhile, but it inadvertently points out a major advantage of using test scores rather than labor market returns to measure student outcomes: Test scores are available at the time the education is provided, while earnings and labor market histories are not available for years or decades.[7] Fortunately, test scores are also a proxy, albeit imperfect, for future success. They are clearly a good indicator of the probability of additional schooling, which has been shown to affect future income. In addition, test scores are among the variables that predict later earnings of those students who do not continue beyond high school. For example, Richard Murnane, John Willett, and Frank Levy show that cognitive ability in math, as measured by math test scores, is a determinant of the wages of 24-year-old men whose education ended with high school. Also of interest is their finding that the effect of cognitive ability on labor market returns has been increasing over time, making test scores a better predictor of future performance now than in the past.[8]

Economists emphasize the effects of education on labor market outcomes. However, to many others, cognitive ability is an end in itself. From this perspective, test scores serve as reasonable measures of the outcomes of education if the tests adequately measure what society wants children to know and be able to do. Standardized tests are clearly imperfect measures of these cognitive skills, especially with respect to higher-order thinking skills. Many states have begun to experiment with alternative forms of assessment. Nonetheless, standardized tests remain the best available measures of output that are valid for comparisons over time and across schools.

6. Card and Krueger (1992).
7. In fact, some skeptics make the case that the linkages between educational inputs and labor market returns implied in the Card and Krueger study are so long and tenuous as to be implausible. See, for example, the conclusions of Speakman and Welch (1995).
8. Murnane, Willett, and Levy (1995). Also see evidence on test scores as predictors of racial differences in earnings in Ferguson (1995).

Specification

The production function approach to education, as already mentioned, generally models student learning as a joint product of measured school inputs, student characteristics, and family and community background variables, and a variety of influences that are hard to measure, such as student motivation.

But notice that this specification implies that the input variables all come from the same time period as the measure of outcomes. This assumption raises questions. After all, learning is a cumulative process. Achievement during a given school year will depend not only on the current-year schooling and background variables but also on values of those variables from prior years. Only if the current-year schooling and background variables can reasonably represent values from prior years would the problem of omitting variables from earlier years not be a major concern. For example, if differences across districts in the level of school inputs and background variables had remained relatively stable over time and the pattern of schooling inputs across grades were similar across districts, then district averages of school inputs and background characteristics would capture the effects of both present and prior variables. This condition might be plausible for a model explaining differences in average student achievement across school districts. In fact, if values of school inputs and background characteristics have changed little over time, it could be problematic or even inappropriate to include values for prior years in a production function approach; including separate variables that are very similar over time can create a problem of multicollinearity.

However, when the values of school inputs and background characteristics have changed over time, then an alternative solution is needed. There are several possibilities. One is to argue that a student's learning is determined not only by this year's school inputs and background characteristics, but by all past values of school inputs and background characteristics as well.[9] An alternate possibility is to ask how this year's combination of school inputs and background characteristics affected not the level of a student's achievement, but the gain that the student has made during the last year; this formulation uses only current variables for inputs to education, but looks at change in output.[10] However, these formulations have

9. See, for example, Hanushek and Taylor (1990).
10. Actually, these two formulations can be identical, provided that achievement in year $T - 1$ is determined by a model similar in structure to achievement in year T. To see why, consider the following model of the learning of the ith student in year T: $A_{iT} = \alpha_T S_{iT} + \beta_T F_{iT} + \sum_{t=1}^{T-1} \alpha_t S_{it} + \sum_{t=1}^{T-1} \beta_t F_{it} + \epsilon_{iT}$. According to this model, achievement in year T depends not only on the student's schooling experience measured

their difficulties as well. Complete information for all past years is difficult to accumulate and time-consuming to estimate, and, as mentioned before, problems of multicollinearity can easily arise. Using the gain in achievement from one year to the next implies the generally unrealistic assumption that achievement in the current and previous periods are commensurate, so that the difference between them represents learning from one period to the next. It also assumes that past learning does not decay naturally, for example, during the summer vacation.

A closely related specification deals with many of these problems. The achievement of student i at time T appears on the left-hand side of the equation as the dependent variable A. Present achievement then depends on the level of achievement in the previous time period, a vector of school input variables summarized in S, a vector of background characteristic variables summarized in B, and a constant, δ. The task of the researcher is then to estimate the parameters in the regression equation:

$$A_{iT} = \delta + \gamma A_{i,T-1} + \alpha_T S_{iT} + \beta_T B_{iT} + \mu_{iT}.$$

Notice that because of the coefficient before last year's achievement level, there is no longer any need to assume that last year's achievement has not decayed or is immediately comparable to this year's achievement. However, the level of past achievement captures the effect of past inputs into education.

Some authors assert that this value-added formulation also solves the potential bias problem caused by the omission of other unmeasured characteristics, such as student motivation or ability, that might otherwise be correlated with included variables, because the past achievement variable will also capture these effects. However, it does so only under the unrealistic assumption that the omitted variables affect the level of achievement and not its rate of growth.[11] In the more realistic situation in which motivation or ability affects the rate of learning as well as the level of learning, researchers using the value-added form of the equation continue to face the challenge of including a sufficient set of student background variables

---

by S and background characteristics B in year T but also on past history of schooling and family characteristics, as well as on unmeasured factors such as motivation and ability included in the error term, ϵ_{iT}. Now, subtract prior-period achievement from current period achievement, which yields $A_{iT} - A_{i,T-1} = \alpha_T S_{iT} + \beta_T B_{iT} + \mu_{iT}$, where μ_{iT} is the difference between the error term in period T and that in period $T - 1$.

11. For example, in the special case in which the unmeasured variable for each student has a constant effect on achievement in each year, the variable cancels out in the change form of the equation. This is the special case used by Hanushek and Taylor (1990).

to minimize the problem of bias from the omitted variables, like motivation or ability, that may be correlated with included regressors.

The analysis of this chapter uses this value-added specification for the equations that treat students as the units of observation. Our school input variables are all measured for a specific grade in a specific year within a school. Because we have data on test scores for individual students and can match a student's test scores to prior-year test scores, our achievement equations include the prior-period test scores of the identical students whose achievement we are trying to explain. Moreover, we can restrict the sample of students to those who were enrolled in that grade in that school throughout the year. Given our goal of determining the effect of school inputs on student achievement, it would be inappropriate to include in the sample students who entered or left the school in the middle of the year. We include a variety of family and school background variables: some are from administrative data at the school level and others are from the census at the level of the zip code area or the school district.

For our district-level analysis, we again focus on the learning of a specific group of students over a well-defined period of time, from the fourth to the ninth grade. However, we are forced to rely on a proxy for prior-period achievement: the test scores of current third and fourth graders, rather than the third and fourth grade scores of current ninth graders five years earlier. Although this synthetic cohort procedure would be unacceptable at the school level, because it would not account for the mobility of students, it is more acceptable at the district level, since it can be regarded as an adjustment for the pre-existing level of learning in the district (see note 31). The analysis below that uses districts as the units of analysis is less precisely specified than the analysis that uses individual students and schools, but it is, nevertheless, in the spirit of a value-added approach.

Aggregation

Various researchers have noted that the quality of a student's school experience varies greatly not only across districts, but also across schools within districts and, what is even more important, among classrooms in specific schools. This observation has led some people to argue that school input variables should be specified at the classroom level, provided that other variables can be appropriately measured.[12] Working in the other direction, however, is the possibility of excessive variation or noise in the

12. See Monk (1992).

explanatory variables when disaggregated analysis is used. That noise can be reduced by aggregating the school input variables to a higher level such as the school, the district, or the state. For this reason, the literature on education production functions yields mixed advice on the appropriate degree of aggregation of the school input variables.

Eric Hanushek, Steven Rivkin, and Lori Taylor have recently explored the aggregation issue in the presence of omitted-variable bias.[13] They point out that in studies that use aggregated school data, relevant family or community control variables are left out of the equation. For example, if the study is based on a national survey of youth, community variables are often unavailable since they would require that the location or name of the school be identified. The direction of the bias cannot be unambiguously predicted. However, based on data from the survey High School and Beyond, they conclude that the coefficients of the school input variables that are aggregated to the state or district level are biased upward. Based on this argument, they discount the production function studies that use district- or state-level school variables. Given that a higher proportion of such studies exhibit positive and statistically significant coefficients than is true for the more disaggregated studies, Hanushek, Rivkin, and Taylor conclude that their analysis supports Hanushek's earlier conclusion that school inputs exert no systematic effects on student test scores. These authors are correct that the use of relatively disaggregated school input variables should be preferred to the use of more aggregated variables whenever key control variables are omitted.

However, their criticism falls short of a general indictment. Our empirical work in this chapter is designed to shed light on the aggregation issue through our estimation of equations based on both aggregated and disaggregated data. Our finding that measured school inputs have effects on achievement in both the student- and the district-level analysis counters the conclusion that positive findings emerge only in misspecified models.

Measurement of School Input Variables

Much of the literature concerns the effects of three key measures of schooling inputs: class size, teachers' experience, and teachers' postcollege education. Some studies, however, also examine the role of teacher quality as measured by teacher test scores. Several studies have documented that

13. Hanushek, Rivkin, and Taylor (1995).

teachers with higher test scores tend to increase the learning of their students more than teachers with lower scores.[14] Moreover, Ferguson has shown that, other things being equal, school districts have to pay more to attract and retain teachers with higher test scores.[15] Hence we believe it is important to include measures of teachers' skills, and we do so in the equations reported below.

Instead of using a direct measure of class size, most researchers use a proxy: pupils per teacher, or its inverse, teachers per pupil. Pupils per teacher is an imperfect proxy for class size for at least two reasons. First, it understates the true average class size by 20 to 25 percent, because not all teachers are in the classroom all the time. Some have administrative duties, and many have some time away from the classroom during the day. A second problem is that the pupil-teacher ratio typically represents an average across all teachers and students in a school or district. Because some teachers may be teaching special education students in small classes while others are teaching regular students in much larger classes, the average could represent a highly misleading picture of the class size for the typical student who is subject to the standardized tests.[16] Moreover, these factors vary across both schools and districts, which creates a measurement problem and may produce estimates of the effect of class size that are biased toward zero. Clearly, a direct measure of class size is preferable to the use of pupils per teacher, especially when the units of analysis are at a disaggregated level such as a grade within the school, and we use such a measure in this chapter.

Disaggregated Student-Level Analysis

The disaggregated analysis reported in this section is consistent with the criteria set out above for a methodologically sound investigation of the links between school inputs and student outcomes, and thus provides an excellent test of whether school resources matter. We focus on a single cohort of students, those in the fourth grade in Alabama in 1990–91, which consists of 29,544 students in 690 schools.

14. Ferguson (1991a, b); Ehrenberg and Brewer (1995).
15. Ferguson (1991a).
16. Typically, special education students are not tested. Only those who are mainstreamed into the regular class take the standardized tests. Hence the appropriate measure of class size is the one that is experienced by the students who are not in special education programs.

Model and Data

The particular version of the value-added model that we use appears as follows:

$$TS_{ij} = \alpha + \beta S_j + \gamma X_{ij}(1 + \lambda Z'_j) + \delta Z_j + \mu_j + \epsilon_{ij}.$$

The dependent variable *TS* refers to a student's test score in reading or in math, where the students are indexed with a subscript *i* and the districts are indexed with a subscript *j*. The students included in the sample are those for whom we have fourth grade scores in reading and math on the Stanford Achievement Test (SAT) and third grade scores in the same subjects on the Basic Competency Test (BCT). All student test score data have been standardized across all students in the state who took the particular test to have a mean of zero and a standard deviation of one. Because the students are not identified by name or number in the test score data sets, we matched students by their birthday, gender, grade, and school. In other words, test score data for a fourth grade student were matched to test score data for a third grade student if that student was in the same school and had the same birth date and sex.[17] Although this process may generate some errors, the errors are likely to be small and to exert no obvious bias.

S is a vector of four school input variables, measured for the fourth grade: three teacher variables and class size. All four variables were calculated from teacher files that include teacher responses to a series of questions about their teaching responsibilities, including the size of the classes they teach. We included regular fourth grade teachers; we excluded teachers who taught special education or who were not teaching in the regular classroom. In the absence of data on a student's specific teachers, we assigned to each student in the sample the average characteristics of the fourth grade teachers in the student's school and the average fourth grade class size in the school.

The three variables that measure the characteristics of teachers are the percentage of teachers with more than five years of experience, the percentage of teachers with a master's degree, and average teachers' test scores. The five-year experience horizon reflects the conventional wisdom that new teachers face a learning curve that flattens out after about five years, although experimentation with other cutoffs yields comparable results. Data for teachers' test scores come from the ACT exams that teachers took

---

17. If a double match occurred, we dropped both students from the sample to minimize the chances of including students who were incorrectly matched.

in the process of applying to college.[18] The teachers' test scores have been standardized to have a mean of zero and a standard deviation of one across all teachers of fourth graders for whom we have ACT test scores. Unfortunately, data are available for only one quarter of all the fourth grade teachers and for all the fourth grade teachers in each school in only 35 of the 690 schools in the sample.[19] Where test scores for some, but not all, fourth grade teachers in a school were available, we simply averaged the scores for fourth grade teachers that were available for that school. When no test scores were available at the school level, we substituted the mean of the fourth-grade teacher test scores at the district level. This procedure generated three different variables for teachers' scores, each representing a different degree of completeness in the sample of scores. Of course, the estimates for the variable representing the 35 schools with full data on scores should yield the best estimates of the effect of teacher quality.

X is a vector of student-specific variables, including third-year test scores, and age, race and gender. The age of the student is included to control for whether a student has been held back. Z is a vector of school or district characteristics, while Z' is a subset of the school or district characteristics that are interacted with some of the student-specific variables. In the absence of student-specific data on family income and educational background of the students' parents, the model includes family background measures reported at the zip code level based on 1990 census data or reported at the school level based on administrative records. On average, there are about three schools per zip code area. The parental education variables include the percentages of adults with sixteen or more years of schooling, with twelve to fifteen years, nine to eleven years, and with less than nine years.[20] Family income is proxied by the log of per capita income

18. Access to these data was arranged by state officials during the summer of 1992 to facilitate Ferguson's participation in a court challenge to the constitutionality of Alabama's system of public schooling. Given the importance of teachers' test scores and other schooling inputs in predicting student performance in Texas (Ferguson 1991a, b), the purpose of the analysis was to discover for the plaintiffs whether the importance of resources in prior results for Texas applied to schools in Alabama as well.

19. The sample of 690 schools includes 69 for which we had to fill in some missing data for some of the control variables. Data were sometimes missing on parental education at the zip code level and, in a few cases, for the percentage of students on free or reduced-price lunch. To fill in the missing parental education data, we used districtwide values from the census. For the free and reduced-price lunch variables, we used other socioeconomic variables in the model to predict the missing values. Note that any school that teaches fourth grade but not third grade is excluded because we had to match students by school. Had students been identified by number on the files, these schools could have been included.

20. The first three of the parental education variables are available from the census at the zip code level. The last one, the percentage of adults with less than a high school

at the zip code level and the percentage of students in the school who are approved for either free or reduced-price lunch.[21] The model also includes one other school-level variable—the percentage of students in the school's fourth grade who were not at that same school in the third grade—as a measure of the mobility of students into the school, and four other district characteristics: district enrollment, the percentage of students in public schools, the percentage of the district that is urban, and a variable to indicate whether the district is a city district in contrast to a county district.

Finally, α, β, γ, and δ are scalars to be estimated in the equation. ϵ is a student-specific error term, and μ is a school-specific error term. Both μ and ϵ are assumed to be independent of the included explanatory variables and to be uncorrelated across units of observation.

Because students are grouped within schools, we estimated the equation as a hierarchical linear model rather than as a standard regression model. The advantage of a hierarchical linear model is that it explicitly embeds the student-level model within a school- or district-level model, and thus allows us to account for grouping of students by schools.[22] (See the appendix for the full model and description of all the variables.)

Results for Control Variables

This equation explains from 54 to 62 percent of the variation in test scores among students and from 59 to 80 percent of the variation among schools. The four school input variables are clearly the focus of our analysis. But before discussing them, we briefly summarize the effects of some of the other variables. A complete summary of regression results appears in the appendix.

At the student level, the model includes prior-year test score variables; indicator variables for being African American, other nonwhite, or male; and an age variable, with the latter four interacted with some school-level variables. Prior-year reading and math scores are each entered as two variables to allow for the possibility that students who performed well on the third grade test may have gained at a different rate compared with those who performed poorly. In each case, the third grade test score variable

---

education, is available only at the district level.

21. Because the state does not collect school-level information on the number of students approved for free or reduced-price lunches, we worked with the Alabama Department of Education to collect this information directly from every district in the state.

22. See Bryk and Raudenbush (1992).

is split at its mean of zero, with above-average test scores generating an additional coefficient to be added to the coefficient on the basic variable. Third grade reading scores emerge as an important predictor of both reading and math scores in the fourth grade. Third grade math scores are also a significant predictor but, not surprisingly, math skill seems to be less important for reading than reading is for math. In addition, the positive coefficients on the third grade test scores for students scoring above average indicate that students who scored well in the third grade appear to retain more and to gain more during the fourth grade than their fellow students.

African American students typically perform less well than white students even after controlling for the other variables in the equation, a pattern that Ferguson has shown becomes even more pronounced in later grades.[23] In interviews, teachers and other community-based professionals who work with African American youth suggest that attitudes and behaviors that interfere with academic performance operate most strongly in urban environments and tend to become more prevalent (especially for boys) when children reach the ages of 9 or 10—around the fourth grade. At this age, they argue, community-based interventions can make a tremendous difference.[24]

If various attitudes and behaviors cause the academic performance of African American boys to drift downward beginning in the middle elementary years, and if the same behaviors are more prevalent in urban than in rural environments, then one would expect to observe some interaction effects between race and gender and between race and urban residence. We find such effects. The estimated coefficient on the interaction of race and urban residence indicates that differences in test scores between African Americans and whites are larger in districts that are more urban. Further, while males on average do less well on fourth grade tests than do females of the same racial group, male fourth graders in schools where high percentages of the students are African American do even less well relative to their female counterparts than males in schools with fewer African Americans. Although these interaction effects are not very large, they are statistically significant and they probably foreshadow trends that continue beyond the fourth grade.

As noted earlier, all of the variables that represent socioeconomic indexes are measured at the group level. Among the parental education variables, only the presence of a large proportion of college-educated adults

23. Ferguson (1991b).
24. Ferguson (1994).

appears to exert a consistent and positive effect on student test scores. The percentages of students receiving free or reduced-price lunches enter negatively, as expected, but with more consistency and precision for the free-lunch than the reduced-price lunch category. Per capita income adds no explanatory power. In the math equation, the negative coefficient on the fraction of students who were new to the school in the fourth grade indicates that the demands of accommodating new students have adverse effects on the learning of students continuing from the previous year. The district-level variables contribute little with the exception of district enrollment; this coefficient implies that students in large districts perform better, all else being equal, than their peers in smaller districts.

Effects of School Inputs

The estimates here show that measurable school inputs—specifically teacher quality, percentage of teachers with master's degrees, and class size—do affect student test scores.

The first measure of teachers' test scores (and the only one based on complete data) enters with a positive and statistically significant coefficient in the reading equation.[25] The coefficient in the math equation is positive but smaller relative to its standard error.[26] Measurement error in the other two test score variables suggests their coefficients are downward biased and can be largely discounted.

How large is the effect of teacher quality, as measured by test scores? The 0.10 coefficient for reading implies that a difference of one standard deviation in the distribution of teacher test scores would generate a difference of 0.10 standard deviations in the distribution of student test scores. To put this figure in perspective, consider two schools, one serving pre-

25. We experimented with two additional indicator variables that are not reported here. One variable equaled one for observations that used the school-level measure for teachers' scores and was zero otherwise. The second equaled one for observations that used the district-level measure and zero otherwise. The omitted base category was for the thirty-five schools that had test scores for all fourth grade teachers. These indicator variables had very small coefficients with *t*-statistics well below one. Other coefficients were essentially unchanged.

26. The lack of precision is not surprising, given the limited number of schools for which complete data are available. Recall that the coefficient is estimated based on a sample of only thirty-five schools.

dominantly African American students with low-quality teachers and one serving predominantly white students with higher-quality teachers. Our results imply that an increase of one standard deviation in the quality of the first school's teachers could offset about half of the average negative effect on reading scores estimated for an African American student relative to a white student in a school district that is 50 percent urban.[27] For the combined math and reading results, the coefficients suggest that the increase in teacher test scores would offset about two-thirds of the average difference between being African American and being white in a 50 percent urban district.

Alternatively, the effect of teacher test scores can be compared with the estimated effects of the socioeconomic characteristics of the community. For example, the estimated coefficients imply that it would take an increase of 25 percentage points in the percentage of college-educated adults (which is equivalent to slightly less than a two–standard deviation change) to achieve the same gain in reading test scores that could be obtained by substituting teachers with test scores one standard deviation higher than those of the school's current teachers.[28]

Although the fraction of teachers with master's degrees appears to have little or no effect on reading scores, it exerts a small positive effect on student math scores: a one–standard deviation increase in the fraction of teachers with a master's degree (0.33 points) would increase student test scores by 0.026 standard deviations, about one-quarter the effect of a standard deviation increase in teacher test scores. In contrast, the teacher experience variable, teachers with five or more years of experience, apparently exerts no significant effect in either subject.[29]

27. Calculated from the reading equation as $-0.156 + 50 \times -0.001$.
28. The effect of the socioeconomic status of the community should be distinguished from that of the student's family. We predict that if data had been available on the education level of the student's parents, larger estimated effects of adult education would have emerged. The results for the community-level education variable correspond to the following thought experiment: they measure the effects of taking a child (and her family) out of a poor environment, for example, an urban housing project, and putting that child down in a school in an upper-class neighborhood where a much larger proportion of the adults have a college education, while holding all else constant, including school input measures.
29. Although this latter finding may well represent the true relationship, a cleaner test of the relationship between teacher experience and student learning requires more complete data on teacher test scores. Within our sample, teacher test scores are negatively associated with experience, presumably because many teachers with high scores do not remain in the profession. Because old teachers are underrepresented in the data on ACT scores, the experience variable may be picking up some teacher quality effects as well as experience, which would bias the coefficient downward.

Figure 8-1. *Effect of Lower Class Size on Reading and Math Test Scores for Fourth Graders*[a]

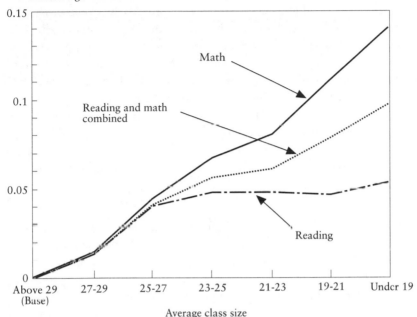

Predicted gain in score

a. The endpoints of the graph correspond to the estimated coefficients for the largest and the smallest class sizes (reported in table 8A-1). The intermediate points are averages of the coefficients of the specified class size and the next larger and next smaller size.

Class size is specified as a series of variables, which allows us to examine the pattern of effects as class sizes are reduced over the relevant range. Each estimated coefficient represents the difference in student test scores relative to the base class size of over twenty-nine students. Although the pattern in the coefficients is not completely monotonic, the general trajectories are clear and are shown graphically in figure 8-1. For math, class sizes of under nineteen generate student test scores that exceed those for the base by 0.14 standard deviations. For reading, the estimated effects are somewhat smaller, about 0.05 standard deviations, and for the combined scores, about 0.10 standard deviations. For reading, the gains level off at a class size in the mid-twenties. But for math and for the combined scores, gains in test scores occur throughout the relevant range of reductions in class size. More learning apparently occurs in smaller fourth grade classes than in larger classes, especially in math. Further investigation of the math gains indicates that the gains from smaller classes are greater for girls than for boys; a class size of less than nineteen increases girls' math scores by 0.17 standard deviations relative to the base case, while a similar class size increases boys' scores by only 0.10 standard deviations.[30]

This student-level analysis supports the view that various measurable school inputs affect student learning. In particular, teacher quality—as measured by test scores and the proportion of teachers with master's degrees—and class size appear to affect learning. In contrast, we have no evidence that more teacher experience, all else held constant, generates gains in student learning. These measurable effects at the micro level for fourth graders are supported by similar findings from analysis at the district level for eighth and ninth graders.

District-Level Analysis

Compared with the student-level analysis, the district-level models we present here are potentially subject to more methodological criticism. Nonetheless, we believe they contain some useful information. Our analysis of student test scores for 127 public school districts in Alabama indicates once again that students learn more when their teachers are more skilled as measured by their own test scores, when a larger proportion of teachers have master's degrees, and when class sizes are smaller. Once again, teacher experience has no measurable effect. These effects emerge for both reading and math. For economy of exposition, we report here only the results for math, which tend to be a bit stronger than those for reading. The consistency of results between the student-level and the district-level findings suggests that the assumptions underlying the district-level analysis are plausible.

The Model and Data

At the district level, we estimate gains in learning between the fourth and the ninth grades as a function of, among other things, the school inputs

30. For girls, the relevant coefficients (and *t*-statistics) on the six class-size variables, in descending order, are 0.007 (0.16), 0.057 (1.40), 0.034 (0.82), 0.063 (1.38), 0.107 (2.13), 0.169 (3.05). For boys, they are 0.024 (0.58), 0.074 (1.78), 0.057 (1.37), 0.105 (2.28), 0.103 (2.00), and 0.105 (1.86). These results emerge from models not reported here that are estimated separately for girls and boys. Coefficients for the other school inputs, such as teacher test scores and master's degrees, are virtually identical for girls and boys.

available to students at the intervening grade levels. The choice of grades was dictated largely by the availability of test data. The state administers the Stanford Achievement Test in grades 4 and 8 and the Basic Competency Test in grades 3, 6, and 9. We define the dependent variable as the average composite of math scores from the SAT for the eighth grade and from the BCT for the ninth grade for the 1989–90 school year. The SAT, BCT, and composite scores have all been standardized to have a mean of zero and a standard deviation of one across districts.

Because we have data at the district level for only one year, 1989–90, we are unable to implement a true value-added model. Instead, we include as explanatory variables reading and math scores based on the average of the third grade BCT and the fourth grade SAT during the 1989–90 school year. One can view these as the scores of the younger brothers and sisters of the current eighth and ninth grade students and, therefore, as proxies for the scores that the current eighth and ninth graders would have earned when they were in the third and fourth grades.[31]

Like the disaggregated analysis, the equations include four school input variables: three teacher variables and class size. Except for the teacher test score variable, the input measures are based only on regular classes and regular teachers in grades 4 through 9. For example, class sizes are based on the responses of teachers who taught in one of those grades rather than on those of all teachers in the district. Because of the large amount of missing data on teacher test scores, the average teacher test score variable is based on all teachers teaching regular classes in the district rather than just those in grades 4 through 9.[32] Like the scores for the students, the test scores

31. This approach is reasonable if the following assumptions are met. First, the position of each district relative to all the other districts in terms of the distribution of families by socioeconomic status remains relatively constant over the five-year period. From this assumption, it follows that the backgrounds of the students in each district in the third (or fourth) grade in 1984–85 would be similar to the backgrounds of third (or fourth) grade students in the district in 1989–90. Second, the position of each district relative to all other districts in terms of the school resources available in each grade remains relatively constant over the same period, which implies that the third and fourth grade students in 1984–85 would have been exposed to the same school effects in the earlier grades as third and fourth grade students in 1989–90. Third, the exposure to learning during grades 4 through 9 in each of the following years can be measured by the resources available in each grade in 1989–90. Although these assumptions are quite strong, we believe that they hold in an approximate way for data at the district level. They would clearly be much less acceptable at the school level.

32. Moreover, the district average was calculated as a weighted average of the actual average for young teachers and an estimate for more experienced teachers. We used this procedure because teacher ACT scores were available for about 60 percent of the relevant teachers who had less than five years of experience but for only a much smaller proportion of more experienced teachers. For the young teachers, we used the actual average ACT

for teachers have been standardized across districts to have a mean of zero and a standard deviation of one.

In addition to the school input variables, the equation includes parental education variables, per capita income, and a family poverty variable (the percentage of families with children ages 5 to 18 living in poverty) to control for the socioeconomic backgrounds of the students. All of these data come from the 1990 Census of Population. Conveniently, school districts in Alabama have boundaries that correspond to either cities or counties, so that data from the census cover the appropriate geographic areas. The equation also includes two enrollment variables—total enrollment and percentage of students who are nonwhite, with the latter also interacted with the percentage of the district that is urban—and three other district characteristics: the percentage of students in public schools, the percentage of the district that is urban, and a variable to indicate if the district is a city district.

The regressions are based on data for the 127 of the 131 districts for which complete data are available. Each observation is weighted by the square root of the district's enrollment, the standard correction for heteroskedasticity when observations are averages of groups that differ in size.

Results

The coefficients for various multivariate regression models were estimated using weighted least squares. The complete results are reported in the appendix. But the clear conclusion emerges that measurable school inputs affect educational outcomes. Only teacher experience has no estimated effect. A difference of one standard deviation in teacher test scores increases student test scores by about 0.25 standard deviations. Given that the analysis covers five years of schooling, the magnitude of this effect is proportionate to the smaller (and less precisely estimated) figure of 0.055 for math from the student-level analysis, which applies to a single year.

The fraction of teachers with master's degrees exerts a positive effect on student learning. A difference of 8 percentage points in the proportion of

scores within each district. For the more experienced teachers, we regressed their average test scores by district on the average scores for the younger teachers and the average experience of the older teachers for whom we had test scores, and used the regression to predict the average test scores of all the older teachers within each district. We then calculated the district average as the weighted average of the average ACT scores for young teachers within the district and the estimated average for old teachers, weighted by the district-specific shares of young and old teachers.

such teachers (equivalent to one standard deviation in the distribution across districts) is associated with a difference of 0.11 standard deviations in student test scores (0.08 times 1.43). These effects are smaller than those for teacher test scores, but not trivial.

Within the range of average class sizes in the sample, smaller class sizes typically generate higher test scores. When class size is measured as a simple average across the district, a reduction of three in average class size (say from twenty-seven to twenty-four) would increase student test scores by 0.26 (three times the coefficient), a magnitude only slightly smaller than the effect of an increase of one standard deviation in teacher test scores. These results are robust to different specifications. For example, when we estimated these equations *without* using the third and fourth grade test scores as a control, it remained true that the school input variables were significant and of the expected direction. To check for nonlinearities in the relationship and the possibility of a threshold class size below which no further gains would be obtained, we entered class size as a series of variables. We found that reducing class size from an average of twenty-six to twenty-five or twenty-four is associated with increasingly higher math test scores. There are few observations below that number, which makes the results unstable, but it is fair to say that we find no evidence that eighth and ninth grade test scores are higher as students are exposed to class sizes below twenty-three. Specific results for these alternate regressions are also presented in the appendix.

With respect to the control variables, we note that neither per capita income nor the poverty rate among families with children enters with a statistically significant coefficient. This lack of effect emerges despite the fact that the simple correlation between the log of per capita income and test scores for math is large and positive ($r = 0.59$) and that between the poverty rate and test scores for math is large and negative ($r = -0.57$). Presumably, any effects of income operate through the correlation of income with other variables in the equations, such as the fraction of adults with a college education, the fraction of the population that is urban, or the fraction of students who are African American. Using the percentage of students on free and reduced-price lunch does not change any of the results.

The relative importance of the estimated effects is shown in table 8-1. The table shows the contributions of each type of variable to the predicted difference between districts that score in the top quartile and those that score in the bottom quartile of the distribution of district-average math scores. The actual difference between the high- and the low-scoring dis-

Table 8-1. *Components of the Predicted Difference in Eighth and Ninth Grade Math Scores*

Component	Contribution to predicted difference (percent)
School inputs	
Teachers' ACT scores	15.1
Teachers with master's degrees	6.1
Teachers with 5 or more years' experience	2.8
Average class size	7.5
Other determinants	
Adults with 16 or more years of schooling	17.0
Poverty rate	2.1
Percent nonwhite	3.3
Interaction of percent nonwhite with percent urban	7.1
District enrollment characteristics (enrollment, city versus county, percent public schools, percent urban)	8.2
Third and fourth grade reading and math scores	30.9

Source: Based on coefficients in column 2 of table 8A-2 and mean values of explanatory variables for districts in the top and bottom 25 percent of the distribution of district-average math scores for eighth and ninth grades.

tricts in the math scores for eighth and ninth graders is 2.77 standard deviations. The predicted difference is 1.57 standard deviations. Hence the prediction captures more than half of the actual difference. The school input variables combine to account for 31 percent, with teachers' scores accounting for half of this contribution. Race, parental education, and variables that control for characteristics of the district account for an additional 38 percent of the predicted difference. The third and fourth grade scores contribute 31 percent of the total predicted difference in eighth and ninth grade scores.

The contributions of the school input variables reflect input levels that vary between the low- and high-scoring districts. Expressed in standard deviations of each input variable, the differences between the high- and the low-scoring districts are 1.22 for teachers' ACT scores, 1.53 for the share of teachers with master's degrees, 0.55 for the share of teachers with over five years' experience, and 0.76 (1.74 students per class) for average class size. The analysis implies that a narrowing of these differences in school inputs would lead to smaller differences in student test scores between low- and high-scoring districts. Because the three schooling inputs that exert some explanatory power—teachers' test scores, teachers' education, and class size—all cost money, our finding that they affect student test scores means that money matters as well. We now address the importance of money more directly.

Instructional Spending

One additional benefit of carrying out the district-level analysis is that it allows us to generate estimates of how changes in instructional spending could affect students' test scores. The obvious approach here is simply to use the same basic specification and the same dependent variables, but to replace the school input measures with the level of per pupil spending. However, this approach will not work well, because spending cannot be treated as an exogenous variable. In Alabama, there is compensatory spending in districts where student performance on standardized tests is the poorest. Thus, not only does spending affect performance, but student performance affects spending. As a result, no systematic relationship emerges between student test scores and actual instructional spending.

The reverse causality is confirmed by formal tests for endogeneity. Specifically, a Durbin-Wu-Hausman test for endogeneity (not shown here) clearly rejects the null hypothesis that spending is exogenous. In contrast, the same test implies that teachers' test scores are exogenous to student performance. Results for class size, teachers' experience and master's degrees are more mixed, but our judgment is that these variables should also be treated as exogenous to student performance for the present analysis.[33] Spending is the only measure of schooling resources for which the null hypothesis of exogeneity is clearly and persuasively rejected.[34]

To find the effect of spending on student performance, we use an instrumental variable approach that provides estimates of instructional spending

33. When an instrumental variables estimate for class size is used along with the unadjusted numbers for the other variables, the estimated effects of class size are even larger than those reported here. Similarly, when instrumental variables estimates for teacher experience or master's degrees are used, the measured effects are stronger for some, though not all, specifications. When instrumented estimates for class size, experience and master's degrees are entered together, an F-test for joint significance shows statistical significance but collinearity among the three that makes their separate effects difficult to distinguish.

34. The endogeneity of spending can be reconciled with the exogeneity of class size as follows. A close look at the districts that rank in the bottom 10 percent of the test score distribution shows that such districts actually spend 12 percent more per student for instruction and 17 percent more per student for noninstructional inputs than would be predicted by the exogenous explanatory variables reported in table 8-2. While these eleven districts clearly spend more money than the equation would otherwise predict, they do not have smaller class sizes than predicted. Thus the additional spending is apparently not being allocated to smaller class sizes for the typical student.

Table 8-2. *Determinants of Instructional and Noninstructional Spending per Pupil*[a]

Dependent variable	Ln (instructional spending per pupil)	Ln (noninstructional spending per pupil)
Ln (property value per student)	0.079	0.111
	(3.68)	(3.59)
Ln (per capita income)	0.192	0.035
	(5.16)	(0.65)
Enrollment in the district	−0.005	−0.012
	(4.55)	(7.25)
Number of schools in the district	0.003	0.007
	(3.35)	(6.59)
Constant	4.683	5.743
	(16.08)	(13.68)
Adjusted R [a]	0.453	0.401
N	129	129

a. Estimated using weighted least squares. Numbers in parentheses are absolute values of *t*-statistics. Dependent variable is natural logarithm of instructional or noninstructional spending per pupil, by district.

that are purged of the reverse causation from poor student performance to more spending. Our predictors for (the natural logarithm of) instructional spending per pupil, and also for comparison, noninstructional spending, are shown in table 8-2. Property value and per capita income represent demand variables: the greater the local wealth, the greater is likely to be the local financial support for education. The other two variables represent cost variables. Larger enrollment will lead to lower costs per student if there are economies of scale. Controlling for enrollment, more schools may mean higher costs because of the fixed costs of running each school. These variables enter with the predicted signs and are statistically significant. The only anomaly is the income variable in the noninstructional spending equation, which might possibly be explained by high noninstructional costs associated with the administration of special education programs. The high correlation between instructional and noninstructional spending and the stronger conceptual link between instructional spending and student performance led us to include only instructional spending in the equation that predicts students' test scores.

The new equation for test scores uses the same basic specification and the same dependent variables as before, but replaces the school input measures with the *estimated* measure of spending. We tried two different ways of specifying the spending variable: log-linear form and a form that allows the effect of spending to vary depending on whether spending is below or above the median.[35] Complete results from the estimation are available in the appendix.[36] We conclude that, all else held constant, districts with lower estimated spending have lower test scores.

Consider the estimated effect of a 10 percent difference in instructional spending, which would represent about one and one-half standard deviations in the distribution of predicted instructional spending across Alabama districts. With the linear specification of the spending variable, this difference in spending would correspond to a difference of 0.356 standard deviations in average scores across districts. The nonlinear specification indicates that the effect of increased spending is concentrated among the districts whose spending levels are below the median: for these districts, the jump would be 0.881 standard deviations. This large effect approximates the difference between the tenth percentile and the median of student test scores. When spending is above the median, the estimated effect of higher spending is small and not statistically different from zero. This general pattern holds true whether or not third and fourth grade scores are included in the regression.

The implicit consequences for individual students are not trivial. The student-level data used above for the third and fourth grades show that the standard deviation of BCT scores in the student-level data is about twice the standard deviation of the district-average score. For the SAT, the student-level standard deviation is three times the district-average deviation. If the same proportions hold for eighth and ninth graders, a 10 percent difference in spending for districts that are below the median in spending

35. If instructional spending is above its median value, the marginal effect of spending is the sum of the estimates from the first and second row of the table. To implement this specification, the supplementary variable to which the second coefficient for instructional spending applies equals zero when the log of instructional spending is below its median value. Above the median spending level, it equals the log of instructional spending minus its median value. Hence the variable to which the second coefficient applies "turns on" at the median value of instructional spending. Alternative specifications that allowed for changes in slope at the first and third quartiles of instructional spending showed no statistically significant changes in slope at these points.

36. Because the coefficients of per capita income were small and insignificant in table 8A-2, we treated it as an exogenous instrument for the purposes of modeling instructional spending and excluded it from the equations explaining test scores reported in table 8A-3. Its negative correlation with student test scores, all else held constant, means that its inclusion in the table 8A-3 equations strengthens the conclusion that instructional spending affects test scores. When per capita income is included in the equations of table 8A-3, its coefficient is always negative with *t*-values that range from −1.0 to −1.92. All of the coefficients on instructional spending become larger by about 20 percent.

corresponds to roughly one-third to one-half of a standard deviation of change among individual students in the statewide distribution.

The predicted effects of spending in Alabama, especially for districts below the median in terms of per pupil spending, are remarkably large. Because most other states spend more than Alabama, we would not expect to find such large spending effects in other states. But Alabama has been among the states spending the least for education for decades, and districts at the bottom of the Alabama distribution of spending are surely among the most weakly staffed and poorly equipped in the country. For such districts, our results suggest that sustained additional funding can make a substantial difference. Current spending patterns suggest that the state is now addressing some of the historical inequalities in spending.

Conclusions

Our analysis of the determinants of student test scores in Alabama provides strong support for the hypothesis that measurable school inputs affect student learning. Moreover, the results for the district-level analysis confirm and reinforce Ferguson's 1991 results for school districts in Texas. Given our attention to good data, a large sample, and a sound specification, we believe that these results are credible and deserve attention.

Three of the four school input variables we consider—teacher test scores, teacher education, and class size—appear to affect student learning. The skills of teachers as measured by their test scores exert consistently strong and positive effects on student learning despite the fact that the data are limited and test scores are an imperfect measure of teachers' skill, which suggests that teacher skills are extremely important. The primary unresolved issue is the level of the class size threshold below which further reductions would lead to no additional systematic gains in student learning. If a threshold exists, we are confident that it is no higher than the mid-twenties—in the range of twenty-three to twenty-five.

Finally, the finding that measurable and costly school inputs affect learning means that money matters. Our direct analysis of the effects of instructional spending based on an instrumental variables approach reinforces this conclusion, especially for low-spending districts. Of course, we are not suggesting that additional spending will always or immediately increase student learning or that it is a prerequisite for learning gains. In some schools, significant gains may come not through additional funding, but rather through school restructuring.[37] Indeed, significant restructuring may well be a more productive alternative for schools that already have relatively high quality teachers or small class sizes but still perform poorly. However, restructuring and higher spending are not mutually exclusive; there will be times to focus on one, or the other, or on a combination of the two.

Some other suggestive findings emerge from our analysis. For example, we find that introducing new students into schools at the fourth grade reduces the performance of students in those schools who are continuing from the third grade. If this finding is borne out in other studies, it would suggest that housing and education policies designed to reduce the frequency with which students change schools may improve test scores even for the students who would not have been among the movers.

In addition, this study hints that it may be beneficial to devote resources to activities that strengthen the academic commitment of students who are prone to disengage from classroom learning. Even after controlling for measured school and community inputs, African American children—and especially boys in urban areas—have smaller test score gains between the third and fourth grades than whites. These findings may reflect systematic social forces that operate inside and outside of the classroom to reduce the academic commitment of a disproportionate share of African American children. Hence, in addition to delivering adequate and equitable levels of the educational inputs upon which this chapter focuses, it may also be necessary to allocate resources to identify, to understand, and to confront destructive social forces that operate in and around local school communities.

Appendix

The hierarchical linear model takes the following form where all variables other than the dependent variable Y are defined in table 8A-1. Y is the math, reading, or composite test score for the ith student in the jth school. As can be seen, we implemented the model as a random-intercept model, which limits the error terms to two types, one that appears in the level 1 model (R) and one ($U0$) that appears in the equation for $B0$ at the second level. Other coefficients in the second level are estimated as fixed effects, or in other words, without error terms.

37. As examples of restructuring, see chapter 9 in this volume.

Level-1 model:

$$Y = B0 + B1 \times (ZR90) + B2 \times (ZM90) + B3 \times (ZR90H)$$
$$+ B4 \times (ZM90H) + B5 \times (BLACK) + B6 \times (OTHER)$$
$$+ B7 \times (AGE91) + B8 \times (MALE) + R.$$

Level-2 model:

$$B0 = G00 + G01 \times (ZREALACT) + G02 \times (ZREALSCH)$$
$$+ G03 \times (ZREALDIS) + G04 \times (CS2728)$$
$$+ G05 \times (CS2526) + G06 \times (CS2324) + G07 \times (CS2122)$$
$$+ G08 \times (CS1920) + G09 \times (CSLT19)$$
$$+ G010 \times (P5PLUS4) + G011 \times (MASTER4)$$
$$+ G012 \times (LTHS) + G013 \times (PCTHSGZ)$$
$$+ G014 \times (PCOLGRZ) + G015 \times (PLUNCHF)$$
$$+ G016 \times (PLUNCHR) + G017 \times (PCTPUBS)$$
$$+ G018 \times (PCTURB) + G019 \times (CAME)$$
$$+ G020 \times (CITYDIST) + G021 \times (ENRL) + U0.$$

$$B1 = G10$$

$$B2 = G20$$

$$B3 = G30$$

$$B4 = G40$$

$$B5 = G50 + G51 \times (PCTURB)$$

$$B6 = G60 + G61 \times (PCTURB)$$

$$B7 = G70 + G71 \times (PCTURB) + G72 \times (SBLACK)$$
$$+ G73 \times (SOTHER)$$

$$B8 = G80 + G81 \times (PCTURB) + G82 \times (SBLACK)$$
$$+ G83 \times (SOTHER).$$

Table 8A-1. *Determinants of Reading and Math Test Scores for Fourth Graders in Alabama Schools*[a]

Variable	Reading	Math	Reading and math combined
School input variables			
Teacher ACT score (average for schools with scores for all teachers)	0.103** (2.01)	0.055 (0.85)	0.079 (1.52)
Teacher ACT score (average for schools with scores for some teachers)	0.011 (0.96)	0.003 (0.19)	0.007 (0.56)
Teacher ACT score (district average for schools with scores for no teachers)	−0.011 (0.37)	0.004 (0.11)	−0.003 (0.09)
Teachers with master's degrees (proportion)	0.016 (0.52)	0.080** (2.05)	0.048 (1.54)
Teachers with 5 or more years' experience (proportion)	−0.016 (0.40)	−0.044 (0.87)	−0.030 (0.73)
Class size			
29 and over	Base	Base	Base
27 to 28	0.013 (0.44)	0.014 (0.31)	0.013 (0.42)
25 to 26	0.055* (1.83)	0.069* (1.74)	0.062** (1.98)
23 to 24	0.048 (1.62)	0.048 (1.74)	0.048 (1.56)
21 to 22	0.030 (0.90)	0.085** (1.96)	0.057* (1.67)**
19 to 20	0.055 (1.50)	0.107** (2.23)	0.079** (2.10)
Under 19	0.053 (1.31)	0.140** (2.71)	0.097** (2.35)
Student level control variables			
Third grade reading score	0.213** (27.07)	0.084** (10.84)	0.149** (22.36)
Third grade reading score if greater than 0 (add coefficient to previous coefficient)	1.201** (59.84)	0.791** (40.09)	0.997** (58.86)
Third grade math score	−0.008 (0.95)	0.187** (22.90)	0.090** (12.80)
Third grade math score if greater than 0 (add coefficient to previous coefficient)	0.499* (28.73)	0.825** (48.26)	0.663** (45.18)
African American, 0-1 variable	−0.156** (7.35)	0.016 (0.77)	−0.070** (3.84)

Table 8A-1 *(continued)*

Variable	Reading	Math	Reading and math combined
African American, interacted with percent of district that is urban	−0.001** (3.06)	−0.001** (2.79)	−0.001** (3.39)
Nonwhite, non-African American, 0-1 variable	0.052 (1.18)	0.064 (1.46)	0.058 (1.55)
Nonwhite, non-African American, interacted with percent of district that is urban	−0.002** (2.91)	0.001 (1.44)	−0.000 (0.88)
Age of student (years)	−0.171** (13.85)	−0.148** (12.15)	−0.159** (15.28)
Age of student, interacted with percent of district that is urban	0.000 (0.20)	0.000 (0.54)	−0.000 (0.20)
Age of student, interacted with fraction of African American students in fourth grade in the school	0.011** (1.98)	0.018** (2.73)	0.015** (2.86)
Age of student, interacted with fraction of nonwhite and non-African American students in fourth grade in the school	−0.002 (0.17)	−0.006 (0.39)	−0.004 (0.30)
Male student, 0-1 variable	−0.015 (1.01)	−0.052** (3.54)	−0.033** (2.66)
Male student, interacted with percent of district that is urban	−0.000 (0.66)	0.001** (2.66)	0.000 (1.17)
Male student, interacted with fraction African American in grade in school	−0.007 (0.29)	−0.050** (2.22)	−0.028 (1.47)
Male student, interacted with fraction nonwhite and non-African American in grade in school	−0.101 (0.94)	−0.109 (1.04)	−0.103 (1.14)
Group variables[b]			
Adults with 16 or more years of school (percent) (Z)	0.004** (3.58)	0.004** (2.63)	0.004** (3.33)
Adults with 12–15 years of schooling (percent) (Z)	−0.002 (0.98)	−0.001 (0.25)	−0.001 (0.64)
Adults with 9–11 years of schooling (percent) (Z)	Base	Base	Base

Table 8A-1 *(continued)*

Variable	Reading	Math	Reading and math combined
Adults with less than 9 years of schooling (percent) (D)	0.003 (0.75)	0.014** (3.00)	0.008** (2.25)
Per capita income (logarithm) (Z)	−0.017 (0.24)	0.009 (0.10)	0.001 (0.01)
Students receiving free lunch (percent) (S)	−0.003** (4.68)	−0.003** (3.09)	−0.003** (4.34)
Students receiving reduced-price lunch (percent) (S)	−0.003 (1.04)	−0.001 (0.26)	−0.002 (0.65)
New students as percent of fourth grade students (G)	−0.201 (1.46)	−0.487** (2.74)	−0.347** (2.46)
Public school students as percent of all students (D)	0.001 (0.18)	−0.000 (0.03)	0.000 (0.09)
Urban population as percent of district population (D)	0.000 (0.10)	0.001 (0.43)	0.000 (0.33)
City district (not county), 0-1 variable, (D)	0.004 (0.08)	0.031 (0.54)	0.015 (0.33)
District enrollment (D)	0.001* (1.73)	0.003** (3.39)	0.002** (2.92)
Intercept	1.42** (2.09)	0.715 (0.81)	1.02 (1.47)
Number of observations (students)	29,544	29,544	29,544
Number of schools	690	690	690
Variance components			
Student level			
Unconditional variance	0.8301	0.8313	0.7179
Conditional variance	0.3798	0.3660	0.2697
Proportion explained (percent)	54	56	62
School level			
Unconditional variance	0.1877	0.1890	0.1738
Conditional variance	0.0404	0.0774	0.0474
Proportion explained (percent)	79	59	73

*Significant at the .1 level.
**Significant at the .05 level.
a. Based on a random-intercept hierarchical linear model. Dependent variable is fourth grade Stanford Achievement Test Scores. Numbers in parentheses are absolute values of *t*-statistics.
b. Z = zip code; D = district; S = school; G = grade.

Table 8A-2. *Determinants of Eighth and Ninth Grade Math Scores in 127 Alabama Districts*[a]

	Linear class size		Nonlinear class size	
Variable	Without scores for grades 3 and 4	With scores for grades 3 and 4	Without scores for grades 3 and 4	With scores for grades 3 and 4
Teacher ACT score	0.251** (3.38)	0.223** (3.19)	0.278** (3.60)	0.248** (3.47)
Teachers with master's degrees (percent)	2.442** (2.96)	1.430* (1.81)	2.326** (2.71)	1.172 (1.44)
Teachers with 5 or more years' experience (percent)	0.754 (0.77)	0.859 (0.96)	1.13 (1.13)	1.236 (1.34)
Class size, average	−0.086** (2.98)	−0.078** (2.94)	...	...
Class size				
Over 26	...	...	Base	Base
25–25.9	...	...	0.355** (1.95)	0.349** (2.11)
24–24.9	...	...	0.383** (2.06)	0.444** (2.63)
Under 24	...	...	0.460** (2.76)	0.489** (3.24)
Adults with 16 or more years of schooling (percent)	0.064** (2.58)	0.032 (1.32)	0.064** (2.55)	0.31 (1.24)
Adults with 12–15 years of schooling (percent)	0.022 (0.76)	0.006 (0.22)	0.019 (0.65)	0.002 (0.81)
Adults with 9–11 years of schooling (percent)	Base	Base	Base	Base
Adults with less than 9 years of schooling (percent)	0.055 (1.05)	0.029 (0.61)	0.052 (0.98)	0.002 (0.08)
Per capita income (natural logarithm)	−0.281 (0.303)	−0.484 (0.56)	−0.317 (0.33)	−0.530 (0.60)
Poverty rate for families with children aged 5–18	−0.009 (0.51)	−0.004 (0.21)	−0.007 (0.37)	−0.002 (0.09)
Nonwhite students (percent)	−0.007 (1.15)	−0.002 (0.28)	−0.007 (0.37)	−0.001 (0.20)
Enrollment, total (in thousands)	0.022** (3.87)	0.018** (3.38)	0.021** (3.72)	0.018** (3.45)
Public school students as percent of all students	0.003 (0.13)	−0.015 (0.67)	0.001 (0.04)	−0.018 (0.79)
Urban population (percent)	−0.007* (1.72)	−0.005 (1.30)	−0.008* (1.93)	−0.005 (1.39)

Table 8A-2 *(continued)*

Variable	Linear class size		Nonlinear class size	
	Without scores for grades 3 and 4	*With scores for grades 3 and 4*	*Without scores for grades 3 and 4*	*With scores for grades 3 and 4*
Interaction between percent nonwhite students and percent urban	−0.0002** (2.59)	−0.0001* (1.77)	−0.0001** (2.57)	−0.0001* (1.88)
City district (0-1 variable)	1.48** (5.36)	1.03 (3.78)	1.55** (5.34)	1.06** (3.79)
Reading scores, grades 3 and 4	. . .	0.319* (1.72)	. . .	0.330* (1.77)
Math scores, grades 3 and 4	. . .	0.187 (1.58)	. . .	0.209* (1.76)
Constant	0.164 (0.02)	5.257 (0.54)	−1.809 (0.17)	3.76 (0.38)
Adjusted R^2	0.71	0.75	0.70	0.75

* Significant at the .1 level.
** Significant at the .05 level.
a. Estimated using weighted least squares. Numbers in parentheses are absolute values of t-statistics.

Table 8A-3. *Effect of Instructional Spending on Eighth and Ninth Grade Math Scores in 127 Alabama Districts*[a]

Variable	Without scores for grades 3 and 4		With scores for grades 3 and 4	
	Linear spending	Nonlinear spending	Linear spending	Nonlinear spending
Ln (predicted instructional spending per student)	4.07** (2.79)	10.36** (3.37)	3.56** (2.72)	8.81** (3.19)
Ln (spending above median)[b]	. . .	−11.00** (2.31)	. . .	−9.19** (2.15)
Adults with 16 or more years of schooling (percent)	0.042* (1.62)	0.053** (2.14)	0.011 (0.48)	0.021 (0.87)
Adults with 12–15 years of schooling (percent)	0.016 (0.54)	−0.002 (0.05)	0.005 (0.18)	−0.010 (0.37)
Adults with 9–11 years of schooling (percent)	Base	Base	Base	Base
Adults with less than 9 years of schooling (percent)	0.045 (0.83)	0.027 (0.50)	0.027 (0.55)	0.011 (0.23)
Poverty rate for families with children aged 5–18	0.007 (0.39)	0.016 (0.89)	0.010 (0.64)	0.018 (1.10)
Nonwhite students (percent)	−0.013** (2.17)	−0.013** (2.14)	−0.005 (0.91)	−0.005 (0.85)
Enrollment, total (in thousands)	0.010** (1.99)	−0.013** (2.14)	0.008* (1.77)	0.013** (2.55)
Public school students as percent of all students	0.032 (1.37)	0.022 (0.93)	0.009 (0.42)	0.0007 (0.031)
Urban population (percent)	0.004 (0.88)	0.0007 (0.16)	0.004 (1.10)	0.0015 (0.40)
Interaction between percent nonwhite students and percent urban	−0.0001** (2.54)	−0.0002** (3.18)	−0.0001** (1.80)	−0.0001** (2.41)
City district (0-1 variable)	0.845** (2.80)	1.15** (3.54)	0.419 (1.50)	0.682** (2.26)
Reading scores, grades 3 and 4	. . .	. . .	0.193 (1.01)	0.210 (1.12)
Math scores, grades 3 and 4	. . .	. . .	0.339** (2.84)	0.317** (2.69)
Constant	−35.02** (2.99)	−79.22** (3.55)	−28.20** (2.66)	−65.13** (3.24)
Adjusted R^2	0.65	0.67	0.73	0.73

**Significant at the .05 level.
a. Weighted least squares. Numbers in parentheses are absolute values of t-statistics.
b. Add coefficient to previous coefficient if spending is above its median.

References

Bryk, Anthony S., and Stephen W. Raudenbush. 1992. *Hierarchical Linear Models: Applications and Data Analysis Methods.* Sage Publications.

Card, David, and Alan B. Krueger. 1992. "Does School Quality Matter? Returns to Education and the Characteristics of Public Schools in the United States." *Journal of Political Economy* 100 (February): 1–40.

Ehrenberg, Ronald G., and Dominic J. Brewer. 1995. "Did Teachers' Race and Verbal Ability Matter in the 1960s? *Coleman* Revisited." *Economics of Education Review* 14 (June): 291–99.

Ferguson, Ronald F. 1991a. "Paying for Public Education: New Evidence on How and Why Money Matters." *Harvard Journal on Legislation* 28 (Summer): 465–97.

————. 1991b. "Racial Patterns in How School and Teacher Quality Affect Achievement and Earnings." *Challenge: A Journal of Research on Black Men* 2 (May): 1–35.

————. 1994. "How Professionals in Community-Based Programs Perceive and Respond to the Needs of Black Male Youth." In *Nurturing Young Black Males,* edited by Ronald B. Miney, 59–98. Washington: Urban Institute Press.

————. 1995. "Shifting Challenges: Fifty Years of Economic Change toward Black-White Earnings Equality." *Daedalus* 124 (Winter): 37–76.

Hanushek, Eric A. 1986. "The Economics of Schooling: Production and Efficiency in Public Schools." *Journal of Economic Literature* 24 (September): 1141–77.

————. 1989. "The Impact of Differential Expenditures on School Performance." *Educational Researcher* 18 (May): 45–51.

————. 1996. "School Resources and Student Performance." In *Does Money Matter? The Link between Schools, Student Achievement, and Adult Success,* edited by Gary Burtless. Brookings.

Hanushek, Eric A., and Lori L. Taylor. 1990 . "Alternative Assessments of the Performance of Schools: Measurement of State Variations in Achievement." *Journal of Human Resources* 25 (Spring): 179–201.

Hanushek, Eric A., Steven G. Rivkin, and Lori L. Taylor. 1995. "Aggregation Bias and the Estimated Effects of School Resources," Working Paper 397. University of Rochester, Center for Economic Research.

Hedges, Larry V., Richard D. Laine, and Rob Greenwald. 1994. "Does Money Matter? A Meta-Analysis of Studies of the Effects of Differential School Inputs on Student Outcomes," *Educational Researcher* 23 (April): 5–14.

Monk, David H. 1992. "Education Productivity Research: An Update and Assessment of Its Role in Education Finance Reform." *Educational Evaluation and Policy Analysis* 14 (Winter): 307–32.

Murnane, Richard J. 1991. "Interpreting the Evidence on 'Does Money Matter.'" *Harvard Journal on Legislation* 28 (Summer): 457–64.

Murnane, Richard J., John Willett, and Frank Levy. 1995. "The Growing Importance of Cognitive Skills in Wage Determination." *Review of Economics and Statistics* 77 (May): 251–66.

Smith, Marshall S., Brett W. Scoll, and Jeffrey Link. 1995. "Research-based Reforms: The Clinton Agenda." U.S. Department of Education.

Speakman, Robert, and Finis Welch. 1995. "Does School Quality Matter? A Reassessment." Texas A&M University, Department of Economics.

CHAPTER NINE

Economics of School Reform: Three Promising Models

W. Steven Barnett

REMARKABLY LITTLE RESEARCH has been conducted on the economics of fundamental school reform or restructuring.[1] In this chapter I review three prominent model programs designed to improve educational outcomes for disadvantaged students. The three models are among the best known and most widely disseminated school reform efforts today: Accelerated Schools, Success for All, and the School Development Program.[2]

All three programs begin with the belief that the educational achievements of poor and minority children can equal those of other children. All of them specify a process of schoolwide change designed to produce increased achievement. All were initially developed for elementary schools but have since been extended to middle schools. If these programs (or others like them) were to be successful on a large scale, they would dramatically change the process and outcomes of education of disadvantaged children in the United States. Moreover, the developers of these programs claim that they can produce large improvements in educational outcomes without large increases in educational costs.

The Three Reform Efforts

Although the three reform efforts share the goal of increasing the educational achievement of disadvantaged children, they approach this goal

The author is grateful to Toyce Collins and Deborah S. Jewett for assistance with the research, Helen Ladd for extensive comments and suggestions, Richard Murnane and William Clune for their comments at the Brookings conference, and Henry Levin, Robert Slavin, Larry Dolan, James Comer, and Norris Haynes for information about the reform models.
    1. For exceptions, see King (1994); Guthrie (1992).
    2. On Accelerated Schools, see Levin (1991a); Hoffenberg, Levin, and Associates (1993). On Success for All, see Slavin and others (1992). On the School Development Program, see Comer (1980); Haynes and Comer (1993).

from different perspectives. Accelerated Schools focus on the need to reorganize school governance and to link reorganization with fundamental changes in a school's approach to teaching and learning. Success for All focuses on instituting specific changes in the technology of instruction. The School Development Program focuses on fostering children's social and emotional development and improving the school climate.

However, the programs also share many elements identified in the literature on effective schools as important for achievement.[3] They all emphasize a challenging curriculum and high expectations for academic achievement; a coherent vision of education focused on high achievement to which staff, students, and parents are committed; staff development focused on achieving the vision; an instructional leader or change agent with clear responsibility for reform; a planning, implementation, and evaluation cycle conducted by school leaders and staff; increased attention to the needs of individual students; instructional methods known to be highly effective; and family support and parent involvement.

Accelerated Schools

The Accelerated Schools project began in 1986 as the result of a five-year study of the education of at-risk students, defined as those who begin school without the experiences that provide the foundation for school success. According to Henry M. Levin, schools traditionally approach such students with low expectations and tedious, unimaginative instruction, which causes their initial educational deficit to widen rather than narrow.[4] In contrast, Accelerated Schools aim to bring at-risk students' performance up to grade level as soon as possible—at the latest, by the end of third grade.

Levin identified three changes that must take place to accomplish this goal: establishing a unity of purpose among the members of the school community; empowering the school community to make essential decisions regarding operation of the school; and building on the strengths of students, staff, and parents.[5] Unity of purpose is established through the development of a common vision and an action plan, which become the focus of the activities of all the school participants, including parents,

3. Purkey and Smith (1983); Walberg (1992).
4. Levin (1991b).
5. Levin (1991b).

teaching and nonteaching staff, and students.[6] School participants assume responsibility for significant educational decisions including "curriculum, instructional strategies, instructional materials, personnel, and allocation of resources inside the school."[7] The role of the central office changes from controlling decisionmaking—which Levin argues has stifled the initiative of school-based staff—to providing support services to the school. Finally, rather than focusing on the shortfalls in their resources and the limitations of the students, parents, and staff, Accelerated Schools treat all students as gifted and talented. The strengths of school personnel and parents are fully utilized by freeing personnel from many of the constraints of regimented school processes and by enlisting parents in support of school activities.

The Accelerated Schools model includes a governance structure, an inquiry process, curriculum specifications, and the involvement of parents in all aspects of the school, including governance, inquiry, and instruction.[8] The governance structure consists of a steering committee to monitor progress toward goals, refine ideas for schoolwide improvements, and relay information from smaller working groups called "cadres" and the whole school to each other and to administrators. Steering committees and cadres both are composed of teachers, support staff, administrators, parents, students, and community members. Decisionmaking is to be based on consensus. The inquiry process involves a planning and evaluation cycle. Cadres identify problems, develop and implement solutions, evaluate performance, and reassess solutions. The steering committee engages in a similar process for the school as a whole, and individual teachers and students can be thought of as engaging in the same kind of process in their classrooms. The approach to curriculum explicitly stresses active learning. It also emphasizes language development across all subjects, early introduction of reading and writing for meaning, high expectations for all, and relating learning to the students' cultures. Peer tutoring and cooperative learning are recommended, as are ways of meeting individual needs while keeping all children in regular classes rather than using pullout programs.

Levin estimates that complete transformation to an Accelerated School takes about six years.[9] Therefore, although over 500 schools in thirty-five

---

6. Levin (1991b).
7. Levin (1991b, p. 2).
8. These elements of the model are described in detail by Hoffenberg, Levin, and Associates (1993).
9. Levin (1991b).

states have begun this process, few schools have fully completed it. The Accelerated Schools model is introduced into schools through a "coach" who is trained by the National Center for Accelerated Schools at Stanford University or newly developed university-based satellite centers at Texas A&M University, the University of New Orleans, California State University at Los Angeles, San Francisco State University, and the University of Washington.[10]

Success for All

Success for All is based on the assumption that virtually all children are capable of achieving school success.[11] The model prescribes two types of activities for elementary schools: prevention and early intervention. Prevention includes high-quality preschool and kindergarten programs, improvements at all grade levels in curriculum and instruction (including cooperative learning and better management of instructional time), frequent assessment of student performance, and establishment of a cooperative school-parent environment. Students who do not succeed even with such preventive efforts require intensive early intervention. This includes one-to-one tutoring by experienced, certified teachers. A family support team works with social service agencies and with the families of struggling students to solve social problems that are obstacles to school success.

Reading is assigned an especially high priority, because it is considered essential for success in primary grades. The emphasis on reading skill is reflected in the use of reading tutors and the organization of the reading program. Tutors provide one-to-one help that is coordinated with the students' regular reading program: it is done during twenty-minute sessions taken from regular social studies lessons. Since the goal is to prevent failure, first graders get priority for tutoring. All students receive reading instruction for a ninety-minute period each day. During this time, reading tutors are used to reduce class size to fifteen to twenty students. For this period, grades 1 to 3 are regrouped into smaller classes on the basis of reading level. A comprehensive reading, writing, and language arts curriculum begins with thematic units, the story telling and retelling program (STaR), and Peabody language development kits in preschool and kindergarten. The approach includes the teaching of specific reading skills, reading for meaning, cooperative learning activities, writing, and teaching of

10. King (1994).
11. Slavin and others (1992).

metacognitive strategies.[12] Reading teachers complete an assessment for each student every eight weeks to assure that each is being assigned to the appropriate group and receiving the appropriate instruction.

As a matter of policy, Success for All minimizes placement of students in special education classrooms through intensive intervention. When students are placed in special education classrooms, the programs are designed to be as consistent as possible with the Success for All model.

Since the initiation of Success for All in its first school in Baltimore in 1986, the program has been implemented in hundreds of schools in twenty-three states.[13] In addition, the model has been refined and expanded in the last several years by the development of "Roots and Wings," which provides math and social studies or science curricula. This expanded model was first available to schools for implementation in 1994–95.

School Development Program

The School Development Program originated in a joint effort by the Yale University Child Study Center and the New Haven school district to bring about reform in two of New Haven's most troubled elementary schools.[14] In the view of the model's developers, children from low-income families behave in school in ways that teachers interpret as revealing either deficiencies in ability or intractable problems with attitude and motivation. However, this behavior often reflects family stress and children's social skills that are appropriate in other contexts but not in school. As a result of this lack of connection, inner-city schools become divided institutions, with adversarial relationships between teachers and the children and their families and low expectations by everyone.

The School Development Program is designed to provide school staff with knowledge and skills in child development, especially the development of the mainstream social skills needed to succeed in school; organization and management skills for changing school policies and practices; and organizational structures to promote problem-solving relationships among all school participants. By improving relationships in the school, the program seeks to create a school climate that facilitates the academic and social growth of students.[15] More specific program goals are to create

---

12. Center for the Social Organization of Schools (1993).
13. Personal communication from Robert Slavin, 1995.
14. Comer (1980).
15. Comer (1980).

a social and psychological climate in the school that facilitates learning; to improve achievement in basic skills, particularly reading and mathematics; to increase motivation for learning and thereby raise students' academic and occupational goals; to develop a feeling of shared responsibility and decisionmaking among parents and staff; and to develop an organizational relationship between child development and clinical services and the educational program.[16]

The School Development Program specifies three new organizational structures that must be put in place: a governance team, mental health team, and parents' program.[17] The governance team brings together representatives of parents, teachers, and support staff to work with the principal to develop a comprehensive plan for achieving a specific social climate and academic goals, to provide for the necessary staff development, and to conduct assessments that allow the staff to adjust plans and activities periodically. The governance team is designed to provide a sense of direction, coordinate activities, and promote a broad sense of ownership among all participants. The mental health team addresses the mental health needs of students as individuals, in the classroom, and schoolwide. A member of the mental health team serves on the planning and management team to promote an understanding of child development issues and human dynamics in leading the school. Pullout programs are provided to give intensive help to students with the most serious behavior problems. The parents' program works to maximize the number of parents involved in the school and the extent of their participation. The model recognizes that parent participation must be actively sought and that parents must get something they value from activities such as representation on the governance team, participation in social activities and the parent organization, and employment as volunteers or paid assistants.

The School Development Program has been adopted in over 200 schools in twenty-three states.[18] The model has been introduced to several middle schools and high schools as well as elementary schools. To facilitate dissemination, the Yale Child Study Center has produced a fourteen-part "how to" videotape series and is developing partnerships with other organizations to expand training and support for the model.

16. Comer (1980, pp. 67–68).
17. Haynes and Comer (1993).
18. Haynes and Comer (1993).

Resource Requirements and Costs

I estimated the resource requirements for applying each program in an elementary school of 500 students, using national average prices in 1994–95 dollars. This approach facilitates comparisons across the three models and estimation of the costs of nationwide reforms. The estimated resource requirements are for four general categories: external training and technical support, new staff, new activities for existing staff, and added programs such as preschool or extended day programs. A critical issue is the extent to which new activities require additional time and effort or can be accommodated through reallocation of existing time and effort.

Accelerated Schools

As a governance and curricular reform that aims to improve the allocation of school resources, the Accelerated Schools model requires little or no increase in existing school resources. The only resource requirements specified by the sponsors are for training and a part-time coach, or change agent, to facilitate the introduction of the model to the school. The training is conducted by a national center or satellite centers in universities, and there are state training and support networks in at least three states (Illinois, Texas, and Missouri). The training centers screen schools for commitment and coaches for suitability. To be accepted, schools must commit 20 percent of the time of a school or district staff person to serve as a coach and agree to have the school engage in five to six full days and some partial days of training as well as weekly follow-up during the first year.[19] First-year external training and support for the coach consists of eight days of intensive initial training, regular follow-up by telephone and fax, several site visits, and an end-of-year retreat. Support and assessment of coaches continues in future years on a declining scale.

Two estimates of resource requirements and costs for the first year of an Accelerated School are shown in table 9-1. The first estimate assumes that the model is implemented as recommended with a 20 percent-time coach and training at the school accommodated by reallocating time from other activities. The second estimate, an upper bound, assumes a 50 percent-time coach and training with an increase in staffing. For the first year, the basic cost estimate is $34 a student and the upper bound $160 a stu-

19. Keller (1994).

Table 9-1. *Estimated Resource Requirements and Costs for a First-Year Accelerated School*[a]
1994–95 dollars

Resource	Basic	Upper bound
External training for coach[b]	5,000	5,000
Coach[c]	12,000	30,000
Training school staff	0	45,000
Total	17,000	80,000
Cost per student	34	160

Sources: Educational Research Service (1993); National Center for Education Statistics (1994).

a. Estimates are for a school of 500 students in grades K–5. They assume a salary of $47,800 for the coach with fringe benefits equal to 25 percent of salary (average for an elementary school assistant principal) and a teacher-child ratio of 1:20 (slightly worse than the national average of 1:19). To convert to 1994–95 dollars, salaries and wages were increased by 2.6 percent a year from 1992–93 or 1993–94 based on the GNP deflator for state and local government purchases.

b. Eight days of initial training, 1.5 site visits, and a two-day annual retreat. Costs include round-trip travel ($400 each), hotel and per diem ($150 a day), $1,000 for eight-day training, and $180 a day for staff time on site visits and annual retreat.

c. Allows 0.2 full-time equivalent in basic program, 0.5 in upper bound.

dent. As the need for training declined in subsequent years, costs would be lower. The estimated cost figures in table 9-1 do not include costs for the Accelerated Schools training and support network itself. However, these costs would be trivial on a per student basis.

The changes required by the Accelerated Schools process could be accommodated without any increase in the total resources used by the school. Levin reports that the Accelerated Schools process requires all previously allocated faculty meeting, staff development, and committee time.[20] Teachers in many other countries spend far less of their workday teaching in the classroom and far more planning together and preparing to teach.[21] These internal reallocations would not increase the cost of schooling.

Reports on Accelerated Schools such as Hollibrook Elementary School in Houston describe tremendous concerted efforts by the principal, staff, students, parents, and other community members.[22] This suggests that all participants may be working harder and longer rather than just more efficiently. Whether this increase in effort represents an increase in costs would depend on whether the resources were viewed as having been slack

20. Levin (1991b).
21. Organization for Economic Cooperation and Development (1995).
22. McCarthy and Still (1993).

or underemployed before the introduction of the Accelerated Schools model. Accurate estimates of changes in effort and time are not available.[23]

Success for All

To implement the Success for All model, title 1 and other federal and state funds targeting economically disadvantaged and low-achieving children are reallocated.[24] Schools qualify for title 1 based on the number of poor children, but receive funding allocations based on the number of children who are low achievers. Estimates of resource requirements and title 1 funding are shown in table 9-2 for three schools that vary in the percentage of students who qualify for title 1 funding.

A full-time program facilitator is essential to oversee planning and scheduling, assist reading teachers and tutors, and address other instructional issues. The number of tutors increases from one to four per school as the number of poorly achieving children in the school increases. To work with families, a social worker and a parent liason are allocated to the most disadvantaged schools, only a liaison to the others. First-year costs for the program include $20,000 for materials, $7,500 in fees for twenty-five days of training, and $6,000 to pay for release time for staff to participate in training. Project staff estimate that materials and training costs decline by half from years 1 to 2 and 2 to 3 and are zero in the next two years.[25]

As table 9-2 shows, all or nearly all of the first-year costs of Success For All typically can be covered by the reallocation of title 1 funding, which averages about $1,000 per eligible student.[26] Title 1 funds would not be sufficient to cover the costs of additional services recommended by Success for All—preschool programs and full-day kindergarten—for schools that did not already have these programs. Based on an average per pupil current expense of roughly $5,200, estimated marginal costs are $3,680 ($2,600 plus $600 for an aide and 15 percent for facilities) per preschool student

23. Jenifer A. King (1994) estimates that Accelerated Schools teachers increase their work time by 3.5 to 7 hours a week (for a school of twenty-five teachers, two to five full-time equivalents), but her estimates are based on interviews that are of questionable validity for estimating time use, for reasons explained by Juster and Stafford (1985).

24. Title 1, the federal compensatory education program for low-income students, was recently reauthorized under the Improving America's Schools Act of 1994. During the 1980s, title 1 was known as chapter 1.

25. Personal communication from Larry Dolan, 1995.

26. Chambers and others (1993).

Table 9-2. *Estimated First-Year Resource Requirements and Costs for Success for All, by Percentage of Educationally Disadvantaged Students*[a]
1994–95 dollars

Resource	Percentage of students qualifying for title 1 funds		
	75	50	25
Facilitator	60,000	60,000	60,000
Tutors[b]	180,000	90,000	45,000
Social worker	45,000	. . .	. . .
Parent liaison	22,000	22,000	22,000
Materials and training	33,500	33,500	33,500
Total	340,500	205,500	160,500
Title 1 funds	375,000	250,000	125,000
Cost above title 1	0	0	35,500
Cost per student	0	0	71
Resources beyond title 1			
Preschool	184,000	184,000	184,000
Cost per student	368	368	368
Full-day kindergarten	195,000	195,000	195,000
Cost per student	390	390	390

Sources: Center for the Social Organization of Schools (1993); Educational Research Service (1993); National Center on Education Statistics (1994).

a. Estimates are for elementary schools of 500 students. They assume a salary of $47,800 for the facilitator, salaries of $36,000 for teachers and social workers, hourly wages of $8.80 for aides, and fringe benefits equal to 25 percent of salary and wages. To convert to 1994–95 dollars, salaries and wages were increased by 2.6 percent a year from 1993–94 based on the GNP deflator for state and local government purchases.

b. Four in schools with 75 percent of students qualifying, two in schools with 50 percent, and one in schools with 25 percent.

and $2,600 per kindergarten student.[27] Assuming that two-thirds of the children attend the preschool program, the added annual costs to the school from both preschool and full-day kindergarten would be $379,000. To add preschool and full-day kindergarten, a school would need an additional $760 per pupil (based on 500 pupils), roughly 15 percent of average current expense per pupil.

Success for All schools feature several administrative bodies—like an advisory committee and a family support team—that require staff time. For the most part, it seems reasonable that their activities could be achieved by reallocation of time. However, increases in parental involvement will represent real costs to parents.

27. The estimated cost of $3,680 is reasonably accurate for adding a typical half-day preschool program operating two sessions a day, but it is not necessarily optimal. Head Start spent $3,748 a child in 1993 while paying lower salaries than the public schools (Head Start, 1994). Preschool programs with the strongest evidence of effectiveness have been in existence for several years, had single sessions a day, and had much smaller group sizes and ratios than the typical public school or Head Start program (Barnett, 1992).

Table 9-3. *Estimated First-Year Resource Requirements and Costs for the School Development Program*[a]
1994–95 dollars

Resource	Basic	Upper bound
Program facilitator[b]	15,000	60,000
Mental health specialist[b]	15,000	60,000
Pullout program staff[c]	22,500	45,000
Training	5,000	10,000
Parents	. . .	44,000
Total	57,500	219,000
Cost per student	115	438
New resources	15,000	219,000
Cost per student	30	438

Sources: Educational Reseach Service (1993); National Center on Education Statistics (1994).

a. Estimates are for a school of 500 students in grades K–5. Lower-bound estimates assume that parents donate their time and that only the facilitator position is filled by hiring a new person (and serves four schools) rather than by reallocating time of existing staff. Upper-bound estimates assume that four parents are paid as half-time aides and that all positions are in addition to existing staff. The training cost estimates assume that external training is quite limited and provided to only one or two staff persons. Unfortunately, even a rough description of the training process was not found. Estimates assume a salary of $47,800 for the facilitator and mental health specialist, a salary of $36,000 for teachers, hourly wages of $8.80 for aides, and fringe benefits equal to 25 percent of salary and wages. To convert to 1994–95 dollars, salaries and wages were increased by 2.6 percent per year from 1993–94 based on the GNP deflator for state and local government purchases.

b. Allows 0.25 full-time equivalent in basic program, 1.00 in upper bound.

c. Allows 0.50 full-time equivalent in basic program, 1.00 in upper bound.

School Development Program

Information on the resource requirements for the School Development Program is very limited, making it difficult to produce confident estimates. For the New Haven schools, it is difficult to separate program activities and costs from the costs of developing the program.[28] Outside of New Haven, the model has not been implemented with the same intensity of new resources.[29] Since the School Development Program seeks to reallocate resources to accomplish its ends, it may require little or no increase in spending in most schools. Although increases in parents' time and effort are expected, measures of time commitments by parents are not available.

Given the uncertainties, lower- and upper-bound estimates for resource requirements and costs are presented in table 9-3. Key program staff are a facilitator, mental health specialist, and instructional staff for pullout programs for children experiencing extreme difficulties. Conceivably, a single staff person could be hired to fill all three needs, or perhaps the mental health leader and pullout program staff could be existing staff who reallocate part of their time. The lower-bound estimates correspond to exam-

28. Comer (1980).
29. Haynes (1994); Haynes, Gebreyesus, and Comer (1993).

ples based on maximum use of existing staff, so only the part-time facilitator and out-of-pocket expenses for training are new costs.[30] The upper-bound estimate corresponds more closely to the description of the original School Development Program in New Haven. The training requirements were not determinable from existing data, so as a rough estimate, I assumed for the lower bound that costs were the same as for the Accelerated Schools model and doubled this amount for the upper bound. Cost per student is estimated at $115 to $438 for all resources, but, because some can be obtained by reallocation, marginal cost is estimated at $30 to $438.

Effects of the Models

Can these reform models produce substantial improvements in school processes and student outcomes, under at least some circumstances? Is it likely that they can produce large improvements in American schools generally?

In answering these questions, all three models face some common difficulties. If more capable and enthusiastic administrators and teachers choose or are assigned to schools implementing reform models, then it is difficult to distinguish the reform from the talents of the people administering it, and impossible to generalize the result to other schools. Further, no one knows exactly how the schools in which process and outcome studies have been conducted compare with the typical schools serving disadvantaged children. Nor does anyone know how schools that have successfully implemented a model differ from those that have failed, or what percentage may be expected to fail and why. The students in these programs may not be a random mix, either. At least some families choose the schools their children attend on the basis of perceived school quality, which could include whether a school is participating in a reform program. Moreover, when achievement tests are used as outcome measures, schools can vary to the extent that low achievers are excluded from the reported assessments, either because they are in special education and not tested or are retained in grade and no longer compared with their age cohort. Finally, all of these models are relatively new and it takes time for reforms to be implemented adequately and for their long-term effects to be studied in even a few sites. With these concerns about internal validity and generalizability in mind, let me now consider the evidence on these three programs.

30. Haynes (1994).

Accelerated Schools

Few schools have been implementing the Accelerated Schools model long enough to fully develop an Accelerated School; thus few outcome studies have reported results to date. However, several Accelerated Schools have reported large improvements in both school processes and standardized test scores, although such scores are viewed as poorly attuned to the goals of the model.

The Daniel Webster School in San Francisco was one of two schools in which the Stanford team piloted their model in 1986. Before the project, Webster ranked sixty-fifth out of sixty-nine San Francisco schools in test score achievement. By 1992 Webster's rank had risen to twenty-three, and it had shown the largest improvement in test scores in the city in every subject area.[31] Other schools have reported similar gains in standardized test scores and improvements in attendance, self-esteem, and participation in more advanced course work.[32]

The most complete data on implementation and outcomes have been reported for Hollibrook Elementary School in Houston. In the mid- to late 1980s Hollibrook experienced a large increase in the number and percentage of students who were disadvantaged. Student turnover rates became extremely high, discipline and vandalism were serious problems, and parents were largely uninvolved.[33] In 1987 a new principal, together with the school staff, introduced and developed an Accelerated School model with little outside assistance. Jane McCarthy and Suzanne Still summarize the results:

> While the minority population at Hollibrook shifted from 67 percent in 1988 to 91 percent in 1991, and the population changed from 64 percent low SES [socioeconomic status] to more than 92 percent low SES in 1991, test scores increased dramatically. In 1988, the fifth graders at Hollibrook were scoring at the 4.3 grade level on composite scores on the SRA standardized tests. They were scoring at the 3.7 level in reading and language arts. In early spring 1991, fifth graders scored at the 5.8 grade level for a composite score and reading and language arts scores have risen to 5.2 and 5.6, respectively, a gain of almost two grade levels in just two and one-half years. Even more remarkable is the fact that students are scoring at about grade level in all subjects and 1 year above grade level in mathematics (6.6).[34]

31. Hilary Stout, "Remedial Curriculum for Low Achievers Is Falling from Favor," *Wall Street Journal*, July 30, 1992, pp. A1, A8.
32. Hoffenberg, Levin and Associates (1993).
33. McCarthy and Still (1993).
34. McCarthy and Still (1993, p. 80).

Other indicators improved. Vandalism declined. Student mobility decreased from 104 percent in 1987 to 47 percent in 1990, though it rebounded to 63 percent later, probably because of changes in the housing market. Parent volunteers rose from zero to 250, and community volunteers from zero to 60. Over the same period, achievement test scores fell at a school in the same district selected for comparison.[35]

Enthusiasm for the findings is tempered by a recognition of the limitations of the evidence. First, it would be desirable to have data on enough Accelerated Schools to estimate the percentage in which implementation is successful and to generalize about the range of effects and conditions under which success was most likely. Second, the evaluation designs used to date—premodel to postmodel changes in aggregate test scores at a given school, or sometimes with a comparison school—are a relatively weak basis for inferences about the effectiveness of the model.[36]

A systematic analysis would want to take into account any changes in a school that might influence outcomes measures: for example, new leadership, new preschool education or extended-day programs, large changes in the number of students, increased funding and staffing, changes in the composition of the school population, changing test or test administration practices, or changing the population for whom test scores are reported. Hollibrook illustrates many of these issues. It received a new leader who introduced the Accelerated Schools model at a low point in the school's performance. This makes it difficult to rule out regression to the mean and the effects of new leadership per se as potential sources of improvement. The school population declined between 1987 and 1991, so the student-teacher ratio fell, and per student operating expenditures increased from $1,866 in 1986–87 to $2,640 in 1990–91.[37] A preschool program was introduced in about 1985, and its effects gradually would have been felt at higher grade levels.[38] These changes might account for at least some of the observed improvements in student outcomes. Similar changes could have occurred at the unidentified comparison school, but such data are not presented.

Of course, one should not conclude that the Accelerated Schools model did not produce the observed improvements just because other factors may

35. McCarthy and Still (1993, pp. 79–81).
36. Cook and Campbell (1979); Cook (1991).
37. Spring Branch Independent School District, *Annual Performance Reports,* 1987–91; Texas Education Agency, *Academic Excellence Indicator System Reports,* 1987–91.
38. The date of the introduction of the preschool program was obtained from a telephone call to the Hollibrook school.

have influenced the results. Hollibrook's performance can also be assessed with data provided by the Texas Academic Excellence Indicators System (AEIS). Although Hollibrook's funding grew over the relevant period, funding also grew in other schools, and Hollibrook's funding level was not substantially higher than that of comparable elementary schools ($2,475 in 1990–91).[39] Preschool programs had also become common in comparable elementary schools. Yet in the early 1990s, Hollibrook performed better on the statewide tests than comparable schools (as designated by the AEIS).

Hollibrook also illustrates the potential for self-selection to influence test scores in urban schools as a result of changes in the student population. Student mobility was very high over the entire period, even though it declined after Hollibrook became an Accelerated School. Thus it is unclear how test scores may reflect changes in the school's population, how much the decrease in student turnover itself might contribute to the improvement in test scores, or even how long the children tested had attended Hollibrook. Possibly the Accelerated School model decreased turnover, and the greater stability in school attendance further increased the model's effectiveness, but the available data cannot confirm this point.

Finally, it is important to assess the extent to which the costs of the model at a given school are typical. Hollibrook implemented the model with no significant added resources and required little support from the model developers.[40] Similar information on other Accelerated Schools with outcome data is highly desirable, but little is available.

Success for All

The developers of Success for All have emphasized the need for research to produce valid quantitative estimates of the program's effects on student outcomes.[41] A series of longitudinal studies will provide evidence of the model's effects on students. In these studies, each school adopting the model is matched with a nonparticipating school that has similar demo-

39. In 1990–91 average operating expenditures in Hollibrook and comparable schools (those serving largely disadvantaged students) were substantially lower than the statewide average of $3,557. The average in Hollibrook's district was even higher at $3,967 a child (Texas Education Agency, *Academic Excellence Indicator System Report*). This difference is only partially explained by the fact that the state average includes high schools, which tend to receive more money per student than elementary schools.

40. McCarthy and Still (1993).

41. Slavin and others (1994).

graphic characteristics. These studies provide considerable data on the effects of the Success for All program in various stages of implementation. Consistent with the model's focus on reading as the key to school success, assessment has focused on individually administered, age-appropriate, standardized tests of language and reading achievement. Data also have been reported on retention, special education placements, and attendance. Recently, broader outcome data—standardized test scores in math, social studies, and science—have been provided for some schools.[42]

Outcome studies have been reported for sixteen Success for All schools in six cities.[43] Some of the studies were performed by the model sponsors and some by an independent group. All found large effects, about 0.5 standard deviations, on reading scores. Figure 9-1 summarizes the results by grade level for all sixteen schools (note that the number of participating schools varies by grade level). When comparisons were limited to the 25 percent of the students with the lowest pretest scores, the estimated effects for these students were even larger.[44]

The five Baltimore schools in which Success for All began provide a picture of effects over time for children from grades 1 to 5. Student reading achievement was significantly higher by approximately three months in grade 1, five months in grade 2, eight months in grade 3, and a full year at grade 5. Although Success for All children fall somewhat below grade level by grades 4 and 5, they are much closer to grade level than the comparison children. Estimated effects tended to be slightly larger in the other cities.[45]

The model was found to be similarly successful in attaining other goals. In the Baltimore Success for All schools, retentions were greatly reduced in some schools, referrals to special education were less frequent and intensive than in comparison schools, and attendance improved.[46] Data from other schools support the findings on special education, and special education and limited English proficiency students appear to gain more than others.[47] The estimated effects on math scores are about the same size as those on reading, although the effects for social studies and science are positive but lower.[48] In addition, Success for All children were more likely to be

42. Slavin and others (1992); Slavin and others (1994).
43. Slavin and others (1994). The cities are Baltimore, Philadelphia, Charleston, Memphis, Fort Wayne, and Montgomery.
44. Slavin and others (1994).
45. Slavin and others (1994).
46. Slavin and others (1992).
47. Slavin and others (1994).
48. Slavin and others (1994). Information on test scores in areas other than reading were obtained from Maryland's statewide accountability program.

Figure 9-1. *Cumulative Mean Reading Grade Equivalents and Effect Sizes for Success for All and Control Schools, 1988–94*[a]

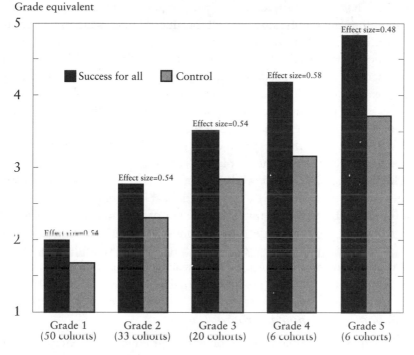

Grade equivalent

Source: Slavin and others (1994, figure 13).
a. Data are from comparisons of matched children in sixteen pairs of schools. The number of school pairs compared by grade are sixteen in grade 1, fourteen in grade 2, seven in grade 3, six in grade 4, and, six in grade 5.

tested, probably because schools had less reason to believe that these children would perform poorly and less reason to exclude them from testing. These findings indicate that Success for All's emphasis on reading did not cause other areas to suffer, but actually had a positive effect on other measures of student performance.[49]

Resource use in the Success for All schools studied appears to be roughly comparable to the earlier estimates in table 9-2. Some schools had more

49. One study compared two Success for All schools with a school using another intervention model, Reading Recovery (Slavin and others, 1994). It found no significant differences on first grade reading for students generally, but did find an effect for special education students who participated in Success for All but not in Reading Recovery. How the two models compare as children move through the grades remains to be seen. Because Reading Recovery is a program of one-to-one reading tutoring in first grade, comparisons as children progress through later grades might be more favorable to Success for All, as noted by Hiebert (1994).

resources for the program, at least in the first few years of operation, because of external funding, and there is some indication that the Baltimore sites that had more resources in the early years, enabling them to employ more tutors and family support staff, produced larger achievement gains, especially for students at greatest risk.[50] One school had fewer resources to reallocate for Success for All because it did not receive title 1 funding, and therefore it used specially trained paraprofessionals as tutors, rather than teachers.[51] Estimates of the contributions of preschool and full-day kindergarten programs are not available, but it should be noted that the results reported in figure 9-1 control for pretest scores obtained *after* the preschool years, so they do not include the contribution of the preschool program (at least as measured at kindergarten).

Research on Success for All has been extensive and rigorous. Advantages include the collection of "pretest" data at kindergarten entry, testing of the same students over time, and the use of individually administered tests. Further improvements could be obtained by administering tests in more subjects and reporting data for Success for All and comparison schools on expenditure levels, student-teacher ratios, staff turnover, and student mobility. I discuss possible alternatives below.

School Development Program

Research on the School Development Program includes extensive studies that provide substantial evidence that the model can be implemented as designed and that it has produced large effects on school climate.[52] Studies report extremely large effects on student self-concept and, for some schools, sizable effects on achievement (0.5 standard deviations and larger) and moderate effects on student behavior (0.25 standard deviations). However, results for student achievement and behavior varied considerably across studies.

Some of the most impressive evidence of success is based on work with the Martin Luther King School and Katherine Brennan School in New Haven. From 1969 until 1984, student achievement by fourth graders climbed steadily in reading and mathematics and rose above national norms.[53] The

---

50. Madden and others (1993).

51. Slavin and others (1994).

52. For example, see Comer (1980); Cauce, Comer, and Schwartz (1987); Haynes, Comer, and Hamilton-Lee (1989); Haynes and Comer (1990); Haynes (1994); Haynes, Gebreyesus, and Comer (1993); School Development Program (1991). Much of the research on effectiveness has been summarized in Becker and Hedges (1992).

53. Comer (1980, 1988).

achievement level appears to have been sustained since the withdrawal of Yale Child Study Center staff from the schools in the early 1980s. Attendance rates and test scores compare favorably not only with other title 1 schools but with all schools in New Haven. However, some other schools in New Haven with populations comparable to King and Brennan had similar achievement test scores.[54] Moreover, the model appears to have failed to take hold in a third New Haven school where it was attempted.

Estimated effects on test scores and on prosocial and deviant behavior were largest in the New Haven schools that had worked longest with the program. This suggested that the program might have been less successful elsewhere or that it requires more time to be fully implemented. Estimated effects on achievement were even larger in long-term follow-ups when children were in middle school, including those at one of the distant sites. Larger achievement effects in middle school are plausible if self-concept and attitudes toward school formed during elementary school become more important for achievement in middle school.

Although their overall findings are highly positive, School Development Program evaluations have important limitations that raise questions about estimated effects on students. Betsy J. Becker and Larry V. Hedges state:

> We would emphasize that the research conducted so far should be considered as suggestive and not definitive because the research designs used provide little control over selection effects. Such effects are surely present and it is difficult to estimate their magnitude on the results obtained. Similarly, many of the outcome measures used may be subject to artificial effects not directly related to the constructs they purport to measure.[55]

Selection effects that would be expected to create an upward bias in estimated effects could have occurred through families' initial choices of schools, mobility in the school population, and attrition in follow-up. Some of the studies matched schools, but none matched students within schools at entry; thus there is much less protection from selection bias than in the studies of Success for All. Perhaps the most serious problem is that many outcome measures were based on assessments of schools and students by school staff who knew that the program was being evaluated.

The validity of the comparisons of grade-level outcome measures for matched schools could be enhanced by providing more information on school characteristics before and after the model was implemented. In two extensively researched sites—Benton Harbor, Michigan, and Prince

54. Comer and others (1986).
55. Becker and Hedges (1992, p. 27).

George's County, Maryland—the School Development Program was part of court-ordered processes that brought new resources to the schools. For example, in Prince George's County, changes included reduced child-staff ratios, full-day kindergarten, additional support staff, after-school tutoring, and other efforts to improve the schools.[56] Such circumstances raise questions about attributing improvements in school climate and student outcomes solely to the School Development Program.

Conclusions and Recommendations

The Accelerated Schools Program, Success for All, and the School Development Program are three of the best developed and tested models of education reform, particularly of structural change in urban elementary schools serving large disadvantaged populations. Results of research on the costs and effects of the three models provide a basis for conclusions about the models' success and costs in practice and their potential to produce similar results for disadvantaged children in schools throughout the nation. In addition, they provide a basis for recommendations for further research.

Evidence on Success and Costs

Research on the three models demonstrates that existing knowledge about what makes schools effective can be used to restructure at least some urban schools. Substantive restructuring can occur remarkably quickly and can be sustained for a considerable number of years.

The evidence for the models' effects on educational outcomes for disadvantaged children is more ambiguous. All of the research has employed quasi-experimental designs that have important limitations.[57] The research designs used to study the effects of the Accelerated Schools model and the School Development Program have severe limitations. The research design applied to Success for All schools provides considerably more confidence that this model has produced large gains in student performance. However, all three models do incorporate key elements of effective schools practices, and the effective schools literature generally can be considered to provide empirical support for the efficacy of the models.[58]

56. Grady (1990).
57. Cook (1991).
58. Purkey and Smith (1983); Walberg (1992); Slavin, Karweit, and Wasik (1994).

It is reasonable to conclude, based on the resource and cost estimates, that all three models can be implemented as described by their developers without substantial increases in per pupil school expenditures. Success for All provides the clearest and most complete estimates of resource requirements and the extent to which they can be accommodated through resource allocation in schools serving disadvantaged populations. However, the data have important limitations. Thorough cost studies have yet to be conducted in conjunction with outcome studies, and important aspects of implementation (such as training requirements) are not well documented for all of the models. In particular, it is difficult to determine the extent to which various reforms increase the time and effort of staff, parents, and students and the extent to which such shifts should be considered as higher costs. After all, even parents' activities in the school and at home helping with homework may be viewed as improving the parents' well-being if they are rewarding and enjoyable.

Questions about increased time and effort and their cost implications are essentially questions about how the reforms work. Do they teach people to work better, motivate them to work harder, or both? If people work harder in these models, is it at least partly because the work is more rewarding? The answers seem clearer for Success for All, which focuses on instructional techniques, than for Accelerated Schools and the School Development Program, which focus on governance and organizational change. Yet the models could be more similar in practice than in theory. Studies of alternative approaches to education have found more variation within than across models.[59]

It is important to point out that the cost estimates presented here do not take into account the savings that occur if the reforms decrease grade retention and special education. All of the models seek to do so. In the case of Success for All, this is policy rather than an outcome and may be considered guaranteed.[60] As over 10 percent of all students are in special education and a quarter of all children in high-poverty area schools repeat at least one grade by grade 4, the potential savings are relatively large.[61]

Generalization

The research provides a less satisfactory basis for assessing the generalizability of cost and effectiveness estimates to all elementary schools serv-

59. Rivlin and Timpane (1975).
60. Slavin and others (1992).
61. U.S. Department of Education (1992, 1993).

ing large disadvantaged populations. Only a small fraction of the schools attempting to implement the models have been studied, and there is little information about how often and under what conditions the models can produce impressive improvements in schools and student outcomes. One cannot assume that the commitment to change that is evident in the schools adopting the models exists everywhere. The participating schools are not only volunteers, but they have also been screened by the sponsors.[62]

One important issue regarding generalization is the extent to which re-source requirements might be greater as the programs are expanded be-yond the schools that were first to implement them. For example, if the early implementers benefited from highly capable leadership or teachers, the training requirements might be considerably higher in other schools. This is a particularly important concern for the Accelerated Schools model, which stipulates a relatively small training requirement but requires teach-ers to adopt a curricular approach different from the one that most teachers know and use.

Widespread implementation of these models may require an extensive training and support infrastructure that would add to costs. The networks of model schools and training centers that have already evolved (such as the Accelerated Schools National Center and satellite centers) may be the beginnings of such an infrastructure. However, the need to fund such net-works should not present a serious financial problem, because even large increases in training and support would have little effect on per student costs. For example, a permanent full-time trainer for every five schools at a cost of $100,000 a trainer (including support staff, travel, and materials) would cost only $40 a student. Also, the cost estimates in tables 9-1 to 9-3 are for the first year, so those costs would be expected to decline over time as teachers are trained and schools gain more experience.

An issue specific for Success for All is the availability of title 1 funds. Recent changes in the law make it easier for many schools to use title 1 funds to support Success for All (and the other models), and its overall funding level provides roughly $1,000 for every poor elementary school child.[63] However, not all funds are spent on elementary school children, not all the children served are disadvantaged, and not all schools serving large numbers of disadvantaged children receive title 1 funds. Without im-proved distribution of these funds, a 10 to 20 percent increase (less than $2 billion) in title 1 funding might be required to ensure that every school

62. Keller (1994, p. 16).
63. Children's Defense Fund (1995).

serving large numbers of disadvantaged students could afford a model like Success for All.

How much, if any, additional resources are required to duplicate the levels of achievement (as opposed to the net effects) of the models is difficult to assess, because of the lack of information about resources in the schools studied. In the case of preschool programs and full-day kindergarten, estimates were made of their effects on costs. Adding both programs to a school would raise its average per pupil operating expenditure by about 15 percent. Roughly half the disadvantaged population is already served in preschool programs, including Head Start.[64] Assuming that about half also receive full-day kindergarten, expanding preschool and full-day kindergarten to serve all disadvantaged children would require an 8 percent increase in national current expenditure on elementary schools. This suggests that adequacy of resources generally is not an impediment to substantial improvement in the achievement of disadvantaged children. It does not mean that more resources would not be beneficial. Modest increases in resources for restructured schools might be required for disadvantaged students, on average, to achieve at grade level through the end of elementary school.

Economic theory provides several reasons that public schools might operate inefficiently, which makes it plausible that the models can accomplish their goals on a large scale with little or no increase in resources.[65] However, economic theory also suggests a reason why all schools have not already adopted some version of these reforms. It suggests that the fundamental problem is a lack of economic incentives for schools (and, possibly, parents and students) to adopt more effective practices, especially if doing so requires increased effort.[66] By themselves, the models cannot address this problem.

Research Needs

The promising results obtained so far warrant further research on the implementation, costs, and effects of these and similar reform models. Opportunities for research will grow as more sites have time to develop the models and generate long-term data on child outcomes. To make the most of these opportunities, government and private philanthropy might fund

64. West, Hausken, and Collins (1993).
65. Levin (1976); Wolf (1993); Hanushek (1994b).
66. Hanushek (1994a); Owen (1995).

an independent research organization to conduct multisite randomized trials with long-term follow-ups. Over five to ten years, such an organization could greatly increase knowledge about the costs and effectiveness of these models.

A number of easily implemented improvements in research can be recommended for future studies, beginning with more precise descriptions of the schools. Even simple year-by-year statistics on per student expenditure, student-staff ratios, and class sizes in model and comparison schools would be a substantial improvement. Basic descriptive studies could answer questions such as: Where does the time allocated to new activities come from? How much time is actually spent by staff in meetings of various sorts? How much time do students spend in various learning activities and in transitions or other down time? How do staff, parent, and student effort and time allocations change?

Another important area for further study is how the adoption of a reform model might change the school's population. Perhaps the models help schools to attract more capable staff and students and to reduce turnover, both of which could contribute to improved performance. Tracking such effects would help to sort out changes in the mix of staff and students from changes in the performance of a given set of staff and students.

Further research on outcomes should employ stronger quasi-experimental models where true experiments do not seem possible. The research model followed by Success for All has much to recommend it over alternatives. Even this model might be strengthened by applying its matching and follow-up procedures to the first-grade cohort from a year before model adoption. Additional attention should be given to obtaining representative samples of schools and to the use of designs that would reduce the potential effects of initial selection. An interesting contribution could be made by the use of a study design in which one or a few schools are randomly selected for reform from a large pool of schools for which data are collected over time.[67]

Future research might produce data on costs and outcomes that would permit comparisons of the relative cost effectiveness of the reform models. In addition, such research might examine the relative cost effectiveness of variations in program components within models, such as the gain from additional tutoring or preschool education,[68] or the extent to which partic-

---

67. Campbell (1991).
68. Some research suggests a synergy between preschool and improved elementary education for disadvantaged children. For example, see Reynolds (1992).

ular components are necessary or sufficient for obtaining strong improvements in achievement. Questions also should be asked about the effects of preexisting levels of resources on the outcomes of reform and how much can be gained by providing additional resources to restructured schools serving disadvantaged students.

Finally, researchers must address some critical public policy issues. Are there policy changes that could enhance efforts to introduce the reforms on a large scale? One barrier to reform is legal provisions that prevent schools from combining funds from various programs for disadvantaged and disabled children. Recent changes in title 1 that facilitate the use of funds for schoolwide changes in instruction (as opposed to targeted pull-out programs) and that remove the risk that increases in student performance would jeopardize funding could serve as examples for similar state programs. Another important issue is how systemic reforms might increase incentives for the development and implementation of innovative school restructuring models. Would schools be more likely to adopt some of the models suggested here if accountability testing included all children and if elementary schools were evaluated on the basis of their students' performance at entry to middle school? Are charter schools more likely than other public schools to adopt these models or to innovate and restructure on their own in effective ways? Answers to these questions would shed light on the ways public policy can be used to encourage the adoption and success of reform in all schools.

References

Barnett, W. Steven. 1992. "Benefits of Compensatory Preschool Education." *Journal of Human Resources* 27 (Spring): 279–312.

Becker, Betsy J., and Larry V. Hedges. 1992. *A Review of the Literature on the Effectiveness of Comer's School Development Program.* Report prepared for the Rockefeller Foundation. Michigan State University, College of Education.

Campbell, Donald T. 1991. "Quasi-Experimental Research Designs in Compensatory Education." Paper prepared for OECD Conference on Evaluating Intervention Strategies for Children and Youth at Risk.

Cauce, Ana M., James P. Comer, and David Schwartz. 1987. "Long-term Effects of a System-Oriented School Prevention Program." *American Journal of Orthopsychiatry* 57 (January): 127–31.

Center for the Social Organization of Schools. 1993. "Information to Schools Considering Adoption of *Success for All* and *Roots and Wings.*" Johns Hopkins University, Center for the Social Organization of Schools.

Chambers, Jay, and others. 1993. *Translating Dollars into Services: Chapter 1 Resources in the Context of State and Local Resources for Education.* Report to the U.S. Department of Education. Palo Alto: American Institutes for Research.

Children's Defense Fund. 1995. *The State of America's Children: Yearbook 1995.* Washington: Children's Defense Fund.

Comer, James P. 1980. *School Power: Implications of an Intervention Project.* Free Press.

————. 1988. "Educating Poor Minority Children." *Scientific American* 259 (November): 42–48.

Comer, James P., and others. 1986. *Yale Child Study Center School Development Program: Developmental History and Long Term Effects.* New Haven: Yale Child Study Center.

Cook, Thomas D. 1991. "Clarifying the Warrant for Generalized Causal Inferences in Quasi-Experimentation." In *Evaluation and Education at Quarter Century,* edited by Milbrey W. McLaughlin and Denise Phillips, 115–44. National Society for the Study of Education.

Cook, Thomas D., and Donald T. Campbell. 1979. *Quasi-Experimentation: Design and Analysis Issues for Field Settings.* Houghton-Mifflin.

Educational Research Service 1993. *National Survey of Salaries and Wages in Public Schools, 1993.* Vols. 2, 3. Arlington, Va.

Grady, Michael K. 1990. *Report on the Academic Effect of Educational Equity Efforts in Prince George's County.* Upper Marlboro, Md.: Prince George's County Schools, Office of Research and Evaluation.

Guthrie, James W. 1992. "National Education Goals: Can We Afford Them?" Paper prepared for annual meeting of American Educational Research Association.

Hanushek, Eric A. 1994a. "A Jaundiced View of 'Adequacy' in School Finance Reform." *Educational Policy* 8 (December): 460–69.

————. 1994b. "Money Might Matter Somewhere: A Response to Hedges, Laine, and Greenwald." *Educational Researcher* 23 (May): 5–8.

Haynes, Norris M., ed. 1994. *School Development Program Research Monograph.* New Haven: Yale Child Study Center.

Haynes, Norris M., James P. Comer, and Muriel Hamilton-Lee. 1989. "School Climate Enhancement through Parental Involvement." *Journal of School Psychology* 27 (Spring): 87–90.

Haynes, Norris M., and James P. Comer. 1990. "The Effects of a School Development Program on Self-Concept." *Yale Journal of Biology and Medicine* 63 (July–August): 275–83.

————. 1993. "The Yale School Development Program: Process, Outcomes, and Policy Implications." *Urban Education* 28 (July): 166–99.

Haynes, Norris M., Sara Gebreyesus, and James P. Comer. 1993. *Selected Case Studies of National Implementation of the School Development Program.* New Haven: Yale Child Study Center.

Head Start. 1994. "Project Head Start Statistical Fact Sheet." U.S. Department of Health and Human Services, Administration on Children, Youth and Families.

Hiebert, Elfrieda H. 1994. "Reading Recovery in the United States: What Difference Does It Make to an Age Cohort?" *Educational Researcher* 23 (December): 15–25.

Hoffenberg, Wendy S., Henry M. Levin, and Associates. 1993. *The Accelerated Schools Resource Guide.* San Francisco: Jossey Bass.

Juster, F. Thomas, and Frank P. Stafford, eds. 1985. *Time, Goods, and Well-Being.* University of Michigan, Survey Research Center, Institute for Social Research.

Keller, B. M., ed. 1994. *Accelerated Schools Newsletter* 3 (Winter). Stanford University.

King, Jenifer A. 1994. "Meeting the Needs of At-Risk Students: A Cost Analysis of Three Models." *Educational Evaluation and Policy Analysis* 16 (Spring): 1–19.

Levin, Henry M. 1976. "Concepts of Economic Efficiency and Educational Production." In *Education as an Industry: A Conference of the Universities,* edited by Joseph T. Froomkin, Dean T. Jamison, and Roy Radner, 149–91. Cambridge, Mass.: National Bureau of Economic Research.

————. 1991a. "Accelerating the Progress of ALL Students." Paper prepared for Nelson A. Rockefeller Institute of Government Educational Policy Seminar

————. 1991b. "Learning from Accelerated Schools." Pew Higher Education Research Program, *Policy Perspectives.* Philadelphia: Pew Charitable Trusts.

McCarthy, Jane, and Suzanne Still. 1993. "Hollibrook Accelerated Elementary School." In *Restructuring Schooling: Learning from Ongoing Efforts,* edited by Joseph Murphy and Phillip Hallinger, 63–83. Newbury Park, Calif.: Corwin Press.

Madden, Nancy A., and others. 1993. "Success for All: Longitudinal Effects of a Restructuring Program for Inner-City Elementary Schools." *American Educational Research Journal* 30 (Spring): 123–48.

National Center for Education Statistics. 1994. *Digest of Education Statistics 1994.* U.S. Department of Education, Office of Educational Research and Improvement.

Organization for Economic Cooperation and Development. 1995. *Education at a Glance: OECD Indicators.* Paris.

Owen, John D. 1995. *Why Our Kids Don't Study: An Economist's Perspective.* Johns Hopkins University Press.

Purkey, Stewart C., and Marshall S. Smith. 1983. "Effective Schools: A Review." *Elementary School Journal* 83 (March): 427–52.

Reynolds, A. J. 1992. "Mediated Effects of Preschool Intervention." *Early Education and Development* 3 (April): 139–64.

Rivlin, Alice M., and P. Michael Timpane, eds. 1975. *Planned Variation in Education: Should We Give Up or Try Harder?* Brookings.

School Development Program. 1991. *Summary of School Development Program Documentation and Research.* New Haven: Yale Child Study Center.

Slavin, Robert E., and others. 1992. "Policy Implication of Success for All." Paper prepared for annual meeting of American Educational Research Association.

————. 1994. "Success for All: Longitudinal Effects of a Systemic School-by-School Reform in Seven Districts." Paper prepared for annual meeting of American Educational Research Association.

Slavin, Robert E., Nancy L. Karweit, and Barbara A. Wasik. 1994. *Preventing Early School Failure: Research, Policy and Practice.* Allyn and Bacon.

U.S. Department of Education. 1992. *Eleventh Annual Report to Congress on the Implementation of the Education of the Handicapped Act.* Office of Special Education and Rehabilitative Services.

————. 1993. *Reinventing Chapter 1: The Current Chapter 1 Program and New Directions: Final Report of the National Assessment of the Chapter 1 Program.* Office of Policy and Planning, Planning and Evaluation Service.

Walberg, Herbert J. 1992. "The Knowledge Base for Educational Productivity." *International Journal of Educational Reform* 1 (January): 1–10.

West, Jerry, Elvie G. Hausken, and Mary Collins. 1993. *Profile of Preschool Children's Child Care and Early Education Program Participation.* NCES 93-133. U.S. Department of Education, Office of Educational Research and Improvement.

Wolf, Charles. 1993. *Markets or Governments: Choosing between Imperfect Alternatives.* MIT Press.

CHAPTER TEN

Alternative Approaches to Measuring the Cost of Education

William Duncombe, John Ruggiero, and John Yinger

Sᴵɴᴄᴇ ᴛʜᴇ ʟᴀɴᴅᴍᴀʀᴋ *Serrano* v. *Priest* decision by the California Supreme Court in 1971, many states have faced lawsuits challenging the equity of their school finance systems. For the most part, the school finance debate has focused on differences in school districts' fiscal capacity, and aid formulas typically make some effort to compensate low-capacity districts. In contrast, educational cost differences across school districts, which have a major impact on educational outcomes, have been virtually ignored by the courts and are often excluded from recent discussions of educational reform. The courts have focused on equalizing expenditure per pupil and not on adjusting expenditure for differential costs. When cost adjustments are made by states, they tend to involve ad hoc adjustment factors, such as "weighted pupil measures" to account for high-cost students and scale factors to compensate small, rural school districts.[1] Aid formulas based on these cost factors are likely to underadjust for actual cost differences and indeed may even magnify existing disparities instead of easing them.

Several scholars have developed methods for constructing indexes of educational costs. The need to account for education cost factors is widely acknowledged, but scholars disagree about the best way to define and measure costs. As we use the term, *cost* refers to the expenditure or outlay needed by a district to provide a specified level of education attainment or outcome, not to actual expenditure. In other words, cost refers to the value of the resources a district must consume in the production of a given level

---

1. For a good discussion of past court challenges, see Odden and Picus (1992). Gold and others (1992) provide a good overview of state aid systems in the early 1990s.

of student achievement. Cost differentials reflect both the costs of inputs and the harshness of the production environment.[2] Actual expenditure, on the other hand, reflects the influence not only of cost factors but also of demand factors, such as community income, and of institutional factors.

Our objectives in this essay are to develop a method for estimating a comprehensive district-level educational cost index that builds on the existing literature and can be implemented with available data—and then to estimate this index using data for New York State. Although we do not explicitly consider state aid, methods for incorporating cost indexes such as ours into state aid formulas are well known.[3] The main contribution of our approach is the development of new methods to select educational outcome measures and to control for school district efficiency. Moreover, the application to New York is instructive because school districts in this state have a wide variety of educational environments, from sparsely populated rural areas to large central cities.

Our approach is consistent with many of the principles underlying recent educational reform efforts. In particular, many states have moved from process-oriented to outcome-oriented policies, such as the development of common standards and achievement measures. Moreover, many states have implemented programs designed to encourage school choice and efficiency.[4] Despite this new focus, recent reform efforts have not recognized, for the most part, that outcomes and efficiency cannot be accurately compared across districts without a viable method for measuring educational costs. Some reforms, including those in South Carolina and Dallas, acknowledge that performance measures will be worse, on average, for low-income than for high-income schools and incorporate ad hoc adjustments to account for this cost-related effect (as explained in chapter 2). However, these reforms do not explicitly recognize the role of input costs or environmental factors, and their adjustments do not accurately account for cost variation across schools or school districts. The cost models we develop can incorporate the new performance measures that have been developed in recent education reforms, so that cost differences can be considered in broad school reform efforts.

2. Ladd and Yinger (1991).
3. See Ladd and Yinger (1994) for an overview of adding costs to several types of aid formulas.
4. For general discussion of education reform and school choice, see Fuhrman, Elmore, and Massell (1993); Cooper (1993); Hanushek (1994).

Educational Production and Costs

Our approach builds on the large literature on educational production functions and educational costs. We review the key elements from this literature, discuss the unique features of our approach, and present our empirical analysis.

Educational Production Functions

The literature on the technology of public education focuses on educational production functions. The dependent variable is a measure of educational service or outcomes, such as a test score or a dropout rate. The independent variables used to explain differences in outcomes include a vector of inputs, such as teachers and classrooms; a vector of environmental factors, such as the share of students with learning disabilities; and often a variable to capture the possibility that unobserved characteristics of the school and its pupils make a difference.[5] It is also common to use a lagged value of the measure of educational services as an independent variable, to capture the continuing effect of inputs, environmental factors, and random errors in previous years on this year's output.[6]

The environmental factors also have been called external inputs, that is, inputs not controlled by school officials. The term *environmental factors* is taken from the literature on local public finance, whereas the term *external inputs* is taken from the literature on school production functions.[7] Al-

---

5. Unless a variable like this is included, the unobserved school-specific effect can be a source of omitted-variable bias.

6. This literature is reviewed in Hanushek (1986), Cohn and Geske (1990), and Monk (1990). As an example, consider a linear form of this relationship: $S_{it} = \alpha I_{it} + \beta X_{it} + \delta S_{it-1} + e_i + \mu_{it}$. The subscripts i and t indicate school and time, respectively; S is a measure of educational service or output; I is a vector of education inputs; X is a vector of environmental factors; e is a set of unobserved characteristics of the school and its pupils; μ is a random error term; and α, β, and δ are parameters to be estimated. This error structure assumes that the error component, e, does not vary over time, an assumption that may be inappropriate if the error component includes student cohort effects as well as school effects. The coefficient δ on the lagged value of S measures how fast the output from the previous year deteriorates between school years. The concept of service "deterioration" is discussed at length in chapter 8. Note that the specification with a lagged value of S also can be derived by including lagged values of I, X, and μ and then subtracting the equations for two succeeding years. With this approach, the coefficients for the lagged values of I and X must "deteriorate" over time at the same rate such that $\beta_{t-1} = \delta' \beta_t$, where β_t is the coefficient vector for these variables in year t.

7. On local public finance, see Bradford, Malt, and Oates (1969); Bradbury and others (1984); Ladd and Yinger (1991).

though these two literatures developed separately, these two terms refer to exactly the same concept. Several recent studies have brought these two strands of literature together.[8]

If observations for each school are available at three points in time, this equation can be transformed into change form. In this case, the dependent and explanatory variables are expressed as the change from the previous year, and the unobserved school-specific effects, which may be a source of bias in the standard approach, cancel out.[9] Since this approach requires at least three years of data, it has not been used by any production function study of which we are aware. The empirical analysis in chapter 8 of this volume, for example, is based on one of the most complete data sets in the literature and includes a lagged dependent variable, but it does not estimate a production function using the full change form.

This production function approach can be applied to school districts, schools, classrooms, or even students.[10] The more micro levels of focus make it possible to isolate the variables that influence the interaction between students and teachers that is at the heart of this technology.

This approach also has some disadvantages, like the fact that extensive data are required. The principal disadvantage for our purposes, however, is that it focuses on one output at a time. Schools are complex institutions that provide many different joint outputs that are likely to share inputs and influence each other.[11] This limitation is crucial for us because our objective is to determine the differences in technology and the associated differences in costs for the unit that is evaluated and aided by state govern-

8. These studies include Ratcliffe, Riddle, and Yinger (1990); Fenner (1992); Downes and Pogue (1994).

9. For an example parallel to that in note 6, a linear form of a change equation would be: $S_{it} - S_{it-1} = \alpha(I_{it} - I_{it-1}) + \beta(X_{it} - X_{it-1}) + \delta(S_{it-1} - S_{it-2}) + (\mu_{it} - \mu_{i,t-1})$.

10. As pointed out by Summers and Wolfe (1977) and Hanushek (1979), among others, in applying this model to individual students one must distinguish between individual and family background variables, peer-group variables, and school variables.

11. Multiproduct production functions have typically assumed separability between outputs so that each can be estimated in a separate equation (possibly allowing correlation across error terms by using a seemingly unrelated regression method). On the other extreme, some studies in the public sector have estimated simultaneous production functions that assume that each output simultaneously influences the other. (See Boardman, Davis, and Sanday [1977].) If the production of outputs share some inputs but do not necessarily cause each other, then a production function that allows for jointness of production is the most appropriate. (See Chizmar and Zak [1983].) Recently, canonical regression has been used to estimate joint production functions. (See Gyimah-Brempong and Gyapong [1991]; Ruggiero [forthcoming a].) However, no one has yet shown how to use this approach to develop comprehensive educational cost indexes.

ment, namely, the school district. We need an overview of educational technology in a district, not the specific classroom technology for a single educational output.

Educational Cost Functions

This problem leads us to the principal alternative method for studying educational technology: an analysis of school spending or costs, defined as the sum of input purchases.[12] Associated with every production function is a cost function. However, cost functions are observed only at the district level, in effect after the cost functions for various educational outputs have been aggregated. In this framework, overall expenditure E for a given district at a point in time is the dependent variable. The explanatory variables include an index S^* of the educational outputs achieved by that district; a vector P of input prices; a vector X of environmental or external factors; and error terms. In algebraic terms, $F_{jt} = h(S^*_{jt}, P_{jt}, X_{jt}, \epsilon_j, v_{jt})$, where the subscript j indicates the school district and t indicates time. Also, ϵ is a set of unobserved district-specific variables, and v is a random error term. (This formulation excludes past history, S^*_{jt-1}, for the moment.)

Before estimating this equation, we must deal with three major conceptual issues. The first issue is that S^* clearly is endogenous; school districts make spending and service quality decisions simultaneously.[13] Fortunately, the literature on the demand for public education provides extensive instruments to use in a simultaneous-equations procedure for this equation. In particular, the standard median-voter model of education demand shows how public service quality, S^* in our approach, depends on income, intergovernmental aid, tax share (usually specified as the ratio of median to mean property values), and preferences.[14]

Several studies have used an alternative, reduced-form approach, in which these instruments replace service quality on the right-hand side of

12. Recent examples of this approach include Downes and Pogue (1994); Gyimah-Brempong and Gyapong (1992); Fenner (1992); Callan and Santerre (1990); Ratcliffe, Riddle, and Yinger (1990). Earlier studies are reviewed in Cohn and Geske (1990); and Monk (1990).

13. Despite the obvious endogeneity of service quality, we know of only two studies of educational costs that treat service quality as endogenous: Baum (1986) and Downes and Pogue (1994).

14. For a detailed discussion and literature review on these issues, see Ladd and Yinger (1991). The specific instruments we use are presented below.

the equation.[15] However, this reduced-form approach has a major disadvantage compared with estimating the structural equation: environmental factors influence a voter's tax price, which is the voter's tax share multiplied by the marginal cost of public services, and therefore environmental factors are demand factors themselves. Hence, the coefficients of environmental variables in the reduced-form approach reflect both their direct effect on educational costs, which is the effect we are looking for, and their indirect effect through demand. These effects cannot be untangled without assuming specific functional forms for the relationships in the model, and these forms cannot be tested.[16] We prefer the structural approach because it requires no such assumptions.

The second issue concerns how to measure the index of educational outputs. One possible approach is to include every possible measure of school outputs and let the regression procedure determine how they are weighted to form S^*. This approach has two serious problems. First, because output measures often are highly correlated with each other, it introduces extensive collinearity into the regression. This collinearity may make it impossible to estimate any coefficients with precision, including the coefficients of the cost variables. Second, this approach undermines our ability to identify the model, since every new (endogenous) output measure requires another instrument. As a practical matter, therefore, the key problem is how to pare down the set of school output measures in a sensible way.

A partial solution to this problem is to use outcomes that are related to demand variables like income, intergovernmental aid, tax share, and preferences. After all, when analyzing district spending, one is interested in school output measures that households care about, as reflected in their demand for public services. School output measures that are uncorrelated with demand variables do not fit the bill. This is only a partial solution to the problem, however, because some outputs people care about at a district level may not be correlated with demand variables, at least not with ones we can observe. Hence evidence that an output variable is correlated with

15. To put it another way, our approach is based on the auxiliary equation $S_{it}^* = d(D_{jt}, \psi_{jt})$, where D is a vector of demand variables and ψ is a random error term. This equation can be substituted into the equation in the text to provide an alternative to our approach. For an example, see Ratcliffe, Riddle, and Yinger (1990).

16. This point is made by Schwab and Zampelli (1987) and Downes and Pogue (1994). A detailed exposition of the necessary structure is provided in Ladd and Yinger (1991). One important assumption that is required to identify cost parameters in a reduced-form model is constant returns to scale with respect to changes in S^*. See Duncombe and Yinger (1993) for a detailed discussion of this point.

demand variables must be combined with judgments about the importance of various output measures based on previous literature. Our judgments on this issue are presented below.

The third issue is that the equation includes two error terms, which we do not observe and which might be a source of bias. The district-specific effect, ϵ, which captures all unobserved variables that do not vary over time, can in theory be eliminated through differencing, as discussed earlier.[17] For our purposes, however, differencing has two serious limitations. First, this procedure makes it impossible to observe the effects of input and environmental factors that do not vary over time; these effects are buried in the district-specific effect. Because many input and environmental factors vary slowly over time (and often cannot even be observed every year), this approach may mask most of the variation in costs across districts. Thus it is not appropriate when one's objective is to obtain a comprehensive cost index.

Second, differencing does not eliminate omitted variables that do vary over time. These variables are likely to include many inputs and environmental factors, along with unobserved outputs, a district's past service quality, and its degree of inefficiency.[18] Unless these variables are accounted for, estimated coefficients for input and environmental factors that are included are likely to be biased, even with differencing, and the direction of this bias is uncertain.

To deal with these problems, we estimate the undifferenced form of the cost function with a new control variable designed to capture all the systematic components of both ϵ and v. This variable is based on a technique called data envelopment analysis, or DEA, which has been used to measure school district inefficiency.[19] Cost inefficiency is the extent to which a district is spending more than necessary to obtain its output level. This inefficiency consists both of using too many inputs for a given amount of output (technical inefficiency) and of using the wrong combination of inputs given input prices (input allocative inefficiency). Further explanation of DEA is provided in the appendix.

17. A first-differencing approach is used by Downes and Pogue (1994). They are aware of the fact that differencing eliminates some cost variables and explicitly develop cost indexes for only two cost variables, the fractions of students receiving subsidized lunches and those with limited English proficiency.
18. Hanushek (1986, p. 1166) points out that inefficiency may make it appear that "expenditures are unrelated to school performance." Ruggiero (forthcoming a) finds evidence that inefficiency dampens the observed effect that school inputs have on outputs.
19. See, for example, Grosskopf and Yaisawarng (1990); Ruggiero (1994).

As it turns out, a standard DEA "efficiency" measure captures the effect of any factor that influences the relationship between service quality and costs—not just district efficiency. All else being equal, an efficient district can obtain the same service quality as an inefficient district at a lower cost. However, the relationship between service quality and costs is also affected by environmental factors.[20] Consider two equally efficient districts, one of which has a much harsher environment than the other. The district with the harsher environment will have to spend more to obtain the same service quality. Hence a standard DEA measure picks up the effect of environmental factors as well as of efficiency. The same logic applies to any other unobserved systematic factor in either error term of our structural equation. Districts that made relatively high investments in education in the past, for example, will have a favorable legacy that allows them to obtain the same service quality as other districts at a lower cost.[21] Thus including a standard DEA "efficiency" measure will eliminate the potential bias from the unobserved, and hence omitted, noncost variables included in the two error terms in the structural equation.[22] To put it another way, our DEA variable is a comprehensive insurance policy against omitted-variable bias.

Unfortunately, however, this insurance policy has a price: a resulting duplication of contemporaneous input and environmental cost variables.[23] To be specific, input prices and environmental factors are included as the Xs in the structural equation as well as in the DEA variable. As a result, some of the full effects of input prices and environmental factors on costs will be captured by the estimated coefficients of the Xs and some will be captured by the DEA variable's coefficient. We do not know exactly how these effects will be divided, but we do know that the true effects will not

20. Ruggiero (1994) has shown how to measure inefficiency controlling for the environment in a DEA framework through the use of multiple cost frontiers (as discussed in the appendix). As explained below, however, this solution is not appropriate here.

21. Downes and Pogue (1994) account for past history by including both twelfth grade test scores and eleventh grade test scores for the same cohort. This is analogous to the service-quality term on the right side of the equation in note 9 and picks up the history of cost factors, as well as of other variables.

22. One important criticism of DEA is that the outputs on which it is based are selected by the researcher, not by some statistical test. See Hanushek (1986). This criticism does not apply to our equations because the outputs used in the DEA procedure are the same ones used in equation 5, where a statistical test of their significance is provided.

23. In principle, one could avoid this duplication by using the Ruggiero procedure to correct for environmental cost factors. However, this approach is not practical here because DEA cannot handle as many cost factors as are required for our procedure without a much larger sample of school districts than exists in any state, including New York. See Ruggiero (1994).

be fully captured by the Xs, that is, by the observed values of the input prices and environmental factors. Our cost indexes are based solely on the coefficients of the X variables and are not affected by the coefficient of the DEA control variable. It follows that our approach inevitably provides an underestimate of the effect of input prices and environmental factors on costs; some of the true effect of the environment is buried in the DEA coefficient.

The DEA efficiency measure also might be endogenous; that is, some of the same factors that influence decisions about spending might also influence decisions that lead districts to act in an efficient manner. To account for this possibility, we identify an instrument for district efficiency and treat the DEA measure as endogenous.

In addition, our approach focuses on the role of contemporaneous input prices and environmental factors and ignores past values of these variables. One could argue that a cost index should capture past as well as current values of these variables. A district should be compensated, the argument might go, for the lingering effects of a relatively harsh environment in the past as well as for one in the present. This argument has some appeal, but it also raises many unresolved issues, such as how far back in history to go. To the extent that contemporaneous values of input prices and environmental factors are highly correlated with past values, our approach may pick up some past history. But neither our approach nor any previous research produces cost indexes that include a comprehensive treatment of each district's history of input prices and environmental variables.

In short, our approach provides a conservative estimate of the effects of contemporaneous input prices and environmental factors on school district costs.

Cost Indexes

For the purposes of designing intergovernmental aid formulas, one needs a measure of the cost, based on factors outside a district's control, of providing a given quality of education.[24] Educational quality is defined by the educational outputs, S. Because the structural equation determines the effect of input and environmental costs on spending holding S constant, it is ideally suited for calculating a cost index. This approach has been applied both

24. For a detailed discussion of the use of cost indexes in education formulas, see Ladd and Yinger (1994).

for school and nonschool spending.[25] Our cost indexes use the estimated regression coefficients to calculate the amount each district would have to spend to obtain average-quality public services.

An alternative approach to cost indexes based on compensating wage differentials also has appeared in the educational literature. According to this approach, some districts have to pay higher wages than other districts to attract teachers of the same quality. Several studies have estimated the extent to which teachers' wages vary across districts based on factors outside a district's control and then calculated a wage index based on this estimation.[26] The problem with this approach is that it minimizes the role of the school environment. A comprehensive cost index needs to account not only for the fact that some districts must pay more than others to hire teachers of any given quality, but also for the fact that some districts must hire more teachers than others to provide the same educational outputs for their students. Indexes based on wages alone therefore inevitably provide an incomplete and potentially misleading picture of cost variation across districts.[27] We will demonstrate this problem using our New York data.

Empirical Analysis of Costs in New York School Districts

We estimate cost models and education cost indexes for 631 school districts in New York in 1991.[28] This section describes our measures, data sources, and empirical analysis of education costs and provides a comparison of alternative education cost indexes.

---

25. For nonschool spending, see Bradbury and others (1984); Ladd and Yinger (1991). For school spending, see Ratcliff, Riddle, and Yinger (1990); Downes and Pogue (1994).

26. See, for example, Chambers (1978, 1980); Fleeter (1990); Wendling (1981).

27. Monk and Walker (1991, p. 174) argue that a more comprehensive approach "presupposes an ability to reach agreement about the nature and level of outcomes schools are expected to produce." We agree that one must select output measures in order to implement our structural equation, but we think that reasonable procedures can be developed for making this selection. Moreover, the fact that a step may be difficult is a poor excuse for not attempting it, particularly when the conceptual case for it is so strong. Finally, one can estimate cost indexes without selecting output measures if one substitutes demand variables for outcomes in the cost model.

28. There were 695 school districts in New York in 1991. Because of missing observations, including New York City and Yonkers, we limited the sample to 631 observations. The remaining sample appears representative of the major regions in New York State.

Cost Model Results

We estimate our education cost models using a modified Cobb-Douglas form. This function imposes several restrictions on the production technology for educational services, but its simplicity and conceptual plausibility, along with its frequent successful application in empirical research, outweigh its potential limitations. The cost models were estimated using linear two-stage least squares, with outcome measures, the efficiency index, and the price of labor treated as endogenous.[29]

The dependent variable for expenditure is the log of approved operating expenses (AOE) per pupil, which is provided by the New York State Department of Education. AOE includes salaries and fringe benefits of teachers and other school staff, other instructional expenditure, and all other expenditure related to operation and maintenance of schools.[30] Average AOE per pupil for the sample was $6,054.

Our initial specification, called model 1, is presented in the first column of table 10-1. The first three explanatory variables are measures of educational outcome. Our data set includes many outcome measures, including average achievement test scores, which are the focus of most previous studies.[31] As discussed previously, however, collinearity severely limits the number of outcomes that can be included in a cost model. We used a two-step process to select a reduced set of outcome measures. First, we identified outcomes that appear to be related to voters' willingness to pay for education by regressing each potential outcome measure on a set of education demand variables, including income and tax share. Second, from the set of outcomes correlated with demand factors, we identified subsets of variables that, based on previous research, appeared to be reasonable measures and then, where appropriate, calculated an average across the variables in such a subset.[32]

29. The Cobb-Douglas cost function restricts the elasticity of substitution between all factor inputs to be one and assumes homotheticity between costs and outputs. Since we include only one factor price in the cost model, the factor substitution restriction is not a serious limitation. An alternate approach is to estimate a translog or flexible functional form. This approach is taken by Jimenez (1986); Callan and Santerre (1990); Gyimah-Brempong and Gyapong (1992); Duncombe and Yinger (1993). In this case we believe that it would add complexity without significant insight.

30. This measure of expenditure excludes transportation expenses because we do not have any data that would allow us to measure the environmental factors that influence the cost of transporting children to school. In addition, most debt service is excluded from approved operating expenses.

31. See the review in Hanushek (1986).

32. An R-squared of 0.1 or higher was assumed to indicate a significant relationship to voters' willingness to pay. We also used factor analysis to determine whether the selection

Table 10-1. *Education Cost Model Results, 631 New York State School Districts, 1991*[a]

	Three outcomes		Two outcomes	
Variable	Model 1	Model 2	Model 3	Model 4
Intercept	−7.7095	−8.0172	1.5291	−1.8377
	(−2.67)	(−2.68)	(0.92)	(−0.56)
Pupil evaluation	2.3472	2.3986	2.1877	2.9261
program scores[b]	(1.49)	(1.52)	(3.24)	(2.11)
Percent non-dropouts	7.1626	6.4159	5.2284	. . .
	(2.68)	(2.35)	(4.00)	
Percent receiving	1.2432	1.3156	. . .	1.5275
regents' diploma	(2.73)	(2.85)		(3.78)
Efficiency index	−0.9930	−0.9337	−1.5660	−1.1436
(percent)	(−4.49)	(−4.02)	(−13.84)	(−5.09)
Log of teacher salaries	0.8913	0.9936	0.1530	0.9657
	(2.16)	(2.38)	(0.92)	(2.63)
Log of enrollment	−0.5331	−0.5552	−0.2503	−0.5397
	(−3.73)	(3.75)	(−3.76)	(−4.02)
Square of log of	0.0329	0.0338	0.0163	0.0309
enrollment	(3.81)	(3.78)	(3.68)	(3.70)
Percent of children in	0.8306	0.7903	0.4812	0.5036
poverty	(3.99)	(3.76)	(4.53)	(2.69)
Percent female-headed	2.1166	1.9823	0.6033	1.7162
households	(4.26)	(3.95)	(2.36)	(3.82)
Percent of students with	0.3903	. . .	. . .	. . .
disability	(1.11)			
Percent of students with	. . .	0.9656	0.5295	0.4460
severe disability[c]		(1.66)	(1.88)	(0.93)
Percent with limited	2.5236	2.5844	1.3943	3.0664
English proficiency	(2.11)	(2.10)	(2.26)	(2.84)
Percent of students in	0.2945	0.3438	0.4451	0.3756
high school	(1.10)	(1.26)	(3.34)	(1.51)
SSE	24.82	26.05	6.50	22.08
Adjusted R^2	0.51	0.48	0.87	0.56

a. Cost model estimated with linear two-stage least squares regression using instruments described in the text. The cost model is based on a modified Cobb-Douglas production function with the square of the log of enrollment. The dependent variable is the log of per pupil approved operating expenditures. Numbers in parentheses are *t*-statistics.
b. Percentage of students above standard reference point.
c. Students are in special class instruction or special programs for at least 60 percent of school day.

The first variable identified by this process is based on pupil evaluation program (PEP) tests given to all third- and sixth-grade students in reading and math. The specific measure is the average percentage of students performing above a standard reference point on these four exams. The standard reference point is used to identify students requiring special assistance (and chapter 1 funding from the federal government). The second variable is the percentage of students receiving a special regents' diploma upon graduation from high school.[33] To balance this measure of achievement, the third variable is the inverse of the dropout rate, the percentage of students not dropping out of school. Notice that all of these measures capture the tails of the student achievement distribution instead of the average.[34] In model 1, the outcome measures all have positive coefficients, as expected, two of the three coefficients are statistically significant, and the third is almost significant with a *t*-statistic of about 1.5.

The next explanatory variable in model 1 is an "efficiency" index for each school district based on AOE per pupil and the three outcome measures, constructed using the the DEA method discussed above and in the appendix. As explained earlier, this index captures not only efficiency but also environmental cost factors and past school decisions that shift the cost frontier facing a school district. Because this index is held constant in constructing the cost indexes, we are being conservative in our estimate of costs; that is, our cost indexes ignore any cost effects picked up by the DEA index instead of by the input and environmental variables in the cost model.[35] The "efficiency" index has, as expected, a negative coefficient and is statistically significant; greater efficiency in a school district is associated with lower expenditure, all else being equal.

The next eight variables are cost variables. To measure input price differences, we estimated a teacher salary index, which adjusts for differences

---

and clustering of our outcome measures adequately captured the variation in the data across all potential such measures. (Specifically, a principal-component analysis with a varimax rotation was performed on the eighteen remaining outcome measures.) The size and pattern of the factor scores strongly supports our choices.

33. The regents' diploma is awarded to students who pass a relatively difficult set of standardized competency exams in different subject areas. Because not all students are required to take regents' exams, it was not possible to use these test scores directly as outcomes because of sample selectivity problems. Student test scores and dropout rates are developed by the New York State Education Department (1991).

34. Conceptual arguments for the importance of such measures are given by Hanushek (1986) and Brown and Saks (1975).

35. The average "efficiency" score is 0.66; 23 districts (4 percent) had an index of 1 and 350 districts (55 percent) had an index below 0.7.

in teacher experience, education, and certification to reflect differences in the cost of teachers of equivalent quality.[36] A potential problem with the index is endogeneity arising out of the relationship between teacher salaries and spending decisions.[37] It is possible that some of the variation in teacher salaries reflects discretionary decisions by district administrators, not underlying differences in opportunity wages for teachers. To avoid this problem, the index is based on salaries of teachers with five years or less of experience. Even if excessive expenditures are used primarily to increase teachers' salaries, this benefit is less likely to accrue to the most recently hired teachers. Moreover, as explained below, this wage variable is treated as endogenous.

We use both enrollment and the square of enrollment as variables, because many studies find that per pupil expenditures are a U-shaped function of enrollment.[38] The education production literature has highlighted the importance of family background and student characteristics.[39] Our data set allows us to measure several environmental variables in these categories, namely the percentage of children in poverty, the percentage of households with a female single parent, the percentage of children with

36. Teacher salaries are highly related with other professional salaries in New York school districts. The correlation is 0.7 or higher with salaries for principals, assistant principals, and superintendents. Salary information on nonprofessional staff is not available. Salaries and teacher characteristics are collected in the Personnel Master File of the Basic Education Data System (BEDS) of the New York State Education Department. BEDS is a self-reporting survey completed by professional staff in schools. Salaries were adjusted to control for teacher characteristics. To be specific, our salary variable is the residual from a regression of teacher salaries on years of experience, level of education, type of certification, and tenure. A number of districts were missing information on salary levels. We filled in for these missing observations by assuming that a district had the same average adjusted salary level as other districts of the same type (such as suburban or rural) in its county.

37. To the best of our knowledge, only one previous study, Downes and Pogue (1994), recognizes that teacher wages are endogenous. However, their study fails to eliminate endogeneity bias because one of the instruments in their simultaneous equations procedure is an index of teacher experience, which also is endogenous.

38. Because we use a double-log functional form, we actually include the log of enrollment and the square of the log of enrollment. Either enrollment or average daily attendance (ADA) could be used as the measure of the number of pupils. An argument can be made for each being the most directly related to costs (Monk, 1990). We selected enrollment because school districts are likely to budget resources for close to full attendance. However, the correlation between enrollment and ADA is close to 1.0 in New York, and there was little change in the cost indexes when ADA was used.

39. See Bridge, Judd, and Moock (1979); Hanushek (1986). These variables and others are discussed in the reviews mentioned earlier. One example of a production study that uses all three of these environmental factors is Ferguson (1991).

limited English proficiency, the percentage of students with a disability, and the percentage of total enrollment that is high school students.[40]

Six of the eight cost variables have statistically significant coefficients with the expected signs. The teacher salary variable is positively related to expenditure and its coefficient is quite large. Both enrollment variables are statistically significant and indicate a U-shaped per pupil expenditure function. Based on these results, the "minimum cost enrollment" falls at a district enrollment of about 3,300 pupils.[41] Child poverty rates and the percentage of female-headed households are both positively related to expenditure and statistically significant, and we find a positive and significant relationship between spending and the share of high school students with limited English proficiency. The percentage of students who have a disability and the percentage who are in high school have the expected signs, but their *t*-statistics are just above 1.0.

Service outcomes, the efficiency index, and the price of labor are all determined simultaneously with district spending through discretionary decisions made in the annual budgeting process. To control for this endogeneity, our cost model is estimated using two-stage least squares, with an appropriate set of additional instruments. Following a standard median-voter model,[42] we use median income as a fundamental determinant of voter demand. Demand also depends on intergovernmental aid; our state aid variable, basic operating aid, is the principal form of noncategorical aid provided to school districts in New York.[43] The standard tax price facing the median voter equals the voter's tax share multiplied by the marginal cost of educational services. The marginal cost component is already in the

---

40. The source of most of these variables is the 1990 Census (U.S. Bureau of the Census and U.S. Department of Education, National Center for Education Statistics, 1994). The remaining variables come from the New York State Education Department's Basic Education Data System.

41. These results suggest that if consolidation of small districts is not possible, it is appropriate to control for the cost effects of scale in an education cost index. See Duncombe, Miner, and Ruggiero (1995) for an analysis of the benefits of school district consolidation in New York State. They found that the number of districts that might benefit from consolidation in New York and the potential cost savings from consolidation were quite small.

42. See, particularly, Ladd and Yinger (1991); Rubinfeld (1987); Inman (1979).

43. Although on paper the operating aid formula used in New York is similar in design to a matching percentage equalizing grant, in actual practice it is closer to a lump-sum foundation grant. Since aid is lump sum and is distributed based on a measure of fiscal capacity, it is likely to be exogenous to local district spending decisions. See Miner (1990) for a good discussion of school aid formulas in New York State.

cost model (in the form of the input price and environmental factors), but the tax share makes a suitable instrument. We measure the tax share with the ratio of median to mean residential property value and with an estimate of the district's ability to export some commercial and industrial property taxes onto nonresidents.[44] Finally, we include several socioeconomic variables that are likely to be related to demand for education, namely the percentage of households with children, the percentage of households living in owner-occupied housing, and the percentage of adults with a college degree.[45]

We also use instruments associated with the price of labor or the efficiency index. Since comparable private-sector prices for teachers were not available, we use 1990 county population as a instrument for teacher salaries. Our choice of this instrument is based on the stylized fact (and a central prediction of urban economics) that the cost of living, and hence the cost of hiring workers, increases with metropolitan population. Identifying instruments for the efficiency index is more difficult. Although there is a large literature on bureaucratic behavior, there is little associated empirical literature examining the causes of inefficiency.[46] The bureaucratic models suggest that greater inefficiency will be associated with larger and wealthier school districts, those facing less competition, and those with poorer performance incentives for their employees. Enrollment and median income already have been included as exogenous variables. Good measures of private school competition are not available, but competition also may come in the form of voter referenda on school budgets. In New York, all school districts are required to have budget referenda except for city school districts, where the budget is set entirely by elected city officials. A dummy

---

44. Borrowing from Ladd and Yinger (1991) and Duncombe (1991), the tax share is represented as $V_m/V = (V_m/V_l)(1-e)$, where V_m and V_l are the median and average local residential property values and e is the percentage of property taxes borne by nonresidents. We construct the export ratio, e, using information on the distribution of property values by type (from the New York State Department of Equalization and Assessment) and estimates of property tax exporting by type of property from Ladd and Yinger (1991). Similar results are obtained using a set of property composition variables instead of the export ratio.

45. One could argue that the percentage of adults with a college degree is an environmental cost variable; more educated parents do more to reinforce the lessons their children learn in school. When this variable is treated as an environmental cost factor, however, it has the wrong sign (positive) so we cannot reject the hypothesis that it has no effect on costs. A similar procedure ruled out children per household and median income as cost variables.

46. See, for example, Niskanen (1971, 1975); Wyckoff (1988, 1990).

variable for city districts therefore is included as an instrument for the efficiency index.[47]

Thus the results reported in table 10-1 reflect a two-stage least squares regression using the instruments just described. Overall, this regression provides strong confirmation of our approach; by controlling for (endogenous) outcome measures, efficiency, and past history, one can precisely measure the effect of many contemporaneous input and environmental cost variables on school district spending.

Variants of the Basic Model

We also estimated several variants of this model to determine the robustness of our results. In model 2, presented in the second column of table 10-1, we explore one possible explanation for the insignificance of the disability variable, namely, the heterogeneity of the students in this category and the associated variation in the special services they need. Using disaggregated information on students with disabilities in New York by the level of service they receive, we examined several disability variables in the cost model.[48] The percentage of students who have severe disabilities, requiring special services out of the regular classroom at least 60 percent of the school day, does have a statistically significant positive effect on district expenditures (with a one-tailed test). A 1 percentage point increase in the number of these students raises per pupil expenditures by close to 1 percent. The other outcome and cost factors remain statistically significant with little change in their coefficients. This model 2 is our preferred specification and is used to construct our principal cost index.

Because one of our outcome measures is not statistically significant, we also estimated cost models using two different pairs of outcome measures. The resulting models 3 and 4 in table 10-1 each include a DEA efficiency index based only on the two outcome measures in the model. In both cases, the coefficient of the PEP scores variable is statistically significant with a

47. See Duncombe, Miner, and Ruggiero (forthcoming) for a more complete discussion of factors associated with cost inefficiency. Contrary to expectation, they found a negative relationship between the relative number of private school students (or schools) and the level of cost efficiency.

48. Categories of students with disabilities are organized by the level of special services they receive. Categories include students requiring special services 60 percent or more of the day or using private schools for services, students requiring special services at least 20 percent of the day, student requiring consultant teacher services, and students using two periods a week in special services. Several New York State education aid formulas use total weighted pupil units (TWPU), which assigns different pupil weightings to these categories.

Table 10-2. *Correlations between Education Cost Indexes for 631 New York State School Districts, 1991*

| | Direct cost indexes[a] | | | Indirect cost index (no efficiency index)[b] | Cost index based on weighted pupils[c] | Teacher salary cost index[d] |
	Endogenous efficiency	No efficiency index	Exogenous efficiency			
Distribution and correlation						
Standard deviation	16.93	26.11	10.85	15.33	8.88	12.75
Maximum	239.62	356.11	191.84	253.94	264.00	143.55
75th percentile	105.26	109.53	103.21	105.74	102.94	111.61
25th percentile	89.56	83.89	93.77	90.50	96.96	89.81
Minimum	77.50	70.70	83.83	77.05	44.68	68.37
Correlations						
Direct cost indexes						
Endogenous efficiency index	1.00	...	...	...	...	...
No efficiency index	0.94	1.00	...	...	...	...
Exogenous efficiency index	0.84	0.74	1.00	...	...	...
Indirect cost index (no efficiency index)	0.63	0.55	0.39	1.00	...	...
Cost index based on weighted pupils	0.14	0.15	0.13	0.08	1.00	...
Teacher salary cost index	0.47	0.57	0.32	-0.08	0.06	1.00

a. Indexes are based on three-factor cost model (model 2 in table 10-1) with the state average equal to 100.
b. Index is based on a reduced-form model where the demand instruments—income, tax share, and households with children—are substituted into the cost model for outcome measures.
c. Index is based on a ratio of weighted pupils over total enrollment; extra weight is given to secondary pupils and pupils with special needs or disabilities.
d. Index is based on the relationship between teacher salaries and family and student characteristics.

magnitude similar to that in model 1. These results reinforce the importance of controlling for elementary student performance in the construction of cost indexes and suggest that it may be collinearity that keeps down the significance of the PEP variable in models 1 and 2. Because it provides a broader range of outcome measures, we will use the three-outcome model to construct our education cost indexes.

Comparison of Education Cost Indexes

The cost models in table 10-1 can be used to construct educational cost indexes. Our cost index is designed to capture the key cost factors outside a district's control, including the underlying cost of hiring teachers (the opportunity wage), district size, family background, and student characteristics. Variation in expenditure among districts that reflects differences in service quality, efficiency, or past history is eliminated from the calculations. To be specific, we multiply regression coefficients by actual district values for each cost factor (and by the state average for outcomes and efficiency) to construct a measure of the expenditure each district must make to provide average-quality services given average inefficiency.[49] Our cost indexes express this required expenditure relative to the state average.[50]

Table 10-2 presents a variety of cost indexes. Our principal cost index, which is based on model 2 in table 10-1, is shown in the first column. This index has a range from 78 to 240 with a standard deviation of 17. Seventy-five percent of the districts have indexes below 105, and 75 percent have indexes above 90. Columns 2 and 3 present cost indexes based on alternative cost models; the cost model in column 2 has no control for district efficiency, and the one in column 3 treats district efficiency as exogenous. The standard deviations in these columns reveal that, compared with our preferred model, ignoring efficiency tends to magnify cost differences across districts, whereas treating efficiency as exogenous tends to dampen them. By omitting efficiency, the index in column 2 may be affected by omitted-variable bias and may therefore overstate cost differences across districts. Treating efficiency as exogenous introduces another possible bias, endogeneity bias. As it turns out, the correlation between the indexes

49. Since the price of labor is treated as endogenous in the cost model, a predicted wage is used to construct the cost index. The predicted wage is based on the predicted value of a first-stage regression between the price of labor and all exogenous and instrumental variables used in the cost model.

50. These cost index calculations are similar to the ones used by Downs and Pogue (1994) although, as explained earlier, our cost model differs from theirs in several respects.

in the first two columns, 0.94, is higher than the correlation between the indexes in columns 1 and 3, 0.84. This result indicates that a cost index correcting for efficiency, which is difficult to obtain, is roughly proportional to a cost index without an efficiency correction. However, the actual distribution of aid using these two cost indexes may be quite different because the efficiency correction lowers variation in costs.

Table 10-2 offers several other cost indexes: one based on an alternative approach from the education literature, and two others that are widely used in practice. The "indirect cost index," discussed earlier, is derived from a reduced-form expenditure model in which demand variables are substituted for service outcomes.[51] Most states use some form of weighted pupil measure in the allocation of aid. In New York, for example, students with special needs or disabilities or those in secondary school receive heavier weights in the distribution of aid. By taking the ratio of weighted pupils to total enrollment, we construct a cost index that indicates the level of cost adjustment in a typical state aid formula. This approach is likely to understate overall cost differences because it focuses on only a few cost-related student characteristics.

The most common cost index proposed in education research focuses on the relationship between socioeconomic factors and teacher salaries. Teachers are expected to command higher salaries if they are of higher quality (or have characteristics rewarded in union contracts), or if they have to work under more adverse working conditions. Working conditions can be affected by district decisions concerning resource utilization (pupil-teacher ratios) or by socioeconomic factors out of the district's control that reflect the harshness of the education environment (such as a relatively high incidence of special-needs or disadvantaged children). By holding teacher quality, demand variables, and discretionary resource factors constant, these studies have constructed education cost indexes to reflect the wage differentials required to compensate for an adverse socioeconomic environment.[52] Although a compensating wage-based cost index may capture cost factors associated with higher teacher salaries, it does not control for

---

51. This approach has been applied to education costs by Ratcliffe, Riddle, and Yinger (1990); Downes and Pogue (1994).

52. To construct a teacher salary cost index, we regressed actual teacher salaries on factors associated with differences in teacher quality (experience, certification, level of education, and tenure), demand for educational services, county population (as a proxy for private wages), and student and family background characteristics. All factors were held at the state mean except the county population and student and family background characteristics.

differences across districts in resource usage (including hiring of teachers) required to provide a given level of service outcomes.

The indirect cost index, which does not control for inefficiency, has slightly lower variability than our preferred cost index in column 1.[53] The least variability appears in the weighted pupil and teacher salary indexes, largely because these indexes are capturing only a portion of actual cost differentials.

Correlation coefficients in the bottom half of table 10-2 reiterate the substantial differences among these indexes. The correlation between our preferred index and the indirect index is 0.63, which suggests that the indirect approach may not do a good job of controlling for service quality differences and may therefore result in biased cost indexes.[54] The correlation between our preferred index and the weighted-pupil index is extremely low, only 0.14; the approach used by New York State therefore misses most of the actual variation in costs across districts. Finally, the correlation between our preferred index and the teacher salary index is 0.47, indicating only a moderate correlation between the factors that push up the salary needed to attract a given quality of teacher and the factors that push up the cost of providing a given quality of educational services. The teacher salary index is not related to either the indirect cost index or the weighted pupil index.

To provide a more disaggregated view of various cost indexes, table 10-3 presents average index scores by region, enrollment size, and income and property wealth of school districts. The direct cost index with endogenous efficiency, our preferred measure, identifies the large upstate central cities and downstate small cities as having the highest costs. (The large downstate cities, New York City and Yonkers, are not included in the sample because of missing data.) This result reflects higher teacher salaries in downstate districts and higher environmental cost factors in upstate cities. Upstate suburbs and rural districts have below-average costs. The results in this table also clearly show the U-shaped relationship between costs and enrollment and reveal that costs tend to be slightly higher for both the

---

53. We estimated an indirect cost model with efficiency, but because none of the variables in the model were statistically significant we do not present the results.

54. This result contradicts the finding in Downes and Pogue (1994), whose direct and indirect approaches yield cost indexes that are highly correlated. This difference may reflect our inability to incorporate efficiency into our indirect approach. Downes and Pogue do not have to deal with this issue because, as noted earlier, they account for efficiency by differencing. However, the Downes and Pogue cost index is based on fewer cost factors, so their direct and indirect cost indexes might differ if more factors were included.

Table 10-3. *Distribution of Education Cost Indexes, by Socioeconomic Factors, for 631 New York State School Districts, 1991*

		Direct cost indexes[a]		Cost index based on weighted pupils[b]
Social characteristics	Number of districts	Endogenous efficiency	No efficiency index	
Region type				
Downstate small cities	7	130.0	142.0	102.6
Downstate suburbs	130	111.4	125.0	101.6
Upstate large cities	3	179.2	190.2	100.3
Upstate rural	212	98.4	93.5	99.9
Upstate small cities	48	105.5	101.2	100.6
Upstate suburbs	231	91.9	89.2	99.0
Pupil size class				
Under 100	1	156.6	166.1	120.3
100–500	61	108.8	110.8	101.1
500–1,000	113	101.0	100.1	99.4
1,000–1,500	131	94.6	92.2	98.5
1,500–3,000	182	96.7	95.9	100.7
3,000–5,000	80	97.2	99.6	99.6
5,000–10,000	54	108.8	111.4	101.1
Over 10,000	9	139.4	149.0	100.9
Income class (percentile)[c]				
Under 10th	62	106.3	118.5	100.5
10th–25th	95	99.8	105.4	100.2
25th–50th	157	98.5	98.7	99.4
50th–75th	159	98.7	95.7	99.5
75th–90th	94	99.0	94.1	100.6
Over 90th	64	102.6	96.6	101.0
Property values (percentile)[d]				
Under 10th	63	109.7	122.9	100.1
10th–25th	94	105.2	112.0	100.1
25th–50th	158	99.8	100.5	99.5
50th–75th	158	94.1	89.6	100.0
75th–90th	95	96.7	91.0	99.7
Over 90th	63	103.0	97.5	101.3

a. Indexes are based on three-factor cost model (model 2 in table 10-1) with the state average equal to 100.
b. Index is based on a ratio of weighted pupils over total enrollment; extra weight is given to secondary pupils and pupils with special needs or disabilities.
c. Based on estimated per capita adjusted gross income in 1991.
d. Based on per capita market value for all property in 1990.

poorest and the richest districts, measured by either income or property wealth. Higher-income or wealthier districts, particularly in downstate New York, may have a relatively favorable educational environment, but they must pay relatively high teacher salaries.

Of course, one can also examine the distribution of alternative cost indexes for each of these socioeconomic categories. As shown in the last two columns of table 10-3, the cost differences across types of district are magnified somewhat with the no-efficiency index and dampened considerably with the weighted-pupils index. Cost differences are also dampened with exogenous-efficiency, indirect, and teacher salary cost indexes, which are not included in this table. Comparing the two types of cost indexes in table 10-3 by pupil-size category reinforces the similarity between our preferred index and the no-efficiency index. However, substantial differences exist between our preferred index and the others (shown in table 10-2). In general, the other indexes fail to pick up the relatively high costs of small districts and understate the costs of the largest districts.[55] Comparisons based on income class or property value class also identify several distinct differences between indexes. Although our preferred index shows little variation across income (and property wealth) classes, the no-efficiency and teacher salary indexes show substantially higher costs in low-income districts. These differences are difficult to interpret because they could reflect either inefficiency or unobserved environmental cost factors.

What types of districts tend to have particularly high or low costs and which environmental factors principally account for these cost differences? To answer this question we examined the 10 percent of school districts with the highest and lowest costs according to our preferred index. Table 10-4 compares average values for environmental factors in these districts and in the state as a whole. For high-cost districts, costs average 52.7 percent above the state average, $3,046 per pupil. All upstate large cities and over 70 percent of downstate small cities qualify as high-cost districts. Over 10 percent of downstate suburbs and upstate small cities also fall in this category. Enrollment, percentage of children in poverty and with limited English proficiency, and percentage of single-parent female-headed households are all well above the state average in these districts.

Combining the environmental indexes with the regression coefficients for model 2 in table 10-1, we can identify which environmental factors have a particularly strong effect on costs. Higher teacher salaries and a relatively high number of female-headed households each account for over

---

55. Part of the reason that the teacher salary index does not demonstrate a U-shape is because we do not include enrollment variables in this cost model. Although some studies in the past have included enrollment, no scholar has provided a convincing reason why teacher wages should be directly related to variation in enrollment. Interestingly, all these studies find an inverted U-shaped function between enrollment size and salaries. See Chambers (1978); Wendling (1981); Fleeter (1990).

Table 10-4. *Effect of Input Prices and Environmental Variables on Education Costs in Districts with Highest and Lowest Costs*[a]

	10 percent of districts with highest costs		10 percent of districts with lowest costs	
Cost variable	Index (state average = 100)	Percent of cost difference due to variable	Index (state average = 100)	Percent of cost difference due to variable
Total cost index	152.7	...	81.1	...
Per pupil difference from average district (dollars)	3,046	...	-1,091	...
Teacher salaries	111.2	30.67	96.0	-20.03
Log of enrollment	198.3	-13.20	128.0	-18.85
Percent of children in poverty	161.6	13.98	49.4	-22.86
Percent female-headed households	170.9	36.16	75.3	-21.24
Percent of students with severe disabilities[b]	177.7	9.43	54.3	-9.90
Percent with limited English proficiency	407.6	22.47	39.3	-7.77
Percent of students in high school	94.9	-1.38	101.3	0.64

a. Cost index based on three-factor cost model (model 2 in table 10-1). Indexes for costs and environmental variables relative to state average are based on average values for 10 percent of districts with the highest and lowest per pupil costs. The percentage cost difference due to cost variable i, say Pc_i, is based on three cost indexes: a total cost index for the high- (or low-) cost districts (A); a cost index with all variables set at the state average (B); and a cost index with cost variable i set at the average for the high- (or low-) cost districts and all other variables set at the state average (C). Then, $Pc_i = (C - B)/(A - C)$.

b. Students are in special class instruction or special programs for at least 60 percent of school day.

30 percent of the higher costs in these districts. Limited English proficiency and poverty are also important factors driving up costs. The higher enrollments in some high-cost districts may actually lower per pupil costs, because their enrollments are closer, on average, to the cost-minimizing enrollment.

The 10 percent of districts with the lowest costs have costs 20 percent below average, $1,091 per pupil. Most of these districts are upstate suburbs or rural districts, where poverty, female-headed households, students with severe disabilities, and students with limited English proficiency are all relatively uncommon. Lower teacher salaries, lower poverty rates, fewer female-headed households, and higher enrollments each account for 20 percent of the lower costs in these districts.

Conclusions and Policy Implications

The large literature on production and cost in education provides a solid foundation for the development of education cost indexes. This chapter demonstrates the serious flaws in existing ad hoc indexes, which do not build on this foundation, and shows how more acceptable cost indexes can be derived. Our approach focuses on the effects of input prices and environmental cost factors on educational spending, controlling for educational service quality. This approach leads to an index of the amount a school district would have to spend, given the input prices and environment it faces, to obtain average-quality educational services. Our contributions are to develop new criteria for selecting service quality measures and to control explicitly for school district efficiency and other unobserved district characteristics that might lead to biased cost indexes.

When applied to data for school districts in New York State, our approach works well in the sense that most of the regression coefficients are statistically significant and all of them have the anticipated signs. Hence, the cost indexes we estimate control for a variety of service quality measures (as well as district efficiency) and estimate with precision the effects of input prices and environmental factors on educational costs. The major disadvantage of our approach is that it requires the calculation of a complex "efficiency" measure based on data envelopment analysis, which may make our approach impractical as a tool for designing school aid formulas.

We also find, however, that cost indexes based on a model that excludes the DEA index are highly correlated with those based on our preferred cost model. School aid formulas based on this simpler formula might be more acceptable. However, it would be better still to discover simpler methods to control for district efficiency and other unobserved district characteristics, and to include these measures in a cost model. We also find two widely used methods for estimating educational costs, those based on weighted pupils and on required teacher salaries, do not provide reasonable approximations for our method. The weighted pupil cost index used in New York is virtually uncorrelated with our cost index, and the teacher salary index is only moderately correlated, misses the U-shaped relationship between costs and enrollment, and greatly understates the costs in large-city districts. In our judgment, therefore, these approaches are seriously deficient.

At the conceptual level, the importance of educational costs cannot be denied. Through no fault of their own, some school districts must spend more than other districts to obtain the same level of educational outcomes. However, educational cost indexes remain elusive because estimating them involves complex methodological problems. Given the stakes involved—the fair allocation of state educational aid—we believe that overcoming these obstacles is one of the principal challenges facing scholars and policymakers interested in education finance.

Appendix: Measuring Inefficiency in Public Services

The method used for estimating technical and cost efficiency in this chapter, data envelopment analysis or DEA, is based on production theory in economics and has been operationalized since the late 1970s. One major advantage of DEA is that it is nonparametric: that is, it requires no a priori specification of the functional form. One disadvantage is that the technique is nonstochastic.[56] These methods have been extended to analyze costs and economies of scope in public-sector production. The relevant mathematical programs are solved to compare the expenditure of a given local government with the expenditure of other local governments producing the same level of services. If the local government is producing at the cost-minimizing level, then no other local government (or linear combination of local governments) is producing the same level of services with lower expenditure.[57]

One problem with existing DEA methods for estimating inefficiency is the maintained assumption that the technology can be represented by one frontier. This assumption presumes that all deviations from the cost frontier are attributable to inefficiency. Although DEA has been commonly employed to examine public organizations such as school districts, the assumption of one cost frontier is not consistent with the nature of public production.[58] As explained in the text, input prices, P, and exogenous socioeconomic variables, X, can have an important influence on the translation of government activities into service outcomes. As a result, there will be multiple cost frontiers reflecting differences in P and X. Estimates of the

56. The concepts used in DEA were conceptualized by Farrell (1957) and developed by Charnes, Cooper and Rhodes (1978) and Färe and Lovell (1978) to analyze multiple output production correspondences. For a discussion of strengths and weaknesses of DEA, see Seiford and Thrall (1990).

57. See Grosskopf and Yaisawarng (1990) for one of the first applications of DEA to cost frontiers. Grosskopf and Yaisawarng limit their sample so that all producing units face the same cost environment.

58. See, for example, Bessent and Bessent (1980); Färe, Grosskopf, and Weber (1989).

minimum level of costs and cost inefficiency that do not control for these cost factors will be biased.

Recently, a method has been developed for estimating technical and cost efficiency that allows for multiple frontiers.[59] Efficiency estimates should be made in reference to the correct frontier. A local government is said to be cost efficient if the observed level of expenditure is equal to the minimum total cost of providing the observed level of services, given resource prices and environmental conditions.

Although this method provides a more realistic estimate of relative cost efficiency among school districts, it can handle only a few fixed cost factors, and these fixed cost factors must be selected before estimation of the cost model. Selected cost factors may turn out to be statistically insignificant, so that a complex iterative procedure would have to be developed to make the regression and the DEA consistent. To avoid these problems, we use the unadjusted cost efficiency index, which compares all districts with the cost frontier for the efficient district with the most favorable environment. Specifically, our measure of cost "efficiency," θ, is equal to C/E, where C equals minimum costs and E equals actual expenditure to produce a given level of outcomes. If local governments are cost efficient and face the most favorable cost environment, then expenditure reflects the minimum cost of providing services and θ equals 1.0. In any other case, that is, with either inefficiency or unfavorable fixed factors, θ is less than 1.0.

---

59. See Ruggiero (1994; forthcoming b).

References

Baum, Donald N. 1986. "A Simultaneous Equations Model of the Demand for and Production of Local Public Services: The Case of Education." *Public Finance Quarterly* 14 (April): 157–78.

Bessent, Authella M., and E. Wailand Bessent. 1980. "Determining the Comparative Efficiency of Schools through Data Envelopment Analysis." *Educational Administration Quarterly* 16 (Spring): 57–75.

Boardman, Anthony E., Otto A. Davis, and Peggy R. Sanday. 1977. "A Simultaneous Equations Model of the Educational Process." *Journal of Public Economics* 7 (February): 23–49.

Bradbury, Katharine L., and others. 1984. "State Aid to Offset Fiscal Disparities across Communities." *National Tax Journal* 37 (June): 151–70.

Bradford, David F., Robert A. Malt, and Wallace E. Oates. 1969. "The Rising Cost of Local Public Services: Some Evidence and Reflections." *National Tax Journal* 22 (June): 185–202.

Bridge, R. Gary, Charles M. Judd, and Peter R. Moock. 1979. *The Determinants of Educational Outcomes: The Impact of Families, Peers, Teachers, and Schools.* Cambridge, Mass.: Ballinger.

Brown, Byron W., and Daniel H. Saks. 1975. "The Production and Distribution of Cognitive Skills within Schools." *Journal of Political Economy* 83 (June): 571–93.

Callan, Scott J., and Rexford E. Santerre. 1990. "The Production Characteristics of Local Public Education: A Multiple Product and Input Analysis." *Southern Economic Journal* 57 (October): 468–80.

Chambers, Jay G. 1978. "Educational Cost Differentials and the Allocation of State Aid for Elementary and Secondary Education." *Journal of Human Resources* 13 (Fall): 459–81.

———. 1980. "The Development of a Cost of Education Index: Some Empirical Estimates and Policy Issues." *Journal of Education Finance* 5 (Winter): 262–81.

Charnes, A., W. W. Cooper, and E. Rhodes. 1978. "Measuring the Efficiency of Decision Making Units with Some New Production Function and Estimation Methods." *European Journal of Operational Research* 2 (November): 429–44.

Chizmar, John F., and Thomas A. Zak. 1983. "Modeling Multiple Outputs in Educational Production Functions." *American Economic Review* 73 (May): 17–22.

Cohn, Elchanan, and Terry G. Geske. 1990. *The Economics of Education.* 3d ed. New York: Pergamon Press.

Cooper, Bruce S. 1993. "Educational Choice: Competing Models and Meanings." In *Reforming Education: The Emerging Systemic Approach,* edited by Stephen L. Jacobson and Robert Berne, 107–30. Thousand Oaks, Calif.: Corwin Press.

Downes, Thomas A., and Thomas F. Pogue. 1994. "Adjusting School Aid Formulas for the Higher Cost of Educating Disadvantaged Students." *National Tax Journal* 47 (March): 89–110.

Duncombe, William D. 1991. "Demand for Local Public Services Revisited: The Case of Fire Protection." *Public Finance Quarterly* 19 (October): 412–36.

Duncombe, William, and John Yinger. 1993. "An Analysis of Returns to Scale in Public Production, with an Application to Fire Protection." *Journal of Public Economics* 52 (August): 49–72.

Duncombe, William, Jerry Miner, and John Ruggiero. 1995. "Potential Cost Savings from School District Consolidation: A Case Study of New York." *Economics of Education Review* 14 (September): 265–84.

———. Forthcoming. "Empirical Evaluation of Bureaucratic Models of Inefficiency." *Public Choice.*

Färe, Rolf, and C. A. Knox Lovell. 1978. "Measuring the Technical Efficiency of Production." *Journal of Economic Theory* 19 (October): 150–62.

Färe, Rolf, Shawna Grosskopf, and William L. Weber. 1989. "Measuring School District Performance." *Public Finance Quarterly* 17 (October): 409–28.

Farrell, M. J. 1957. "The Measurement of Productive Efficiency." *Journal of the Royal Statistical Society* 120 (3): 253–81.

Fenner, Richard. 1992. "The Effect of Equity of New York State's System of Aid for Education." Ph.D. dissertation, Syracuse University.

Ferguson, Ronald F. 1991. "Paying for Public Education: New Evidence on How and Why Money Matters." *Harvard Journal on Legislation* 28 (May): 465–98.

Fleeter, Howard B. 1990. "District Characteristics and Education Costs: Implications of Compensating Wage Differentials on State Aid in California." Ohio State University, School of Public Policy and Management.

Fuhrman, Susan H., Richard F. Elmore, and Diane Massell. 1993. "School Reform in the United States: Putting It into Context." In *Reforming Education: The Emerging Systemic Approach,* edited by Stephen L. Jacobson and Robert Berne, 3–27. Thousand Oaks, Calif.: Corwin Press.

Gold, Steven D., and others. 1992. *Public School Finance Programs of the United States and Canada, 1990–91.* Albany: American Education Finance Association, Nelson A. Rockefeller Institute of Government.

Grosskopf, Shawna, and Suthathip Yaisawarng. 1990. "Economies of Scope in the Provision of Local Public Services." *National Tax Journal* 43 (March): 61–74.

Gyimah-Brempong, Kwabena, and Anthony O. Gyapong. 1991. "Characteristics of Education Production Functions: An Application of Canonical Regression Analysis." *Economics of Education Review* 10 (1): 7–17.

—————. 1992. "Elasticities of Factor Substitution in the Production of Education." *Economics of Education Review* 11 (September): 205–17.

Hanushek, Eric A. 1979. "Conceptual and Empirical Issues in the Estimation of Educational Production Functions." *Journal of Human Resources* 14 (Summer): 351–88.

—————. 1986. "The Economics of Schooling: Production and Efficiency in Public Schools." *Journal of Economic Literature* 24 (September): 1141–77.

Hanushek, Eric A., with Charles S. Benson and others. 1994. *Making Schools Work: Improving Performance and Controlling Costs.* Brookings.

Inman, Robert. 1979. "The Fiscal Performance of Local Governments: An Interpretative Review." In *Current Issues in Urban Economics,* edited by Peter Mieszkowski and Mahlon Straszheim, 270–321. Johns Hopkins University Press.

Jimenez, Emmanuel. 1986. "The Structure of Educational Costs: Multiproduct Cost Functions for Primary and Secondary Schools in Latin America." *Economics of Education Review* 5 (1): 25–39.

Ladd, Helen F., and John M. Yinger. 1991. *America's Ailing Cities: Fiscal Health and the Design of Urban Policy.* Updated ed. Johns Hopkins University Press.

—————. 1994. "The Case for Equalizing Aid." *National Tax Journal* 47 (March): 211–24.

Miner, Jerry. 1990. "A Decade of New York State Aid to Local Schools." Metropolitan Studies Program Occasional Paper 141. Syracuse University, Maxwell School, Center for Policy Research.

Monk, David H. 1990. *Educational Finance: An Economic Approach.* McGraw-Hill.

Monk, David H., and Billy D. Walker. 1991. "The Texas Cost of Education Index: A Broadened Approach." *Journal of Education Finance* 17 (Fall): 172–92.

New York State Education Department. 1991. "Comprehensive Assessment Report."

Niskanen, William A. 1971. *Bureaucracy and Representative Government.* Chicago: Aldine-Atherton.

———. 1975. "Bureaucrats and Politicians." *Journal of Law and Economics* 18 (April): 617–43.

Odden, Allan R., and Lawrence O. Picus. 1992. *School Finance: A Policy Perspective.* McGraw-Hill.

Ratcliffe, Kerri, Bruce Riddle, and John Yinger. 1990. "The Fiscal Condition of School Districts in Nebraska: Is Small Beautiful?" *Economics of Education Review* 9 (1): 81–99.

Rubinfeld, Daniel L. 1987. "The Economics of the Local Public Sector." In *Handbook of Public Economics,* edited by Alan J. Auerbach and Martin Feldstein, 571–645. Vol. 2. New York: Elsevier Science Publishers.

Ruggiero, John. 1994. "Nonparametric Estimation of Cost Efficiency in the Public Sector: With an Application to New York State School Districts." Metropolitan Studies Program Occasional Paper 165. Syracuse University, Maxwell School, Center for Policy Research.

———. Forthcoming a. "Measuring Technical Inefficiency in the Public Sector: An Analysis of Educational Production." *Review of Economics and Statistics.*

———. Forthcoming b. "On the Measurement of Technical Efficiency in the Public Sector." *European Journal of Operational Research.*

Schwab, Robert M., and Ernest M. Zampelli. 1987. "Disentangling the Demand Function from the Production Function for Local Public Services: The Case of Public Safety." *Journal of Public Economics* 33 (July): 245–60.

Seiford, Lawrence M., and Robert M. Thrall. 1990. "Recent Developments in DEA: The Mathematical Programming Approach to Frontier Analysis." *Journal of Econometrics* 46 (October–November): 7–38.

Summers, Anita A., and Barbara J. Wolfe. 1977. "Do Schools Make a Difference?" *American Economic Review* 67 (September): 639–52.

Wendling, Wayne. 1981. "The Cost of Education Index: Measurement of Price Differences of Education Personnel among New York State School Districts." *Journal of Education Finance* 6 (Spring): 485–504.

Wyckoff, Paul Gary. 1988. "A Bureaucratic Theory of Flypaper Effects." *Journal of Urban Economics* 23 (January): 115–29.

———. 1990. "The Simple Analytics of Slack-Maximizing Bureaucracy." *Public Choice* 67 (October): 35–47.

Comments on Chapters Eight, Nine, and Ten

William H. Clune

My COMMENTS emerge from the perspective of research I have been doing on "adequacy" in school finance, especially as regards disadvantaged children.[1] Adequacy is an outcome (or output) standard and refers to the level of resources needed to produce specified educational outcomes. In contrast, equity is an input standard that is based on equalization of resources relative to some other benchmark district or school.

All three of these chapters are quantitative studies of educational adequacy. Ferguson and Ladd use production function analysis to investigate whether educational spending and specified inputs, like class size and teacher qualifications, are associated with gains in student achievement, controlling for other factors. Duncombe, Ruggiero, and Yinger employ cost analysis to determine how much the cost of producing demanded educational outcomes is driven up by costly factors in the school environment, like needy pupils. To disentangle the effects of cost and inefficiency, they then calculate the additional resources required by districts to reach average levels of outcomes assuming average efficiency. Barnett's chapter, in the tradition of research on cost effectiveness, reviews available research and data on outcomes and costs in three well-known and reputedly successful models of school restructuring for disadvantaged children: the Accelerated Schools approach associated with Henry Levin, the Success for All model of Robert Slavin, and the School Development program of James Comer.

From my perspective, at the risk of oversimplification, the chapters might be seen as looking at the cost of achievement for the average child in a state (Ferguson and Ladd), the cost of average achievement for needy

---

1. Clune (1995a; 1994a).

children (or at least the average child in certain needy districts) assuming average efficiency (Duncombe, Ruggiero, and Yinger), and the cost of high minimum achievement assuming the maximum efficiency of leading-edge models (Barnett).

My research has focused on the needs of high-poverty schools, usually in urban areas, because these schools typically serve the overwhelming majority of students in a state where levels of student achievement fall massively below what the state has determined as necessary for full functioning in society. High-poverty schools are thus prime candidates for special treatment by the legislature and prime targets for school finance litigation based on minimum state educational standards. From this perspective, I asked myself what answers are given by the three chapters to five important questions.

1. Should poor children and high-poverty schools receive extra resources? The most direct and complete examination of extra costs is the chapter by Duncombe, Ruggiero, and Yinger, which looks at cost data from almost all school districts in New York state. The 10 percent of districts with the highest costs include all large upstate cities and over 70 percent of downstate small cities. The factors associated with higher costs in these districts are higher teacher salaries, high percentage of female-headed households, limited English proficiency of students, percentage of children in poverty, and percentage disabled. Higher enrollments in these districts actually have the effect of lowering costs. The composite picture in this chapter is a good match with the characteristics of high-poverty schools: higher costs for qualified teachers (also a characteristic of suburbs), lack of educational advantage in the family, and special educational needs. The cost model employed by the authors finds that districts with these characteristics spend more to produce student achievement, controlling for efficiency.

The Barnett chapter also is directly relevant because all three models of school restructuring that he reviews are designed to raise achievement and have been implemented exclusively in schools serving disadvantaged children. Although he concludes that a large increase in resources is not required, at least in some schools, all three models do require some extra resources. Ferguson and Ladd do not calculate the extra costs of raising achievement of poor students but do make a number of related findings. First, demographic factors associated with poverty—parental education, percentage urban, percentage African American—account for about one-third of the variation in student achievement. Second, the two most powerful school inputs, teacher ability and teacher education, are known to cost money, especially in high-poverty locations. Another powerful input variable, reductions in class size (or extra staff), has been shown to be effective in raising the achievement of disadvantaged children when the extra staff are used in a properly designed program of accelerated instruction that relies on small classes and individual tutoring, as shown in the Barnett chapter and in other research.[2]

2. *How much money is necessary to reach a high, minimum level of educational outcomes?* In my work, I have been using a figure of $2,000 per pupil as the cost of extra staff, management, and teacher training needed for effective accelerated instruction among disadvantaged children. Other costs would be additional: for example, preschool and full-day kindergarten, qualified and adequately trained teachers, social and family services, and building maintenance and construction. The total of all needs, I suggested, might well reach $5,000 per pupil above an average national spending of about the same amount (in other words, a total of $10,000 per pupil).[3] Because these figures were rough estimates, the more precise cost numbers derived in these chapters are of great interest.

Duncombe, Ruggiero, and Yinger find that extra costs in the 10 percent of districts with highest costs are about $3,500 per pupil in a state with an average per pupil spending of about $6,000. This includes higher costs for teachers as well as spending to meet greater educational need (such as extra staff). This figure seems roughly in line with the $5,000 figure guesstimate in my work. By the logic of this chapter, costs in high-poverty schools should be substantially greater because the poverty rates in such schools are much greater than in the districts studied in the chapter. The absence of New York City and Yonkers in the data base, coupled with aggregation at the district level as opposed to the school level, probably results in an understatement of the impact of poverty factors. For example, the percentage of children in poverty in the Duncombe districts ranged from 2.6 to 38 percent. However, schools are usually considered high in poverty when they reach 40 percent, and the bulk of low-scoring students in New York City attend schools in the range of 60 percent to nearly 100 percent poverty (and minority) composition.[4] Also, neither this chapter nor the others includes capital spending, and schools with disadvantaged children have

2. In the Barnett chapter, see in particular the discussion of the Success for All program. Also see Madden and others (1991).
3. Clune (1994b).
4. Berne (1994).

been shown to have a backlog of such needs, which acts as a drain on new resources.[5]

Ferguson and Ladd find that a 10 percent increase in spending is associated with an increase of test scores from the 10th percentile to the median. For purposes of comparison to the findings of Duncombe, Ruggiero, and Yinger, 10 percent in New York would be about $600 per pupil. However, the Ferguson and Ladd figure does not make any correction for poverty but rather represents an average estimate for all districts below median spending. Also, Ferguson and Ladd interpret the large effect of dollars on achievement in Alabama as the probable result of extreme low funding in Alabama's poorest districts. Restoring the most basic elements of adequate schooling is likely to have a larger effect than refinements at a higher level. This interpretation is plausible and represents a good argument for a state-wide minimum of educational funding to provide horizontal equity for all students, but it also means that gains would be more expensive at higher levels of spending. Poor schools in New York City, for example, spend a little less than the state average. The combination of not focusing on high-poverty schools and getting a big effect from low-spending districts means that $600 is likely to be quite a low estimate of the needs of high-poverty schools in other states.

Barnett finds the cost of training and accelerated instruction ranges from about $100 to $1,000 per pupil. Funding preschool and an extra half-day of kindergarten would on average add about another $800. At various points, Barnett also discusses why these figures may not be representative and may need to be revised upward; but, even so, for reasons discussed further below, I think he understates the problem. I would argue that the data strongly support the interpretation that we are looking at a few schools at the low cost—high performance end of a production frontier. First, in contrast to the other two chapters, Barnett's reports data on a small handful of schools with exceptional performance. Second, not all schools in which the models are implemented are successful, so that the average level of outcomes produced by the intervention at existing levels of resources may fail to meet the adequacy standard. Third, it appears that many of these schools benefit from large amounts of volunteer effort, which would have to be paid for in other schools and which, because of burnout, may decline over time. Fourth, substantial initial selection effects due to the fact that schools are preselected by both the models' sponsors and the staff of each school may be compounded by further selection effects

5. Firestone and others (1994).

when better teachers and students gravitate toward successful programs, a point dealt with extensively by Barnett. Fifth, in notable contrast to the chapter by Duncombe, Ruggiero, and Yinger, practically all of the most elementary data on costs are simply missing, including initial and subsequent measures of spending per pupil, availability of preschool and kindergarten, teacher qualifications, and class size.

In one sense, the lack of data and experimental controls is not surprising. The sponsors of these models considered themselves as operating under the cost constraint of the existing level of resources and designed programs to increase the technical efficiency of education within those limits. Only the Slavin program seems to have introduced deliberate variations in resources in some sites, and the results suggest greater effectiveness at higher levels of resources.[6] As Barnett notes, from previous research on effective schools we could expect substantial gains in some schools from process changes that all of the models have in common, such as high academic expectations, a strong curriculum, and strong instructional leadership. What we may see in the more cost-efficient schools is an unusual combination of effective leadership, qualified teachers, and volunteer time. It is interesting in that regard that the model with the best data and broadest implementation, Slavin's Success For All schools, is also the most expensive. Finally, none of the models includes capital costs.

In sum, without disagreeing with Barnett's conclusion that "substantial" gains can be made in some schools without "major" increases in spending per pupil, the data from these studies do not alter the two main conclusions I reached in an earlier assessment about the average costs of full minimum adequacy: we desperately need more replications of restructured school experiments involving variations in program and funding, and a range of expenditure from about $2,000 to $5,000 per pupil above the statewide average, including social services and capital costs, is not an unreasonable estimate for supplementary funding. Duncombe, Ruggiero, and Yinger offer one important qualification to this conclusion, by pointing out that the most common method used by states for distribution of compensatory aid, the weighted pupils method, is practically uncorrelated with an adequately constructed cost index, at least in New York State. Put simply, districts receiving aid under the weighted pupil method are not high-cost districts.

3. Which educational inputs seem most important in producing educational outcomes? Beyond the universal input of sheer dollars, we can ask

6. Madden and others (1991).

which specific inputs purchased by dollars have the largest influence on educational outcomes. Of course, the whole point of site-based restructuring is that each school must manage inputs in its own way. Even a relatively standardized intervention like Slavin's has been found to raise literally thousands of discrete problems in each school.[7] Nevertheless, a plausible argument can be made that the three chapters point to three kinds of strategically important inputs: skilled teachers and teacher training, extra staff (or time) to reach individual students, and skilled management or coordination aimed at student achievement and efficient use of resources.

As already mentioned, the Barnett chapter synthesizes the changes made by the three reform models in terms of earlier research on effective schools, the essence of which is the more efficient organization of the time of teachers and students around higher academic expectations. The explicit costs of the reform models involve teacher training, with teacher qualifications left unexamined in the background. Ferguson and Ladd give us the most direct examination of the input question. They find teacher qualifications as the most important explanatory variable, followed by class size. A possible interpretation of these findings would be the traditional notion that skilled teachers can make use of smaller classes to reach more students more effectively, although Ferguson and Ladd do not analyze the interaction effect. Duncombe, Ruggiero, and Yinger can be interpreted in a similar way. Teacher salaries are the major component of higher input costs, and factors associated with disadvantaged students (like the prevalence of single-parent families) are the major environmental factor. Of course, the cost of these key inputs is a different question, depending on such things as the amount needed and market cost. Barnett's chapter, for example, suggests plausibly that teacher training and skilled management are not large costs relative to total per student spending. In contrast, qualified teachers are likely to be an expensive input.

4. Is school restructuring necessary and widely possible? "Restructuring" here refers to changes in school organization and process that make the school more efficient at using any level of resources to produce desired educational outcomes. The three chapters offer an interesting range of interpretation about the need for school restructuring. Ferguson and Ladd say that restructuring might lead to even greater gains, but their data show substantial gains are available from increases in key inputs even without restructuring, at least in resource-limited districts where the input levels are low to begin with. Duncombe, Ruggiero, and Yinger find that imposing

7. Slavin, Dolan, and Madden (1994).

a standard of average efficiency on districts makes only a modest difference compared with an index based on input costs alone. Barnett makes the strongest case, arguing that restructuring, not money, is the primary factor affecting achievement in the reform schools. Indeed, Barnett suggests that the greatest puzzle raised by the restructuring models is why the great preponderance of schools seem to lack incentives to do better.

Barnett's argument for the feasibility of powerful restructuring on a wide scale is not completely explicit but could be framed as follows. First, the process of restructuring in the model programs seems to use a relatively inexpensive input, training of teachers and expert coordination of teaching and learning. Although the costs of this input are not trivial, neither are they large relative to the daily operating expenses of the school. Second, the technology for producing substantial gains in efficiency does not seem to be esoteric or beyond the grasp of the ordinary teacher. Indeed, Levin's Accelerated Schools models builds on the premise that the existing staff of most schools have many skills that are repressed by negative expectations and organizational obstacles. Exactly what is this new, highly efficient teaching technology? Much remains to be explored, but the common elements seem to be a focus on specifically defined learning objectives and the marshaling of all available resources around achieving those objectives for the students of the particular school. Compared to this model, the "slack" or inefficiency in ordinary schools would seem to lie in the presence of multiple uncoordinated and even regressive goals for learning (implemented by default through the teaching that occurs "at random" in individual classrooms but also embodied in fragmented academic "programs"), inefficient teaching methods (like rambling lectures), lack of feedback on student progress and appropriate response, and a large amount of unfocused time (distractions from what is commonly called "time on task").

Stated this way, the common model of restructuring does seem to have potential for wider implementation. But there are also some obvious questions. Regarding the cost of inputs, one rival hypothesis is that the higher performance depends on staff spending more time with the learning problems of individual students: in other words, the "volunteer effort" problem discussed earlier. To the extent that the models do not require a greater quantity of teaching time, another more expensive possibility is that highly skilled teachers have found ways to reach individual students more effectively within existing time constraints. Barnett raises the possibility that the staff or restructured schools may be working harder rather than longer (intensity of effort rather than length of time or skill in teaching). But he also notes that the presence of high levels of effort immediately raises questions about incentives. What explains the fact that the staff of particular schools are willing to work at a faster pace, with more focus and less down time? A formula that requires exceptional leadership or workers may not be equally and inexpensively available in all schools.

Even if the adoption of common learning goals creates economies of coordinated effort, a question about broad-scale implementation remains. The process of getting teachers to accept common goals is somewhat mysterious and leads back to the unexplored question of incentives. Is Levin correct in his vision that teachers are thirsting for common goals and greater effectiveness, or is there a substantial amount resistance and inertia? The answer may be a puzzling "both of the above." Andrew Porter once summarized a long tradition of research on school improvement with the following proposition: The great majority of interventions pushed by outside change agents are readily adopted and produce substantial initial change in both process and outcomes, but usually persist for only a short time.[8] Before concluding that restructuring is widely feasible, we need to understand more about what makes high performance a transient, atypical phenomenon, in other words, more about what is now being called the problem of "scaling up."[9] In the meantime, giving more resources to existing schools looks easier than getting large numbers of schools to be substantially more efficient.

    5. *Do these papers provide reliable guidance for policymakers and answer concerns about "throwing money at schools"?* One of the most interesting questions about these three chapters is an unstated question in the background about the policy significance of production functions, cost analysis, and research on cost effectiveness. For many years, Hanushek and others have argued against spending more money on schools on grounds of lack of a consistent relationship between inputs and outcomes.[10] At the conference where the chapters in this volume were originally presented, I asked whether we could properly advocate an increase in spending once research began to establish such a relationship. I was surprised to hear several of the authors and participants argue that the research could not be relied on in this way, that spending should not be increased, and that "anyone doing production function research comes with a political agenda."

---

8. Verbal comments to author. See Porter and Brophy (1988).
9. Slavin, Dolan, and Madden (1994).
10. For example, see Hanushek (1991).

This is a bleak view of some of our most sophisticated research techniques and one that I believe misunderstands the proper role of social science in policymaking. The key point is comparative advantage. We now spend billions of dollars on education, using a variety of allocation formulas to decide how much tax money is allocated to which districts and schools. The assumptions and models underlying these spending decisions are simplistic, politically motivated, and subject to demonstrable political bias. The chapter by Duncombe, Ruggiero, and Yinger shows that the existing "weighted pupils" method of computing compensatory aid in New York State bears practically no relationship to more competent methods of estimating costs. In general, a cumulative body of objective research has a clear comparative advantage over politics and guesswork.

Although the crude idea that money simply does not count is receding into the background, these papers do highlight two remaining areas of uncertainty: the validity of complex quantitative estimates and the extent of feasible efficiency-oriented restructuring. In a sense, society is still concerned about throwing money at schools, but the emphasis has now shifted to the amount. The discussion by Duncombe, Ruggiero, and Yinger, for example, is somewhat apologetic about the complexity of its efficiency correction and suggests that a simpler index might capture most of the variation in costs. The Barnett paper is reasonable in asking how the inexpensive restructuring demonstrated in some schools might be made more widely available.

It seems to me that the answer to both of these concerns is to begin with conservative assumptions about the importance of resources. A conservative policy agenda for compensatory aid would have two parts: a program of universal funding based on conservative estimates of excess costs, and a series of educational experiments designed to ascertain the cost of adequacy under various conditions of restructuring and funding. Even many of those who are skeptical of higher funding levels for schools seem to agree with the suggestion (explicitly made in the Barnett chapter) that our society should begin a program of systematic, sustained experimentation aimed at establishing the cost of socially desired educational outcomes. As have previously argued, giving every poor child an extra $5,000 per year extra could cost a politically difficult $25 billion; but beginning an experimental program with 10 percent of poor children funded at different levels from $2,000 to $5,000 would cost less than one-tenth of that amount, while generating political support instead of resistance.[11]

11. Clune (1995a).

The importance of such a program of experiments in educational adequacy becomes much greater in light of the fact that our society seems to be actively engaged in the opposite agenda: aggressively reducing costs without regard to the effect on outcomes, through tax limits, downsizing, and inexpensive choice plans that lack accountability. There is a danger that educational adequacy will become politically moot before it can even be seriously considered. To counter this understandable political resistance, society should guarantee that poor children receive at least a conservative estimate of compensatory funding on a universal basis. The only way to answer concerns about efficiency is to invest some resources in finding out. At the moment, a systemic program of experimentation seems to be the most promising strategy. Of course, political and ethical problems could be involved in true random assignment of students. Even if that is true, much could be learned simply by following Barnett's suggestion of employing better quasi-experimental designs, including the elementary step of longitudinal tracking of resources and achievement scores. In the meantime, careful replication of the work by Ferguson and Ladd and by Duncombe, Ruggiero, and Yinger focused on high-poverty schools would also seem useful. I am not aware of any database that systematically collects relevant data on high-poverty schools on a national basis. Labor market research on the costs of qualified teachers in high-poverty schools also would be useful, as well as the development of a research design on the neglected question of underfinanced capital needs.

References

Berne, Robert. 1994. "Educational Input and Outcome Inequities in New York State." In Robert Berne and Lawrence O. Picus, eds., *Outcome Equity in Education,* 1–23. Fifteenth Annual Yearbook of the American Education Finance Association. Thousand Oaks, Calif.: Corwin Press.

Clune, William H. 1994a. "The Cost and Management of Program Adequacy: An Emerging Issue in Educational Policy and Finance." *Educational Policy* 8 (December): 365–75.

———. 1994b. "The Shift from Equity to Adequacy in School Finance." *Educational Policy* 8 (December): 376–94.

———. 1995a. "Educational Adequacy: A Theory and Its Remedies." *University of Michigan Journal of Law Reform* 28 (Spring): 481–91.

Firestone, William A., and others. 1994. "Where Did the $800 Million Go? The First Year of New Jersey's Quality Education Act." *Educational Evaluation and Policy Analysis* 16 (Winter): 359–73.

Hanushek, Eric A. 1991. "When School Finance 'Reform' May Not Be Good Policy." *Harvard Journal on Legislation* 28 (Summer): 423–56.

Madden, Nancy A., and others. 1991. "Success for All." *Phi Delta Kappan* 72 (April): 593–99.

Porter, Andrew C., and Jere Brophy. 1988. "Synthesis of Research on Good Teaching: Insights from the Work of the Institute for Research on Teaching." *Educational Leadership* 45 (May): 74–85.

Slavin, Robert E., Lawrence J. Dolan, and Nancy A. Madden. 1994. "Scaling Up: Lessons Learned in the Dissemination of Success for All." Paper prepared for the Center for Research on the Education of Students Placed at Risk, Johns Hopkins University.

Comments on Chapters Eight, Nine, and Ten

Richard J. Murnane

DISCUSSION OF the relationship between school resources and student learning has been contentious, with most of the debate focused on whether it is possible to extract a parsimonious, reliable message from the large number of studies done over the past thirty years. Ronald Ferguson has been the only person in recent years who has focused on bringing new data to bear on the question of whether money, and the resources schools purchase with money, affects student achievement. This chapter in this volume with Helen Ladd based on Alabama data follows work that Ferguson did with Texas data.

One can view the chapter by Ferguson and Ladd from three perspectives: as a contribution to the theory of how to study relationships between school resources and student achievement, as a set of new results about relationships between particular school resources and student achievement, and as a basis for drawing inferences about how to improve schooling for American children.

I begin with the first perspective. The chapter makes several valuable contributions to the literature on how studies of this type should be done. Most important, the authors show that expenditures per pupil should be viewed as jointly determined with student achievement, rather than as determining achievement. After all, lower student achievement will lead to higher expenditures per pupil if school districts that serve large numbers of low-income children with low achievement receive compensatory federal and sometimes state education funding. The implication of this alternative causal relationship is that it makes no sense to use ordinary least squares to predict whether expenditures per pupil predict student achievement, as so many studies in the past have done. Another contribution of the chapter by Ferguson and Ladd is emphasizing the importance of distinguishing class size from the student-teacher ratio. Other researchers have pointed out this problem, but the Ferguson-Ladd discussion and their strategy for dealing with the difference between the two concepts are especially thoughtful.

Viewed from the perspective of providing new substantive results, I have a cautiously positive reaction, with more interest in the student-level analyses than in the district-level analyses. Before reading the paper, I made a list of the methodological characteristics of a "gold standard" study. My list was long, and no study to date meets this gold standard. However, the Ferguson and Ladd analyses of individual student data do satisfy many of the "gold standard" characteristics. In particular, the authors use longitudinal test score data for individual children. They also use hierarchical linear modeling (essentially generalized least squares) to get the correct standard errors in the presence of data from different sources—some pertaining to students, some to schools. The importance of obtaining the correct standard errors cannot be overemphasized, given their central role in hypothesis testing.

One limitation of the data available to Ferguson and Ladd for the student-level analyses is that it is not possible to match students to individual teachers. Instead, the authors must attach the average characteristics of the fourth grade teachers in a school and the average fourth grade class size in the school to a child's characteristics, which creates the possibility of bias from measurement error. Another limitation is the absence of test score data for a majority of the teachers. The authors are creative in using the available teacher test scores, but I wonder about the validity of estimates of teacher test score effects when the critical variable is missing for more than half of the relevant teachers.

I have more questions about the methodology used in the district-level analyses of the achievement of eighth and ninth graders. Ferguson and Ladd are ingenious in using the data they were able to collect, but a great many assumptions are needed to interpret their results as providing unambiguous information about the impact of school resources on the learning of individual children. In the district-level analyses, the dependent variable is a composite of the mathematics scores of eighth and ninth graders in a school district in the 1989 school year. The variable used to control for prior achievement is a composite of the average reading and math achievement of third and fourth graders in the district *in that same year,* rather than five years ago, when the eighth and ninth graders were in the third and fourth grades. Many assumptions are necessary to interpret coefficients in a model estimated with these data as indicative of the impact of school resources on the learning of individual children—which is the the real question.

I encourage the authors to write out the gold standard model they would estimate if they had unlimited resources and access to data, and then to work out the assumptions under which the models they estimate with available data provide unbiased estimates of the parameters of the gold standard model. I think the assumptions would include that interdistrict student mobility patterns did not change between 1985 and 1990, that funding levels within districts did not change over this period, and that the effectiveness with which funds were used by districts did not change during this period. These assumptions are all quite strong.

Another way to examine the validity of the assumptions would be to take a data set that does provide longitudinal data on the achievement of individual students, estimate school resource effects using an appropriate value-added model, and then aggregate the data to construct variables that look like the ones used in the chapter. These aggregated data would then be used to estimate the type of models reported in this chapter, and the results of the two approaches could be compared.

What about the authors' substantive results? I find most striking the consistent pattern that student achievement is higher in grades and districts staffed by teachers with relatively high test scores. This pattern has appeared in all of the studies conducted over the last thirty years that have had measures of teachers' academic skills. Also intriguing is the pattern that, above a threshold, class size is negatively related to student achievement. This certainly fits the beliefs of many school teachers and parents. I also find especially notable the finding that student mobility has a negative impact on the achievement of children who do not move. This makes sense since teachers in classes with high rates of student mobility must devote large amounts of instructional time to assessing the skills of newcomers.

As mentioned earlier, I have questions about the instruments the authors use in predicting per pupil expenditures. However, I find plausible the results that instructional expenditures per pupil are positively related to student achievement. In fact, I have always been puzzled by findings that expenditures were unrelated to student achievement. If schools do use resources inefficiently, as Eric Hanushek has argued, this means that they do not get as much output out of the money they spend as they could if they used the money more wisely. It does not mean that additional funding would have no impact on student achievement.

This leads me to the third perspective from which to view the Ferguson-Ladd chapter: what does it it tells us about how to improve schooling for American children? I realize that this is not a question the authors set out to answer, but their results will be used by those who want to defend a particular answer to this question.

I think it would be a mistake for the authors to interpret their results as supporting the argument that providing more funding for low-spending districts to use in conventional ways—lowering class size, hiring more teachers with master's degrees—is a powerful strategy for improving student achievement. Why? One reason is that these conventional strategies are expensive, and the standard errors around the point estimates of effects on achievement are sufficiently large that the benefit-cost ratio from such conventional strategies may be very unfavorable. Also, as Steven Barnett's chapter explains, it appears that school-based reforms can have a large impact on the achievement of low-income children. These changes are of a quite different nature than simply providing more resources to be used in conventional ways.

The Barnett chapter shows that while the three reform strategies of Levin, Slavin, and Comer differ, they share a common set of ideas and practices. In his words:

> They all strongly emphasize a challenging curriculum and high expectations for academic achievement; a coherent vision of education focused on high achievement to which staff, students, and parents are committed; staff development focusing on achieving the vision; an instructional leader or change agent with clear responsibility for reform; a planning, implementation, and evaluation cycle conducted by school leaders and staff; increased attention to the needs of individual students; instructional methods known to be highly effective; and family support and parent involvement.

Implementing any of the school-based reform strategies Barnett describes requires additional resources. The resources could go for more experienced teachers or for lower class size; but these changes are part of a coherent effort to change what happens in schools. If the work by Ferguson and Ladd is used to support this claim, this makes sense to me. Of course, the challenge remains of figuring out how to stimulate the type of school-based reform initiatives that Barnett describes. As several chapters in this book document, designing incentives to stimulate reform efforts is extremely difficult.

The Barnett chapter provides an interesting description of three reform strategies. When Barnett turned to estimating what these programs cost, he found it very difficult to get reliable numbers for making comparable estimates—and his work on the costs of preschool programs illustrates that he is good at putting together reliable cost estimates. The numbers he does present are a start at understanding what these programs cost, but I think he would agree that the evidence is woefully thin. The same is true for evidence on the effectiveness of these programs. They are tough to evaluate. They take a long time to bear fruit; for example, Henry Levin estimates that it takes six years to complete the transformation to an Accelerated School. Moreover, some schools that try one of the reform efforts drop out after a year or two. Given this selective attrition, evaluating a program on the basis of the student achievement in the schools that stick with the program is not appropriate.

I close with a research question, motivated by reading the chapters on state-sponsored systemic reform and the Barnett chapter on school-based reform. It seems important to learn more about the extent to which state-sponsored systemic reform efforts promote or hinder school-based reform efforts such as those that Comer, Levin, and Slavin advocate. Given that the school-based reformers have sites in many states, this is a question one could fruitfully investigate.

Conference Participants

(with affiliations at the time of conference)

HENRY J. AARON
Brookings Institution

CHARLES H. ABELMANN
Harvard University

NABEEL ALSALAM
U.S. Department of Education

W. STEVEN BARNETT
Rutgers University

LAURIE BASSI
Georgetown University

JOHN H. BISHOP
Cornell University

ROLF K. BLANK
Council of Chief State School Officers

MARK BRAY
The World Bank

PATRICIA BROWN
National Governors Association

CHARLES T. CLOTFELTER
Duke University

WILLIAM H. CLUNE
University of Wisconsin

DAVID K. COHEN
University of Michigan

MICHAEL D. COOK
Brookings Institution

WILLIAM D. DUNCOMBE
Syracuse University

RONALD G. EHRENBERG
Cornell University

RICHARD F. ELMORE
Harvard University

JULIE I. ENGLUND
Brookings Institution

RONALD F. FERGUSON
Harvard University

JAMES N. FOX
U.S. Department of Education

SUSAN H. FUHRMAN
Rutgers University

ALAN L. GINSBURG
U.S. Department of Education

STEVEN H. GOLDMAN
Ball Foundation

JANE HANNAWAY
The Urban Institute

ERIC A. HANUSHEK
University of Rochester

E. D. HIRSCH, JR.
Core Knowledge Foundation

CAROLINE MINTER HOXBY
Harvard University

JACK JENNINGS
*Institute for Educational
Leadership*

THOMAS J. KANE
Brookings Institution

SHEILE N. KIRBY
The RAND Corporation

HELEN F. LADD
Brookings Institution

HAMILTON LANKFORD
*State University of New York,
Albany*

MARLAINE E. LOCKHEED
The World Bank

JENS LUDWIG
Georgetown University

LINDA MCNEILL
Rice University

ROBERT H. MEYER
University of Chicago

FREDERIC MOSHER
*Carnegie Corporation of New
York*

LANA D. MURASKIN
SMB Economic Research, Inc.

RICHARD J. MURNANE
Harvard University

SHEILA E. MURRAY
University of Maryland

DANIEL H. NEWLON
National Science Foundation

MACONDA BROWN O'CONNOR
The Brown Foundation, Inc.

MARTIN ORLAND
The Finance Project

SUE ROSS
U.S. Department of Education

JOHN RUGGIERO
University of Dayton

ISABEL V. SAWHILL
The Urban Institute

MAX B. SAWICKY
Economic Policy Institute

ROBERT M. SCHWAB
University of Maryland

DAVID L. STEVENSON
U.S. Department of Education

JOHN TYLER
Harvard University

ANTONY WARD
*Carnegie Corporation of New
York*

NANCY BROWN WELLIN
The Brown Foundation, Inc.

ALEXANDRA K. WIGDOR
*National Research Council,
National Academy of Sciences*

JOHN F. WITTE
University of Wisconsin, Madison

JAMES H. WYCKOFF
*State University of New York,
Albany*

JOHN M. YINGER
Syracuse University

Index

Abbott, Robert D., 224n
Abelmann, Charles H., 6–7, 18, 129, 130, 134–35, 143
Accelerated Schools program, 10, 299–302; effects of, 310, 311–13; evidence on success and costs, 318–19; further research, need for, 321–23; generalizability issue, 319–21; resource requirements and costs, 305–07. *See also* Economics of school reform
Accountability systems, 6–7, 134–35; acceptable performance definition, 73–75; accreditation systems, 66–67, 69–71; "authentic" assessments and, 13–14; backlash against, 88–89; capacity development, 95–96; complexity problem, 14, 73, 75–77, 92–93; components of, 65; delays in implementation, 67–68; design issues, 13–15, 69–77, 84–85; experimentation and evaluation, need for, 17–19; goals and standards, focus on, 3–5; impetus for, 1–3; implementation issues, 77–85; incentives used in, 77–81, 94–95; inspection methods, 67; lowest-performing students, assistance for, 81; parental confusion about, 89–90; perverse consequences, 80–81; political issues, 85–91, 96, 135; process regulations, persistence of, 90–91; prospects for, 91–96; public and press scrutiny, 78–79; resource constraints, 87–88, 95–96; sanctions used in, 67, 79; school-oriented, 11–12, 75; socioeconomic status, controlling for, 13, 81–82, 93–94; state-level intervention, 83–84; student-oriented, 11–12, 65; teacher-oriented, 11–12; undesirable side effects, 14, 43–46, 140–41; writing outcomes, 78. *See also* Recognition and reward programs
Accreditation systems, 66–67, 69–71

African American students: in magnet schools, 153; recognition and reward programs and, 52; school inputs and performance, 276, 278; social forces and learning, relationship between, 289; voucher programs and, 193, 194, 196, 198, 199, 201
Almaguer, Ted O., 33n, 34n
Alston, Ethel, 72n
Americans with Disabilities Act, 3
Anderson, Mark, 44n, 47n
At-risk students, 300. *See also* Accelerated Schools program
Attendance, recognition and reward programs and, 55
"Authentic" assessment, 13–14, 25, 73

Badillo, Herman, 228n
Baker, Regina, 183n
Ball, Deborah L., 113n
Baltimore schools, 303, 314, 316
Barnett, W. Steven, 9–10, 17, 18, 308n, 357–66, 371–72
Basic Competency Test (BCT), 273, 281
Basic Skills Assessment Program (BSAP), 30, 84
Baum, Donald N., 331n
Becker, Betsy J., 316n, 317
Benson, Charles S., 128n, 132n
Berne, Robert, 359n
Berninger, Virginia W., 224n
Bessent, Authella M., 352n
Bessent, E. Wailand, 352n
Bishop, John H., 11, 12, 43n
Blank, Rolf K., 153n, 161
Boardman, Anthony E., 138n, 330n
Borland, Melvin V., 186n
Borman, Jennifer, 104n
Bound, John, 183n
Bradbury, Katharine L., 329n, 336n
Bradford, David F., 329n

Schwab, Robert M., 158n, 166–67, 207n, 332n
Schwartz, David, 316n
Schwille, John, 107n
Scoll, Brett W., 265n
Scott, W. Richard, 107n, 110n
Seiford, Lawrence M., 352n
Serrano v. *Priest*, 327
Shepard, Lorrie A., 73n, 138n
Sheu, Tian Ming, 31n, 32n
Site-based management, 28
Sizer, Theodore R., 28n
Slavin, Robert E., 10, 299n, 302n, 303n, 313n, 314n, 315n, 316n, 318n, 319n, 362n, 364n
Smith, Marshall S., 100n, 108n, 109n, 138n, 265n, 300n, 318n
Socioeconomic status, 289; controlling for, 25–27, 31–32, 33, 34, 56, 81–82, 93–94, 133–34
South Carolina Educational Improvement Act of 1984, 28–29
South Carolina schools: measures of school performance, 137, 141, 142, 144; recognition and reward program, 23, 28–29, 30–32, 34, 36, 37–42, 45, 56; systemic reform, 104, 108
Speakman, Robert, 267n
Special education: disabilities covered by, 223–24, 225; enrollment growth, 225; identification of students, 226–27, 237; placement settings, 225, 226; Success for All program and, 303
Special education spending, 3, 8–9, 221–22, 258–62; budget allocations, 239–48; crowding-out effect, 245–47, 249; enrollment projections and, 247–48; future prospects, 248; good use of additional dollars, 244–45; growth in, 234–39, 249; incentives to categorize students as needing special education, 227, 237–39, 249, 259; legislation on, 222; national expenditures, 224–25; per pupil over time, 228–34; and spending on regular students, 228–34; reimbursement formulas, 227; state funding formulas, 222–23
Spending on education, 2, 130–31; data on, 221; growth in, 2–3; test scores and, 285–88; voucher programs and, 179–81, 192–93, 194–95, 200–01. *See also* Special education spending

Spillane, James P., 104n, 105, 106n, 107n, 108n, 109n, 111n, 112n, 113n, 114n, 118n
Stafford, Frank P., 307n
Staiger, Douglas, 183n
Stanford Achievement Test (SAT), 71, 273, 281
State governments: accountability systems and, 83–84; systemic reform and, 103–05, 107
Still, Suzanne, 306n, 311, 312n, 313n
Stock, James H., 183n
Stout, Hilary, 311n
Student accountability, 11–12
Success for All program, 10, 299–300, 302–03; effects of, 310, 313–16; evidence on success and costs, 318–19; further research, need for, 321–23; generalizability issue, 319–21; resource requirements and costs, 307–08. *See also* Economics of school reform
Sugarman, Stephen D., 170
Summers, Anita A., 330n
Systemic reform, 5, 7, 99–102, 135; accountability issue, 117–22; assumptions of, 100–01; components of, 100; conflicting goals, 108–09, 122–23; federal government and, 102–03; guidance for instruction, 102–11; local responses, 105–06, 107; obstacles to implementation, 110–11, 124–25; political issues, 108–09, 117–22, 124–25; popular support, lack of, 123; private-sector organizations and, 107–08; standards, lack of consensus on, 109–10; state versions of, 103–05, 107; teaching practice and, 111–17; variability in implementation, 106–11

Taylor, Lori L., 138n, 268n, 269n, 271
Teachers: merit pay programs, 11, 27, 46, 131–32; quality of, and student outcomes, 277–78, 282–83; recognition and reward programs' effect on morale, 46; systemic reform and, 111–17
Teaching to the test, 25, 27, 43–44, 140
Tennessee schools, 144
Test scores, 2; class size and, 279–80, 283; as measure of educational outcomes, 266–67; recognition and reward programs and, 24–25; spending on edu-